WORDS TO
OUTLIVE
US

WORDS TO OUTLIVE US

EYEWITNESS ACCOUNTS
from the
WARSAW GHETTO

edited by MICHAŁ GRYNBERG

translated and with an introduction by PHILIP BOEHM

Granta Books
London

Granta Publications, 2/3 Hanover Yard, Noel Road, London N1 8BE

First published in Great Britain by Granta Books 2003
Published in the US by Metropolitan Books 2002
Originally published in Poland in 1988 under the title *Pamiętniki z getta warsza-
wskiego: fragmenty I regesty* by Państwowe Wydawnictwo Naukowe, Warsaw

A CIP catalogue record for this book is available from the British Library.

1 3 5 7 9 10 8 6 4 2

ISBN 1 86207 623 5

Printed and bound in Great Britain by Mackays of Chatham PLC

"And they will ask if this is the truth. I will answer in advance: No, this is not the truth, it is a only a small part, a tiny fraction of the truth. The essential truth, the real truth, cannot be described even with the most powerful pen."

—FROM THE ACCOUNT OF STEFAN ERNEST

Contents

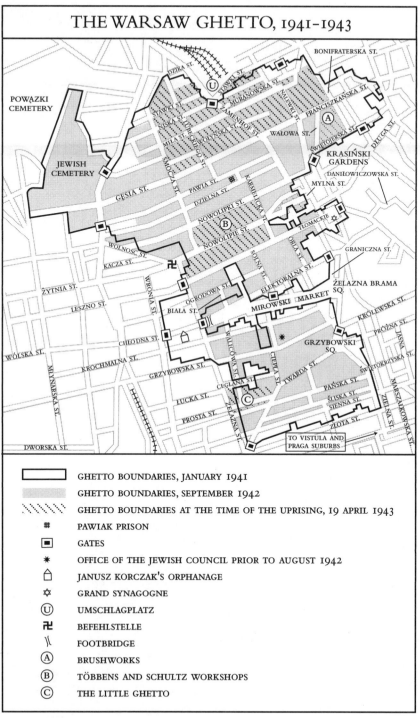

THE WARSAW GHETTO, 1941-1943

GHETTO BOUNDARIES, JANUARY 1941

GHETTO BOUNDARIES, SEPTEMBER 1942

GHETTO BOUNDARIES AT THE TIME OF THE UPRISING, 19 APRIL 1943

PAWIAK PRISON

GATES

OFFICE OF THE JEWISH COUNCIL PRIOR TO AUGUST 1942

JANUSZ KORCZAK'S ORPHANAGE

GRAND SYNAGOGNE

UMSCHLAGPLATZ

BEFEHLSTELLE

FOOTBRIDGE

BRUSHWORKS

TÖBBENS AND SCHULTZ WORKSHOPS

THE LITTLE GHETTO

WORDS TO
OUTLIVE
US

Introduction
by Philip Boehm

Within the world of terror we now call the Holocaust, the Warsaw
Ghetto was a particularly horrible microcosm. As the largest Jewish community under German control, its complex development
from 1940 to 1943 was both a reflection of evolving Nazi policies
and a reaction to them. Reliable estimates suggest that 489,000
Jews lived in the ghetto at some time; 100,000 of them died from
disease, malnutrition, or execution before the mass deportations of
July 1942. About 42,500 people are thought to have escaped the
ghetto: The rest, perhaps 347,500, were murdered, primarily at Treblinka. These figures do not include an estimated 50,000 who
chose to mask their Jewish identity and live illegally on what was
called the Aryan side of Warsaw. Of this last group, an unknown
number perished, either at the hands of the Nazi police or later
during the Warsaw Uprising of 1944. By that time the ghetto itself
had been completely razed, much of the rubble sorted, and all
usable material stored or shipped away to bolster the German
war effort.[1]

Today, even as the number of surviving witnesses dwindles
away, their individual experiences continue to be subsumed into a

larger collective memory. English readers have access to diverse books chronicling ghettos in Eastern Europe, the most important source for the Warsaw Ghetto being the journal of Emanuel Ringelblum, a professional historian who launched the secret project Oneg Shabbat inside the ghetto to document its existence and bear witness to the crimes being perpetrated daily.[2] Before the uprising of April 1943, the archives were sealed in milk cans and other containers, and buried inside the ghetto; two out of three receptacles were unearthed from the rubble in 1946 and 1950.

Words to Outlive Us provides a compelling personal counterpoint to Ringelblum's more dispassionate record. This extraordinary collection, presented for the first time outside Poland, is drawn from twenty-nine eyewitness testimonies, which—like the Ringelblum material—are housed in the Jewish Historical Institute in Warsaw, where they were compiled and edited by longtime affiliate Dr. Michał Grynberg, a leading Polish scholar of the Holocaust. Nearly all the accounts were written during the war, by Jews either confined to the ghetto or hiding in Warsaw on the Aryan side. In only a few cases do we know what became of the author; in some we lack even a name.*

The variety among these witnesses reflects some of the diversity within the ghetto, albeit weighted in favor of the educated intelligentsia, who were more inclined to record their experiences. Nine out of the twenty-nine accounts cited were written by women; three were originally in Yiddish. The authors range in age from eleven-year-old Marysia Szpiro to the engineer Henryk Bryskier, forty-five in 1944. They include philologists such as

---

*The institute's archives contain two collections apart from the Ringelblum collection: One, labeled *Pamiętniki*, Diaries, contains some 272 accounts, of which 65 concern the Warsaw Ghetto. Another group consists of 7,000 memoirs written after the war. With one exception, the testimonies in this book are drawn from the first group. One account, that of Całel Perechodnik, has appeared in English.

Chaim Hasenfus, shopkeepers such as Pola Glezer, and doctors such as the anonymous woman who wrote while hiding outside the ghetto with her four-year-old son. Of particular interest are the five accounts written by members of the *Służba Porządkowa,* or SP, the Jewish police force under the auspices of the *Judenrat.*

The stories of the documents themselves are just as varied. Only a fraction of the authors actually delivered their manuscripts to the Jewish Historical Institute after the war. Some papers were found in the rubble of the ruined city, in attics or basements; many passed from hand to hand before finally reaching the archives. The documents further vary in form: Some were written as diaries, others as simple narrations, while still others offer social and psychological analysis. The styles range from exceedingly simple to overtly literary; one account is written as a dialogue, and one was transcribed from dictation immediately after the war.

Out of these various points of view, a collective story unfolds—in apartments, shops, and offices, on alleyways and city squares. The creation, existence, and destruction of the ghetto involved a perverse civic planning, as the blueprints of annihilation were mapped onto a real world of schools and playgrounds, churches and synagogues, hospitals, restaurants, hotels, theaters, cafés, and bus stops. These loci of urban life—which figure prominently in the testimonies that follow—acquired entirely new associations: Residential streets changed into sites of executions; hospitals became places for administering death; cemeteries proved to be avenues of life support.

Under the German occupation, everyone in Warsaw became a topographer. Jews especially—whether inside the ghetto or out—needed to know which neighborhoods were "quiet," where a roundup was being conducted, or how to navigate the sewer system to reach the Aryan side. Consequently, the accounts abound with names of streets and districts, each of which would have involved associations lost in the distance of time and translation. The map of the ghetto included in this edition should help readers in their attempt to visualize the specific layout.

During the late 1930s, the Polish capital was home to some 1.3 million people, of whom 380,000, or nearly 30 percent, were Jews—the largest Jewish population in any city outside of New York. These Warsaw Jews comprised not one but several worlds, which varied tremendously in their degree of assimilation and acculturation and which were reflected in language, dress, religious practice, and social customs. While certain boundaries among groups were clearly demarcated, such as that dividing the pious-charismatic Hasidim from their more scholastic opponents, the Misnagdim, other distinctions were overlapped or blurred: Within a single family, for instance, one generation might speak Yiddish while another preferred Polish; one person might be a devout Hasid while another might decide to convert. Ongoing industrialization and the importation of ideas from Russia and Western Europe spawned a host of political allegiances and ideologies.

Naturally, lifestyle varied greatly according to class; the rarefied world of a financier living in a manorial house in a fashionable district had little in common with the poor crowded neighborhoods around Krochmalna Street, with their jumble of backroom shops and courtyard cheders, such as described by I. B. Singer:

> All the garbage bins were high with refuse. Dyers dyed clothing, tinsmiths patched broken pots, men with sacks on their shoulders cried, "Ole clo's, ole clo's, I buy rags, ole pants, ole shoes, ole hats; ole clo's, ole clo's." Here and there a beggar sang a song—of the *Titanic,* which had gone down in 1911, of the striker Baruch

Shulman, who had thrown a bomb in 1905 and been hanged. Magicians were performing the same stunts they had in my childhood . . .³

While Jews were scattered throughout the city, the traditionally Jewish neighborhoods were just outside the boundaries of the Old Town, in the southwest central part of the city, particularly in and around the Muranów, Powązki, Leszno, and Grzybowski square.

Although the integrated and largely assimilated intelligentsia often preferred Polish, most of Jewish Warsaw spoke Yiddish; I. B. Singer's own works derive from the great Yiddish literary ferment catalyzed by I. L. Peretz. By the mid-1930s, Warsaw, the largest Yiddish-speaking center in Europe, had also become the recognized center of Yiddish literature. Nevertheless, many educated Jews considered Yiddish little more than a pidgin German; following the late-nineteenth-century trend toward assimilation, more and more of the Jewish intelligentsia preferred Polish—which is one reason why these documents were almost entirely written in that language. Moreover, many who spoke Yiddish did not necessarily write in that language. Some Jews—especially those loyal to the Haskalah movement, or Jewish Enlightenment—continued to embrace German as the language of culture, while others—for instance those from Lithuania—were apt to speak and read Russian. With the growth of Zionism, Hebrew too began to gain adherents as the language of the Jewish future.

Warsaw Jews were similarly divided in their political orientations; myriad parties from the Assimilationists to the Zionists represented combinations of socialist, Zionist, and religiously orthodox agendas. The advocates of assimilation, whose influence peaked during the last decades of the nineteenth century, lost ground following World War I, and groups such as the Yiddish liberal Folkist Party gained new adherents. Some Jews threw in their lot with the Communists, while others joined the social-democratic Bund, which maintained close relations with the Polish Socialist Party (PPS). Zionist groupings from right and left also vied for seats on the local *kehilla* or *Gmina* (Jewish Community Council), on the Warsaw city council, and in the national parliament, or Sejm. Knowing of this wide array of allegiances is crucial to understanding the development of the Warsaw Ghetto, the programs advocated by its administrators, and the lack of a coordinated policy of resistance during its first years.

Perhaps the only thing the Jewish groups had in common was their opposition to the anti-Semitic Polish political party known as the Endecja, or National Democrats, a group also opposed by Marshal Józef Piłsudski, the dominant political power in the new state. Piłsudski, who after the Treaty of Versailles had helped establish Poland as a parliamentary republic, decided in 1926 to end what many citizens considered an irremediable political crisis simply by taking over. Because of his firm opposition to the National Democrats, most Polish Jews supported the coup, and indeed the new government extended the jurisdiction of the *kehillot* and consistently suppressed anti-Semitic agitation. Many Jews continued to support Piłsudski even as his regime became increasingly authoritarian.

In the financial life of the city, Warsaw Jews had long played an important role, especially as industrialists, professionals, and artisans, and had helped rebuild the economy following World War I and the Polish-Soviet War of 1919–1921. The disruption brought on by these wars was exacerbated by the loss of the Russian market and the inflation of the early 1920s, and the Great Depression proved disastrous for many people who had barely managed to stave off poverty before. A rigidly laissez-faire fiscal policy further hampered recovery until more interventionist measures were introduced in 1936. The depressed market fueled fierce competition, and Christian shopkeepers and tradesmen lobbied for anti-Semitic restrictions to gain the upper hand over their Jewish counterparts. Throughout the country, Polish nationalists organized boycotts of Jewish businesses—a practice openly condoned by the Catholic Church.[4]

In those years, a typical blue-collar worker earned a monthly wage of 120 zloty; a white-collar professional could make two or three times as much. A kilo of sugar cost about one zloty, a kilo of potatoes sold for a mere ten groszy (.10 zloty). Meat ran about 1.5 zloty per kilo; electricity cost around one-half zloty per kilowatt-hour. Twenty-two zloty could buy a man's hat, while an Underwood typewriter could fetch well over a thousand. For a long time the zloty remained tied to a gold standard; its value fluctuated between 8.91 per U.S. dollar in 1928 to 5.31 per dollar in 1939.

Despite economic hardship and political turmoil, the cultural life of the Warsaw Jews flourished. Jewish periodicals in Yiddish and Polish achieved impressive circulations, although the Hebrew press declined somewhat as many of its writers left for Palestine. Yiddish literature continued to thrive with authors such as I. B. Singer and Sholem Asch, and numerous writers of Jewish heritage made significant contributions to Polish literature. The University of Warsaw boasted a chair in Jewish History (filled by the eminent scholar Majer Bałaban, who is mentioned in the accounts), and an independent Judaic Institute was also established. The government set up a system of universal primary education with special schools for Jewish children, closed on Saturdays but not Sundays. A number of Jewish organizations also developed networks of private schools aligned with their particular agendas.

The death of Piłsudski in 1935 led to a crisis within the Polish government and a rapid deterioration in the position of Jews throughout the country. Right-wing nationalists reemerged and became more and more vociferous, openly calling for a boycott of Jewish businesses and other anti-Semitic actions. In an attempt to win the support of some of these groups, the government considered discriminatory measures such as a restriction on kosher slaughter, while the autonomous university introduced a system of quotas specifically for Jews.

In 1938, however, this trend reversed itself somewhat when the democratic opposition, including several Jewish parties, showed substantial gains in local elections. Today we can only guess whether Poland would have managed to establish a permanent genuine democracy or whether an authoritarian system would have prevailed. Nor can we know for certain what either event would have meant for Polish Jews. In the end, the German invasion and subsequent Nazi policy of genocide leave little room for speculation.

Terror accompanied the German attack of 1 September 1939, both in the random acts of individuals and as part of a planned campaign. Anti-Jewish pogroms were quickly organized in the territories occupied by the Wehrmacht, and leading Polish intellectuals were rounded up and sent to labor camps or shot in a systematic effort to "decapitate" the nation.

On the very first day of the blitzkrieg, German airplanes bombed Warsaw; subsequent air and ground attacks inflicted heavy casualties on civilians and wrought tremendous destruction. Jewish Varsovians actively participated in the defense of their city.

The national government, though, abandoned the capital soon after the bombardment began. Many officials of the Warsaw kehilla, including president Maurycy Mayzel, joined the thousands of refugees fleeing before the advancing German armies, so Mayor Stefan Starzyński, charged with overseeing the defense of the capital, appointed longtime activist Adam Czerniaków to fill the empty position. The city held out until 28 September 1939.

The last Polish armies surrendered days later, and the country was partitioned between the Germans and their Soviet allies. Some of the lands under German occupation passed directly into the Reich (including Silesia and the area between Łódź and Poznań renamed the Warthegau), while the central part of the country, including Warsaw, was declared a separate entity, the Generalgouvernement, headed by Hans Frank. The capital was moved to Kraków, and Ludwig Fischer was appointed governor of Warsaw.

As early as 21 September, Reinhard Heydrich, head of the RSHA, the Main Office of Reich Security, had issued a clear directive to the *Einsatzgruppen* (task force) leaders in the occupied territories. These secret orders called for all Jews to be removed from regions annexed directly to the Reich and relocated to the Generalgouvernement. Specific towns were to be designated as centers of concentration, where a Judenrat, or Jewish council, was to be set up and charged with carrying out subsequent agendas, including the resettlement of Jews from smaller communities. Judenrat councillors, or elders, were to be drawn from leading males in the community; on 4 October 1939, the Germans declared the formation of a Judenrat in Warsaw and ordered Adam Czerniaków to select twenty-four other men.

In this way the machinery was set in motion to establish Jewish ghettos with Jewish administrations responsible for carrying out the orders of the Nazis. The planned concentration of Jews in selected towns was clearly seen as the first step in the achievement of the final goal of their removal—although at that point the Nazis were still considering options other than extermination. As we now know, the ultimate objective became clarified in a program of mass murder presented at the Wannsee Conference in January 1942.

The Germans moved quickly to implement sanctions against Polish citizens, Jews in particular. The 1935 Nuremberg race laws were put in force and restrictions imposed on education and cultural life. Jews were subjected to public humiliation, rounded up for forced labor, beaten and robbed, raped, and murdered—by the Germans themselves, by the *Volksdeutsche* (ethnic Germans living in Poland), by the Polish rabble, and, later on, by Ukrainian, Latvian, and Lithuanian auxiliaries.

While the idea of a closed Jewish district in Warsaw was mentioned as early as November 1939, nearly a year passed before the ghetto actually took shape. The first ghetto in Poland, in Piotrków Trybunalski, was officially set up in October 1939; the first ghetto in a major city was in Łódź, proclaimed in February 1940 and sealed off on 30 April of that year. With their penchant for timing disaster to coincide with Jewish holidays, the Nazis informed the Warsaw Jews of the new decree establishing a ghetto there on 12 October 1940—Yom Kippur. Most of the area set aside for this purpose consisted of working-class or lower-middle-class neighborhoods in the Muranów district, with a smaller enclave around the Mirowski marketplace—sections that had suffered heavy damage during the German bombardment.

At first, nearly 400,000 people were confined to a space of approximately 1.3 square miles—just about the size of New York City's Central Park—creating a population density astronomically higher than elsewhere in Warsaw. An average of seven residents lived per room, mostly in large buildings of two to four stories constructed around a central courtyard, with shops on the ground level along the street and living spaces above and in the rear wings of the building. An entryway led from the street into the courtyard, where entrances provided access to separate stairwells. While there were also more spacious residences of relative luxury, a typical apartment consisted of a kitchen and one or two rooms. Toilets were often communal, and many buildings had no baths so residents had to use public facilities. City utilities had been badly damaged during the shelling, and people throughout Warsaw faced chronic problems with water, electricity, and waste removal.

As soon as the ghetto was established, the Nazi authorities began transferring Jews there, both from the Reich and from nearby towns and provinces, which made bad conditions even worse—particularly because so many of these people arrived completely stripped of their belongings, without adequate clothing, and infested with lice. These "refugees" were housed in public shelters that soon became breeding grounds for typhus and other diseases that ravaged the ghetto. In a bitter twist of fate, German policy thus unleashed the very epidemic that had been invoked as the rationale for sealing off the Jewish district in the first place. Famine led to typhus, typhus was followed by tuberculosis, and after that came the deportations. In the words of author Stefan Ernest, "When the three horsemen of the Apocalypse summoned by the invader—pestilence, famine, and cold—proved no match for the Jews of the Warsaw Ghetto, the knights of the SS were called in to complete the task."

The accounts themselves reveal exactly how the Nazi plans were put into effect, from the immediate perspective of the victims. Compiling and editing them for publication during the 1980s, Dr. Grynberg sought to document all aspects of the Warsaw Ghetto, from its inception to its savage annihilation, and grouped the texts thematically and chronologically to present specific topics: Nazi agendas; Jewish efforts to cope with hunger, overcrowding, and disease; roundups and deportations; life in hiding; and organized armed resistance.

This book follows the second Polish edition, although some minor changes have been made for English readers: The chapters have been streamlined and equipped with brief introductions. Certain explanatory glosses have been expanded or added. A very few passages included in the Polish book have been abridged: for example, where a long list of Warsaw street names threatened to tax even the most patient of readers. Also, ellipses present in the Polish edition have been discarded, and bibliographic references have been moved to the back of the book.

To introduce specific authors, a thumbnail biographical note precedes the first citing of a particular source; readers are invited to consult the fuller sketches at the end of the book for additional information. Where possible, these notes also trace the history of the given document. This biographical information is constantly being updated; readers able to supply additional information are kindly requested to contact the publisher.

Beyond their value as factual sources, the documents confront the reader with personal and emotional realities often lost in scholarly presentations. They help us visualize the complexity of the events and grasp the web of complicity that ensnared otherwise innocent victims and bystanders. They depict the daily struggle for survival and the hourly challenges to ideals, to human bonds, to faith in God. They explain both those men and women who were reluctant to resist and those who took up arms. They help us distinguish between compliance and collaboration, and defy our tendency to oversimplify and judge.

The accounts are challenging on a linguistic level as well, because the Nazis also invaded with words: an entirely new vocabulary of persecution, terror, and genocide camouflaged in colorless bureaucratic German euphemisms. These words infiltrated the local languages—in the case of the Warsaw Ghetto, Yiddish and Polish—and gradually became declined, conjugated, and abbreviated into a horribly quotidian grammar.

In order to maintain the dissonance of such invasive expressions as *Umschlagplatz* and *Aktion,* which in the original accounts often appear polonized as *Umszlag* and *Akcja,* I have chosen for the most part to keep the German forms.* Like most modern bureaucracies, the offices dealing with the ghetto used a number of

---

*Umschlagplatz (literally "transshipment station") was where the ghetto residents were collected for deportation; Aktion was used for military or police operations, and in the ghetto, for systematic roundups.

acronyms and abbreviations—HSSPF, KdS, Sipo, Kripo—which, by depersonalizing the agendas being carried out, helped the perpetrators to veil their misdeeds in anonymity. The shortened versions gained currency among the victims as well, largely through sheer repetition but perhaps in part by answering their own need to establish some psychological distance from the horror.

The story of the Warsaw Ghetto, like the history of the Holocaust in general, was a tragedy spanning many cultures. Nazi policies of forced resettlement extended the cultural and linguistic mix that had existed in Jewish Warsaw before the war, as the ghetto absorbed Jews from Germany, Czecho-Slovakia, and Greece and a large group of Roma. It is important to bear this in mind while reading the accounts, which despite all their variety cannot speak for those others who had no voice: who were foreign, illiterate, or too young to leave a record of their brief existence.

But perhaps these testimonies will help us to envision even the lives of those unnamed, to put faces on the cold statistics, and, through our own imagination, to help save at least the memory of people otherwise consigned to oblivion.

*"With all these apartments being swapped, the streets were an
incredible sight: Handcarts and wagons moving in all directions…"*

Chapter 1

LIFE WITHIN THE WALLS

The Germans moved quickly to identify and isolate the Jewish population of Warsaw. On 23 November 1939, less than three months after Poland was invaded, Governor Hans Frank ordered that all Jewish-owned businesses in the Generalgouvernement be clearly marked; mere days later, Jews in Warsaw were required to wear armbands with the Star of David. Schools were closed and restrictions placed on Jewish professionals. Economic sanctions were imposed and property confiscated indiscriminately. Jews were banned from certain public spaces, subjected to public humiliation, and pressed into hard labor, such as removing rubble.

Physical segregation began as well; the predominantly Jewish districts near the center of the city were posted with signs warning of an epidemic. Although the earliest outbreak was of typhoid fever and was by no means confined to Jewish neighborhoods, it was the far deadlier louse-borne typhus that Nazi propaganda sought to associate with Jews, whom the quarantine was designed to further stigmatize and alienate from the local population.

After months of unclear signals, on 12 October 1940 Warsaw's German governor Ludwig Fischer informed the Jews that they would be confined to a ghetto, which officially came into existence on 15 November—although the borders of the new district remained in constant flux. Over ten *miles of walls went up—built by Jewish labor and paid for by the Jewish community, along a seemingly random zigzag boundary that closed off streets in the middle of a block or occasionally bisected them lengthwise. The wall was usually eight to ten feet high and topped with broken glass; a few stretches were fenced off only with barbed wire. Some 80,000 Christian Poles were moved out of the area and about 140,000 Jews were forced in from other parts of Warsaw and nearby areas, so that by January 1941 nearly 400,000 people were confined to the ghetto.*

*ALL WE KNOW ABOUT **STANISŁAW SZNAPMAN** IS THAT HE escaped from the ghetto in July 1943 and went into hiding on the Aryan side of Warsaw, where he wrote his "diary." He is assumed to have died there in unknown circumstances.*

Monday, 25 September 1939. The bombardment of Warsaw began around six in the morning, both from the air and from the ground. It lasted all day and night without stopping and went on the next day and night as well. Even if a person had managed to hold on until the bombing, by Monday he would have had a nervous breakdown. People were running around like mad, looking for cover underground in shelters and cellars; some were completely overcome with terror and took off in a panic with no idea where they were going. Women were wailing and children were crying as they prayed out loud, kneeling in the doorways of their apartments.

On the morning of Wednesday, 27 September, things quieted down; at noon we heard that Warsaw had surrendered. Those two days of shelling had inflicted terrible damage: The water plant, the power plant, the gas works, and the radio station had all been hit, among other places. Warsaw was without water, electricity, gas, or radio. The streets were covered with rubble and shards of glass. The city was pockmarked with huge craters. The air was thick with dust and soot.

When the bombing stopped, everyone sighed with relief and started coming outside to examine the wreckage. Everywhere you turned there were demolished homes, walls torn open or riddled with holes, or else the charred skeletons of apartment houses, their burned-out window frames gaping like empty eye sockets. Here and there piles of ash and debris were still smoldering, and a few buildings continued to burn. There was no question of putting out the fires, because there wasn't any water.

As things quieted down, people began to grasp the enormity of the disaster that had befallen our country. Their first reaction was to curse the government and its leaders, but this judgment proved overly hasty. It's always easy to criticize. The inexperienced Polish army fought heroically; unfortunately, there was little it could do against an enemy many times stronger, led by experienced veterans. While the enemy was motorized and equipped with vast quantities of the latest weapons, our army had few motorized units and was only modestly armed. This was an enemy that had gone hungry for nearly two decades, doing nothing but manufacture cannons, tanks, and military equipment, an enemy for whom war is a craft and who sees this war as a way to take back the land lost in the last one.

One of the first things these "honorable" German troops did was to conduct night raids on Jewish homes, where they demanded money and jewelry at gunpoint, all the while beating and kicking the residents. Anyone brave enough to visit the command post the next morning and file a complaint never again saw the light of day—having dared to impugn the honor of a German soldier. These uniformed heroes also searched homes for weapons and confiscated whatever struck their fancy. The Gestapo began to run riot.

Most important was a decree forbidding Jewish families from keeping more than 2,000 zloty in cash. Anything above that amount had to be taken to the bank immediately. All Jewish capital in the banks was seized. Gestapo officers began paying visits to the wealthier Jewish families, stealing money and other valuables, after subjecting the residents to meticulous searches in which women were made to strip naked while their underclothes were examined under a light. Orders were enforced by a pistol pointed at the victims' heads. Anyone who dared object was shot for "possession of weapons." German soldiers made the rounds of Jewish shops, taking the best and most expensive wares without paying a penny. To add insult to injury, they would compel the owners to write a statement that the items had been given to them as gifts.

The gendarmes would stop Jews on the street in broad daylight and take whatever they had, down to their last cent. The rabble, realizing what it could get away with, also began vandalizing and looting Jewish shops and assaulting Jewish pedestrians.

Household possessions were the next to go, as the Germans went from one Jewish apartment to the next, systematically and according to plan, seizing furniture, appliances, linens. Some people were stripped of everything; others lost only part of their belongings. Under threat of being beaten, they were forced to carry their own property to the waiting cars. Doctors were robbed of their microscopes and other instruments. Wealthier families with better-furnished homes were evicted on the spot, so their apartments and everything in them could be handed over to Volksdeutsche: Polish citizens of German descent who had now become a new aristocracy. As soon as the Germans entered Warsaw, these people, who had been passing as true patriotic Poles, revealed themselves to be German zealots consumed with hatred for anything Polish. It turned out that these Volksdeutsche had built up an entire army of spies who betrayed secrets to the Germans. Unfortunately, this included military information as well, since there were many such "patriots" in the higher ranks of the Polish armed forces. The Volksdeutsche also removed Jews from their businesses. In other words, if one of these new dignitaries took a liking to a particular Jewish enterprise, he would throw the Jew out on the street with no compensation whatsoever, take his place behind the counter, and run the shop himself.

Countless regulations began to appear curtailing the rights of Jews. One order prohibited them from managing their own real estate or collecting rent. To enforce this order, the Germans appointed commissars to Jewish-owned buildings. Jews were also forbidden to employ Aryan domestic help.

On the streets, the Germans demanded that Jews step aside and bow to them; anyone who failed to do so was kicked and beaten to a pulp.

The labor camps began receiving their first shipments—more than twenty thousand young people were sent away. Working conditions there were so bad that some died on the spot from being starved or beaten, while those who did come back were so crippled they were no longer fit either for work or for life in general.

To drive a wedge between Poles and Jews and to thwart possible joint action against their common enemy, the Germans launched a huge propaganda campaign designed to vilify Jews in the eyes of Poles. Walls were covered with posters depicting Jews as repulsive and dangerous criminals or as vampires sucking Polish blood. Special free films were shown that demeaned and ridiculed Jews. Public lectures were held asserting that Jews were immune to typhus but functioned as carriers of the disease and could pass it on to Aryans. People with Semitic features were deployed throughout the city, where they could be seen littering streetcars and public places with small bottles and boxes filled with lice.* No wonder that so many Poles, unaware of these devious plots, began to curse the Jews.

And so the days passed, filled with persecution, humiliation, and hideous torments. No one felt safe day or night. Unwanted visitors could barge into any home at any moment: uninvited guests

---

*This information has not been confirmed.

answerable to nothing and no one, masters of life and death. They could seize whatever they chose, beat the residents unconscious, take them away or kill them on the spot, rape the women and small children. Whoever ventured outside was never sure when or whether he might come back. In other words, Jews were placed outside the law. A non-Jew could do to a Jew whatever he pleased, take his property or even his life, with complete impunity. It was a tragic situation.

The only thing keeping our spirits up was our great hope that, by the spring of 1940, England and France would settle scores with the enemy and bring us freedom. The Germans were surprised, considering the harshness of the persecution, that there weren't more suicides, as there had been among the Jews in Austria. What stopped us was precisely this hope. Despite our tremendous misfortune we were confident, optimistic, and full of faith that these two great democratic powers would crush the black monster that was smothering the whole of Europe.

May 1940 arrived, and with it the beginning of the end. The news was bleaker and bleaker. We were stunned. We couldn't believe it. We could not fathom what had happened. We had deluded ourselves into thinking that the tide would turn at any moment, that the Germans could not possibly succeed, the world could not possibly be plunged into the dark abyss, and civilization could not step backward thousands of years.

But the sad, tragic reality came to pass: France surrendered. Boundless despair and hopeless depression descended upon us. It was then that we broke down, and the suicides began. We shuddered at the thought that England might give up the fight and sue for peace.

STEFAN ERNEST *WAS LIVING IN HIS NATIVE* WARSAW *AT THE time of the German invasion. Having escaped from the ghetto in*

January 1943, he too went into hiding on the Aryan side. He must have perished shortly after writing his account, which he ended with the words: "A pit inside the German district, May 1943."

The doorways and display windows of Jewish businesses and shops are being marked with rectangular signs showing a blue Star of David against a white background.* Unlike similar stores owned by Aryans, these businesses attract hordes of German soldiers who plunder whatever they can. Some have a sense of honor and pay with German money from the 1923 inflation, about one hundredth part of the price.

For quite a while now, other signs have been going up on the doors of cafés, restaurants, movie theaters, and the like, as well as at a few places of business: JUDEN EINTRITT VERBOTEN—NO JEWS ALLOWED—or JUDEN NICHT ERWÜNSCHT—NO JEWS WANTED.

This was followed by other restrictions on the use of carriages, automobiles, and streetcars; special trams have been introduced exclusively for Jews, with the number of the line displayed against a yellow background.

MAREK STOK, *A LAWYER, LIVED IN THE GHETTO FROM APRIL 1940 until the fighting broke out in April 1943, when he escaped to the Aryan side. He wrote his account in early 1944 while hiding at the home of a Polish couple. Stok survived the war and later emigrated to Brazil.*

It's a strange feeling for someone who has always held his head high and thought of himself as a citizen with the same full rights as everyone else. This nagging sense of degradation, of humiliation,

---

*On 23 November 1939, Governor Hans Frank issued an order requiring all Jewish-owned businesses in the Generalgouvernement to be clearly marked.[1]

is impossible to shake. Any German can hit you or beat you up or brutalize you into carrying out some task, and there's nothing, absolutely nothing, you can do about it. What's emerging is a slave mentality—the first and worst effect of German rule.

What strikes you next are the walls, which are springing up unexpectedly in the oddest places, closing off streets. These walls can be found in the Old Town, on Marszałkowska Street (at Sienna, Świętokrzyska, and Próżna), as well as on Długa Street and elsewhere. What are they for? Nobody knows. The optimists say they're being built for "strategic" purposes, but the pessimists maintain they're part of a future ghetto. That's what everyone's afraid of. Especially the refugees from Łódź, where the Germans savagely herded people under gunfire into a cramped ghetto; now a terrible famine is raging there.*

So we talk about a possible ghetto with apprehension and dread—even though we can't really imagine it will happen. Summer is on its way. The political news is terrible. Norway, Holland, and Belgium have fallen. France is still fighting on. But soon we read about the fall of Paris and the French surrender. Now there's no hope left that the war will end quickly. We'll simply have to adapt and go on living.

But that's not so easy. Jews have been stripped of their possessions. The larger businesses have been taken over and each assigned a German commissar. With the exception of doctors and dentists, all Jews have been expelled from the professions. But now they're showing just how resistant and adaptable they are by nature. Deprived of everything, subjected to constant humiliation, they are bowed but not broken. Merchants are "aryanizing" their businesses by transferring them to Polish acquaintances. In enterprises that have been placed under a commissariat, everything depends

---

*The order to create the ghetto in Łódź was signed by Johannes Schäfer, the chief of police in that city, on 8 February 1940.[2]

on the individual commissar. Sometimes these people retain the Jewish staff, at least in part, and even tolerate the owner. Some such Jewish owners offer their commissars advice, occasionally directing them so adroitly that everyone profits handsomely from the business's being officially a German one. But frequently the commissars are rabid anti-Semites who simply throw owner and staff onto the street. Masses of Jewish tradesmen and especially the intelligentsia are living in poverty. Many of the intelligentsia have found work at two large institutions: the Jewish Council (the Judenrat, or Gmina Żydowska) and the Jewish Welfare Association (Żydowskie Towarzystwo Opieki Społecznej or ŻTOS). The work is by no means lucrative; the Jewish Council pays a tiny salary, and ŻTOS pays most of its employees nothing at all. But everyone wants to work to qualify for an *Ausweis,* an identity card. You feel safer on the streets if you have an Ausweis to prove you are employed.

By the end of summer the Germans have evicted more and more Jews from the central district and the southern part of the city. The evictions are brutal: Residents are ordered to clear the premises within fifteen minutes or half an hour, and they are allowed to take only the most essential personal belongings. All furniture, clothing, appliances, and linens must be left untouched. Given the increasing number of such seizures, people have begun finding apartments outside the walls so they can save what they own. The newspapers are full of advertisements offering to exchange Aryan-owned apartments "inside the walls" for Jewish ones "outside."

The bombshell finally drops at the end of October. All Jews are given two weeks to move into the Jewish district, the borders of which are precisely delineated; similarly, all Aryans within those boundaries must move out. The borders described in the decree don't exactly line up with the newly built walls: the new ghetto territory no longer includes Złota Street, the Old Town, or Długa

Street, for example, so everyone who exchanged apartments in those neighborhoods must now move again. The racket on the streets is incredible. Officially, no one is permitted to take furniture, only hand luggage, but the Germans don't enforce that rule very rigorously, so the streets are full of people rushing madly alongside carts and wagons, mostly pushcarts on two wheels piled with junk. In this way everyone manages to move into the district before the deadline.

By early morning on the designated day, sentry posts have sprung up at several "exits." These are manned by German gendarmes, who are accompanied by members of the Jewish police force recently organized by the Council. Jews are not allowed into town, and Aryans are not allowed inside the ghetto. Period. There's no going back. We're locked in.

BEFORE THE WAR, **HELENA GUTMAN-STASZEWSKA** *WAS A teacher in a public elementary school for Jewish children. In the ghetto she worked for various social institutions, including soup kitchens and child welfare agencies. Gutman-Staszewska survived the war, although her fate remains unknown.*

Soon after the invasion, the Jews began to organize their daily life. At first I worked for the children's soup kitchen at Graniczna 12 sponsored by CENTOS.* The poverty is extreme; more and more children are turning to begging. As a rule the children are frightened, terrified by all the things that keep happening to them. A little later I moved to a cafeteria set up for the intelligentsia at Zamenhof 13.

Toward the end of the summer of 1940 a number of people were forcibly resettled from Łódź. They are full of horrible stories

---

*CENTOS, Centralne Towarzystwo Opieki nad Sierotami, was the Central Association for the Care of Orphans.

about the creation of a separate district. Many of these people spent a long time in transit inside sealed cars. My friend's sister-in-law was one such case; during the passage she caught a lung infection.

In early May a civil engineer working in the municipal administration told me he had been assigned to draft plans for a Jewish district according to German specifications. Initially, things dragged on so long it seemed this might not happen. But by the end of September the idea became reality as the Jewish district began to take shape.

The designated borders underwent constant revision, to the point of being redefined several times in a single day. The building I was living in housed fifty Jewish tenants and ten Christian families. We didn't know for certain whether it would wind up within the Jewish district or not. Then the day of judgment arrived and we learned we had to move out.

According to the official decrees we had the right to exchange our apartments for Aryan ones. Because our building was new— and since even the smallest apartments were equipped with modern appliances—we were besieged as if by a swarm of locusts. From daybreak on there was one inquiry after another about swapping apartments. Down in the courtyard it was awful: People were shouting and crying; one person was swindling another, all sorts of shady characters came creeping around trying to take advantage of the situation. Someone showed up at my elderly neighbor's with the idea of forcing her to give up her apartment for nothing. Apparently she discovered some little clause that allowed her to wriggle out of it. A district chief from the PP—*Policja Państwowa* or State Police—took the apartment belonging to our building administrator, in exchange for a place in some rubble that had been redrawn outside the Aryan district. The administrator protested, but he had no choice; they simply tossed his belongings into the courtyard.

I was afraid I'd lose my mind watching all this, so I stepped outside to calm down. When I came back the concierge told me the commissioner of the Seventh Police Commissariat had reserved my apartment; until his return I was not to leave or exchange with anyone else, or he would have both the new buyer and myself thrown onto the street.

I had already arranged an exchange with an Aryan family living at Ogrodowa 6, so at dawn I snuck out like a thief to move my things under cover of the crowd. I don't know whether the concierge didn't spot me or whether for some reason he just chose to leave me alone. The commissioner did indeed show up at my apartment the next day, accompanied by a sizable escort, but the exchange had already been officially transacted and all he could do was tell off the concierge. In the end I was lucky; I only had to move once. Many people in our building, however, moved from Chłodna 20 to Żelazna 80, from Żelazna to Łucka, and from Łucka to Krochmalna. A relative of mine who lived on Poznańska 22 had already exchanged apartments with a city official at Ogrodowa 52, but since the house on Ogrodowa was reassigned to the Aryan district, the official refused to honor the transaction and sent the Gestapo instead. They beat up my relative and evicted her without letting her take a thing. So she moved from Ogrodowa to Twarda 7, from there to Dzielna 61, and from Dzielna 61 to Leszno 12. With all these apartments being swapped, the streets were an incredible sight: handcarts and wagons moving in all directions and everyone afraid the gendarmes might confiscate their belongings, which often happened.

On 1 November 1940, I started working as a clerk in the Jewish Aid Committee, or JHK, a liaison group that represented all the institutions in the Jewish district to the German authorities and intervened in various affairs. This meant that institutions such as TOZ, CENTOS, Ezra, TOPOROL, the old-age home, the Central Shelter, the orphanage, the Jewish hospital, the maternity clinic on Twarda, ORT, and HIAS all came to us for passes or permits to transport goods while exchanging offices with Aryan institutions.* These exchanges were governed by contracts, which at times were even written out, with lists of any inventory left behind. Naturally these contracts were to apply only for the duration of the war; afterward each institution would return to its former location. In this manner the orphanage at Krochmalna 92 traded places with the Roeslerów school at Chłodna 33. The Central Shelter moved out of its magnificent building on Górczewska Street to the home for invalids at Dzielna 59. The old-age home moved from Górczewska (another fine building) to the Aryan old-age home at Nowolipki 52 beside the church. The Jewish hospital moved from its well-known premises on Dworska Street to Leszno 1. TOZ moved some of its children's kitchens, but I can't remember the exact addresses. These institutional moves were extraordinarily difficult, and not all the gendarmes respected the transport permits; some let things through while others did not.

In the course of moving the orphanage, Dr. Janusz Korczak landed in jail. The gendarme confiscated various things and Korczak went to complain at Daniłowiczowska Street, where he was arrested for not wearing an armband and held for three months.

The worst move involved the Central Shelter, with its huge stock inventory. It was fully equipped to take care of infants, and it was the only place that took in foundlings. About five hundred children had to be moved (among them one hundred infants), without clothing or shoes, in the cold on uncovered wagons. The director couldn't get inside the building, and there was no com-

---

*TOZ, or Towarzystwo Ochrony Zdrowia, was the Society for the Preservation of Health; Ezra, meaning "help" in Hebrew, was a general charity; TOPOROL (Towarzystwo Popierania Rozwoju Rolnictwa wśród Żydów) was the Jewish Agricultural Development Organization; ORT, from the Russian Obshchestvo Remeslennogo i Zemledelcheskogo Truda—loosely, the Trades Manufacturing Development Organization—was designed to increase production among Jewish artisans; and HIAS was the Hebrew Immigrant Aid Society, an American organization created to help Jewish emigrants.

munication. The deadline for closing the old shelter was post-poned several times; things were being moved up to the very last minute. Certain details stick in my memory, like the children from the dormitory at Graniczna 8, all between the ages of four and seven. There was only one coat for several children, and no place to move them to—for a while they were put up in the soup kitchen at Gęsia 9. The shortage of clothing and shoes caused many children to fall sick.

For the moment we have enough passes; our office manager even has one for his son, who is being tutored on the Aryan side. Meanwhile pan Morgensztern, the director of HIAS, was arrested for using official forms without permission and taken to Auschwitz, where he was shot.*

On 25 November 1940, they announced the final deadline for closing the district. We are now surrounded by fences and walls, with only a few exits leading to the Aryan side.

SAMUEL PUTERMAN *WORKED AS A FUNCTIONARY IN THE Służba Porządkowa, or SP, the Jewish police force active within the ghetto. Later he hid at the home of a Polish couple until the Warsaw Uprising of 1944, following which he survived imprisonment at Sachsenhausen and Oranienburg. After the war he emigrated to France, where he died in 1955.*

Although the ghetto had been in existence for several months, it was still an ordeal just to venture a few steps out of the house, especially for more sensitive people. Not everyone could get used to the magnitude and range of poverty on the ghetto streets, which displayed such a variety of beggars it defied belief.

Pan and *pani*—roughly "Mr." and "Mrs."—are used in Polish as polite forms of address and as the formal equivalent of "you."—PB

One well-known case involved a family from Łódź, which at first numbered eight people. Their entire belongings consisted of two baby strollers: The father pushed three children in one, while the mother kept two others on top of the second. They rolled the strollers along the curb and sang old Yiddish songs. They had beautiful voices. He sang and she sang, accompanied by six children's descants. After a while there were only four voices; then there were three, then one stroller disappeared, along with the family's shoes and what was left of their outer garments. Finally only two people and one stroller remained. The father pushed while the mother lay in the stroller, singing to accompany her husband. She was thirty-nine years old but looked one hundred. Together they sang the same songs and were given the same pennies as they had received the year before.

Another figure who stood out from the gray mass of people dying on the streets was Nuchem Lejbkorn. Before the war he had owned a building and a store in Skierniewice; he also had a wife and five children. The Germans transported them to Warsaw. Within a few weeks he had become a beggar. His wife died of typhus. That same week his oldest child died. He moved what was left of his family from the room he was renting to the homeless shelter and from there onto the street. With three children clinging to the remnants of his clothing he would walk around the ghetto, carrying his fourth child high on his shoulders. They walked and sang the same Yiddish song over and over: *"Ich dank dir Got, az ich bin a yid."** Gradually the children died of starvation, but their father had enough strength to go on walking despite his swollen legs. Autumn came, then winter, and still he trudged on without shoes or clothes. All he had left was a down quilt, which he tied around himself with a string. He kept his hands inside, but his legs stuck out from underneath, now horribly

*"I thank you, God, for making me a Jew."—PB

swollen. Sticking out of the top was his small withered face, tightly wrapped in yellow skin and ringed by a little pointed beard. Feathers came leaking out of the down. Even though the streets were always crowded, everyone gave Lejbkorn a wide berth. A few would toss some coins into the tin can he kept tied to a string as he made his way through the crowds, smiling contentedly, like a wise man or an idiot, always singing the same song, *"Ich dank dir Got, az ich bin a yid."*

There was another demented man with an even shorter song: nothing more than the two Polish words *"Jestem głodny"*—I'm hungry. He would sing to the melody of a waltz or a foxtrot; he couldn't carry a tune, but he could move in step and was able to repeat those two words without stopping. The picture was completed by other beggars lying against the building walls, their voices too weak to reach the ears of passersby. Sights such as these pained the eyes of every sensitive soul.

Then there was the king of the Warsaw beggars, Rubinsztejn, also known as *"Alle glajch,"** who went around well fed and happy. This man had really made a career for himself; always full of ideas, he knew how to dress and always gave the crowds something new to stare at. He would appear on the street wearing different outfits, which he then explained with jokes that immediately made the rounds. Why was he wearing a ladies' dress? "I don't have a wife so I guess I'll have to be my own wife today; not bad, eh?" Why the swimming trunks? "Oh, I was just planning a little stroll along the beach; not bad, eh?" For a few days he went around wearing tails because he had to attend a session at the Council or run to the Provisions Department; not bad, eh? He became so popular that the Melody Palace put on a cabaret show entitled *"Alle glajch,"* with the actor Minowicz[†] playing the role of Rubinsztejn. The

---

*Yiddish for "Everyone's equal."—PB
[†]Presumably the actor Edmund Minowicz.—PB

finale featured a live appearance of none other than the most popular madman in the ghetto himself, all turned out in tails.

*CHAIM HASENFUS WAS BORN IN WARSAW IN 1906; HE STUDIED
at the university before finding employment as an accountant in a
bank. His chronicle of ghetto events contains entries from late 1939 and
the first half of 1941. What became of the author remains unknown.*

12 JANUARY 1941

Today I visited pan Dreihorn, a refugee from Ozorków near Łódź
who once worked as a dentist and owned several buildings. Pan
Dreihorn read to me aloud from his impressions written in
Yiddish—so what if he writes with more moralizing than facts?

27 JANUARY 1941

Yesterday I attended a wedding in the ghetto. The reception was
unusually elegant; my former neighbor from Nowogrodzka Street,
the elegant Kubuś T, twenty-eight years old, married Ewunia Z,
age twenty-one.

3 FEBRUARY 1941

These are very stressful days. There's been a third registration of
Jewish men born between 1881 and 1926. The purpose is to place
them in labor camps. Apart from that, two German civilians
showed up today looking for furniture; fortunately they didn't find
anything they liked. Beggars have been pounding on the door saying that thousands of Jews from the provinces have been resettled
in Warsaw, which could spark a typhus epidemic.

26 MARCH 1941

I spent the day running around like a dog with its tongue hanging
out, didn't earn a penny, but maybe something will come of it.

This is my second year working as an intermediary and middleman, which brings in a little every now and then.

Yesterday I read in the DAZ [*Deutsche Allgemeine Zeitung*] an article with the headline NOT A JEWISH STATE BUT A JEWISH RESERVATION, written by Alfred Rosenberg, one of the chief propagandists and the author of *Blut und Boden* and *Mythus des XX. Jahrhunderts.** The piece evokes a mixture of terror, pity, disdain, and laughter. Driven by his consuming hatred, the author proposes that 15 million Jews be placed in a kind of wildlife preserve under the supervision of experienced German police, who would force them to do hard labor. This would bring salvation to the world by cleansing it of Jewish blood and delivering it from Jewish bankers. As further justification for his argument, the author quotes a letter to Lord Lansdowne from the *Diaries of T. Herzl,* in which the Zionist leader writes that the creation of a Jewish state would earn England ten million loyal subjects, currently scattered throughout the world. In Rosenberg's opinion, Palestine cannot solve the Jewish question as it cannot possibly house all the Jews; only a reservation will do. Evidently Rosenberg is vexed that England has a world empire while Germany still doesn't. The idea has nothing positive; the whole piece sounds like the ravings of a clever madman with sadistic tendencies.

Life has become distressing and depressing. There are dismaying rumors going around—about relocating the Jews in barracks outside Warsaw or kicking them out of Sienna Street. Living conditions in the ghetto, where it's difficult to find paid work, are desperate.

*Rosenberg was sentenced by the Nuremberg Tribunal and hanged in 1946.—PB

2 APRIL 1941

Yesterday at eight in the morning, along with everyone else born in 1906, I reported to 12 Prosta Street, where the commission has been set up to register people for the labor camps. By the time I was finished with all the formalities it was four in the afternoon. What struck me most while waiting was the number of people buying and selling places in line; several men, mostly fairly young or fairly old, had come early to hold a place, which they then sold for fifty groszy or a zloty or even two zlotys, depending on the client. The vendors weren't doing too bad either, selling bread and rolls, pretzels, candy, cigarettes, and hot coffee. The Jewish SP had their work cut out for them, keeping the unruly element in check, since there were many cases of latecomers trying to cut in. The police weren't receiving official pay, but they did manage to make something off the crowd; evidently, all you needed was a few zlotys to skip the line and move ahead more quickly. The people waiting in line realized what was going on but didn't make a fuss—after all, the police have to make a living as well. But the ones who profited most were the people from the Jewish Council and the medical commission, since everyone had to report to them. Referrals to a specialist cost 5 zloty 50 groszy (2 zloty for poor people); an exam without a referral cost 10 zloty, while 5 zloty would buy a deferment. The photographers and building administrators must have been in on the take as well, since everyone had to have two photos, officially stamped.

Tens of thousands of Jews have been relocated from the provinces and crammed into a closed district inside Warsaw, which was already packed with half a million. The move has meant the ruin of many families. Add to that the range of economic prohibitions, and it's no wonder that people are turning to begging and thieving. Most of the beggars are old women and children, although there are old men as well, and even some young men and boys.

They dress in filthy rags to arouse pity and weep and whine and groan, appealing to your conscience or else to God.

There's one young beggar in a fragile state who laughs merrily and cries despondently at the same time. Another person, ragged, dirty, and unshaven, keeps calling out the one word *Brojt*—bread—with maniacal repetition. Many are lying in the mud, listless and apathetic, but they still expect passersby to toss them a few groszy. Occasionally some poor hungry man will snatch a loaf of bread from someone else and eat it on the run. A crowd usually gathers: Sometimes they'll shove the man around, and sometimes he manages to get away with his loot. Any given beggar may have a proletarian background; he may be a former artisan or a merchant or occasionally even a member of the intelligentsia. One bespectacled intellectual keeps repeating in German that he is a refugee, a German Jew, in need of financial assistance. Another tries to appeal to your conscience by resorting to high-flown phrases. There's one old Jew who sits in front of the courthouse on Leszno Street reading psalms and praying out loud. Whole families stand outside the courthouse for hours with their poor, pitiful children—hungry, scared people trying to move the passing crowd by calling out or showing their swollen legs.

The street performers are also worth noting. There's one singer with a pince-nez who has an outstanding voice. His wife pushes a stroller containing their child to collect donations. Another man with a good voice sometimes makes the rounds of the stairwells singing religious songs. A girl on Ciepła Street intones hymns in Hebrew, while a tall beanpole of a girl from an educated family sings in a piercing voice: "This miserable life has laid me low, this fate so wretched, so vile/Don't pass me by, sister, lend me your hand, and stand by my side for a while." Occasionally for the sake of variety she sings "Sienna Street" or "I Made a Date with Her at Nine." Her mother stands by her side. There are musicians as well. A typical group consists of one lame trumpet player and two blind singers performing in Yiddish about "the city of Jerusalem." There are several violinists, though only a few are good.

All these people just want to live, but life in the ghetto is becoming more and more horrific, it's so hard to earn a living. A well-known beggar named Rubinsztejn calls himself a "wise fool" and has a number of witty sayings to offer. From time to time he calls out *"Alle glajch"*—All are equal. Who knows? Maybe we'll all end up as beggars.

24 APRIL 1941

Something happened to me today that has become rather common: I was going down Walicowa Street when a German soldier struck me on the head with his rubber nightstick and ordered me, along with several other Jews, to load gravel onto a truck. The work lasted half an hour.

I frequently walk through the ghetto from Sienna down Żelazna to Leszno, Solna, Karmelicka, and Pawia—hardly a cheerful or relaxing stroll; on the contrary, the whole thing is quite nerve-racking. Until recently you had to doff your cap to the guards; now you no longer have to do that, but there's a good chance you'll get caught in a roundup and sent to work. Which is why your heart pounds whenever you go outside and why it's considered an amazing success if you manage to get where you're going without incident. People are so wound up that the sight of a German truck is enough to set off a panic and send everyone scurrying. The streets are full of people bustling about, vendors selling candy, cigarettes, and cake. A regular market has sprung up on the corner of Ciepła and Grzybowska.

11 MAY 1941

I was at the cemetery today and have to say that, compared with the ghetto, the place is orderly and even full of joie de vivre. On Smocza Street I saw a boy collapse from hunger and bought two pretzels to give him. I was told they wouldn't help, as he was already in his death throes. At every step you see emaciated people weakened by hunger, tottering about and fainting. On Pańska Street there was another common sight: Some urchin wanted to make off with a woman's loaf of bread, but people stopped him and shook him up a little. On Sienna someone was beating a beggar for being too pushy. A group of gendarmes were strolling through the ghetto amusing themselves by kicking pedestrians.

I had a conversation—typical of the times—with three ladies who had recently been released from prison. They had been sent there for several months for not wearing armbands or for living outside the ghetto. All three were wealthy and well educated; all three were Catholics—one was even born into that faith. The Germans turned them back into Jews. One of the ladies explained that most of the women in prison were Jews who had been christened—the wives of Polish officers. Twenty-five people are kept in one cell. The daughter of the second lady is still in prison, and the husband of the third was sent to a prison in Siedlce. All three talked about passing secret messages, and the whole experience of prison made such an impression on the youngest that she's collecting literary accounts of prison experiences. They claimed that in general they were much better off there than in the ghetto.

26 JULY 1941

Because thousands of people have been thrown out of work, various social organizations have been created to attend to their needs. The basic units of this philanthropic operation are the building committees, elected by the residents of individual buildings. The committees primarily collect food and clothing, as well as donations for specific funds. Very high taxes have been imposed on everyone living in the ghetto. From time to time the committees organize artistic events to help raise money. The women's groups and youth circles excel in this and help each other's efforts. The chairmen, secretaries, and committee members are clearly becoming the social activists of the future; for the time being, however, they often pass the time in their meetings by playing cards.

Entertainment: There isn't much going on in the ghetto; the Melody Palace or the little theater Femina sometimes have good concerts, and "Szafa Gra" is known for its clever satirical sketches.* The Polish production of *Mirełe Efros* was a great hit; they also put on *Got fun nekome* by Asch.† But conditions in the ghetto are more conducive for performing penance than indulging in entertainment. It's not so much fun sitting in a café reading the anemic newspapers; even so, at least there it's possible to savor the aesthetic delights of solitude.

MAREK STOK. It's the hard winter of 1941. Despite all its various activities, the Council is unable to keep the situation under control. The hunger and misery are so shocking it's beyond imagining. Every day the Germans bring in thousands of poor Jews resettled from small towns in the provinces. The population keeps growing. There's no room; the shortage of living space is appalling, so these masses of people are put up in *punkty,* communal shelters converted from movie houses or whatever else happens to be available. The filth in these places is horrendous. There are thousands of miserable beggars permanently camped on the street, looking more like phantoms than human beings: ghostly figures in dirty tattered rags, with swollen legs and feverish eyes inside their emaciated faces. They're everywhere: in the courtyards, on the streets and sidewalks, leaning against the building walls. They moan and shout and beg for handouts. There's no way to help them and no

*A literal translation from the Polish would be "The music box is working," a Warsaw expression for "Everything's fine."—PB
†The first is a play by Jacob Gordin (1853–1909); the title is a woman's name. The second piece refers to *God of Vengeance* by Sholem Asch (1880–1957).

way to shake them off. You can't carry food across the street without some beggar running over, tearing it out of your grasp, and stuffing pieces of bread into his mouth as fast as he can. He has to hurry because as soon as the others see what he's up to the whole pack descends on him to knock him down and try to wrest the remaining booty from his hands. Then they're all rolling around in the street, beating each other, tearing at the bread, cramming it into their mouths, and screeching to high heaven. After a while the bread is finished; they get up calmly, no grudges, and await the next victim. If there's a corpse on the street in nothing but rags, people simply walk by and avert their eyes until some merciful soul covers the body with newspaper. Men, women, children—corpses are lying on nearly every street. In the morning they're collected en masse and carted to the cemetery. Given all the hunger and filth, a typhus epidemic is bound to break out come spring. Maybe that's how the Germans plan to get rid of us. Because within a year we'll all be felled either by typhus or starvation.

*THIS **ANONYMOUS WOMAN** WAS AN ACTIVE MEMBER OF HER building committee, helping to set up soup kitchens and distribute food. In 1942 her husband worked in a hospital ward, where the author, along with her four-year-old son, survived several roundups. In February 1943, mother and son escaped to the Aryan side. We have no further information beyond 21 June 1943, the date of her last entry.*

The Germans came to the ghetto with trucks to haul away the furniture. Most possessions—furniture, pictures, carpets, and the like—had been collected from the majority of the Jewish apartments even before the district was closed off. Practically every German visit to a Jewish home was accompanied by some brutality. They kicked and beat the inhabitants at every opportunity: if someone was a little too slow answering questions, or if he didn't carry the furniture adroitly enough, or mostly for no reason at all. One German gentleman punched my fifty-year-old neighbor in the eye because she took too long to find the whisk broom he had requested, even though the hallway was completely dark. They squeezed her husband's nose with pliers because he didn't say good-bye; the punishment was for a lapse of courtesy. Similar incidents could be listed ad infinitum.

The Germans didn't stop plundering inside the ghetto until the typhus epidemic began to gain strength. The disease had broken out in the first months after the Germans entered Warsaw, clearly due to the growing hunger and poverty. Food rations were incalculably small: Other than dark bread, which was supplied irregularly, and vegetables, which were scarcely ever available, there was practically nothing to eat, especially no meat or fat of any kind. People were undernourished; their nerves were exhausted; they neglected their apartments, which became increasingly filthy. If they didn't have money to buy their children a bit of bread, how were they going to pay for a bar of soap?

I know this side of life in the Warsaw Ghetto very well because I spent a long time working with the building committee on Ogrodowa Street. Assigned to my building were about thirty families (approximately 150 people) who lived in a small wooden shack set off at right angles to the main building and who had no electricity, gas, or water. Among them were a carriage driver whose horses had been taken by the Germans, a seamstress with two children whose husband—a provincial schoolteacher—had been killed, a bakery worker with ten mouths to feed, and so on. Ten or twenty people were crammed into each room: old parents, small children, or young people who had been removed from their places of work and were trying to earn a few pennies for bread by trading on the streets. They struggled with the difficult conditions as well as they could, but it was an uphill battle. Prices kept rising, while their strength and resources kept dwindling. Shortages of shoes and clothing left a severe mark. Hunger and cold often kept people confined to bed for weeks on end. The building committee organized a kitchen to feed the children, distributed packages for the holidays, paid for medicine and medical treatments, offered whatever aid or loans it could, procured clothes, sought employment for those able to work, and maintained a heated and lit community room where people could sit during the day. More than a dozen building committees set up a public kitchen on Ogrodowa Street, which served soup daily to several hundred of the poorest people.

Not only did the building committees fill an important role by bringing aid to the impoverished populace, they frequently also helped awaken their political consciousness. The committees were headed by people with ties to the working masses and were generally opposed by the Judenrat, which disapproved of independent programs. The Judenrat wanted to transform the committees into agencies that would implement its own agenda by pressuring the residents in their charge. To this end the Judenrat imposed a variety of payments and taxes on the committees, clearly designed to reduce the committees' available funds.

Whereas some committees continued operating several months into the liquidation actions, the one on Ogrodowa ceased operations when a new shift in the ghetto's boundaries relocated the street to the Aryan side. This was in 1941. The soup kitchen was closed at the same time, depriving many people in the neighborhood of a hot bowl of soup and needed nutrition. Hunger grew increasingly severe. More and more patients complained to their doctors of swelling due to hunger, and more and more corpses lay on the ghetto streets. Pale, emaciated children with huge, horribly hungry eyes sobbed and moaned and asked for bread. Living skeletons covered in rags became an increasingly common sight. There was scarcely a night when you didn't hear the groans of people dying on the street. The typhus spread. Doctors made superhuman efforts to control the disease: daily rounds of assigned buildings, lectures maintaining hygiene, attempts to obtain soap rations and disinfectants, and long hard hours in the hospital. But the epidemic grew, owing to the conditions inside the ghetto. Hundreds of dirty, starving Jews who had been declared unfit for work in the labor camps were relocated in Warsaw, and even more people were resettled from the provinces. Typhus decimated the population—in private homes, public shelters, children's boardinghouses, and in the punkty.

These last shelters for homeless refugees had their own desperate, tragic story. They housed masses of people who had been deprived of their homes and shipped in from outside the city without any possessions or means of support. The agency responsible for their welfare put these people up wherever it could and struggled to keep them alive. But what kind of life was it, with over a dozen—or even several dozen—people to a room, lacking even the most primitive cots for sleeping, and, worst of all, with no food, no hope for tomorrow, no energy to go on living? A few lucky ones managed to break out and move in with some distant relative, miraculously discovered, where they would add to the poverty already reigning in that household. Some stayed put for as long as it took for a merciful death to bring an end to their suffering.

The mortality rate rose. On average, some four thousand people died each month. As the poverty and hunger worsened, tuberculosis also became epidemic and wrought horrible devastation up to the very end of the ghetto's existence. It was impossible to fight. Thousands of adults and children died because they were getting no fat, no milk, no sugar. The hospitals were overflowing and the doctors despaired at their powerlessness.

Life in the ghetto never flowed smoothly. News of every event, regardless of its significance, was passed from mouth to mouth. One day a small Jewish boy was killed on Biała Street as he attempted to pull a carrot lying in the gutter on the Aryan side through a hole in the fence. A German spotted him, inserted his gun in the hole, and killed the boy with one well-aimed shot. Was it so strange that this incident should have moved thousands of people? Another case involved a notorious gendarme known as Frankenstein, who had vowed he would personally kill a thousand Jews. From a window of the building at Elektoralna 6, I once saw this murderer at work in the courtyard, killing the concierge, who refused to say where another Jew had run off, supposedly a smuggler who had caught Frankenstein's eye.

During the winter of 1942, people were going barefoot on the streets. But that no longer made much of an impression; by then the ghetto residents had grown indifferent even to the dry shriveled faces and dull stares of children who were alive but unable to walk, whose mouths could no longer form words, and whose speech was reduced to a terrifying gibberish. Their eyes showed neither tears nor hunger, but only death, painting its features inside their faces. For the most part these children sat near the courthouse; people learned to pass by these living human horrors calmly, just as they passed the corpses.

The Germans started filming inside the ghetto.* One day they drove to the Judenrat and ordered a lavish banquet to be staged in the home of the council president, with a number of elegantly dressed guests. That was filmed along with several other banquets staged in various other apartments. They also filmed in restaurants and cafés. They even took the camera to the Jewish bathhouse, or mikvah, but that day no dirty, starving Jews were allowed inside;

---

*In May 1942 a German film crew visited the Warsaw Ghetto. Scenes were set up showing Jews living a life of luxury, with declining ethical and moral norms and wanton sexual mores.

the Germans rounded up well-dressed people from off the street. They filmed a Jewish funeral as well. Inside the ghetto, especially in 1942, all funerals followed the same pattern. A collective hearse—a large box divided into two floors, each of which held three or four litters—arrived for the corpse; it could be pulled by a single person if there was only one deceased. The German film crew staged a different kind of funeral. The hearse was decorated with flowers and pulled by two beautifully festooned horses, while a sumptuously dressed rabbi led the procession. Of course no funerals like that ever happened in the ghetto. It was obvious that the films were designed as propaganda.[3]

STEFAN ERNEST. Numerous sporadic cases of typhus preceded the epidemic that broke out in full force in the summer of 1941 and continued unabated for almost a year, until the spring of 1942.

The epidemic claimed dozens of victims every day; during the peak months of October, November, December, and January the daily mortality rate approached two hundred. The official statistics for each of these months refer to six thousand registered deaths. And that's not counting all the nameless wretches who died of cold and starvation on the streets and were buried inside the Jewish cemetery in common unmarked graves, their passing never recorded.

Poverty, hunger, and the camps select the weakest and poorest. But typhus is more democratic. It reaps its victims from all classes, professions, and walks of life. By some odd decree of fate, poor people seemed more resistant to the disease than the ones better off—the likely winners in the economic war.

Typhus had provided the Germans with a legal pretext for creating the ghetto, although there were no cases of true typhus at the time, and the minor outbreak of typhoid fever in the fall and early winter of 1939 affected Poles and Jews and German soldiers alike.

What caused the epidemic were the walls, which enclosed half a million people in poverty, hunger, and cramped conditions. For a long time it was forbidden to dispose of sewage and refuse outside these walls, so the inhabitants inside were forced to subsist in filth.

It's no surprise that lice found an excellent breeding ground, especially considering that the number of hosts was swelling geometrically with the constant forced arrival of people from the provinces. These new refugees being squeezed in behind the walls were invariably already ridden with lice.

War was declared on the epidemic. Despite the lack of resources and outside aid, people managed to organize quarantines for new arrivals, periodic "steam baths" for apartments, houses, and entire buildings, and individual disinfections of people, possessions, and apartments carried out by mobile sanitation units equipped with gas and protective clothing. Numerous public baths were opened; lectures were held; appeals were posted on the streets, in the offices, and at the entrances to buildings calling on people to keep clean, keep clean! Every case of typhus had to be reported to the Department of Health, whereupon the infected apartment was immediately sanitized and the patient taken to the hospital. Doctors were forbidden—under penalty of death—to treat typhus patients in their homes. The hospitals no longer had room for other sick people. Practically all the sections were closed to accommodate the Infectious Disease Ward. Each of the ghetto's four hospitals—Leszno 1, Stawki, Berson-Śliska, and Berson-Leszno/Żelazna—were marked with warning signs saying SEUCHEN-KRANKENHAUS!* Every other building was closed off, guarded by the SP, and posted with a yellow sign—ACHTUNG, ACHTUNG: FLECK-FIEBER—warning that a disinfection was in progress.† Under SP

---

*Epidemic hospital!—PB
†Attention, attention: Typhus—PB

escort, long lines of people snaked through the streets on their way to "steam baths" to be quarantined and disinfected.*

It appeared that the epidemic would finish the job that poverty and hunger had failed to accomplish, even though the latter had soon been joined by severe cold as well, brought on by the ban on fur as much as by the harsh winter.[†][4] And rumors were spreading about cholera and bubonic plague. Clearly, if the epidemic continued at the rate it had progressed in November and December, within five or six years not a single soul would be left inside the ghetto. The invaders rubbed their hands with glee—their work would take care of itself—until they realized that even at that rate things would take too long!

By the spring of 1942, the epidemic had begun to lose strength, both because of efforts to contain it and because it had almost run its course. But when finally the disease died out, it was replaced by a new plague, that has since taken a terrible toll, especially of the children, who, while more immune to typhus, are dropping like flies from tuberculosis! About 200,000 people have contracted typhus; approximately 30,000 have died from that disease, and the cost of containing it is enormous. Doctors have suffered a higher mortality rate than anyone else.

Even so, when the three horsemen of the Apocalypse summoned by the invader—pestilence, famine, and cold—proved no match for the Jews of the Warsaw Ghetto, the knights of the SS were called in to complete the task.

---

*Typhus, and the fear of typhus, led the German authorities to impose many controls—often ineffective or even unsound—that ranged from delousing certificates to quarantines and disinfections carried out on-site or at the public bathhouses.—PB

†On 25 December 1941, Auerswald posted a decree requiring Jews to surrender all articles of clothing containing fur—under pain of death. The measure caused untold suffering during the severe winter.—PB

NATAN ŻELICHOWER, ALSO KNOWN AS JAN KURCZAB, WAS A dental technician in Warsaw before the war. In 1942, after losing both wife and daughter, Żelichower was assigned to the plunder crews known as the Raumkommando, *until that group was sent to Majdanek in April 1943. Żelichower's memoir covers both his life in the ghetto and his harrowing odyssey through the camps. He was liberated from Buchenwald in April 1945.*

The people of the ghetto street formed one huge mass of castaways doomed to extinction, subsisting on a daily diet of anguished news and heart-wrenching notices. With its relentless reports of dead and dying friends and acquaintances, the street served as a constant memento mori, a terrible whip in the hands of a merciless executioner, flogging into sobriety any drunken hopes for a better tomorrow. But the street was also a true life-giving artery. Shadowy figures emerged from the depths of the blackened city to feed off the street like leeches, and these in turn fed others, even to the point of nourishing delusions of a bright future built on easy living and abundant earnings.

Raw nerves cried out at the slightest touch. The most trivial matter would set women crowded around a kitchen stove to quarreling. Every pot became the subject of a spat, every spoon sparked anger, every child's cry triggered a mother's sharp reaction. The ghetto lived in a constant tense clamor that grew worse with every piece of bad news and rarely if ever was silenced. Even the seemingly quiet nights only muffled but did not still this unbroken lament.

Everyone stayed alert. No one left home without first asking, "What's it like out today?" Once outside, people focused trained eyes on their surroundings, searching for danger. Pedestrians traded words of warning that could suddenly shift the direction of traffic. Mere mention of a threat, the slightest gesture, could send a crowd of several thousand back inside, leaving the street empty and bare.

Danger could swoop down like a hawk. A black limousine would pull up at a street corner; a Gestapo officer would step out and casually survey the crowd. He would choose his victims, summon them with his finger, shove them into the car, and speed off toward the destroyed buildings on Dzielna Street, just opposite the Pawiak prison. There they would be subjected to a meticulous search and then shot in the head, while the car would return to the ghetto in search of new prey. This private hunting became a favorite sport among dignitaries of the new regime in need of immediate financial relief. If they appeared on a street the traffic would slow down, although it never stopped altogether. After the limousine left, people would diligently inquire who had been taken away—and then return to business, trading, shouting, haggling, consoling . . . and waiting for the next black limousine.

During the night, soldiers would make the rounds of certain buildings accompanied by members of the SP; they would pound on doors using their rifle butts and nightsticks. Dozens of men whose names had been listed in advance would be dragged from their homes. These dazed, terrified victims would be led to some side street, lined up against a wall, and gunned down on the spot. Then the perpetrators would briskly ring the doorbells of the buildings nearest the corpses and order the concierges to stack the bodies in the entranceways and wash the blood off the pavement. A few hours later, crowds of people would step over the same spot completely unaware of what had taken place there. The only news of these incidents traveled through word of mouth, as people passed along the victims' names—at least for a day or two, until the next execution.

The Jews did not believe in their own extinction. At the very center of their "spiritual refuge" sat God, who, having led them through the Red Sea, would surely knock down the walls of the ghetto. While the executions filled people with terror and wrenched their hearts with fear, there was always some space left for reasoning: Methods such as this might enable the Germans to eliminate a few thousand or, let's say, even tens of thousands, but surely not half a million people! Logically speaking then, since not everyone inside the ghetto was doomed, each person had a chance of escaping alive. And the best defense against executions was faith—an unwavering faith in divine protection, along with vigilance and cleverness to avoid getting caught in a roundup. In time, though, none of these defenses could withstand the cunning techniques devised by the Germans.

SAMUEL PUTERMAN. The second Passover in the ghetto.* Once again the Jewish Council has obtained permission to bake matzoh, the Provisions Department managing to distribute half a kilogram more than last year. Over the past twelve months the ghetto has lost tens of thousands, but these people have been replaced by two or three times that number, as new arrivals are shipped in from small towns in the provinces. Hardly a single family left inside the ghetto has not been touched by death. On the first night of Passover, the Seder, the Feast of Remembrance, families gather at tables covered with white tablecloths. Mechanically, they repeat the words of the Haggadah. What do they care about the fate of their brothers thousands of years ago? Just last year there was a father, a mother, brothers, sisters, husbands. The Traubes take their tablecloth, still spotlessly white, large enough for twenty-four guests, and fold it in half. The faces look familiar—but no, some

---

*The text refers to *Wielkanoc,* which is Polish for Easter but was also used by many to mean Passover (or "Jewish Easter") as well as the general holiday season. In 1942 the two holidays fell close together: The first night of Passover fell on Wednesday, 1 April, while Easter came on Sunday, 5 April.—PB

are missing: Aniela Traube, and Moryc with his Janka. Fela's already a widow, sitting there with her little girls. Mother and daughters discreetly brush tears from their eyes. Everyone is crying. Jakub Traube struggles heroically to stem the sobs rising in his throat. He can no longer chant the words of the Haggadah. Two months ago he lost his brother, who was walking down Karmelicka Street when a German truck came along transporting prisoners to Pawiak. The German sitting to the right of the driver was amusing himself by beating pedestrians; his stout cane happened to land on Abram Traube, who fell to the ground with a fractured skull; concussion was followed by death. He left a wife and four children. Meanwhile pani Gwajfus learned of her husband's death through official channels: The previous summer he had been caught in a roundup and sent to the labor camp at Kawęczyn. Basia's husband, Herman, lost both parents in one week to typhus. Karol's mother died in the Central Jail. The old lady had gone out to buy bread and forgotten to put on her armband. She ran into some gendarmes on patrol who sent her to prison. After two weeks she died of a heart attack.

"Thank you, Lord, for preserving those dearest to me." *Pan* Jakub sighs quietly as he looks tenderly at his wife and children and their spouses. He goes on reading the Haggadah, trying to recover his normal melodious resonance, but his voice is drowned out by the women weeping, by the sobs that are filling every Jewish home this evening. Everyone is worried about what will happen next, and this worry grips each exhausted heart in an iron vise. Fathers close the Haggadah and finish with the words *B'shana haba, b'yerushalayim*—Next year in Jerusalem.

MAREK STOK. Early on the morning of 17 March 1942, we learned that a small pogrom had taken place in the ghetto.* The Germans

---

*Stok, writing in 1944, is presumably referring to the massacre during the night of 17–18 April 1942. Other sources put the number of victims at 52 or 53.[5]

dragged fifty-seven people from their homes and shot them on the nearby streets. The police cleaned up the corpses just before morning, and the bodies were hauled off to the cemetery. Among those shot were Blajman, a well-known baker, and his wife, as well as a printer, a teacher, a smuggler, and so on. The mood in the ghetto was very grim. Everyone wanted to know why those people in particular had been dragged out and killed during the night. Some said it was all part of a campaign against smuggling and profiteering (Blajman and the smuggler); others said the reasons were political (the printer and the teacher). The Jewish Council circulated a reassuring memorandum that said, "According to information obtained from the German authorities, the execution was a singular event and would not be repeated."

And in fact the next two or three nights passed peacefully. But then several days later the nocturnal shootings resumed, and several dozen more people were shot. And that was only the beginning. After that scarcely a night passed in peace. They called these pogroms "executions." Early each morning we would learn whether forty people had been killed or whether it had been relatively quiet, with just a few executions—eighteen people, hardly worth mentioning. Sometimes we'd hear there had been as many as sixty or more. Typically they would let up for a day or two and then resume. Most were carried out in the same manner. First the victim was dragged from his home, where a car was waiting out front, ready to train its headlights. The victim would be ordered to step into the light, and the Germans would fire several rounds into the back of his head. As a rule the corpses were left where they fell, though on occasion the victim was forced into the car, to be killed on some other street and left there.

An increasing number of incidents involved Jews caught on the Aryan side who were brought to the ghetto and shot. This occurred even in broad daylight. In several cases the person was returned right to his doorstep; a Gestapo officer would politely extend his hand in farewell and say, "So now you've made it back safe and sound," but the minute the man turned around to go inside the same officer would dispatch a bullet to the back of his head. The officer would then calmly order the nearest Jewish policeman to take care of the corpse and casually drive away.

Later things got even worse, in a bizarre way. The street roundups ceased. The *Transferstelle* began placing very large orders.* But there was no letup to the shooting and killing. A large car left Pawiak prison every afternoon around one or two and drove down Karmelicka and Leszno while the Germans inside would shoot at people on the street. One officer drove a small sports car. This gentleman would zigzag down Leszno Street, firing all the while at pedestrians. It was a game. The sentries also started shooting from their posts. This had happened before, but never to such a degree. They shot people for attempts at smuggling or for no visible reason at all. All of a sudden a gendarme would grab his rifle and fire a few bullets into the crowd. When he shouldered his weapon there would be several people lying dead or wounded in the street. The gendarme nicknamed Frankenstein—after the character from the horror film—excelled at this game. People said about this particular Frankenstein that he couldn't sleep at night unless he had on his slate for the day at least one murdered Jew.

*The Transferstelle, or Transit Authority, controlled the traffic of goods to and from the ghetto.—PB

Adam Czerniaków

Chapter 2

GHETTO INSTITUTIONS

As early as September 1939, the German Security Police had dictated the establishment of Jewish Councils or Judenräte to maintain order within the newly established ghettos and to help implement subsequent Nazi agendas. The structure and degree of autonomy of these councils varied greatly; in Warsaw its members were largely respected men active in Jewish civic circles. Headed by Adam Czerniaków, the Council oversaw most social services within the ghetto, with nearly complete autonomy over "internal" affairs. Other institutions active in the ghetto included a coalition of independent welfare agencies and branch offices of international groups such as the Joint Distribution Committee (known as the Joint) and HIAS. The people in these agencies struggled against overwhelming odds to control poverty, famine, and epidemics within the ghetto. A more problematic institution was the Jewish police force—here most often referred to by its Polish initials SP, for Służba Porządkowa. Originally set up as an arm of the Jewish Council and charged with maintaining order, most who joined initially believed their participation was the best way to effect positive change. In time, however, the SP became an institutional accessory to murder; the gradual coopting of many of its members forms one of the ghetto's greatest tragedies.

STEFAN ERNEST. Pan *inżynier* Adam Czerniaków, *Der Obmann des Judenrates*—the chairman of the Jewish Council, whom we called the President for short—was a man with a distinguished career of public service in independent Poland: former senator of the republic, councilman for the city of Warsaw, member of the Jewish Community Board, director of the State Accounting Office,* and an active advocate of cooperatives for Jewish craftsmen on behalf of the Artisans Guild,[1] a man who did not hesitate to shoulder the ultimate responsibility for the fate of the unhappiest people on earth, in the hope he might be able to ease their lot.

Czerniaków was undoubtedly a man of the best will, the finest intentions, the highest devotion. With requests, petitions, and other insufficient bureaucratic measures, he struggled to postpone danger, to allay harm, and to remove new threats of repression devised by those in power. Now and then he managed to wangle this or that during official audiences with Leist or Auerswald—although never with SS Untersturmführer Brandt.† Subjected to moral and physical abuse (on more than one occasion he was publicly slapped by Gestapo or SS men), he was clearly willing to sacrifice his life for the sake of the community. He was a martyr who did not mince words, the foremost symbol of an oppressed society. Within the ghetto he fought to preserve the status quo, to keep as many people alive as possible and their social structures intact, so the community would survive the war. Unlike the Jews in Łódź, he ruled out radical or revolutionary programs, and that may have been his gravest tactical error, if it doesn't turn

---

*This information is imprecise. Before World War II, Czerniaków worked in the Foreign Accounting Office.

†Heinz Auerswald, commissar for the Jewish District, 1941–1942, was investigated by West German authorities but not charged. He died in 1970. Ludwig Leist, an early governor of Warsaw, was sentenced by the Polish court to eight years. Karl Georg Brandt, who was not sentenced, is no longer alive.—PB

out that all of Łódź ended up in Treblinka.* He was especially protective of the intelligentsia, professionals, young people, and children—whom he considered the foundation of his people's future in a happier time. At least they would enjoy physical and moral health, thanks to their fathers, who were fated to bear this terrible cross of suffering and humiliations.

For the ghetto's public institutions, he worked to secure as much autonomy as possible, and he generally enjoyed widespread respect and recognition. Indeed, there were some who believed he was a pawn in the hands of a particular clique, while others considered him simply too weak. Given the circumstances, though, could he have been more than he was or done more than he did? Could he have led with a "strong hand"? It was his refusal to be a tyrant that some people read as a sign of weakness and ineptitude. It's true that the Jewish Council was infested with vile and corrupt weeds like the "Thirteen," or the Konhellers and their ilk, who were specially cultivated by the Gestapo and who thrived despite Czerniaków's honest and best intentions.† And if the sprawling administrative apparatus occasionally failed in its duties to the populace it served, this was unavoidable. One thing is certain: The President was the protagonist of a classic tragedy whose terrible finale was rehearsed and staged by a monster.

---

*Chaim Rumkowski, the authoritarian head of the Łódź Judenrat, believed he could save a significant number of the Jews in his charge by mobilizing ghetto productivity and complying with German demands—to the point of calling on Jews to surrender their children for deportation.—PB

†Officially the Office for Combatting Usury and Speculation, the group was known as the Thirteen because of its location at 13 Leszno Street. A concessionary front for the Gestapo, it was run by the collaborator Abraham Gancwajch. Czerniaków struggled against their attempts to infiltrate the Council. Moryc Kon and Zelig Heller used their connections with the Gestapo to obtain various concessions, notably to develop their horse-drawn transportation business.—PB

I can see his powerful looming form, his face frozen in pain and torment, as if mirroring the collective anguish of those he led. Unchanging, deadly serious, he comported himself with a solemnity that commanded respect. Winter or summer he always wore a black coat, whether at his desk or outside the office, in his "official" vehicle or on the street. Never did he smile. Wounds inflicted on his person did not hurt him, but he was truly tormented by the suffering of the ghetto as a whole. He was a pure symbol of his oppressed people.

JAN MAWULT (STANISŁAW GOMBIŃSKI, A LAWYER BY PROfession) directed a department of the SP, the Jewish police force. He wrote his account in hiding during the first half of 1944; after the war he reportedly emigrated to Paris, where he died in the 1980s.

A man sits behind a desk. He looks between fifty and sixty years old, stout, with a fleshy clean-shaven face, drooping cheeks, and a slightly hanging lower lip. He is bald and wears heavy spectacles on his somewhat crooked, flattened nose. At first glance you might say he was a banker, an industrialist, a surgeon—but whatever his profession, it's clear that this is a real human being, a person who loves life and understands it in all its variety, someone who appreciates the aroma of a good cigar, the taste of fine food, the bouquet of a nice dry wine. Discerning, life-loving, he does not abstain from sensual pleasures, but neither does he indulge them in their basest forms. For despite its heavy sensual contours, there are certain aspects of his face—the line of his chin, the shadow of a grimace hidden in the folds around his lips—that bespeak a certain finesse, a subtlety of taste. When he assumes his full height, he is an imposing man who carries his years well, when he walks it is with a rapid, self-assured step, and when he speaks his sentences are coherent and clear.

But when the man behind the desk removes his pince-nez, rubs his tired eyes, and looks directly at his interlocutor, our impression of him changes somewhat. The man's gaze is piercing, circumspect, and kind; for a split second the mask is dropped, offering a glimpse of another, deeper nature.

The man behind the desk is no newcomer to the political arena; as a senator, department director in the State Accounting Office, and energetic spokesman for the Artisans Guild, he has spent many years in public life, and his experience is buttressed by his long tenure as a teacher. He is even less a novice when it comes to Jewish life. He became senator with the support of Jewish craftsmen and was active in the Jewish Artisans Association, serving as a teacher and director of the Jewish Community Trade School. For decades he has lived in the capital, leading the life of most Polish—and particularly Warsaw—Jews. Consequently he has a deep understanding of everyday Jewish affairs; this is his life, and he is bonded to it forever.

Since September 1939 the man behind the desk has been in charge of the largest concentration of Jews in Europe. He was chosen—supposedly at the initiative of Mayor Starzyński*—to fill the chair of the previous Gmina president, and he remained in that office after the Germans occupied Warsaw (proclaiming in their first declaration that neither Jews nor other citizens had any "cause for worry.") This is the man who holds the wheel; he is trying to steer his vessel into port, trying to ride out the storm, so that those in his care may survive.

The man behind the desk is hardly ill-equipped. Being an engineer has always meant more to him than simply having a degree; he is constantly striving to expand his knowledge. Among

---

*As mayor of Warsaw, Stefan Starzyński oversaw the city's defense. He is presumed to have died in Dachau in 1944.—PB

his many assets are his experience as a public servant, his ability to maneuver, and his familiarity with the language, customs, culture, and representatives of the Herrenvolk that he acquired during his student days and consolidated over many years as head of the German department in the Accounting Office (which oversaw all trade between Poland and Germany). Add to that his deep wisdom, high intelligence, and active intellectual life—so rare among men in such demanding positions—and he is a pleasant, captivating, and fascinating conversationalist. This man who at first glance seemed heavy, earthbound, and sensual is surprisingly adept at discussing literature, history, and cultural trends. He is further capable of humor and lightness, ease, and skepticism and can convey more with one word, glance, or gesture than others with whole torrents of speech. On occasion these various traits enable him to display great grace and charm—despite appearances to the contrary.

His attitude toward the Germans is essentially that of an opposing player, but to the gray masses placed under his stewardship he is something else entirely. If "politics" is defined as the art of ruling, he is not a politician and has no aspirations to be one. He tries with all his might to help as many people as possible. He does not strive to transform or improve the lot of the whole, since he doesn't consider this within the realm of possibility. Rather, he struggles for individuals, concentrating on specific cases, though these might involve anywhere from several to several hundred people. And always his primary concern is to address material needs.

He focuses on the fate of different groups in the ghetto and does what he can to come to their aid. He helps the artists by looking for opportunities for them to create. Thanks to him, some have received commissions for paintings, woodcuts, and graphic designs, and pretexts have been found to engage the services of poets, journalists, and singers. The offerings are small in proportion to the need, but at least he is thinking about them, at least he is trying

to help. The list goes on: scholars, professionals, refugees, tradesmen, all headed for ruin, all in a hopeless struggle—or, rather,
being crushed by fate without a struggle. Such a long list of those
in need, and such a short list of resources for helping! But the
man behind the desk never wavers; he works with the limited
possibilities at his disposal. Is there no greatness to his unceasing
forward crawl, his reluctance to yield, his refusal to dwell on the
losses?

Undaunted by repeated disappointments, the man behind the
desk is always on the lookout for new ways and means to cement
his ties with the populace. He greets every initiative in this direction with enthusiasm. Only now and then, when he spies private
interests cloaked in noble words and discerns a different face lurking behind seemingly altruistic plans and lofty motives—only then
does his zeal begin to flag. At such times he says, "I feel as though
I'm stranded on a bank of steadily rising mud. First it's up to my
knees, then my chest, then my neck, until finally it covers my
head—and everything comes to an end."

This inept and superficially sketched portrait is not the creation of legend. This is the way he was: highly cultured, kind, and
intelligent. His only private fault may have been a certain acceptance of byzantine ritual—too much incense. But even if he wasn't
entirely immune to gestures of servility, he was by no means exces-
sive in this regard—after all, he was First Citizen of the ghetto.
And though he was occasionally criticized for this, he played the
role of tribal chief far less than certain others. Moreover, while he
tolerated some degree of sycophancy, he never actively embraced
it. Everyone who came into contact with him, whether personally
or on official business, saw that he was frank and direct, without the slightest sign of bluster. Neither he, nor especially his
wife—a pale, tall, slender lady whose bearing, dress, and appearance reflected her years as a schoolteacher and principal—
displayed any superficial glitter or engaged in social posing. So

his acceptance of a byzantine atmosphere was not an indication of his private personality; rather, it stemmed from his need, being a man in public office, to put up with this or that despite his inner preferences.

Maybe this is where he was wrong; maybe this was his mistake. In his effort to avoid any despotic tendencies, he erred in the opposite direction: He was not decisive enough. He followed no political line; his only mission was to survive. And this might not have been such a bad strategy, had he also been able to communicate his will to his people, had there been some framework for such communication. But there was none, and the absence of such a structure continued uncorrected until events themselves intervened, until fate dictated its own course.

SAMUEL PUTERMAN. The main lobby of the Council is abuzz with activity. The masons have just finished repairing the holes in the stucco; in place of the old ornamental pilasters there are gleaming patches of new plaster. One can smell the paint, feel the light moisture as it dries wafting from the floor despite the strong sun slanting through the open window in full beams. The master artists are bustling about the gigantic hall, focused on their work with an energy that has been suppressed for three years—artistic painting is punishable by death. The artists have forgotten where they are, forgotten all about the ghetto and its walls. Carried away by sacred inspiration, they have forgotten for whom they are working. They have been drafting, sketching, and painting from dawn to dusk. They have forgotten their physical hunger, too, though this is their first chance to satisfy it.

They have even forgotten the proverbial professional jealousy. They are working in one space, constantly checking what the others are doing; their glances flit discreetly from one easel to the next. They form an indivisible whole, welded together by a common passion that has been held captive for three years, confined to endless discussions of art and nothing more. After three years of struggle to survive, jealousy has given way to a growing bitterness toward the society that in the first hour of poverty cast them aside as something completely superfluous—bitterness and also resentment toward those who helped them, who gave them bread and asked that they stand in line and affix their signatures to nothing more than charts, to the glory of a given social agency. Now for the first time they are able to sign their paintings instead of welfare receipts from the Joint or other institutions. They don't mind that they are painting together; they're even proud of their ability to collaborate. Envious criticism has been replaced by mutual critique and carefully weighed corrections.

The largest composition, "Job," is the object of lengthy discussion. For the moment it's only been roughed out, but this will obviously be a wonderful work of art, as long as they don't ruin it. The painters are Frydman, Puterman, and Trachter. The picture is alive with a richness of muted hues and perfect technique. Frydman's dynamics combine with Trachter's expressiveness to expand the picture. Each artist works with his own palette, but all three have the same cultural perspective, the same expertise. Together they create multiple planes that vie with one another in a vibrant struggle that benefits the whole. Like musicians in an orchestra led by a conductor's firm hand, they sit beside one another and call to life a symphony of colors. The figures representing Job's friends come from all four corners of the earth; they carry a hint of faraway places, a weariness of travel, a genuine expression of concern and sorrow for Job's condition.

The central figure is after Michelangelo; the drawing is enhanced by the combination of talents, with the result that the three artists have created a figure worthy of the Renaissance masters. Job's head rests heavily on one hand, expressing the tragedy and torment of a nation that has been damned and oppressed for centuries. His mighty body is doubled over, powerless, but it exudes an inner anguish, a fervor, even a strength that make a striking impression on the viewer. Some titanic force issues from within, the suffering of a great soul who continues to fight even though he has fallen. The painters are modernists who have always steered clear of overtly literary influence, so this is a difficult experiment—but all three will emerge triumphant. Trachter is standing before the painting; his white smock accenting his albino coloring and the angular cut of his jaw. Without stopping what he is doing, he stares wide-eyed in wonder. Then with one subtle stroke he fuses and tempers the work of Puterman and Frydman, pulling everything together into one harmonious whole according to a plan he proceeds to execute in soft, subtle tones. The sun is already setting; the din from the corridors is quieting down. Trachter works in silence, expressionless. His colleagues let him be: no barbs or teasing, no Symchele this or Symchele that. This is not the time for jokes; his colleagues are full of admiration for his divine spark. Suddenly he's finished—that's it for the day. The spell has been broken, and they give his shoulders a friendly pat: Symchele, you must have worn yourself out! But today you've really earned yourself a nice dinner.

The idea is contagious. Everyone is devilishly hungry but in fine spirits. In a few days the lobby will be ready; the Gestapo desk officer for Jewish Affairs, SS Untersturmführer Brandt, is supposed to attend the opening. President Czerniaków suggested he might manage to obtain permission for a one-time exhibition of paintings. The three men leave; outside it's still bright enough to make them blink, and each goes his separate way to have dinner. An hour later they regroup in the Artists Garden.*

---

*This was a café and garden for artists on the former Mylna Street. In Poland, the main meal is served in midafternoon.

JAN MAWULT. On 29 October 1940, Szeryński took office as head of the Służba Porządkowa (*Ordnungsdienst* in German)—the official name of the police attached to the Jewish Council in Warsaw.* The SP was originally designed as one of several departments within the Council. Each department consisted of a supervisor and lower officials, and—in keeping with current practice—was overseen by the Council Commission. Leopold Kupcykier was the councillor chosen to oversee Department Seventeen—the SP.

Before the war, Kupcykier owned a chocolate and candy factory; his previous experience with the Artisans Guild earned him a seat on the Council, even though his new position had little to do with guild work. He was the kind of energetic entrepreneur common among Polish Jews before the war, especially in cities and towns, the type that frequented official bureaus, trade associations, and other institutions, always smooth and elegant, always working for the common good while fervently courting those in power, constantly cultivating the people who mattered and unfailingly respectful toward the authorities. Kupcykier was also a glib poseur, vain and conceited. But he was kind, gentle, and compassionate to those less fortunate; he happily devoted his time to people in need; he showed great interest in others and was eager to assist them—all as long as his efforts were acknowledged and advertised. He was passionately concerned about the fate of the intelligentsia and did what he could to find work for them and help them survive. If this sketch seems full of contradictions, its inconsistencies give a true picture of the man.

Initially the SP was located in what had been the main office of the trade school, on the ground floor of the Council annex at

---

*Lieutenant Colonel Józef Szeryński (formerly Szynkman). A converted Jew, he served as an inspector in the National Police headquarters until the war broke out. Sentenced to death by the resistance, Szeryński was wounded on 25 August 1942, in an assassination attempt by Izrael Kanał of the Jewish Fighting Organization. After the latter group began actively fighting the Germans in January 1943, Szeryński committed suicide.[2]

Grzybowska 26. It occupied two rooms in the left wing: The first served as a receiving area and was manned by functionaries from the former *Straż Porządkowa.** Inherent in the setup was the potential for corruption. In light of the huge number of pending cases, a temporary cap was placed on filing new petitions, but with no supervisory control some of the officials continued to accept them on an "unofficial" basis.

The second room functioned as SP headquarters, where Szeryński and several of his closest collaborators had their offices, and where Kupcykier or Deputy Chief Händel would occasionally "drop in." This room also housed the representatives of the Council Commission who had been charged with receiving petitions before Szeryński took office. These included Councillors Graf and Cukier, the commission secretary. Other members of the Commission included (if I remember correctly) Councillors Zabłudowski, Kobryner, Glicksberg, and Zundelewicz (a lawyer)—as well as Adam Fels, whose role was unspecified and whose presence was probably due to his close acquaintance with the Council President and Kupcykier. Fels was a man of enormous build, at that time close to sixty, from a well-known Warsaw family of merchants. He was involved in the SP throughout the ghetto's existence. He didn't want to sit idly by; he wanted to do something, which is why he attached himself to the Commission. Although I list him as a councillor, he had no official position—I simply want to stress the fact that his work with the SP resulted from his connections with the Council. As soon as the Jewish prison, or *Arrestanstalt,* was organized, he took the prisoners under his wing. Unasked and under no one's orders, he performed acts of kindness, such as delivering letters or packages to family members, and helped in any way he could whenever there was an explosive situation

---

*"Order Guard" (as opposed to the later Służba Porządkowa or Order Service described here).—PB

involving the SP: a roundup, individual detentions, or finally at the terrible Umschlagplatz. He wanted to do something, and he accomplished a good deal; probably everyone he encountered has only the best recollections. He was one of the few—the very few— who shunned all honor or advantage, who shrank from positions of authority, who was always eager to serve, kindhearted, decent, and gentle. And this good, sensitive, and honest man met with a vile and sorry end: In April 1943, on the first day of the uprising, he was accused of being a German flunky and felled by a Jewish bullet. The ghetto had its share of such paradoxes.*

The SP was set up along lines designed by Szeryński, who had taken as his model a similar organization from before the war. The President of the Jewish Council—acting with the Council itself—was to serve as commander in chief; next came the Supervising Councillor and the Council Commission; then the Chief of the SP along with his command, known as the KSP.† Next came the executive sectors.

In reality the KSP was represented by one person throughout its existence: the SP Deputy Chief. Originally there was to be a secretariat headed by a chief—a de facto unofficial second Deputy Chief— and composed of offices under his command. These included a daily records bureau, an archive, and three further divisions:

1. Organization and Administration—with separate specialists overseeing organization and administration as well as service and training
2. Personnel—with specialists assigned to personnel files and disciplinary matters
3. Economic—with specialists in payroll, supply, and main-

---

*The information is imprecise. Fels died as the result of wounds inflicted during a shootout between the resistance fighters and the Nazis. Before he died he supposedly said, "I'm happy to have fallen from the bullets of our brothers."[3]
†The *Kierownictwo Służby Porządkowej,* or Order Service Headquarters.—PB

tenance and, finally, the adjutant services and board of
inspection

In time the desk assigned to disciplinary matters, as well as the
one assigned to service and training, became independent agencies, and new offices were added: an office for combating infectious disease, which was assigned to the new Service Division; an
office for Air Attack Defense, which reported directly to the Chief
of the SP; the Jewish prison; the Hospital Guard Detachment; and
the Fire Department. This last was organized in May–June 1942 by
order of the German authorities and never really managed to start
operation. Eventually, Division 3 organized both the Material Aid
Section (soups and provision rations) and the Financial Aid Section. All these offices had executive sectors in the field.

The most immediate task involved recruiting several hundred functionaries (the number was increased to fifteen or sixteen
hundred) who had to receive at least a minimum of training.
November 15, the day the ghetto was to be closed off, was rapidly
approaching. There was widespread fear that the Germans would
abandon the ghetto entirely to its own devices and that the Polish
police would leave as well.

Thus the first order of business was to establish criteria for the
new recruits. These were determined as follows:

1. Age: 21–40 years
2. Education: six grades of secondary school
3. Physical requirements: generally healthy, minimum height
   170 cm (5½ feet), minimum weight 60 kg (132 pounds)
4. Military service record
5. No prior convictions
6. Recommendations from two people known in the district

Officers were to be drawn from the ranks of former officers and cadets of the Polish army. Szeryński intended that several lawyers who were also reserve officers would fill various directorial posts.

It's difficult to speak of class divisions within the Jewish population of the ghetto, since it was essentially an ungoverned mass— a caricature of a classless society. To some extent the SP organizers achieved their goal and succeeded in recruiting many members of the intelligentsia. Without documentation it's impossible to show the percentage breakdown, either by profession or degree of education. Only one detail sticks in my mind—that 10 percent (roughly two hundred) were lawyers, law school graduates, and students of law.

Anyone reading these pages who lived in the Warsaw Ghetto at that time will undoubtedly stop here. Remembering his own experiences, he will ask—not without a dose of irony and indignation—How did it happen? How did it happen that these recruits, so carefully and meticulously selected, turned out so bad? How could they have inflicted so much harm? Why were they so fervently hated? Let the reader withhold judgment until he has finished these pages—and a thousand others. Let him first study the situation in all its complexity and then attempt for the hundredth, the thousandth, time to grasp the reality in which we lived.

The structure of the KSP was complicated from its inception. Szeryński was chief of the SP, Händel the deputy chief; the lawyer Maksymilian Schönbach was chosen to head up the secretariat. The division heads were as follows: Organization and Administration, Dr. Stanisław Gombiński;* Personnel, former Deputy Prosecutor Nikodem Stanisław Goldstein; and Economic, Czesław Kornblit (also a lawyer). Stanisław Czapliński became Szeryński's adjutant, the editor Stefan Lubliner the head of the chancellery,

*I.e., the author.—PB

while Seweryn Zylbersztajn, a former high commissioner of the National Police, was appointed to head the board of inspection.[4]

This is just a brief overview of the personnel inside the KSP. On more than one occasion, Szeryński stated he felt like the dean of a bar association rather than a chief of police. Indeed, lawyers were abundantly represented inside the SP, especially among the officers. The eldest, about fifty years old at the time, was Maksymilian Schönbach, who had practiced law for thirty years, first in Vienna and then in Warsaw. His presence provided important reassurance to all the other lawyers and jurists.

Schönbach had been a major in the Polish army during the Great War; he had served repeatedly on the board of the Warsaw Bar Association and was held in wide esteem for his spotless reputation, his immense sophistication, his personal charm, his eagerness to help others, his kind heart, and his collegial spirit. He had long been active in Jewish community life, having served for many years as the president of the Children's Hospital of Bersonów and Baumanów; he was also president of the highly regarded Society for the Development of Jewish Agriculture, a member of the Bar Association executive committee, the Achduth Association, and many others. He came from eastern Małopolska, from a well-known patrician family (his father was a landowner from the Lwów district well regarded in Jewish circles there), and throughout his life he succeeded ably in combining his duties as a Pole and as a Jew, an activist and a lawyer, and always did so with dignity. He won the respect, recognition, and affection of everyone he met, and the twenty years he had spent so actively in Warsaw had made him well known among the Jewish intelligentsia.

For many of us—perhaps too many—Schönbach's presence in the KSP provided another significant assurance. A large number of the Polish-Jewish intelligentsia had yet to discover fully what it meant for them to be Jewish. Family traditions, blood ties, and—last, although perhaps most important—social developments in

Poland and in the rest of the world in the years just before the war had forced them to see themselves as Jews. Their Jewishness, however, did not extend beyond a feeling of group solidarity. Many were completely rooted in Polish culture and knew neither the Yiddish language nor the traditions. For them, the road to full participation in the life of the Jewish masses was long and difficult. It's easy to condemn these people, to mock their new "conversion," which had often been imposed on them from outside—and in a very painful way. But that would be too easy, too shallow, because these people were engaged in a very complex undertaking. On the one hand they did not want to abandon the principles and predilections that had been instilled in their souls by their upbringing, their environment, and their life experience as Poles, while on the other hand they wanted to live as active, compassionate, and cooperative Jews.

Was this wish a hopeless fantasy? Was it a question of simply having to make up one's mind, no straddling the fence? Not at all. Because it was possible. Life had proven that such dualism could exist. Many conspired to fight for Poland before the Great War; many followed the Polish Legions into that conflict, sowing the battlefields with their blood and bones, and many fought with the young Polish army along the Vistula, San, or Pripet rivers. And of these there were many who also fought and toiled in the sands along the Jordan.

But sometimes shouldering a gun and sacrificing one's blood is easier than coping with the gray routine of everyday life, which is far less heroic and exalted. Everyday life can present dilemmas that demand not only solutions but above all discernment, and that in turn requires a finely tuned apparatus, a well-functioning, sensitive receiver. Thus Schönbach's presence served as a guarantee that the SP would not drift away from the community, that it would keep in step and march shoulder to shoulder with the general populace of the ghetto.

Maksymilian Schönbach did not live to witness the summer of 1942 and the deportations. That April he died of pneumonia. Hypothetical questions are always tricky, but I am of the sad conviction that, even if he had survived, he could not have altered the course of events.

One of the SP's most important tasks was to determine its relationship with the Polish police in Warsaw—the PP—as well as the German police. The issue was resolved verbally: President Czerniaków went with Szeryński to Szuch Boulevard* to inform SS Untersturmführer Brandt, head of the bureau for Jewish affairs, and his assistant, SS Oberscharführer Mende, that the Służba Porządkowa had been organized, to introduce its new chief, and to establish the chain of command. They were told that the SP was to carry out orders of the Council President as well as act as a surrogate for the German *Ordnungspolizei,* or Order Police, within the ghetto. In this latter function the SP would serve as an auxiliary arm of the PP.

Szeryński received a warm welcome at PP headquarters, owing to his rank and his long service before the war. At an official meeting with the chief of the German Order Police, Colonel Jahrka, the latter declared that his organization had no official connection to the SS, nor would it have in future. He confirmed that the SP would serve both as the Council President's *main armée* and as an auxiliary arm of the PP. Szeryński was to report to the commandant of the PP, who would supervise operations of the Jewish police, in consultation with the Council President.

In this manner the Służba Porządkowa was placed under a new authority: namely, the commandant of the PP for the city of Warsaw. Szeryński was pleased with this arrangement, since he hoped to increase the degree of dependency on and subordination

---

*I.e., Gestapo headquarters in Warsaw, located outside the ghetto.—PB

to the PP. Contrary to expectations, however, the PP did not cease operations inside the ghetto after the district was sealed off, although certain functions that it formerly oversaw, such as the maintenance of streets and buildings and traffic control, did pass to the SP. In other areas, particularly criminal investigations, jurisdiction remained with the PP—at least in theory—which continued to maintain its own commissariats within the ghetto.

As a result of this arrangement, certain basic powers—such as the degree of reliance on the German Order Police, the policy toward profiteering, and the organization of the Fire Department—passed from the SP to the PP.

The hierarchy was quite apparent at the entrances into the ghetto, where members of the SP were stationed 20 to 30 meters away from the German and Polish sentry posts, according to official orders and reinforced by memoranda from both PP and SP headquarters. While it was clear enough in theory, in practice this ruling proved impossible to implement. Because they didn't understand the language, the German police were unable to cope with either the Polish police or with the general public. They would call over someone from the SP to translate, both in official matters or, even more frequently, in unofficial ones. Every German policeman ran his own business, letting things be smuggled into or out of the ghetto, and naturally the terms had to be discussed. Of course the Polish policemen received their take as well.

Perhaps the most important result of the SP's subordinate position was that all personnel files were transferred to the PP. This meant that PP headquarters had the final say in appointments or dismissals, as well as in determining punishment in disciplinary actions.[5]

At its most active, the supervision of personnel was managed as follows. A list of candidates who had passed all the review committees was presented to the Commandant of the PP for ratification before the men could join the SP. Promotions and disciplinary actions followed an identical procedure; in each case the files as well as the verdict would be passed to PP headquarters to await ratification. Sometimes the files would be sent back with a recommendation that further investigation be undertaken, as specified, or that a punishment be stiffened. This typically happened in cases where a member of the SP had committed some infraction together with a Polish policeman or—and this was often at the behest of the German police—if an investigation was being carried out against a Polish policeman and it turned out that a member of the SP had played some role in the matter. In such cases either all or 90 percent of the guilt would fall on the SP man.

Czerniaków accepted the new degree of subordination to the PP, which Szeryński sought to emphasize. Certain Council members, however, voiced their dissatisfaction. The Legal Commission, in particular, objected to the notion that the President of the Jewish Council should require PP approval to make appointments or that the PP should exercise control over disciplinary actions to the point of being able to overturn verdicts. According to the zealous jurists of the Legal Commission, the existing regulations covered appointments as well as disciplinary measures; they did not recognize any outside organ of control for any branch of the Jewish Council. Therefore, they argued, the current practice had no legitimacy. But their vehement opposition proved futile.

Thus the SP came to be a separate group within the body of Council employees (in 1942 the SP comprised one quarter, or more than 2,000), in that they had to answer not only to the Council President but also to the Commandant of the PP. While the situation presented some problems, on the whole we considered it beneficial, since it helped ensure ongoing communication between the ghetto and equivalent institutions in Warsaw, our common city.

*THE FOLLOWING ACCOUNT IS BY AN **ANONYMOUS MAN**, A former lawyer who joined the SP. Although he never revealed his identity, we know this man quit the SP in January 1943 and went into hiding on the Aryan side. We also know he survived the war.*

In the summer of 1941 the President received an order from Szuch Boulevard to set up a Jewish prison. Because of its long history, the building at Zamenhof 19 seemed predestined to play the role. Actually, this was a complex of structures separated by three large courtyards. The building that fronted Zamenhof Street was only one part of the complex; the remaining structures extended along Gęsia Street to the crossing at Lubeckiego Street. Before 1914 the complex had housed the Russian military prison, or *t'urm;* after 1921 it contained the Polish military prison as well as various army offices and warehouses. The structures had been heavily damaged in September 1939; only the one facing Zamenhof Street had been partially restored and converted into private housing and Council offices such as the post office and the SP station for Region Five. (Later, during the deportations of July–September 1942, the Council itself was moved there, and it stayed until the end.) The other wings consisted of long rows of cells that still bore traces of bombshells in their damaged walls. A children's garden had been constructed in one of the courtyards; the other was assigned to TOPOROL.

At first a small building at Gęsia Street was designated as a jail. Capable of holding only a few dozen prisoners, it soon proved insufficient and had to be expanded more and more in the direction of Lubeckiego Street. This initial building was called the "little jail" and after a few months was used to house only a small fraction of the prisoners.

According to instructions, the prison was set up under the auspices of the SP. Dr. Ludwik Lindenfeld of the KSP was

appointed chief warden; his deputy for economic affairs was Lew-
kowicz, a candidate for the bar who served on the Legal Commission. After several weeks he was replaced by Ignacy Blaupapier of
the KSP, who in turn was succeeded by Izaak Rudniański, a
refugee from Łódź and a deputy district chief of the SP. Sylvia
Hurwicz, a lawyer from Łódź, was appointed to head the women's
ward, with a similar rank of deputy district chief.

The prison staff comprised a separate group: They had regular salaries and special ID papers marked A (for Arrestanstalt), with
a number in the middle. Apart from the three executive officers
already mentioned, there were group leaders for the male and
female guards, squad leaders, orderlies, kitchen staff, and auxiliaries. There was also the receiving station, run by a former captain
of the Polish army, Fryderyk Rose—brother of the well-known
pathologist and famous brain researcher at the University of
Vilna, Maksymilian Rose—and the sanitary station headed by Dr.
Frendler and his assistant hygienist.

The pressing need to create a Jewish prison—known officially as the *Zentralarrest für den jüdischen Wohnbezirk* (Central Jail
for the Jewish District)—was caused by the fact that the Warsaw
prisons had a large Jewish population, of whom many required
medical treatment. In fact, 90 percent of these inmates were Jews
caught on the Aryan side, where they could not be contacted
from the ghetto; many were suffering from hunger, and tuberculosis and typhus were rampant. The Prisoners' Aid Board did what
it could to help, its representative occasionally contacting the Jewish Council and the KSP to arrange assistance. The Council had
special funds for this purpose, but everything was in terribly short
supply. In the event of illness, Jewish prisoners held in Warsaw
prisons were transported to a hospital inside the ghetto, from
where they occasionally escaped, being under the guard of a Polish
policeman. One of the more talked-about escapes involved
Gomuliński, the former director of the Provisions Department,

and a man named Szymański. Arrested for failing to register their status as reserve officers of the Polish army, they were being held in Mokotów Prison to face a severe trial when both managed to get sick. They were taken to the hospital at Leszno 1, where they were able to get away. There were several similar escapes. Even though guard duty was officially the province of the PP, the SP was ordered to post sentries as well.

The growing number of sick prisoners being removed for treatment from Warsaw prisons, and later from the Jewish prison, necessitated the creation of a new SP unit, known as the Hospital Guard Detachment, with about thirty to forty functionaries.

Most of the Jewish inmates imprisoned at Pawiak, Mokotów, or Daniłowiczowska for infringements of ghetto regulations were under official interrogation. Misdemeanors were punishable by death; they fell under the jurisdiction of the Special Court and were prosecuted by the German authorities.

While the "little jail" was designed for approximately one hundred people, the expanded prison could accommodate five to six hundred, but soon it had three times that many. The number was always growing, checked only by typhus and tuberculosis, which provided highly efficient population control. Living conditions in both facilities were very harsh. Food rations were well below starvation levels: some coffee and a piece of bread in the morning, soup from the welfare kitchen in the afternoons and evenings. The fare improved somewhat—and significantly for the children in prison—thanks to the Jewish Prisoners' Aid Board, organized by the KSP. Its guiding spirit was Adam Fels, while its titular heads were Czerniaków's wife and Councillor Zundelewicz. No one unfamiliar with such efforts in the ghetto can grasp how difficult it was to obtain food and needed medicine, even for children.

Still, despite the Board's efforts, the prisoners were dying like flies. These deaths created new complications. As official subjects of the German Special Court, even the deceased could not escape

the requirements of proper procedure; their death had to be officially confirmed by an authorized doctor. The death certificate
could leave no doubt as to the cause of death and had to be presented to the German prosecuting authorities in German—only
then was permission granted to bury the remains. Because this
procedure took several days at best, and because every day brought
several deaths, the morgue in the Central Jail soon ran out of
space. And because this all took place during the stifling-hot summer of 1941, burying the dead became a very pressing problem.
Only after numerous memoranda, explanations, petitions, and
reports by the SP and the PP did the authorities finally respond
with "great generosity" and allow the statistics to be telephoned to
the German prosecuting office. Every day in the KSP one could
hear the appointed functionary "reporting" the names of those
who had died in the Jewish prison: sometimes five, sometimes
eight, sometimes ten. With imperturbable solemnity the prosecu-
tors at the other end would hear the litany of names and grant permission for burial. And that's how it went for months.

There were two group executions carried out in the Jewish
prison. Each involved between ten and twenty people of all ages
and both sexes, ranging from practically children to old men and
women. The executions took place in the prison yard, close to the
wall. Guards led the condemned prisoners outside and tied them
to specially erected posts. The SP chief and the warden were both
in attendance; a firing squad of Polish police was standing by. The
German prosecutor and his invited guests drove up in their cars to
witness the rare spectacle. At the prosecutor's signal, the PP officer
in charge of the firing squad gave the command, the rifles were
lowered, a salvo of shots rang out—and justice was done.

There were no distressing scenes, no moans or terrible sobs;
at most a few women fainted on their way to their martyr's stakes,
but merciful as this was, it only prolonged their lives by a few min-

utes: The women were led to the stakes and shot while still half conscious. They were not the only ones to faint, though; many of the orderlies did so as well—true Jewish nerves—as did two Polish policemen from the firing squad. Others who were stronger and tougher managed not to faint, but there were unmistakable symptoms of nausea behind the gate and in the yard itself. This purely physiological reaction was a wonderfully clear sign, inasmuch as vomit is a universal symbol of repugnance and revulsion.

These two executions were actually carried out. Of the several hundred inmates in the prison, many had been sentenced to death, and they waited knowing neither the day nor the hour of their execution. For weeks and months they went to sleep thinking each night could be their last, and they would begin each new morning with the thought, Another day has been granted. When the prisoners Sacco and Vanzetti were kept in a similar state of uncertainty inside an American prison some years ago, the whole world was quick to react with indignation; in Paris and Brussels, Copenhagen and Birmingham, workers took to the streets, and demonstrations were held in dozens of other European cities. But here inside the ghetto, in the Central Jail for Jews, the identical practice failed to elicit the slightest protest, just as there was none against the arrest or the sentence or the punishment . . . all just links in a long chain.

Both group executions occurred in the late summer and early fall of 1941. Between one and two thousand prisoners remained in prison until July 1942, when all inmates were deported, Jews and non-Jews alike—for not all those in the Central Jail for Jews were Jewish. In keeping with the theories of the Herrenvolk, *"Juden und Zigeuner gehören zusammen"*—Jews and Gypsies belong together. Thus the Central Jail held about two hundred Gypsies. God only knows why they had been imprisoned; the documents cited charges of "vagrancy," but in fact there were no regulations that applied to Gypsies inside the Jewish ghetto, nor were there any requiring them to be there at all. For whatever reason, a number of these people wound up in the Central Jail, where they endured great hunger and misery, as they had no family or friends in the ghetto and had to rely solely on the official food ration and help from the Prisoners' Aid Board. They also suffered because they were locked up "among Jews and below Jews," and in the end they died with the Jews during the deportation.

There were no further formal executions; impromptu ones became the norm. Beginning in the fall of 1941, a small car from Szuch Boulevard would appear every few days, stopping for a moment on the even-numbered side of Orla Street. When the car drove away, it would leave behind the corpse of a Jewish man or woman who had been caught on the Aryan side. As a judicial procedure this was highly efficient; it shortened the legal process and reduced the court docket, all quite in the spirit of a judicial system that prided itself on being "flexible and suited to the needs of the time." But what piqued our curiosity most was the stubborn insistence on using the even-numbered side of the street.* Was this in deference to the late Maurycy Kon, of Kon and Heller, the ghetto potentate who lived on the odd-numbered side of Orla? The riddle remained unsolved as the summary executions continued. Among those executed in this manner were Henryk Toeplitz, the septuagenarian president of the Jerzy Majer company. His family was well known in Warsaw; he was the son of Bonawentura Toeplitz, brother of Theodore Toeplitz, the former magistrate, and Józef and Leon Toeplitz, president and director of the Banca Commerciale Italiana. There were many others who had once held very respected positions, as well as ordinary people.

---

*In time, after a few months, this practice changed; executed bodies were found on Pawia, Szczęsliwa, and other streets.—Author's note.

OF **HENRYK SŁOBODZKI** *WE KNOW ONLY THAT HE WAS A doctor who worked in the ghetto at the hospital on Stawki Street, and that he was incarcerated in the Pawiak prison from 20 November to 9 December 1943, where he shared a cell with thirty-three other prisoners. Although he eventually escaped Pawiak, Słobodzki is known to have perished in Warsaw.*

The doors to our cell are torn open. We are standing along the wall, which is steeped in the pale light of early dawn. The hall warden orders us to the washroom in his booming voice. "Let's go, on the double! Make sure you get right back! And who's taking the pisspot?" He yells in rage, and the cluster of keys comes screeching down on Felek's head since he's the first out of the cell. Felek and I heft the little cask that serves as our chamber pot; we step out into the corridor with the others close behind us. "Faster! You're not out for a walk!" the hall warden moves us along with a threatening jangle of keys. We run. Dozens of legs rumble across the metal plate covering the corridor in that spot. We turn. Here it is. A group of prisoners from a different cell is crowding around the two faucets on the wall, and a line forms in front of the large cracked bucket that serves as a toilet. Felek and I try to push our way through to the bucket, so we can empty the chamber pot, but we have to give up right away, since the people in line start foaming at the mouth in indignation and heaping various curses on us. We patiently take our place in line, looking enviously at our cellmates who have managed to fight their way to the faucets and are now splashing themselves with cold water in groups of three or four.

Our line moves ahead slowly, tossing out curses as it does so, hounding the lucky ones already sitting astride the primitive toilet. All of a sudden the warden's angry voice calls out: "Back to the cell! Move it! Müller's coming!" The bundle of keys traces a wide arc in the air. The line breaks up and vanishes. We quickly empty the pot and set it down in order to run over to the faucets that have now been freed from the throng of prisoners. The cold, foamy water is spraying onto the sides of the basin, splashing the tiles on the wall and floor. "Not enough time for you gentlemen?" the booming voice merges with the jangle of the keys which I adroitly dodge as they go whistling by my head to land on Felek's back. We run into the corridor, which is now empty of people. "And who's taking back the pot?" he prods us on, the fury of his voice rising into a hoarse roar: "I'll show you a good wash-up, you little fops."

We hurry back for the little cask standing beside the toilet, the keys keeping striking our backs with a series of loud chinks. We'll be able to breathe a little easier once we're back inside the cell, which now seems to us like a finish line that our pursuer is not allowed to cross. This turns out to be a mistaken notion, as the canvas clothes and sternly pointed mustache of the warden suddenly appear looming at the entrance to our cell. "I'll show you, you aristocratic scoundrels . . ." The epithets he hurls at us seem to vary between extremes of sarcastic exaggeration and vitriolic understatement, and are punctuated by the harsh accent of the keys as they trace their deadly arcs. When the doors finally slam shut we rub our wounds and bruises. I didn't fare all that badly, my father pronounces as he carefully palpates the topography of my head. Felek's eyelid has been slashed, but that doesn't stop him from smiling and composing a few strongly worded, piquant expressions as an ex post facto reply to the warden. We slowly take our seats on the benches.

Our respite does not last long, however, since soon the door swings open once again. We line up in the corridor to receive our small chunks of bread. We catch sight of a steaming pot of coffee. "No coffee for you today; you don't have anything to drink it out of—" says the hall warden, then remarks to his colleague "—besides they should learn some order, they're still unfledged." A Ukrainian emerges from the depths of the corridor—the same one who inspected our clothing the day before. One name at a time he calls out: Bormann, the boy, my father, and me. He orders us to report to cell number 268. We run, frantically searching for the number: 266, 267, 268—there it is.

The warden unlocks the door. We go inside. The stench nearly knocks us off our feet. We are in a large, fairly well-lit cell with three windows. A number of people run over from the straw ticks stacked along the wall and surround us, enclose us. I step back in horror. What kind of people are these? Emaciated figures, with heavily circled eyes and long, bluish noses that stand out against the dark background of their unshaven faces with their hidelike growth of beard. One of the figures comes forward and welcomes us: "Don't worry, nothing's going to harm you here, at least for the moment. That's just the first impression; you'll get used to it." I study the man, who is strongly built, with a gray-streaked beard, and whose oval face looks uncanny with its sunken cheeks. A murmur runs through the group, and turns into shouting. *"Panie inżynierze!*—Tell them everything they need to know. But be quick about it; we want to hear the latest news." The engineer introduces himself and shakes hands with each of us. "My name is Salkind. This is my colleague, inżynier Baumberg." We shake hands with a tall, bald man who inspects us through a pince-nez that keeps sliding down to the tip of his nose. His eyes show the heavy redness often found in myopic individuals. We stand there a moment shaking his bony, trembling hand. "And this is Doctor Reich," Salkind continues; I see a small, slight man whose face is covered by a pair of large dark glasses. "Doctor Warecki"—a tall man steps forward whose beard reaches up to the wrinkled circles beneath his eyes; his toothless jaw is moving back and forth—is he chewing something? No, he's speaking to me, but so quietly that his whisper is drowned out by the general din inside the cell. As his voice fades away the odd old man is brutally brushed aside by someone behind him. "Szuldberg"—I see a tall, older man who tries to twist his pale face into a smile. An entire gallery of prisoners files past us; the names start to get mixed up, evoking all kinds of associations and forming fantastic designs. The prisoners' figures also blend together like so many colored pictures off a lotto gameboard; they attach and split up, appearing and disappearing in a pattern of heads with black, unkempt, and curly hair, a range of beards and long, bluish noses. I see little human figures weaving together in a rapidly trembling chain, then dispersing into individual links, each moving, quivering, drilling into the ground, swaying, bending, dancing. "Lawyer Ganz"—a broad hand is shaking my own. My gaze rests a moment on a corpselike pale face encircled with reddish hair. "Sandberg"—the name seems familiar to me, no, it can't be: I look at the small figure standing in front of me, the elongated head, the short ears sticking out at right angles, the long, unevenly cut mustache. "Come on, Rabbit! Don't keep us waiting so long!" someone shouts and the small man slips off into the surrounding darkness. And then there are more new people, new names, which stack together like blocks into a tall, irregular jumble. Then the circle breaks up. That's it; that's everybody. Salkind takes us to the stack of straw mattresses, he invites us to sit down and make ourselves "at home." Then he begins to explain: "You are in a cell containing thirty people who were staying illegally on the Aryan side. These are people who either confessed to their Jewish background on their own or whose Jewish background has been proven beyond any doubt."

The door to the cell bursts open violently, there is a clanging of keys, and a few people come inside. They are returning from work. Salkind introduces us to our cell leader, a tall man who looks a little better than the others. "So you gentlemen come from the Aryan district as well?" he asks, sizing us up. "If they keep bringing new ones in like this, we'll have less and less a chance of surviving the next selection! What happened to you," he asks me, "did someone put a bullet through your ear?"

"No, that was during interrogation."

"Get your bowls ready for dinner," the order comes from

outside, and two prisoners drag a large, steaming cauldron of soup into the cell.

Lawyer Ganz is lying on a straw tick; my father is helping him hold up his head. "That's better," Ganz answers in a weak voice.

"Clean the cell," the cell leader calls out. "They're going to have roll call right away. Let's make sure we don't have to dance around the corridor on account of that slouch!"

"Zelle 268, raus!" we hear an angry shout outside the door. An SS man is standing in the corridor, his green uniform spic and span. Beside him is an athletically built Ukrainian who starts doling out blows with his powerful fist to the prisoners running by. *"Was macht dieser dort?"*—What's that one doing there? The SS man points his riding crop at a body lying inertly on a straw tick. The cell leader draws himself up to attention in front of Krumschmidt and attempts to explain in broken German peppered with a number of Yiddish expressions that he is very sorry, but cannot be held responsible; after all, there's always one oaf in every group. The riding crop comes cracking down on the cell leader's face; he stoops over and steps back into our group. The Ukrainian runs over to Ganz and with one strong blow of his fist knocks him off the mattress onto the floor; the man's body makes a half-roll and comes to a stop at Krumschmidt's feet. The latter removes a pistol. And then all of a sudden—what? Baumberg breaks off from our group, stands at attention before Krumschmidt and explains in German that the colleague lying on the floor had fainted at his work, that cell 268 is prepared to perform heavy physical exercise by way of punishment, if the life of the unconscious man were spared. Krumschmidt steps back a little and levels his pistol at Baumberg, whose tired, red eyelids begin twitching faster than usual, as he adjusts his falling pince-nez with one quick motion. Krumschmidt lowers his pistol and returns it to his leather holster. *"Wer hat dich eigentlich gefragt, du Lump?"*—Who asked you, you scoundrel? The words come out of his gullet with a hiss of hatred. Baumberg says nothing; only his skin

seems to go one tone paler; he starts swaying and spreads his legs so as not to fall; his eyelids are moving up and down so quickly that it's almost impossible to see his dark, fairly swollen eyes. *"Der Jude hat Frechheit."*—This Jew is insolent, Krumschmidt tells the Ukrainian, who slowly steps up to Baumberg. "Line up!" Salkind suddenly orders our group. A moment later the line of prisoners is stretching down the entire corridor, all at attention. Krumschmidt turns his head and scans our line for a moment; then looks at Baumberg again, then at Salkind, then the cell leader. . . . The Ukrainian is standing right in front of Baumberg: In a fraction of a second his strong fist will come crashing down on Baumberg's head, but no— he just stands there. . . . Krumschmidt bends over and uses his crop to flick off a little thread that had stuck to the shiny leg of his boot. The corridor is silent except for the drizzle of water dripping from the running faucet and the muffled voices coming from the other cells. *"Zu laut ist es dort, zu lustig."*—It's too loud over there, too merry, Krumschmidt tells the Ukrainian, pointing to the long row of white doors leading from the corridor to the cells. The Ukrainian tears away from Baumberg and rushes over to the neighboring cell. We hear some loud crashes coming from that direction, quickly followed by a huge roar that echoes down the long corridor. The roar quiets down and gives way to sporadic groans of pain. Finally the huge figure of the Ukrainian emerges from the cell, practically scraping the ceiling. He slams the door shut. Once again the corridor is silent. Baumberg standing at the threshold of our cell fixes his pince-nez; he is leaning against the door to keep from falling, and now his hand is splayed out, fervently feeling the wall for some protuberance, some handhold. *"Du!"* Krumschmidt addresses him, tapping Baumberg's chest with the handle of his crop and pointing to our line, *"stell dich dort!"*—You! Stand over there! Baumberg quickly staggers over to the end of our line. We are ordered to perform fifty squat jumps. The cell leader counts out the numbers, alternating loud and soft. The long string of prisoners is breathing heavily; they squat close to the ground then straighten back up. I stare at the white door across from me as I do my squat jumps; I can feel the sweat streaming off my body; my shirt is beginning to stick to my back. "Forty-eight, forty-nine"—the voice is getting more and more quiet—"fifty." Finally!

"*Noch zwanzig!*"—Another twenty! comes the next command. The cell leader's voice is growing more and more hoarse; these are no longer real words, just groans and whistles grunted at the moment before squatting. My eyes fog up; I feel the drops of sweat running down my eyelashes into the corners of my eyes. I can no longer distinguish the door from the wall; the cell leader's voice is more and more distant. . . . "Seventy"—I hear more distinctly. For a moment everything is quiet except for the loud panting of the prisoners. I wipe my wet face and see the smiling mug of the Ukrainian not far away. "*Genügt es?*"—Enough? he asks. Silence. "*Zurück in die Zelle!*"—Back in the cell!

*BOTH **ARON CZECHOWICZ** AND HIS BROTHER-IN-LAW **GURMAN** (we have no first name) came from Warsaw, where one sold jewelry and the other ran a tailor shop. We know that Czechowicz survived the war, although his wife and two children perished in Treblinka. The account—mostly written in Yiddish—describes the authors' arrest, interrogation, imprisonment, and remarkable escape from Pawiak.*

Sunday, 22 October 1943. Early in the morning, the Scharführer assigned to our section came and gave the order that as of that day Jews would have to deliver food to all sections. So he took fifteen men led by the *kapo* Janek. They ran at once to the kitchen to get the bread and vat of coffee and deliver them to the other sections. It should be noted that there were more than 2,000 prisoners at Pawiak at that time. Even just hauling the vats of coffee up the stairs was hard work. But that's not what I wanted to tell about now. I'd like to describe the events of that day. The assigned prisoners went to the kitchen and found Scharführer Müller there with his two dogs. Since only Jews were assigned to carry the coffee—each vat weighed about 80 kg.—Müller sicced his dogs on the prisoners. The dogs bit their legs and tore at their clothes. The prisoners barely escaped with bloody legs and a severe nervous shock.

The sadistic Müller should be described in more detail. He was of average height, of squat build, with thick bones and a large head that sat squarely on top of his red neck. Two gleaming eyes bulged out of his fat, bloated face. A little smile was always lurking on his lips. He was permanently assigned to guard the entrance gate. From time to time he would stroll around the courtyard with his dogs. His favorite pastime was siccing them on people, especially Jews. They were especially trained to do this; they would attack their victims and tear their flesh apart with their sharp teeth. And on that morning this same Müller, a rabid dog in human form, looked on with pleasure at the lacerated Jews, whose only fault was that they were Jews who—for no obvious reason—had to trudge around lugging the heavy pots of coffee to all the sections of the prison. With obvious joy he watched as his canine cohorts tore at the bodies of the unfortunate victims, who had no way of defending themselves. Woe to the Jew who dared strike a dog in self-defense. Müller took sadistic pleasure in watching the blood flow from the bitten prisoners. Six were severely wounded; they reported to the doctor, who bandaged them up. Thus the week began under the sign of blood.

On Monday a great deal of work was assigned to the Jewish prisoners. We gladly went out to work; we were only afraid of the dogs running up and down the courtyard. From then on, every time we went to the kitchen to fetch the huge pots of food, our hearts froze in horror of Müller and his dogs. So that was our general mood when we went to work on Monday. The Polish prisoners sympathized with the ones who had been bitten by the dogs. They had heard their cries and watched the whole event from the window. During our walk we noticed Müller promenading around the courtyard showing off his dogs, as if to say: "We sure did a fine piece of work today." We put an end to all conversation, marched around in even step, each person shaking at the thought that Müller might arrange some more entertainment with his dogs. The Polish prisoners were afraid that they might be hurt as well.

Finally we made it through the walk and were happy to go to our workshop. And there was plenty to do there: The Germans were constantly bringing in suits, furs, and shoes to be repaired. The Pawiak storage rooms were filled with piles of clothing that had belonged to prisoners who had been shot. Every German from the prison administration could choose whatever he wanted from the best pieces and take them to the workshop to be altered or refurbished. The Ukrainians also received (or rather stole) whatever they could, ordering us to fix it up; then they would sell the item at the market to have some money for vodka. In a word, business was booming, and we were pleased with the work.

That day we received a few cigarettes from the Ukrainians, for whom we had performed some work. Cigarettes were in short supply in Pawiak; for smokers they were considered a basic necessity. To some extent smoking cigarettes slows the thinking process and provides an escape from reality, and we wanted very much to escape from reality, forget about all the terrible things we had experienced, and above all not think about what was in store for us. If life is suffering we had suffered so much we had little desire to live.

All of a sudden we heard the guard's voice calling "Attention!" We leapt to our feet. A German stepped into the workshop, with a whip in his hand and a large dog at his side. He looked around and muttered: "Keep working." We thought, "What a day with all these dogs, what kind of evil fortune is pursuing us today?" We soon found out exactly who this German was. It was Oberscharführer Bürckl. We watched him out of the corners of our eyes: young, tall, blond hair combed flat to the side, elegantly dressed. But when we looked at his face, his eyes—particularly his eyes that were darting back and forth like a murderer's—we were very afraid. He gave the impression of being a drug addict. After he left, one of the Jewish prisoners came up and told us things about Bürckl that made our hair stand on end. He was the worst murderer in Pawiak, a specialist in torturing prisoners, particularly Jews. They say he would put Jews into the doghouses. At the entrance to Pawiak there was a small garden enclosed by a little fence. They kept dogs there and that's where Bürckl would chase his victims, laughing as he watched the dogs tear to pieces whichever man or woman he had forced inside. He felt a daily need to sacrifice a victim, just like others feel a need to eat. But dogs were not the only things he used for his bloody "entertainment" with the unfortunate Jews. He invented more horrible tortures. He hung a Jewish prisoner upside-down with his hands tied behind his back, then shot him with his pistol. He aimed so that the victim wasn't killed right away, but died a slow, agonizing death. First he would shoot the legs and arms, then he would cut the rope and the victim would fall to the floor, still alive. After that, he would let his dogs in and they would tear at the unfortunate victim until death put an end to his suffering. It was difficult to look at such calculated cruelty, our hearts were torn with pain, and the sight of that beast in human form made our blood boil.

A few weeks later—I can't remember the exact date—we received word that Bürckl had been liquidated, that is to say he had been shot.* That news electrified all the prisoners in Pawiak. For us Jews it was like a balsam to soothe our aching hearts. I can honestly say that if ever I experienced a sense of moral satisfaction, it was my joy at Bürckl's death. I felt content that justice had triumphed, that revenge had been inflicted on the criminal, and that we had lived to see that revenge. Our joy was twofold: First, the torments we had suffered, the sophisticated tortures of those condemned to

---

*SS Oberscharführer Franz Bürckl was sentenced to death and assassinated by soldiers from the AK (Home Army) division headquarters on 7 September 1943.

die, had come to an end, and second, there was a glimmer of hope that our own sufferings might be eased.

Yes, that criminal well deserved to die. We soon learned the details concerning his liquidation: It was an easy death, too easy for the executioner who had caused people so much suffering. I remember that on the day of the event it was the subject of all conversations.

REGISTER OF JEWISH PRISONERS INCARCERATED IN PAWIAK

No.	Surname and Name	Occupation	Prewar Place of Residence
1	Adamska	—	Warsaw
2	Akerman	tailor	Warsaw, Sienna 4
3	Akerman	shoestore owner	Radom
4	Akerman	—	Warsaw
5	Apfelbaum	—	Łódź
6	Aks	son of a tinsmith	Warsaw, Miła Street
7	Atlasowiez	carpenter	Warsaw, Żelazna Street
8	Atlasowicz (son)	—	—
9	Baumgart	driver	Warsaw
10	Bełkin	shoemaker	Gdańsk
11	Bergman	doctor	—
12	Berliński	—	Lublin
13	Bielicki	fish store	Warsaw
14	Blitt (kobieta)	—	Warsaw, Twarda Street
15	Blond	—	Lwów
16	Blum	—	—
17	Bochniarz	—	Warsaw-Praga
18	Bomsztajn	pharmacist	Warsaw
19	Bóg-Maciszek Irena	—	Kraków
20	Brodt	furniture warehouse	Warsaw, Marszałkowska Street
21	Brzezińska	—	Częstochowa
22	Buda	shoemaker	Warsaw, Leszno 7
23	Budzyńska	—	Warsaw
24	Cendrowski	vulcanizer	Białystok
25	Cyngiser	—	Warsaw
26	Czechowicz Aron	—	Warsaw
27	Czesner	—	Warsaw, Pańska Street
28	Datyner	—	Warsaw
29	Dawny	merchant	Łódź
30	Dąb	—	—
31	Dębski	doctor	—

(continued)

No.	Surname and Name	Occupation	Prewar Place of Residence
32	Dębska	—	Warsaw
33	Dyner Hasiek	—	Lublin
34	Dubiocki Chil	lawyer	Wilno
35	Edelist	actor	Łódź
36	Eljaszowicz	tailor	Warsaw, Muranowska Street
37	Eljaszowiez (son)	—	—
38	Elsohn	fur warehouse	Warsaw, Al. Jerozolimskie
39	Fajnbaum	merchant	Częstochowa
40	Federman	miller	Warsaw, Nowolipie 56
41	Federman (son)	—	—
42	Fejgin	jewelry shop	Częstochowa
43	Ferbicz	—	—
44	Ferbicz (son)	—	—
45	Filar	button factory	Warsaw, Nalewki Street
46	Filip	owner of apartment building	Warsaw
47	Fingerhut	engineer	Warsaw
48	Finkelsztejn	shop owner	Warsaw
49	Finkelsztejn	fur warehouse	Warsaw
50	Florian	—	Kraków
51	Fogelman	turner	Warsaw-Pelcowizna
52	Foman	—	Kraków
53	Fraczman	tailor	Radom
54	Frankfurter	tailor	Warsaw, Grzybowska 35
55	Fromberg	tinsmith	Warsaw, Nowolipki Street
56	Fromberg Max (son)	—	Warsaw, Nowolipki Street
57	Fryd	upholsterer	Warsaw-Grochów
58	Frydman	cinema owner	Warsaw
59	Fryszman	—	Łódź
60	Fruchthendler	tailor	Warsaw, Grzybowska 35
61	Garbiński	—	—
62	Gaston	singer	Kraków
63	Gersztman	fur shop	Warsaw
64	Glajchgewicht	—	Warsaw
65	Ginzburg	—	Gdańsk
66	Ginzburg (son)	—	Gdańsk
67	Goldberg	driver	Warsaw
68	Goldfajn	jewelry shop	Radom
69	Goldman	tailor	Warsaw
70	Goldsztejn	driver	Biała Podlaska
71	Goldzimer	shoemaker	Warsaw, Nowolipki 38
72	Gołębiowski	—	Warsaw, Brzeska Street
73	Górka	hosiery factory	Warsaw, Długa Street

74	Grizolik	—	Lublin
75	Grubsztejn	hat shop	Warsaw, Długa Street
76	Grümland	—	Warsaw
77	Grünszpan	—	Warsaw, Nowolipki Street
78	Gurman	—	Warsaw
79	Gutman	leather stitcher	Dobrzyń
80	Gutman	—	Łódź
81	Gutman	—	—
82	Handelsman	—	Ciechocinek
83	Hebedzyński	engineer	Radom
84	Herc	—	Warsaw, Żelazna Street
85	Hochberg	locksmith	Warsaw, Franciszkańska Street
86	Idelman	tailor	Warsaw, Pańska Street
87	Ichzelbst	barber	Warsaw, Freta Street
88	Igelberg	mechanic	Warsaw, Hoża Street
89	Ilitowicz	—	Warsaw
90	Jakubowicz	—	Łódź
91	Jas	—	Rembertów
92	Kacmarek	—	Poznań
93	Kadysiewicz	—	Warsaw-Praga
94	Kahan	—	Warsaw
95	Kanarek	grain trader	Pułtusk
96	Kapitulnik	—	Toruń
97	Kapłan	grain warehouse	Warsaw, Grzybowska Street
98	Kapłan	—	Warsaw, Gęsia 39
99	Karaś	—	—
100	Klinger	lawyer	Warsaw
101	Klotz	tailor	Kraków
102	Kolczewski	butcher	Warsaw
103	Kopelman	—	Warsaw
104	Kordowski	professor	Wilno
105	Korolczyk	blacksmith	Nowy Dwór
106	Krakus	—	—
107	Kramarz	—	Mińsk Mazowiecki
108	Krupnik	plumber	Warsaw, Nalewski 38
109	Kuperman	tailor	Warsaw
110	Lach	—	Warsaw
111	Laks	dental technician	—
112	Lederman	—	Warsaw, Mylna Street
113	Lederman	student at polytechnic	Warsaw, Ogrodowa Street
114	Lerner Janek	—	Warsaw
115	Lewicki	fur shop	Vienna

(continued)

No.	Surname and Name	Occupation	Prewar Place of Residence
116	Lipszyc	—	Kalisz
117	Machsztern	—	Warsaw-Praga
118	Majdan	fruit grocer	Warsaw, Bielańska Street
119	Margulis	saddler	Warsaw
120	Margulies (woman)	—	Warsaw
121	Marecka	—	Gdańsk
122	Majzner	shopkeeper	Warsaw, Elektoralna Street
123	Mazur	—	Vienna
124	Melcer	—	Warsaw
125	Miller	carpenter	Lublin
126	Miłobędzki	—	Warsaw
127	Miłobędzka	—	Warsaw
128	Miodowski Bronisław	—	Warsaw, Śliska Street
129	Miodowski Józef	—	Warsaw, Śliska Street
130	Mizes*	—	Lwów
131	Monderer	shoe shop	Kraków
132	Najman	—	Warsaw
133	Najman	—	Warsaw, Twarda 24
134	Nisencwajg	school pupil	Warsaw, Smocza Street
135	Nowak-Bornsztejn	furrier	Kalisz
136	Nużyc	—	Warsaw-Praga
137	Okonowski	—	Kalisz
138	Oksenberg (woman)	—	Warsaw, Pawia Street
139	Poznański	locksmith	Pabianice
140	Przgoda	clothing shop	Warsaw, Muranowska Street
141	Rabinowicz	—	Łódź
142	Rapaport (woman)	—	Bielsk
143	Ringelblum	historian	Warsaw
144	Roman Józek	—	Sosnowiec
145	Roman Antek	—	Sosnowiec
146	Rotberg	merchant	Łódź
147	Rozen	—	Lwów
148	Rozen (woman)	—	Lwów
149	Rozenblat Jakub	—	—
150	Rozenbaum (woman)	—	Radom
151	Rozencwajg	—	Łódź
152	Ryba	—	—
153	Sawicki	—	Borysław
154	Segal	—	—
155	Senator	tailor	Warsaw, Królewska Street
156	Słuczak	watchmaker	Warsaw-Bródno
157	Sopaj Szloma	—	Warsaw, Muranowska Street

158	Surokumowski	watchmaker	Łódź
159	Szajnberg	—	Warsaw, Puławska Street
160	Szajnberg (son)	—	Warsaw, Puławska Street
161	Szewiec	—	Warsaw, Elektoralna Street
162	Szklarski	—	Warsaw
163	Sznaj	tailor	Warsaw, Wilcza Street
164	Sznyciarz	—	Warsaw-Praga
165	Sztark*	—	—
166	Szwarcband	—	Łódź
167	Tajtelbaum	—	Warsaw
168	Turek	—	—
169	Tykulski	typesetter	Warsaw-Praga
170	Ungersohn	printer	Gdynia
171	Wajcman	—	Biała Podlaska
172	Waksmacher	—	—
173	Wende	engineer	Lwów
174	Wigdorowicz	tailor	Sierpc
175	Wiśnia	tailor	—
176	Wiśnia	—	Warsaw
177	Wiśnia	leather stitcher	Warsaw, Krochmalna Street
178	Witels	student	Lwów
179	Włodawer	merchant	Warsaw, Twarda Street
180	Włodawer (woman)	—	Warsaw, Twarda Street
181	Wolgroch	—	Warsaw
182	Wolteger	—	Warsaw
183	Wołosz	engineer	Berlin
184	Wódka Mosze	tailor	Radom
185	Wróbel	—	Warsaw-Praga
186	Wróblewski	—	Łódź
187	Zaremski	clothing shop	Warsaw, Miodowa Street
188	Zawadowski	engineer	Warsaw
189	Zawoźnik	hardware store	Warsaw, Leszno Street
190	Zylberberg	glazier	Warsaw, Grzybowska Street
191	Zylberman	tailor	Warsaw, Świętojerska Street
192	Zylberman	butcher	—
193	Zylbersztejn	—	Warsaw, Targowa Street
194	Zylbersztejn	—	Henryków

* Indicates Gestapo collaborator.

STEFAN ERNEST. The social organizations CENTOS, TOZ, and HIAS, and above all the Joint, began delivering aid to the victims—children and adults—immediately after the Germans invaded.

These groups set up a coordinating committee to synchronize their efforts and established a network of soup kitchens where the poorest could get a bowl of soup either at no cost or for a nominal payment of 10 or 20 groszy. In time there were more than a hundred of these kitchens, working from morning to night, serving up to 100,000 bowls of soup a day.

The administrative and technical staffs of these kitchens were mostly teachers who had been deprived of their positions. These people would be able to describe the misery of the Warsaw Ghetto better than anyone else, including the Council welfare officers and the workers at the refugee shelters, quarantine stations, bathhouses, and hospitals, where contact with the misery was "official." The soup kitchen staffs would have more to tell not only because they were teachers but primarily because they had the broadest contact with the suffering population.

As time went on—that is to say, as the wretchedness grew—more and more people began visiting the kitchens. For most patrons, the thin soup was their only meal of the day.

Apart from the kitchens, these organizations carried on a wide range of philanthropic activities: collecting clothes and financial aid and maintaining children's boardinghouses—of which Dobra Wola was considered luxurious—just to list a few examples. The self-sacrifice of the people involved should be recorded as one of the brightest pages in the annals of the ghetto. Almost all of them—and there were several thousand—died during the first Aktion, since they always thought of others before themselves. They deserve to be remembered with the deepest respect.

At first, most of the aid came from abroad. The Joint received support from Latvia, Hungary, Holland, Switzerland, and ultimately North America, both in cash and, more often, in kind. That was quite a lot, but when the United States entered the war the funding stopped, and the institutions had to rely on public generosity or the philanthropy of wealthy individuals, who understandably preferred to support those organizations rather than the offices and agendas of the Jewish Council. But some funding came from the Council itself, and occasionally social evenings were organized to raise money. Of course, in the conditions immediately preceding the deportations, the financial state of all these institutions was worse than desperate, severely limiting their ability to help.

JAN MAWULT. Events intervened, and Adam Czerniaków did not steer his vessel into port; it was struck by the storm unleashed on 22 July 1942, in the conference hall of the Judenrat, from lips inflexible and hard. The storm was real; one thunderbolt struck after the next, and soon a hurricane was sweeping down with full force. The man behind the desk kept thinking something could be done; he refused to quit; he went on searching for ways and means, ideas, people to turn to. In doing so, however, he lost precious time, as hours turned into the first day, the second, the third—and all his efforts continued to be in vain; nothing and no one could stem the tide. This was not some sudden upset. Something entirely new was happening; new circumstances had come into play—new people, new rules.

The man behind the desk did not give up all at once; first he tried to fathom what was happening, to decipher the new language as well as its message. For three days they allowed him to study it before a final conversation with one of the perpetrators shattered any illusions. There were no big words, no weighty discussions, just a short memo for him to sign like always, detailing the logistics of the Aktion: the boxcars, the quotas. It was a conversation between two cultures that were worlds apart. It was the same as two thousand years before: a Germanic leader with his *"vae victis"**—and the same humiliation of the vanquished.

And then the man behind the desk, a mathematician by training and inclination, performed some calculations and postulated

---

*"Woe to the defeated"—refers to the sack of Rome by Brennus.—PB

some equations: (1) Jews under German rule do not equal life, (2) Germans as rulers do not equal the fundamental ideals and principles of contemporary Christian civilization, (3) the present development equals a death sentence for the ghetto. And then, like a good mathematician, after he considered each of these equations, he arrived at the conclusion that x could never equal y, where x stood for the bankruptcy of his belief that the vessel could be steered into port and y represented Adam Czerniaków, alive and holding office as president of the Jewish Council.

It was then he reached for the cyanide. He showed not a moment's hesitation, no reluctance, no despair; he simply kept going, kept on working; and when he saw the end was near, he decided to end it himself, not a minute too soon or a minute too late.

SAMUEL PUTERMAN. Three gentlemen entered the office of the Council President: SS Major Höfle,* the leader of the *Vernichtungs-kommando*—extermnation commando—newly arrived in Warsaw, SS Untersturmführer Brandt, desk officer for Jewish affairs in Warsaw, and Oberscharführer Mende. The President rose from his seat and each man offered him his hand. They seated themselves in the comfortable armchairs. With a polite gesture, Brandt signaled the President to sit down as well. For a moment the silence was unbroken; the July sun beat through the stained-glass windows, coloring the office walls with patches of rainbow. For a long time the three SS men studied Czerniaków's face, while Brandt rocked his shiny boot back and forth, accenting the rhythm by tapping a roll of papers. The President seemed completely frozen, motionless. Behind his high forehead, his brain was working furiously. The visit disturbed him—the exaggerated politeness and the courteous, measured gestures of the "guests." Brandt's rather hoarse voice broke the silence:

*Höfle committed suicide in Vienna in 1962, just before his trial was to begin in Hamburg.—PB

"The Warsaw ghetto is overpopulated"—he was weighing every word—"the vast majority of the population is unproductive. Only a fraction is working in the shops that produce goods for the war effort. The rest—"

Here he stopped, as if searching for the right word.

"—aren't doing anything, they're idlers who either deal in illegal goods or trade on the black market or else don't do anything at all. The Warsaw ghetto is overpopulated: Even the streets are overcrowded. Typhus has been running rampant for two years. Despite the measures taken to contain it, the epidemic continues to spread. Smuggling is on the rise regardless of the severe penalties that have been introduced. The stores sell goods that don't grow in the ghetto. A huge percentage of Jews are taking advantage of your social services, they are living at the expense of the Judenrat, and the Judenrat has no money."

The words came more and more slowly. Czerniaków showed no emotion; he seemed hypnotized by Brandt's clenched speech, which now came out in a hissing trickle.

"For all of these things I've mentioned there is only one remedy, which will be for the good of the Judenrat and for the good of the Jews. Resettlement."

The President's powerful figure absorbed the horrendous blow. Only there, inside, his heart stopped beating for one short moment.

"The unproductive element must be resettled, the parasitic part that is living at the cost of others. We will send them east where they will work. And for this purpose"—here again he paused to think a moment—"you will sign these documents."

Brandt leaned forward and slowly placed the Gestapo memorandum on the desk. He opened a large fountain pen and held it out, after first pointing the nib toward himself. Czerniaków took both paper and pen. Something inside him shouted stop, refrain from signing at all costs. That damned heart, pounding away. Now it's up to me to say something. He sighed deeply, caught his breath, and managed to reply in a very calm voice: "You gentlemen will permit me to read the paper before I sign it." Major Höfle fidgeted impatiently at the delay. Brandt, who had known that Jew for two years now, nodded his assent and sank back into his chair.

The letters swam before the President's eyes. "The Judenrat is in a catastrophic state of affairs." He opened his eyes wide: The phrases and sentences began shooting at him from the pages. "The Jewish Council in Warsaw therefore kindly requests that the authorities undertake to resettle . . ." That damned heart, pounding away. He pressed hard on his tormented heart, pulsing with all the blood that had been spilled . . . "to resettle those Jews whom the Jewish Council is unable to provide for." Obmann des Judenrates in Warschau Diplom-Ingenieur Adam Czerniaków.

For a while he pretended to keep reading. He wanted a moment to close his eyelids that had been parched by a sudden fever. He regained his composure. He felt three pairs of eyes boring inside him. The pen was still burning his hand. He put down the papers. "With your permission, gentlemen . . ." The three gentlemen moved in unison, as if they intended to throw themselves at him. He understood.

"With your permission, I'd like just half an hour. In half an hour I'll send you the signed petition." They walked out without looking at him. Deputy Lichtenbaum and some curious council members began filtering into the office.

"Gentlemen, please, leave me alone for half an hour."

All the blood had drained from the President's face, leaving it gray and ashen. Reluctantly, they obeyed. Half an hour later the council members began dropping by. The President's face was still pale, but now it was smiling. The liberating smile of death. He had poisoned himself with a small dose of potassium cyanide powder. The impassioned heart of inżynier Adam Czerniaków, President of the largest Jewish community in Europe, had ceased to beat.

STEFAN ERNEST. When the elegant officers of the SS visited Grzybowska Street to deliver the will of the beast of destruction, the
man who had up to now obeyed every order rebelled for the first
time. For the first time, he said *no!* and refused to sign the decree of
deportation. He took his leave by taking cyanide. With this new
act of cruelty they had crossed the line.

The President's suicide was an act of protest. Or did he want
to teach the dying ghetto to assert its right to choose its own
death? But in this the President committed a major error, possibly
even an act of cowardice. Perhaps at the very last moment he lost
the courage, the strength, the nerve to give his *no* a greater voice,
to turn private reaction into public expression. Believe me, in our
circumstances nothing was easier than choosing to die; deciding
to survive was harder by far. Czerniaków should have lived and
led the rebellion. And if at the age of sixty he felt so worn out by
his three years of struggle that he truly lacked the necessary
strength, he should have at least told people what was in store for
them before he took his leave. For the sake of honor he should
have let them assume responsibility for shedding their own blood.
Because Czerniaków now knew the whole truth. In the end,
though, the people went to their death leaderless, submissive and
ignorant of the fate awaiting them. The man who had been raised
on parliamentarian, democratic, and pacific traditions—the modern humanism of a passing era—was simply unable to grasp the
need for a course of action that required bloodshed. He shied
away from the necessary sacrifice, which he would have had to
help direct.

Throughout the deportations, the ghetto was plastered with
announcements of his death—Adam Czerniaków / Licensed Engineer / President of the Jewish Council of Warsaw / sixty years—
the black-rimmed notices a symbol of the demise of the district he
had led with such devotion. But Czerniaków was not a man of
active resistance.

"They had collected about three thousand people on Zamenhof Street."

Chapter 3

ROUNDUPS, SELECTIONS, AND DEPORTATIONS

At the time of the Wannsee Conference in January 1942, Nazi policy toward Jews in occupied Europe reached a turning point, as proposals for evacuation were abandoned in favor of the mass extermination already under way in territory newly taken from the Soviets. Inside the Warsaw Ghetto, sporadic acts of terror gave way to roundups and forced deportations beginning in July 1942, when the Nazis completed construction of the nearby death camp at Treblinka. With the help of Latvian and Ukrainian auxiliaries and the cooperation of the Jewish SP, the Germans cordoned off the ghetto section by section, subjecting residents to systematic selections. During the first phase of the deportation, ghetto residents who could prove they were productively employed were allowed to stay, while the majority were driven to the freight train depot known as Umschlagplatz and, from there, shipped to Treblinka. Within weeks, however, the workshops themselves became targeted, and by early September the ghetto's population had been reduced to one-tenth its original size and its territory shrunk to a few blocks containing specific factories and Judenrat institutions. During the summer deportation of 1942, 300,000 people were sent to the death camps or killed.

MAREK STOK. On the evening of 18 or 19 July, one of my neighbors, a legal intern by the name of Norbert Feldman, asked me to go with him to see our neighbor Kon—brother of the famous Kon who co-founded the Kon and Heller company. We found the man shaken and pale, his nerves on the edge of breaking. He told the neighbors who had gathered that the deadliest of all SS units had arrived in the ghetto, which meant that all Jews in Warsaw were marked for extermination. Young Kon's brother had connections with the Gestapo and had been told that the Warsaw Gestapo had been conferring with the Transferstelle. Kon's connections claimed that they and the people from the Transferstelle had defended the Jews as best they could, but the leader of this new unit refused to consider less extreme measures. He claimed the fate of the Jews was sealed; they were parasites that had to be destroyed. Kon and Heller had already moved their families out of Warsaw.

We later learned the grim report was true. The newly arrived commission was under the direct command of a certain Globocnik.* He was headquartered in Lublin and answered only to Himmler himself. The unit was acting on explicit orders from Berlin, so the local command could do nothing about it; intervention with Governor General Hans Frank† in Kraków or even with Berlin was pointless. I am getting ahead of myself, but I should note that only a few days after the Aktion began, the new SS men executed Kon and Heller in broad daylight, right in the courtyard of SP headquarters—thereby flaunting their independence of all local authorities.

Of course we didn't know all this that evening at young Kon's apartment. Nevertheless, we were stunned by what he had told us.

---

*[Brigadeführer] Odilo Globocnik directed Operation Reinhard from his headquarters in Lublin. He committed suicide in 1945 at the time of his arrest.—PB
†Governor General of Poland. Executed at Nuremberg, 1946.

We discussed our options. Feldman suggested it was time to cross over to the Aryan side. But most of us, myself included, dismissed that as a fantasy. To whom would we go? How would we live? How long could we hide? After all, anyone caught on the Aryan side was shot on the spot. By the time we left, nothing had been decided. For my part I continued to put my faith in the protection offered by my job at the *Rüstungsbetrieb,* an armaments factory that supplied the Wehrmacht.

The next day the ghetto was in a panic and buzzing with rumors (generally less accurate than Kon's information). The Jewish Council had yet to hear anything official. Even so, masses of people began turning to the factory shops; everyone wanted to sign on for work. For a day or two nothing happened, except that the gendarmes stationed at the guard posts and along the walls were reinforced by Latvian SS units.

On the third day, at about 1 P.M., my wife came running over to the factory. She told me things were bad on Chłodna Street and I shouldn't go home. The Germans were going through the buildings, searching out members of the intelligentsia and shooting them in front of their families. Several doctors and lawyers had been killed, as well as a number of children. My wife had run to find me as soon as the Germans had left her building. Soon similar reports began filtering in from other places where they were killing individuals in their homes and on the streets.

People turned pale with fright, which is what the Germans wanted: to terrorize the ghetto and disorient us completely. We decided to sleep at the factory, where a night shift would be working. The first worker to show up before dawn the next morning was my wife's uncle, pan Eisenberg, a very kind person. He told us the streets were covered with posters from the Jewish Council announcing a "resettlement." We ran to see for ourselves. The posters—issued in the name of the Council—said something to the effect that, by order of the authorities, all Jews living in the Jewish district of Warsaw were to be resettled in the east. They were to report voluntarily to Umschlagplatz—a former railway siding on Stawki Street where the Transferstelle received goods coming into the ghetto and dispatched products manufactured for the outside. Each person to be resettled would receive 2 kilos of bread and 1 kilo of jam to take on the journey. Anyone who failed to report voluntarily would be taken there by force. The following categories were exempt from the resettlement order:

> Workers employed by German companies
> Workers employed by companies supplying the Wehrmacht
> Members of the Jewish Council
> Hospital staff and sanitation personnel
> Trade-school employees
> Employees of ŻTOS and similar organizations

Evidently the vast majority of ghetto inhabitants was subject to "resettlement."

But this resettlement turned out to be another tragic lie. The announcement was signed by President Czerniaków; later that same day we learned he had committed suicide.* He knew what "resettlement" meant; he knew what it would look like, and he preferred to take poison. Most people considered Czerniaków honest but weak-willed. At that time no one thought seriously of putting up organized resistance; that would come later, after everything was nearly over. But I don't want to get ahead of myself.

---

*In fact, this was the proclamation Czerniaków had refused to sign, so that the posters dated 22 July were issued generally in the name of the Jewish Council. Czerniaków committed suicide on 23 July, the second day of the Aktion.

For the moment everyone started rushing to the factories and setting up new workshops wherever possible.

STEFAN ERNEST. Late in the morning of Sunday, 20 July*—a beautiful, sunny day—a dozen or so small cars carrying SS officers showed up on the ghetto streets. The guards at the checkpoints to the Aryan district were doubled. Behind the walls you could see the black uniforms of Latvian sentries who had surrounded the district. Clearly, an unseen hand was directing the spectacle now beginning, and this was merely the orchestra tuning up for the performance of some dreadful danse macabre.

Posters had appeared a few days earlier, dated 15 July and signed by Auerswald, reminding everyone that leaving the district was punishable by death—as if we might forget! That Sunday around 2 P.M. things began to become clear. They arrested a number of Council members; a few were freed right away but others were detained until the next day. The President was "spared." Some were taken to Pawiak where they were held with other hostages who had been randomly picked off the street, mostly doctors and officials.

The game had begun. Fear fell upon the city. Few people slept that Sunday night, although nothing was scheduled—and nothing happened—on that day. Because employment had become a matter of life and death, all attention was shifted to the *Arbeitsamt*—the Office of Employment. Anyone with the slightest claim for employment hurried to the Arbeitsamt to procure a document attesting to his productivity, pay off outstanding fees, update any registration requirements, or apply for papers, be they real or fictional. All were after the so-called *Meldekarte,* or registration card, a pink booklet of six pages that contained personal information, a photograph,

*Sunday was actually 19 July.—PB

and the Arbeitsamt seal with a facsimile of Ziegler's signature.*
Also listed were the name of the employer, the type of work, and
the date of enrollment. When the Aktion began, the Arbeitsamt
had issued approximately fifty thousand registration cards to men
and barely three thousand to women. Masses of so-called *Anweis-
ungen,* or work referrals, had also been distributed, mostly directing
the bearers to the workshops at Többens, Schulz, and Schultz Co.
Ltd., since these places were always turning to the Arbeitsamt for
skilled and unskilled workers—tailors, dressmakers, seamstresses—
and what woman had never threaded a needle at least once in her
life? In addition to this, various administrative offices, institutions,
businesses, work sites, and workshops had their own identity cards,
which continued to serve as the basis for obtaining a Meldekarte.

For the moment, though, few dare go out between eight in
the morning and one in the afternoon, unless they've been sent on
business. The streets are deserted except for passing patrols of SS
men or gendarmes, who have had several companies stationed in
the ghetto since the middle of November (at Zamenhof 44 and
Niska Street) and who have taken over the internal guard posts.
Apart from that there are only Jewish policemen, a few passing
wagons, and small groups of workers.

Around 1 P.M. the city livens up a little, as workers lug their pails
to the kitchens and return with their soup. Little by little the crews
start heading home, first the ones from the *Werterfassungstelle*—
the Office of Value Assessment, which serves as a collecting point
for former Jewish property—whose SS bosses prefer to finish work
early, for reasons we're familiar with. Wild people† begin appearing
on the streets, where they conduct their business more and more
openly as evening approaches. More and more crews return from

---

*Ziegler was an official in the Council Department of Employment.—PB
†Wild people were those without employment certification.

outside loaded down with smuggled food. The bureaus finish their day's work—or, rather, their idle waiting; four o'clock in the afternoon is a boring time in the ghetto. Then the streets fill with traders, people scurry around looking for food, the workers returned from outside the ghetto visit their clients or vice versa, and goods are bought and sold. In the evening, people eat their fill—of good food, too. Some people play cards, some talk about routine business matters or the events of the day. They don't dwell on larger issues—why should they? Very few are inclined to political debates; after all, Stalingrad is pretty far away from Kurza Street in the little ghetto!*

But now and then these conversations do touch on the very real concern of what will happen next. In private, among close friends and relatives, people discuss how best to save themselves. The dilemma is whether to stay or to go. Should we build a shelter here, a hiding place stocked with several weeks' worth of food, or should we cross the wall? But this is like squaring a circle. Because on the other side you need money—or friends. One false step, one act of blackmail, can ruin elaborate plans that were supposed to hold for weeks or even months. Not to mention the danger of being found out in other, even more dramatic ways, or the unbelievable range of difficulties involved in setting up a place to live.

STANISŁAW SZNAPMAN. Early on the morning of Wednesday, 22 July 1942, a sense of foreboding descended on the Jews inside the ghetto. People sensed that something bad was going to happen. At about 11 A.M., word went around that the deportation had begun. The despair was boundless. People were overwhelmed by panic

---

*By July 1942, the ghetto boundaries had been redrawn so that a smaller southern section was cut off from the larger district. A wooden footbridge over Chłodna Street connected the two ghettos.—PB

and dread. Meanwhile, the Germans began riding through the ghetto in their cars and picking men off the street, especially the better dressed; some were killed where they stood. They also arrested most of the Jewish Council members and held them as hostages. Toward noon the Council proclamation appeared, announcing that all Jews would be resettled outside Warsaw, somewhere to the east. Only workers were exempt; they would be quartered where they worked. Everyone subject to resettlement was allowed to take personal belongings weighing up to 15 kilograms. Those who reported voluntarily would receive 3 kilos of bread and 1 kilo of jam; others would be given only 1 kilo of bread and ½ kilo of jam. This enticement was clearly intended to spare the Germans some work. Meanwhile, the Germans decreed that any Aryans caught hiding or otherwise assisting a Jew would also face the death penalty.* The deportations began that same day, on Tisha b'Av, a fast day.†

The first buildings to be vacated were the punkty, the communal shelters that housed people who had been driven out of the small towns. Next came the prison on Gęsia Street, the old-age homes, the children's hostels and orphanages, and the hospitals.

By order of the authorities, all proclamations concerning the deportation were to be signed by the Jewish Council or the SP. Indeed, the Jewish police directed the operation during the first few days. They cordoned off the buildings. People were placed on carts and carried off to the so-called Umschlagplatz, where they were loaded onto freight cars, one hundred or more to a car. The cars were packed so tightly that people had to stand squeezed

---

*In fact, this was a reminder of existing regulations.
†Tisha b'Av, or the Ninth of Av, is a fast day commemorating the destruction of the First Temple in 586 B.C.E. by Nebuchadnezzar, king of Babylon (Zech. 7:5, 8:19). According to tradition, the Romans under Titus destroyed the Second Temple on the same date in 70 C.E.

together, unable to move. There were no benches. People tossed out their knapsacks, suitcases, and packages to save room. All the doors and windows were bolted and sealed. There was a terrible heat wave, so it was absolutely stifling inside the cramped cars, and there was not a drop of water. Many people died in the railroad cars for lack of air.

The decree that workers were to be quartered at their job sites was widely interpreted to mean that workers were exempt from deportation. As a result there was a terrible rush to create new workplaces, known as shops. Many Jewish owners had transferred their businesses to native Germans, along with the entire inventory and large sums of cash. Jews would then sign on as workers at these businesses. They were paid a daily wage consisting of a bowl of soup and 50 to 200 grams of bread; some workshops gave two bowls of soup a day. There was no other pay in any currency. Masses of Jews tried to sign on at workshops belonging to Germans: Többens, Schultz, Brauer, Hallmann, Schilling, Oxaco, Döring, Oschman, and various others. They paid a fee to sign on and had to furnish their own sewing machines or other equipment in the bargain. Upon registering they were given identity cards, which they believed would protect them from deportation. Apart from these shops, there were Jews employed at a number of German worksites on the Aryan side—ammunition, airplane, car parts, and weapons factories—as well as at various military supply houses.

On 23 July, the day after the deportation officially began, President Czerniaków took his own life. Despair and panic reached a peak. People understood that the suicide did not bode well for the future. Meanwhile, the deportation intensified. From early morning through evening they went on sealing off houses, buildings, and entire streets.

Though initially directed by the Jewish SP, the operation was soon taken over by the Germans, supported by Ukrainians, while the Jewish police continued to assist. Buildings or blocks that had been cordoned off one day were often revisited the next day, to discourage people from hiding in places already searched.

The blockades, or roundups, were conducted as follows. First the Germans, assisted by Ukrainians and the SP, would cordon off a block of buildings. Then the SP would go through the houses and summon people downstairs, using whistles and warning that anyone who stayed inside or lagged behind would be shot. Meanwhile the Germans and Ukrainians would start firing their weapons and shouting, to frighten and terrorize people. The residents would rush down to the street, pale and terrified, sobbing and wailing, and show the Germans papers proving they were "employed by German factory workshops." Usually this didn't help. Everyone—man or woman, old or young, even children—was chased outside with a few heavy lashes of the crop to the head or face. Then the Ukrainians and Germans, together with the Jewish police, would check the apartments room by room, chasing out those who lagged or shooting them on the spot. If doors were padlocked or bolted they were broken down with crowbars, those hiding inside were killed, and the apartment was plundered. On the street below, the SS and the police shouted, hit, and fired at people as they assembled into ranks. The convulsive sobs of the women and the loud crying of the children mixed with the swish and crack of whips falling on the heads and faces of the victims. And all that noise was drowned out by the roar of guns and the shouts, curses, and taunts of the perpetrators and their henchmen. It was hell. To inflict maximum torture, and to cause the greatest despair, they ordered the ranks of people to stand or kneel for hours. After thus clearing a specific section of buildings, they surrounded the evicted residents and, to the accompaniment of more shots and snarls, conducted them to Umschlagplatz. Red traces of German bestiality could be seen inside the apartments, in the courtyards, on the sidewalks, and along the streets—puddles of Jewish blood and dozens of motionless bodies of men, women, children, and old people, the innocent victims of the self-proclaimed cultural crusaders, the *Kulturträger* turned savage. Those who'd risked their lives to hide in the attics, cellars, and other hiding places saved themselves for the time being—until the next roundup.

And so, from 22 July on, every day from morning to evening, the barbarians' hapless victims marched through the ghetto streets under a hail of blows from clubs or rifle butts, their faces frozen in pain, their bodies bowed under the weight of their packs and bundles, their last material possessions.

> They march, downtrodden, outcast, and oppressed,
> They march: workers and craftsmen, engineers, and doctors.
> Their wives are marching, their children, their mothers and
>   fathers;
> Bloody Hitler is marching his victims to destruction and death.
> Beaten with rifles and bruised with clubs,
> Lashed with whips that cut like swords,
> They march, and the air resounds with their sobbing.
> And why? What is this for, O Lord?

JAN MAWULT. Posters put up throughout the ghetto and issued by the Jewish Council—now no longer signed by the President—transform conjecture into tragic certainty. Deportation becomes a fact. The proclamations contain over a dozen items cataloging who may feel safe: people employed in factories, workshops, or work-sites; staff members of the Jewish Council and its agencies, employees of JHK, ŻTOS, CENTOS, and TOZ assigned to the factories and work sites—in other words, all the officially recognized social institutions.

On 23 July the SP moves into "battle." Officers equipped with the day's plan of action lead groups of forty to fifty police.

Their first target is the prison on Gęsia Street, followed by the large shelters that house German and Czech Jews.

The refugee settlement is an enclave of absolute misery. The people there don't care what happens to them; they've already hit bottom. It's impossible to imagine a worse life. When ordered to move, they do so at once; they come outside and for a few hundred meters even attempt to keep some kind of order, shuffling along as if marching of their own free will.

It's different with the German and Czech Jews; their sense of order, discipline, and obedience is so engrained they seem more like regular troops than random groups of men and women, old people, and children. They have stowed away whatever they cannot take and carry identical bundles, each labeled with name and place of origin. Every person has a preassigned place and function. They step away in even rows of four, like soldiers in formation. The comparison is apt: Many are wearing their *Frontkämpferzeichen*—ribbons awarded to those who fought at the front during the Great War. Some display medals, such as the Iron Cross, the Austrian *Tapferkeitsmedaille*—Bravery Medal—or other German, Austrian, and Hungarian decorations. They march forward in tight formation, shoulder to shoulder, in perfect step. They're parading for their last review, in anticipation of receiving the supreme medal from the hands of their comrades-in-arms, their colleagues, their superiors—or perhaps these people's sons. Here's a squad of sick people, propped under the arms by their fellow marchers and led by a doctor, a German Jew, who is flanked by two nurses; all three display with visible pride the distinctions they earned in the war. Little has changed since then; twenty-five years ago they brought aid to the wounded and comfort to the dying; they saw action in battle and took part in the most dangerous fighting. Then as now they were under fire. Back then they survived the fire and emerged unscathed. But this is a battle they will not survive. They will not emerge from this fire. Perhaps they sense it; still, they carry themselves proudly, even haughtily, as befits their ribbons and their past. They march well.

The long processions of people head north, toward a place by the Dzika Street checkpoint known as Umschlagplatz. The whole thing is called a roundup, a selection, an Aktion. People learn these words quickly; they're on everyone's lips. You hear the same questions over and over: "Where's the roundup today?" "Where's the Aktion?" "How did the selection go on Gęsia?"

People see all this, but they can't believe their eyes, they can't comprehend, they cannot grasp the events. Another rumor makes the rounds. "It won't last long; they might take forty or fifty thousand people and send them east, but that'll be it." A few irresponsible pessimists maintain that the designated quota is far higher. *"One hundred thousand people?* Don't believe them, that's nonsense. It'll be over sooner than you think—I have it from a reliable source. And it will all turn out just like everyone thought; they'll take the poorest and the weakest and call it quits. You can see for yourself. They're not touching the core; they're only hitting the back streets, driving out the beggars, the paupers, the refugees. Yes, yes, it's true: Old people and children wouldn't survive the journey or the hardships of setting up a new life so far away. But the rest will go to work camps in Russia, where they'll be building roads and rerouting rivers. Sure they'll have their fill of hunger, cold, and misery; sure it's horrible; of course it's a terrible fate, but what can be done about it? These people wouldn't survive anyway; they were dying by the day, by the hour, from hunger, typhus, tuberculosis. So if this is how it has to be, if they're the ones who have to pay for our redemption . . . ?"

That rumor finds many eager ears and willing mouths, and as it is passed around, it grows in significance until it becomes an idea, an agenda, a Reason of State. Soon people are also justifying and excusing the Jewish Council and the Jewish police.

"There was no way out. Any heroic posturing or reckless

declarations of 'We refuse!' would result in total extermination, the complete destruction of the ghetto. So if we can save the whole by sacrificing a part—even a large part—if we have to give up an arm or a leg to save the body, if we have to forfeit a child—the feeble-minded one, say, or the most unfortunate—to save the family, we must not hesitate! The fate of several hundred thousand people is in the balance, and even if the worst pessimists are right and their gloomiest prophecy proves true, even if *one hundred thousand people* were to perish—that would still leave a quarter of a million; the body would still survive, however crippled! There's too much at stake; you can't just follow your heart, play the hero, and proudly march to your death shouting 'All or none!' They had to go along with it, even if that was the more difficult task, even if complying with such orders was a greater burden on the soul. This is the way it had to be—for the good of the whole. Better we do it ourselves: there'll be fewer casualties and less bloodshed."

That's what people are saying; that's what's making the rounds. And as they say these things, many people who count themselves among the saved (although not—God forbid!—among those doing the saving) are really thinking, So it isn't me, it's not my loved ones. Maybe we'll make it through this cataclysm too.

But there are others who think and say the same thing without regard for their own interests and hopes. In fact, an identical rationale has been guiding Jewish politics for nearly three years; it might be called the theory of the lesser evil. No other voice is heard, no indignation or protest; those in the best and only position to speak out keep silent; they say nothing. Naturally the official justification never reaches the "the feeble-minded or the most unfortunate" children, nor does it reach the refugees, paupers, and beggars. They would certainly protest, but—my God!—in times like these who can afford to be bothered by them?

The Aktion continues. Now the Germans are taking part! Two or three SS men show up where the SP is conducting the roundup and terrorize the population with their yelling, their whips, and their shooting. People are killed. It all takes place at a dizzying tempo. Faster, faster, on the double! Soon all the residents are standing in the courtyard; the selection is over; those who will return to their apartments have been separated from those who will never see their homes again. There's no time for going back, no time for a final look around, no time for any last words. Even though the proper pace for funerals is slow and dignified, you aren't allowed to walk slowly. Here you have to run. Faster, faster, on the double!

The Aktion continues without a break. It spreads; now it's moving out of the poor back streets and toward the core. Whole sections have been blocked off on Leszno, Nalewki, Gęsia, Śliska, and Pańska. The German presence is more and more pronounced. All pedestrians and residents caught in the blockade—several thousand people—are chased onto the street and lined up in ranks of four or six. The selection is done right there. One rank after another advances toward the SS man: a quick glance at the papers, the face, and a flick of the crop sends each person either to the left and freedom or to the right and Umschlagplatz. One group stands off to the side—the privileged wives, children, and families of the SP functionaries. They are in possession of a piece of paper, a certificate from headquarters, stamped in the lower left-hand corner with the magic sign and seal of the Sicherheitspolizei, the SIPO or Security Police. The selection proceeds calmly—calmly and politely. The German politely sends the parents to Umschlagplatz, and the daughter to freedom, the daughter politely approaches and asks to accompany her parents; the German politely consents. Politely he splits families, taking wives from husbands, children from parents, parents from children. Politely, calmly, quietly: no moaning, no cries, no convulsions.

By now there are three groups. First, the privileged families of the SP and second, the workers who have passed through the selection. They are allowed home. They are free—for the time being. Third is the group bound for Umschlagplatz, thousands lined up by fours and sitting on their haunches. All those sent to Umschlagplatz are made to crouch in the middle of the street until the selection is finished, as they wait to be joined by more and more people. Is this better to tell the groups apart? To make sure no one will break away and run off? Or is it simply the concoction of some SS mind? No one knows.

The selection is over. The third group is bound for Umschlagplatz—but how, just as they are? It's a hot August day; everyone is dressed as lightly as possible. The women are wearing summer dresses and sandals; the children are barefoot; no one has any other wrap or hat. And that's how they're expected to ride off into the unknown? No fresh shirt, no bundle, not a piece of bread? Impossible! Where are they headed? What does it mean? After all, everyone has to take something; surely they're allowed a minimum of essential items! They're going to a new settlement, not on a few days' vacation or for a picnic in the country. Autumn will be here, then winter, and they have no more than a single shirt or dress. And they're going east, for heaven's sake, to Russia! What's going on here?

There's no time to think. Now there is a great mass of people crouched on the street. "Stand up! Forward, march!" They go, in a gigantic procession, quickly, as they are told. They are surrounded by SP men and Volksdeutsche from the *Sonderdienst**—from the front, from behind, and on both sides—while SS men press in from all directions like hunting hounds. The people march on, in a gigantic procession. As earlier during the selection, they have feverish snatches of conversation with the SP men, whether they

---

*The Sonderdienst, or Special Service, was a German police formation that consisted of Polish-speaking Volksdeutsche.—PB

know them or not—half a word quickly tossed out and quickly caught. "Tell X. My name is Y, I'm the daughter of so-and-so, the wife, sister, mother of such-and-such. Pull me out! Pay off the Volksdeutsche, save me!" These exchanges go on without stopping, and all along the way people are being fished out. Colleagues from the SP hide them behind their backs so the Germans can't see. Now's the time! Go! One jump to the closest doorway and it's done. This goes on during the selection, along the march, in bottlenecks formed by the streets, at the curve of Karmelicka or Dzika. They save many, but it's only a small percentage. They save family, friends, neighbors; they save for the sport of it, they save for money. But the vast majority remains, and marches on, and finally arrives at Umschlagplatz.

*BORN IN 1906, **ADOLF (ABRAM) BERMAN**[1] WAS DIRECTOR OF CENTOS until September 1942, when he fled to the Aryan side with his wife, Barbara. After the war Berman became President of the Central Jewish Committee in Poland and in 1950 emigrated to Israel, ultimately serving as a member of the Knesset. He died in 1978.*

The Germans had generally left the orphanages untouched prior to the roundups. CENTOS kept intervening on their behalf at SP headquarters, so many people maintained the vague illusion they might manage to save these institutions by converting them into children's workshops. But the situation changed drastically as soon as the Germans took direct command of the Aktion and began removing one orphanage after another. At first they took only the children and left the staff behind, but after a few days they also began deporting the workers.

During the savage roundups conducted in the little ghetto, one of the first orphanages to be evacuated was Dr. Korczak's

Orphans' Home.* The entire staff, with Janusz Korczak and Stefania Wilczyńska in the lead, allowed themselves to be deported with the children, despite the fact that the directors were offered their freedom even at Umschlagplatz itself. That same day the Germans took the boys' boardinghouse at Twarda 7, along with Director Dąbrowski and his wife, as well as the girls' boardinghouse at Śliska 28, with Director Broniatowska and her staff. A few boardinghouses managed to stave off deportation by hiding the children or resorting to various ruses. Some of the institutions managed to be released at Umschlagplatz. Little by little, however, despite every possible effort, all the orphanages, hostels, and other shelters were deported. The largest institution, the Children's Home at Wolność 14, was taken within a few days, together with its director Szymański, who before leaving spared his old mother further torment by giving her a dose of poison. Then he went bravely on with the children. At that time the Children's Home housed approximately a thousand children, including the ones transferred from the Central Shelter at Dzielna 39 and the boardinghouse for religious children at Dzielna 15 (which had been relocated to Wolność 14 when Dzielna Street was evacuated during the Aktion). A large portion of the staff accompanied their charges, including the financial manager pani Pullman and her husband, Szymon Pullman, the most outstanding musician and conductor in the ghetto.† That same day they deported the 360 children at the Emergency Shelter for Homeless Child Beggars at Wolność 16—together with Director Goldkorn and the entire staff—as well as 400 children at the model boardinghouse Dobra Wola (Dzielna 61), which had recently been organized by a group of industrialists. One of the last places to go was the exemplary boardinghouse for small children at Dzielna 67,

---

*The orphanage was evacuated on 5 or 6 August 1942.—PB
†Pullman (1890-1942), nephew of the great actress Estera Rachele Kamińska, served as the conductor of the symphony orchestra inside the ghetto.[2]

where director Sara Janowska and her entire staff accompanied the children. Altogether, the Germans removed about four thousand children from thirty orphanages and boardinghouses. By 5 September only two boardinghouses were left, one for boys and one for girls. Some of the charges were employed in the shops or work sites; the rest went into hiding.

A few children's day-care centers and shelters remained in operation well into the Aktion, although they underwent a dramatic shift, as the begging "street children" disappeared and were replaced by children of the shop workers. These children were eagerly received, since so many places had been opened. People also deluded themselves into thinking these children would not be deported, that centers would be tolerated for children of workers. This assumption, too, proved mistaken. Whereas at the start of the Aktion there were instances where even the Germans would turn a blind eye to these assemblages of children, as the roundups became more and more severe they gradually removed both children and staff from these centers.

For a while a few children's soup kitchens also remained in operation, but soon they too were liquidated. Thus the entire child welfare system, consisting of more than one hundred centers and serving roughly 25,000 children, was razed, with both children and staff falling victim to the pogrom. In addition to the personnel who accompanied the children in their care, the Germans took other workers from the central offices, soup kitchens, day-care centers, recreation rooms, and other facilities.

HENRYK BRYSKIER, *A MECHANICAL ENGINEER AND RESERVE officer in the Polish army, was vice president of ŻTOS, the Jewish Welfare Association. In July 1942 he and his wife obtained work in a munitions factory. She later died during the fighting in the ghetto; he was sent to Majdanek. Bryskier managed to escape from the camp;*

he survived the war and served as a department director in the Polish
Ministry of Commerce and Industry until his death in October 1945.

Because working for the war effort was supposed to protect against
being deported, it was no wonder that anyone with two hands
rushed to the shops regardless of qualifications. Everybody hoped
to find some kind of job. Procuring your *Dienstausweis,* or work
papers, as well as a company stamp in your Meldekarte, was the
chief concern of every thinking person. Men who had once been
wealthy merchants were overjoyed to sweep a factory yard; doctors
and engineers were pleased to take the lowliest jobs. The demand
for these papers greatly exceeded both the supply of documents as
well as the available number of workplaces, and shop managers
began to take advantage of the situation, demanding a signing-on
fee that ranged from a few thousand zloty to nearly twenty thousand per head.* Ostensibly this sum was to cover the cost of expand-
ing or creating areas of production to accommodate more workers.

The gentlemen receiving these sign-on fees were brazen
enough to claim they were acting out of a humanitarian impulse
to save people. By hiring huge crews, they said, they were inviting
trouble, since they had to explain to the authorities the sudden
increase in staff.

Tradesmen, merchants, and former industrialists also paid in
kind by bringing whatever equipment, raw materials, and unfin-
ished goods they could; they hoped this would speed things up and
help them obtain official papers and living quarters on the factory
grounds—which was considered a guarantee of personal immunity. In the process, all sorts of previously stashed items began to
emerge, as if the ghetto were a huge underground vault housing all

*During the occupation, the zlotys issued by the German authorities generally had a
black market value of fifty to one U.S. dollar.—PB

kinds of raw materials, partly manufactured goods, and finished products that, because of the new situation, passed "voluntarily" into the hands of the German shop concessionaires if not to the German authorities themselves.

There were workshops with no more than a few hundred positions that took on several thousand workers. It went without saying that no one had any real jobs for these masses of people; the managers were mainly interested in their signing-on fee. Whoever couldn't raise enough cash paid with valuables such as watches or rings. Nor were wedding rings scoffed at, if someone couldn't afford the full fee.

The shop managers—Germans, Poles, and their Jewish assistants—were raking in money hand over fist in exchange for temporary permits. These bore the factory seal stamped on whatever piece of paper was at hand; the companies had had no idea how many forms to print, and the workforce grew at such a rate it quickly surpassed even the wildest guesses of the self-proclaimed "benefactors."

It happened that separate family members applied to different workshops, not so much to compare relative working conditions as to better the chances of landing a position—at least for the person applying. As a result, many families were split up in the desperate rush to find an employer. Parents might take work in one factory, children in another; a husband could be separated from his wife, and so on. But unless they planned everything with the utmost care, family members were later unable to visit one another, since everyone had to live where he was employed. The official work week consisted of twelve hours per day, with no rest on Sundays; it was forbidden to leave the factory grounds except on work-related business, and only then with a permit. An early evening curfew made it impossible to spend time with family or engage in any romantic pursuits.

JEWS EMPLOYED IN EDMUND DŁUŻYŃSKI'S "ZWÓJ" FACTORY
FOR SPRINGS AND WIRE PRODUCTS
ŻELAZNA STREET 58A.
REGISTER OF NAMES AS OF 14 AUGUST 1942

No.	Surname and Name	Duty
1	Ankier Josek	assistant diemaker
2	Beder Aron	diemaker
3	Cajtung Moszek	laborer
4	Cajtung Saul	technician
5	Cymerman Józef	supply
6	Cymerman Ryszard	unskilled laborer
7	Damenstein Jakub	clerk
8	Falk Artur	engineer
9	Falk Johanna	unskilled laborer
10	Falk Emanuel	diemaker
11	Falk Harry	diemaker
12	Falk Doris	cook
13	Falk Jerzy	apprentice diemaker
14	Falk Ewa	—
15	Fiszel Mojsze	laborer
16	Frydrych Majłoch	guard
17	Glejchgewicht Adolf	factory doctor
18	Gleichgewicht Dwojra	unskilled laborer
19	Glikler Pinkus	laborer
20	Grinberg Icchak	unskilled laborer
21	Haltzilber Mojżesz	—
22	Haltsilber Mozes	quality control raw material
23	Haltzylber Wanda	unskilled laborer
24	Hazenfuss Hilel	laborer
25	Hazenfus Mojżesz	assistant diemaker
26	Hinterhoff Maurycy	assembly
27	Hinterhoff Maria	unskilled laborer
28	Hinterhoff Joanna	unskilled laborer
29	Hinterhoff Delfina	unskilled laborer
30	Jonisz Szymon	wagonner
31	Kirszbraun Władyslaw	assistant diemaker
32	Klapersak Wolf	turner
33	Kossower Noe	assistant diemaker
34	Kudasiewicz Herman	laborer

35	Kupercyn Wolf	turner
36	Lederman Gedale	laborer
37	Lederman Ruwin	diemaker
38	Lederman Szmul	laborer
39	Lewkowicz Marian	laborer
40	Limon Chaim	laborer
41	Lewinson Witold	technical draftsman
42	Millenbrand Mordko	laborer
43	Mokotow Jakob	laborer
44	Müller Benjamin	unskilled laborer
45	Najman Julian	technician
46	Najman Zysie	diemaker
47	Najman Dawid	diemaker
48	Nusenbaum Chaskiel	diemaker
49	Perkal Josek	laborer
50	Proszower Marek	technician
51	Proszower Ada	mechanic
52	Rotblat Abram	unskilled laborer
53	Rotblat Chaim	diemaker
54	Rubin Michał	laborer
55	Sarna Hersz	laborer
56	Sarna Fejga	spooling cable
57	Susłowski Józef	diemaker
58	Szlang Stanisław	diemaker
59	Wachman Symcha	laborer
60	Wajcman	—
61	Wajsbard Boruch	diemaker
62	Wertans Wąadysąaw	mechanic
63	Wertans Bogdan	draftsman
64	Wrocławski Jokob	laborer
65	Zwayer Władysław	turner
66	Zylberman Majer	grinder

SAMUEL PUTERMAN. Before the deportations began, there were a number of small tailor shops inside the ghetto where Jews worked for the German firm of Walter C. Többens. The one housed in the former business school on Prosta Street employed 500 artisans; the Schultz shoe works at Nowolipie 42 employed the same number, while the Henryk Wiśniewski metal factory at Stawki 56 had 200 workers. Only a few days into the Aktion, Többens had 10,000 registered workers—who brought the same number of sewing machines—Schultz had 12,000, and Wiśniewski 2,000. New workshops were springing up every day, such as the Rotwand and Wawelberg plants. German entrepreneurs requisitioned buildings and took over entire residential blocks, which they emptied themselves, evicting the residents. Or if their production was considered important enough, they called in the Gestapo, who would clear the area by conducting repeated roundups. In this way the Oschman shop—which laundered and mended uniforms and undergarments—wound up in the Hotel Bristol. Wilhelm Döring took over nine buildings on Prosta Street for the Prehl machine shop; the paper goods factory occupied two buildings at Nowolipie 5 and 7, K. G. Schultz took over the Bror and Rowiński knitting factory at Leszno 78. Garheime et Miller commandeered all of Mylna Street from Karmelicka to Przejazd, and Nowolipie Street from number 18 to Przejazd. That factory was intended to subsume a number of small woodwork shops, locksmiths, and textile mills into one company. The brushworkers took up several buildings on Świętojerska Street. Von Schöne occupied a few houses for producing metal goods, and the Wehrmacht firm Transavia took over the former trade school at Stawki 24. Brauer occupied nine buildings for workshops engaged in various activities: renovating helmets, undergarments, and leather goods.

As soon as they were set up, all these shops were closed off by a temporary wooden fence. Each factory was taking on new workers—a few thousand every day. They couldn't issue papers fast enough to keep up with the demand. Before the offices had a chance to compile a valid list, and before the owner had a chance to sign the registrations, the new employees were being rounded up and sent to Umschlagplatz. The Aktion did not end. Every day the Germans at the selections would declare more and more documents invalid, as the number of people left in the ghetto dwindled.

At first a red Meldekarte was enough proof that the bearer had fulfilled his obligation to the Arbeitsamt; later you also needed a valid workplace registration. After a while the Germans stopped accepting documents from some of the smaller firms, and before long they refused to recognize any. Everything was declared invalid unless verified by the Arbeitsamt, but before the Arbeitsamt could process the documents, thousands were sent to Umschlagplatz. Meanwhile, the sewing machines remained in the shops, along with thousands of updated lists with the names of the new workers whom the freight cars had already taken away.

On the seventh day of the Aktion three thousand officials of the JSS* were told to remove their identifying armbands, as these people were no longer needed. On the eighth day all papers issued by the distribution centers were declared invalid, and on the tenth day the papers of the postal workers. On the eleventh day of the Aktion, the Germans invalidated the certificates of the small workshop owners—which they had hitherto respected—even those who were producing exclusively for the Wehrmacht. Every day different streets were blocked off in various parts of the ghetto. People were chased out of the buildings and onto the street and a German would carry out the selection. People would present documents that one German had declared valid a few hours earlier, only to have a different German choose to send the entire group to Umschlagplatz.

A rush—an open race—for the right papers ensued inside the ghetto. People paid thousands of zloty for a piece of paper that at least seemed legitimate. After all, a few hundred people were freed from Umschlagplatz yesterday, so their documents must have been good.

News of people being freed spread quickly; that same day thousands would crowd into the factory in question. They would use their connections and pay large sums for a document that

*Jüdische Soziale Selbsthilfe, or Jewish Self-Help Agency.—PB

quickly proved to be no more than a worthless scrap of paper. The worst thing was that these people didn't think it necessary to hide on the roofs or in the cellars or in the shelters; they would assemble for selection and then find themselves marching toward Umschlag-platz, completely dumbstruck. Papers from particular shops were traded like stock certificates. By the tenth day the ones with the highest value were Transavia, Többens, and Schultz. But these weren't guaranteed either; their bearers, too, were often sent to the freight cars.

JAN MAWULT. So now the ghetto starts on the even-numbered side of Leszno Street, and all the streets south of this line have been excluded. In the new ghetto all the buildings are occupied; the apartment houses are reserved exclusively for people with official certification—workers from the factories and worksites and offi-cials affiliated with the Jewish Council. As a result, the Többens factory, the largest shop in the ghetto, takes up the entire block of buildings on the even side of Leszno from Żelazna to Karmelicka—in addition to an enclave still in the little ghetto. The Church of the Blessed Virgin Mary has been converted into a warehouse.

A church inside the ghetto is a paradox, an unnecessary object, although the building itself can and ought to be used. If this church were anywhere else, such an act of desecration might provoke worldwide indignation, as has been the case of a certain nation accused of being so barbarous as to convert Catholic and Orthodox churches into museums, cinemas, and theaters. But both the church at Leszno and another one on Nowolipki Street have been put to more practical use, as warehouses for vegetables, furniture, and all sorts of things. Besides, they're in the Warsaw Ghetto, so there's no need to bother about such niceties, no need to put on a show or worry about how we might look; here we can drop the mask and just be ourselves.

The workshops and worksites are very much in flux—they appear and disappear. Apart from the very large enterprises, which existed before the deportation, they are in a constant state of transformation. One moment they are granted certain privileges; the next moment these have been taken away. The number of workers is increased and then cut. Employees are assigned to one block of buildings and then sent somewhere else, amid conflicting orders, arbitrary decisions, confusion, bedlam, chaos.

The buildings inside the district that are not assigned to any workshops are now beyond jurisdiction. They do not exist. No one can live there or even visit them; they are "wild" houses. But it would be a mistake to assume they're empty. The wild houses are occupied by wild people—people with no official living space, no papers, no workshop—old people, and women with children. They live in secret. They spend their days hiding in some secret place with a hidden entrance, a cubbyhole or a garret, and only emerge in the early morning and in the evening. They have visitors—sons, brothers, sisters—people with permission to live, who bring provisions and a few words of comfort. And when they leave the waiting resumes. The wild people wait for evening, just so they can poke their heads out; they wait for loved ones, just to see a sympathetic face, a person to feel close to, another human being who is not bent on taking their lives. They wait for a miracle to happen; they wait for the end. They hide, following the advice a certain German gave a Jew who was proudly showing his papers with all the proper seals and signatures: *"Du dummer Kerl! Das ist alles Quatsch! Der beste Ausweis ist und bleibt der Keller-Ausweis!"*— You dummy! That's all just a lot of rubbish. The best document around is and always will be the cellar.

The thing is, they're right! Papers don't matter; workshops aren't important; seals don't make any difference. So more and more workers start following in the wild people's footsteps, fixing places to hide, and when they hear the cry "assemble in the court-yard," they run to their shelters.

Others venture into the wild homes to steal. They grab what-ever they can, whatever is of value, whatever can be quickly converted to cash. It's not called stealing, though; it's looting, pil-laging. After all, they're not robbing anyone, since there aren't any owners. The building is wild, the apartment is wild, and anything inside is there for the taking. So they continue pillaging, plunder-ing, and looting.

Most people still live in the open, though—in the designated buildings, on the factory grounds, and at selected worksites outside the ghetto. But they don't stay in one place; they don't stick with one company. They move from factory to factory, to a worksite outside the ghetto and then back to another factory. They're look-ing for wherever will be best.

"It's best at the brushmakers'! They're under direct control of the army, and their Germans look after them. Everybody—even the SS—listens to them. After all, it's the army! After the last purge they won't touch a soul; whoever's signed up and really does his job will be able to sit things out quietly until the deportations are over. Or maybe even the war. They're the safest bet, the only one. All the other workshops are doomed."

"No, it's better at Többens! Többens is chairman of a whole consortium of ghetto workshops; he's the most important entre-preneur of all. And what counts even more is that he's Göring's brother-in-law—did you know that? That's right, Göring's own brother-in-law! Do you realize what that means, what kind of influence he has, how much they have to reckon with him? Többens has said that whoever really works—and isn't just going through the motions—can rest assured about himself and his fam-ily. And Többens doesn't just say things lightly! If he said it he knows what he's talking about! Besides, X moved to Többens, Y moved there, and now so did Z. And they're all smart people.

Többens is the one; no question about it. You better sign on with him; it's the only workshop that will survive!"

"And I'm telling you that it's not the brushmakers or Többens or Schultz, it's Hoffmann. He may not be a high official, but he knows how to take care of his business, and that's the main thing. They say he's Brandt's brother-in-law. Ever notice how well he gets along with all of them? They eat together, drink together, go out carousing together. Because he knows it's all well worth it in the long run. You have to keep paying him off, but it's worth it. His shop's pretty small, under a thousand, but he'll take care of his workers; after all, he's living off them. He always knows in advance when and where there's going to be a selection. Things are better at Hoffmann's, I'm telling you."

And the people go on switching like crazy from one shop to the next.

The Aktion continues. They've finished blockading the streets and are now moving to the shops. A detachment bursts onto the factory grounds and chases everybody outside for another selection. They lead away another group: a few hundred, a thousand, two thousand—but other people immediately take their place, and within a few days the number of workers has been restored to the previous level. There's no shortage of candidates; there are still plenty of wild people. The workshops have certain assigned quotas, and they hire replacements. Once again, it's just a matter of money, connections—and the selections.

Meanwhile, every day a long line of people makes its way toward Umschlagplatz; the processions file through streets devoid of any other life. Many drop dead along the way, on the pavement. Corpses are everywhere, they're part of the ghetto; they fit the picture. The funeral carts and wagons rush in to pick up the bodies and haul them away. The funeral workers now have been combined into one large funerary service; they are considered a "productive element." And although even their ranks have been thinned by selections, the black caps still receive a measure of respect.

Living conditions are terrible. There's no money for food. People buy bread, potatoes, and vegetables if and when the occasion presents itself—on the street, early in the morning. Little shops are springing up in the factories, or really just shopkeepers, since they can hardly be called true workshops. The basic diet consists of soup cooked communally in the residence buildings and prepared by the administration in the workshops. The main suppliers of food are the laborers who bring it in from worksites outside the ghetto, as well as the burial crews, who smuggle it inside the hearses on their way back from the cemetery. Because of its location right next to the Powązki Cemetery,* the Jewish cemetery has become a central trading point. SP functionaries make up the third channel of import: If the gendarme at the checkpoint is in a good mood, he'll let them run out and make some purchases a few dozen meters outside the gate. The workshops are the primary wholesale importers—the only ones, really. Smuggled goods are hidden in the provision transports. Prices fluctuate wildly: The cost of food, which is the major commodity being bought, is on the rise, while that of clothing, the major commodity being sold (mostly coats and undergarments) is falling. A whole outfit in good condition is worth about 2 kilos of butter or 25 kilos of potatoes.

Even so, life in the workshops is not as monolithic or uniform as this description might suggest. Here as everywhere else, there are different classes, with the upper class consisting of the shop management, the department supervisors, the officials responsible for the workshop's provisions, the local housing authorities, the warehouse superintendents, and so on. The lower class consists of

*The central Catholic cemetery in Warsaw.—PB

the workers—although these people are usually atypical, many having never worked in a factory before. The genuine shoemakers, tailors, or saddlers among them are few and far between. The boundaries between the upper and lower classes are fluid; many a worker is on close terms with the manager; occasionally the worker might have been the manager's former boss in a completely different line of work. Many are workers only in name; despite scares, threats, and surprise inspections they manage to avoid labor and spend little or no time in the shop. This is not a matter of shirking; it's just that people who've worked for decades as teachers, writers, or artists aren't up to spending twelve hours at a shoemaker's bench or in a harness shop. It's too late for them to learn the right way to hold an awl and twine.

The shop workers continue to be exploited; the administrators invent pretexts to extort bribes. If confronted, the officials justify this by claiming they need to pay off others higher up. There's some truth to this assertion, but it's equally evident that the shop managers occasionally invent reasons to obtain many times more than what is needed. And meanwhile they're lining their own pockets.

The first major controversy involves provisions. Aside from the uniform allotments for all residents, the workshops receive extra food rations. These are manipulated in various ways; some shop managers appropriate the entire quota, while others content themselves with a portion. But no workshop is entirely free from these machinations. The provisions departments constitute a virtual Klondike for anyone with a head on his shoulders.

Rent is a story in itself. Although no one who might be authorized to collect it—even the Real Estate Commission Board— ever asks or is even allowed to ask for fees to cover electricity and gas, fees are collected. But these aren't payments for consumption of kilowatt hours and cubic feet; they're simply "hook-up fees" for "arranging" things. Similar fees are collected for water, sanitation, and trash removal. Then there are separate payments to cover presents given to Them and parties arranged for Their pleasure, for procuring special considerations. The local Germans from a given workshop negotiate with Them, to procure specific favors and privileges.*

Extortion is worst in the factory workshops. The workers at the worksites outside the ghetto are less affected by the new order; usually the only thing squeezed from them are the tributes paid to each group leader and earmarked for specific purposes. The third and smallest group consists of Jewish Council employees, who are relatively shielded from this new unwritten law; the only people they have to pay are the gas and electric installers, who expect something under the table from every building.

Rumors of an organized resistance are circulating throughout the workshops and inside the ghetto. The first sign came when members of this resistance called on certain shop officials and expropriated some of the money the latter had been using to line their pockets. Occasionally groups of young men (some masked) visit the evening haunts of the factory plutocrats—the clublike locales where they eat or play cards—and demand wallets and other valuables from those present.

People are generally doubly pleased to hear about such events. First, they're happy to hear that X—who's been demanding money for every registration number and extracting payments from his workers both during and after the deportation—has been forced to relinquish some of his blood money; someone is doing to him what he has been doing to others. Second, they're happy to hear the whispered rumors: "You know where that money's going? It's to buy weapons; there are armed fighters in the ghetto."

---

*Ringelblum, writing mostly in Yiddish, also refers to the Germans frequently as "They."—PB

No one is sure who's doing this: Some say it's the Bund working with the PPS; others attribute it to Hashomer Hatzair; still others speak of a broad coalition.* Then there are those who contend it's merely a bunch of young daredevils, unallied and unaffiliated, just in it for themselves.

*WHEN THE GERMANS INVADED POLAND, **LEON (ARIE) NAJBERG** was fourteen years old and a member of Hashomer Hatzair. His older brother, Izaak, was killed in 1939, fighting with the Polish Army; his mother, sister, and younger brother all died at the hands of the Nazis. Early in the occupation, Najberg couriered documents to outlying towns and traded goods with the Aryan side. In August 1942 he was transferred to the Adam Oppel munitions factory, and in April 1943 he returned to the ghetto. After the uprising there he hid at the home of a Polish couple. Leon Najberg survived the war; today he lives in Israel.*

Some Jews who had money, equipment, or the right contacts managed to enroll in the workshops, which weren't subject to the selections during the first ten or twelve days of the Aktion. At first it was enough to have a registration paper issued by a given shop; all you had to do was report to the factory and sit things out, pretending to work at one of the machines. You could also hide your family on the factory grounds and return to your apartment at night. But eventually the workshops were closed off with temporary fences, and the management threw out anyone who wasn't registered. Meanwhile, people who did have the proper papers moved into the vacated apartments and remained quartered on the shop grounds. Toward the end of the deportation, all that was left of the little ghetto was Többens's factory, which covered the area

*Hashomer Hatzair (Young Guard), a Zionist youth movement with socialist leanings.

bordered by Żelazna, Pańska, Twarda, Ciepła, and Ceglana streets. The Jews quartered there were forbidden to leave the grounds under pain of death. The rest of the little ghetto remained enclosed by walls, but not a soul was stirring inside. The stores had been broken into—their doors had been left wide open—and the streets were littered with their wares. The apartments were still full of furniture and other belongings, but their owners were absent or dead. The only shopkeepers found in the stores were the corpses of those who had chosen to commit suicide by turning on the gas, the ones no longer willing to be playthings in the hands of the Germans.

After all the Jews had been removed, the little ghetto looked like the site of a terrible pogrom. Months later the area was given to Poles to live in. The walls were razed, but first the SS opened a new workplace for Jews called the Werterfassungstelle. This new "institution" oversaw the systematic ransacking of formerly Jewish apartments. Anything found was looted, sorted, and stored in special depots before being shipped to Germany. The Germans reassured the shop workers that families housed on the shop grounds were not at risk. But the Germans never kept their promises. During the day, while the men and women were at their jobs, the Germans would sneak into the factory apartment buildings and remove the families, as well as any workers from the night shift, and take these people to Umschlagplatz. At this time the Germans also began to liquidate some of the shops that had been created earlier in the Aktion, so that soon only a few privileged factories remained. They did this by surprise, without warning or prior notice, so that practically no one managed to hide. The smaller shops eventually merged with the larger ones, and at the end of August 1942 the only ones left where Jews were still working were a few small islands cordoned off by fences (later replaced by solid walls). Among these were the brushmaking shop surrounded by Bonifraterska, Franciszkańska, Wałowa, and Świętojerska streets; the

Brauer factory at Nalewki 36; Transavia (an airplane part factory) on Stawki; Többens's and Schultz's shops, bordered by Leszno, Karmelicka, Nowolipie, and Smocza streets; the Hallmann woodworks at Smocza and Nowolipki; the East German Carpentry Works at Gęsia 75–79; as well as over a dozen buildings occupied by the Ostbahn, the Eastern Railway. There were also apartment buildings where Jews were hiding who had failed to find places in the shops. The Jewish Council moved to Zamenhof 19, and the Provisions Department to Franciszkańska 30–32. The SP also moved to Zamenhof, and the number of its functionaries was reduced; some were taken to Umschlagplatz.

ANONYMOUS WOMAN. On 12 August 1942 I lost my mother and father. They were taken away from one of the Council institutions. I wasn't the only one to know such pain, not the only one to succumb to despair. I'm sure everyone around me was suffering as well. A terrible fate has severed people from those they love, and those who remained, those condemned to suffer a few more days of fear and misery, felt more and more disheartened.

On 17 or 18 August, new proclamations went up ordering everyone without working papers—and therefore children—to assemble at a designated point. This decree was nothing new; it only increased the general panic and gave the police more license. Unlike the Germans, who were not bound by regulations and could act according to whim, the police had to comply with orders, at least for the sake of appearance. The decree that made these documents the sole legal basis for remaining in Warsaw gave the police the authority to take away women and children who had hitherto been protected by their husbands' and fathers' papers.

Between 19 and 25 August, the Germans left to liquidate other Jewish centers in the provinces, so the Aktion inside the ghetto was carried out exclusively by the Jewish police. Each policeman was ordered to round up five people within a few hours; upon presenting them at Umschlagplatz he was given a receipt, which he turned in at police headquarters. Only then was he allowed to eat, safe from being punished for dereliction of duty. The Jewish police quickly adopted the German methods of shouting and beating.

Watching from the windows of a building on Nalewki, I saw a crowd of women and children being rushed along by a couple of Jewish policemen. So many tears, so much despair, so many blows falling on the women's backs and the children's little heads. The sight was etched deep in my memory.

According to the German decrees, the police were not allowed to enter residential buildings belonging either to the factories or to the Council institutions. They were told instead to search the wild buildings, those not assigned to any work groups. Many people were hiding in these buildings; they had no official employment and thus no valid residency. The Jewish police acquitted themselves splendidly. They ferreted people out of the vacant apartments, cellars, and attics. Showing no mercy, they chased the wretched souls down to the street and escorted them to Umschlagplatz.

From the window of the hospital on Pawia Street, I frequently saw policemen hauling old people and children away on rickshas. I will not forget one little girl, maybe six years old, wearing a small green coat, who cried as she begged the policeman. "I know you're a good man," she said. "Please don't take me away. My mama just went out for a minute. She's coming right back and I won't be here; please don't take me away." But the girl's sobs, which would have moved the heart of a monster, had no effect on the policeman. He cold-bloodedly carried out his duty. Two hours later I saw a frantic woman running down the street toward Umschlagplatz, crying desperately, "My child—Where is my child?"

These buildings were cleared not only of all human remains;

they were also plundered for any material goods left behind. This was done by Germans, Ukrainians, and Latvians. On calmer days rabble from the other side of the wall would also sneak into the ghetto. Most of the abandoned apartments had been left open; where they were locked, the doors were taken off their hinges or broken down. The same thing happened to the stores, which were mostly closed. There was wide-scale looting, and robberies became so common that workers' homes were broken into while the inhabitants were away at their jobs. Neighbor stole from neighbor. The hunger intensified, and prices rose. By the end of August 1942 they had deported around 300,000 Jews. Only then did the first reports manage to reach the ghetto concerning the true fate of those taken "east." Their lives had ended in the horrible death camp at Treblinka.

Although many Jews maintained their illusions, by the end of August the truth concerning the German crime was beyond all doubt. Day after day, the Germans were carrying out the mass murder of tens of thousands of people in the most monstrous way. And just as I could neither understand nor accept the passivity with which the Jews went to their deaths, neither could I understand why no help came from outside, or at the very least why no one protested while an unprecedented tragedy was playing out inside the ghetto and at Treblinka. No voice of indignation came over the waves of ether to the listeners inside the ghetto: not from London, not from Washington, not from the Vatican.

In these circumstances the bombardment carried out by the Soviet Air Force during the first deportation gave the ghetto new faith and encouragement.* To my ears, the roar of bombs exploding around Umschlagplatz was a heartening, joyous sound, and

---

*The Soviet bombardments occurred on the nights of 20 August and 1 September. The targets in August were various points in downtown Warsaw; in September, primarily Wola, Powiśle, Praga, and the park belonging to the *Sejm* (Polish parliament). The bombs scared the Germans into leaving their posts to hide in shelters, enabling some people to escape from the ghetto.

others felt the same way. On occasion the bombs also provided an opportunity to escape (I remember that on the night of 1 September some people managed to cross to the Aryan side or to slip away from Umschlagplatz). Most of all, however, the bombardments had great moral significance. From the east, the embattled Soviet Army was sending its pilots several hundred kilometers to disrupt the Nazis' monstrous crime and oppose the silence of the West.

After a few days' interruption the deportations resumed. Now the roundups reached into the barracks and factories; workers were pulled from shops at random. In one factory a German might decide to take every tenth person; in another they took only the younger workers, while elsewhere they took the older ones.

I myself passed through one of these selections devised and directed by German imagination. They had collected about three thousand people on Zamenhof Street, at the square by the Jewish Council,* including hospital staff, Health Department employees, Council officials, and Provisions Department personnel. A crude-looking German equipped with a riding crop sorted the people into two groups, right and left. To be sent to the right was a death sentence. Documents meant nothing. Occasionally the German asked for a profession; other times he merely glanced at a person's face. His victims grew more and more fearful the closer they came to him.

I didn't have any documents or work papers, and moreover I was holding my small son by the hand. All the other women with children had been directed to the right: that is, to Umschlagplatz. The German asked my husband his profession and then looked at me. I had draped my coat over my son. I think the German saw me do that but for some arbitrary reason, on some momentary whim, he let us go, and our threesome was saved from death. It was then I decided I would hide during the next roundup. While chance

---

*The Council offices were moved from Grzybowska Street during the deportation.—PB

often decided the fate of adults, that of children was sealed in advance: All were taken away. I was determined to protect my child for as long as I could. Besides, like everyone else, I was clinging to the hope that the terrible Aktion had to come to an end. It had been going on for a month and a half.

On the night of 5 September, all remaining Jews were ordered to move into the area bound by Gęsia, Smocza, Zamenhof, and Niska streets, with specific addresses allotted to each institution.* The hospital was assigned to Zamenhof 21. Everyone was told to take food for two or three days. No one knew what this might mean. Everyone was to be at his designated place by 10 A.M. on 6 September; all access to other streets was cut off by heavy German patrols. No one could leave his assigned building or he would immediately be fired on. Within a few hours a rumor started up that the Council had received permission to issue 30,000 "lifesaver" registration numbers and that only those who possessed them would be allowed to stay in the ghetto: The rest would be deported. The Council issued these new numbers to its own employees, to the factory managers, and to the workers. Some people did everything in their power to obtain such a number; others were resigned and made no effort to do so. This time the reduction, or selection, was to be carried out not by the Germans but by Jewish administrators in each institution.

In every courtyard rolls were read out listing those who would receive numbers, the people who would be allowed to leave those houses of death. All the rest were commanded to wait patiently for the Germans to come and take them away to Umschlagplatz. How many tragedies took place in those moments? What happened

---

*In September 1942 the Germans herded the remaining inhabitants of the ghetto into the so-called cauldron bordered by Zamenhof, Gęsia, Lubecki, and Miła streets. This was the continuation of the operation begun on 22 July. The new selection affected workers employed in the factory shops as well as members of the SP.[3]—PB

when a husband received a number but not his wife? What should they do? How should people react? Some chose to split up, others decided not to report for registration and remained with their loved ones to await their common fate. So many tears and so much despair! A son left his mother, a husband his wife, a mother her child. They went to obtain their numbers, some in the hope of returning to hide with their families during the roundup. The numbers were also important for procuring food. But in the end no one who registered ever managed to return. No one was permitted back inside the houses of death; everyone waited, calmly and resigned, although suicides were frequent and often macabre.

ADOLF (ABRAM) BERMAN. On Tuesday, 25 August, the roundups resumed, now directed against the designated residential buildings and the workshops. The first to come under fire were the buildings housing Council employees (in the block between Pawia, Lubeckiego, Gęsia, and Zamenhof). Ukrainians and Jewish policemen cordoned off these streets in the early morning hours and led the residents to the corner of Zamenhof and Gęsia.

They caught all of us together in one apartment. Not expecting a roundup, we were holding a CENTOS staff meeting. When the familiar whistle announcing the roundup sounded in the courtyard, we went down and tried to explain to the Jewish policemen that this particular building housed the directors and staff of CENTOS, who were clearly exempt from deportation. But this time none of our arguments proved effective. Politely but insistently, the policemen demanded that everyone go to the street. When we hesitated, the Ukrainians burst into the courtyard and up the stairs, firing their weapons and beating us with rifle butts, prodding us outside. They also took the opportunity to tear the watches off several colleagues and steal their money. We managed to hide a few people, including the older women and children; the rest of us marched over to Gęsia Street, where we lined up in ranks alongside numerous Council employees from different departments. Then we waited for someone to ask to see our papers.

In fact, some people from the Health and Maintenance departments showed up later and succeeded in freeing a number of doctors, nurses, and maintenance workers (mostly street sweepers shouldering their brooms and spades). But the prevailing German attitude to the social services was so negative that Dr. W. Wielikowski, the head of social services, didn't dare intervene on our behalf, despite the desperate signals we were sending him from a distance. Thus after some time, in an enormous procession, everyone headed off toward Umschlagplatz. On the way, however, we passed a higher-ranking officer of the Jewish police who happened to be an old acquaintance and schoolmate; this meeting would prove to be our salvation. Once we were behind the barbed wire enclosing Umschlagplatz, the situation looked completely hopeless. All the colleagues we might have counted on for help were there with us. But a little bit later an SP officer arrived and pulled us out of the ranks, saying he was doing so on the orders of his superior. For a while we had to hide off to the side. Then the officer reappeared to alert us that we would be able to pass in a moment; all we had to do was produce 200 zloty for the Polish policeman and show some kind of document. We handed him the money and walked through the checkpoint a few steps behind him.

We ran to the Council to intervene on behalf of our colleagues still at Umschlagplatz and managed to rescue most of them, either through the intervention of the Jewish police or else for money. Nonetheless, we were unable to save a few. In this way the number of Council staff was automatically reduced for the second time. That day they took away hundreds of workers, from among those who had remained after the extensive reduction previously conducted by the Council (that had reduced the number of employees by 75 percent, and the number of JHK workers by 90 percent).

Immediately after the Germans "cleansed" the Council apartments, intensive roundups began in the factory workshops and their residences. Some shops were subjected to repeated roundups, day after day, that were conducted insidiously, by surprise. After a relatively mild first selection, the workers were assured there would be no other, so those who remained felt secure. A day or two later, however, a second murderous roundup would take place, and most of the remaining workers and their families would be deported. Certain workshops suffered genuine pogroms during this Aktion and were completely liquidated—mostly the ones lacking either the proper authorization or the necessary connections. But there was no firm rule. Certain shops considered "absolutely" secure (such as Müller's shop and Vinetta) were liquidated. Of the 7,000 workers in the large brushmaker's factory only 3,000 remained after the roundup. Thousands of workers and their families were also removed from the largest factories (Többens and Schultz). We were witnesses to heartrending scenes where a father, who worked in a different shop from his wife and children, returned to his apartment to learn that he had lost everyone he held dear. Mothers came home from work and couldn't find their children. In the evenings the streets were full of people sobbing in despair at having lost children, siblings, or parents.

During this period of the Aktion a significant number of people active in our cultural, social, and artistic life of the ghetto, who had previously found shelter in the workshops, were rounded up. They took almost all the artists (Ostrzega, Waintraub, Śliwniak, Tykociński, and others) and well-known poets (Lerer, Kirman, and others), as well as several highly regarded women volunteers (Rotner, Mokrska).

On Saturday, 29 August, we were alarmed by the news that neither the Polish police nor the Warsaw municipal officials would have access to the ghetto from Sunday through Tuesday. We interpreted this to mean there would be some decisive action against the remaining Jews—a pogrom or complete deportation to some other place. It turned out, however, that our alarm was premature. The restrictions applied only to the little ghetto, where no Jews were left; there was to be a so-called furniture Aktion—that is, an organized plundering of the apartments. In all likelihood the Germans wanted to do this without witnesses or accomplices. The furniture Aktion took place at the appointed time: Supposedly the Germans searched the little ghetto with police dogs and uncovered a few hundred people who had been hiding; these were killed on the spot. The event had no effect on the deportations taking place in the big ghetto.

On the night of Tuesday, 1 September, the Soviets launched a second bombing raid. This time it was somewhat expected, in conjunction with the anniversary of the outbreak of the war. Many bombs fell on the ghetto; our building was hit as well. No one was killed because everyone was on the ground floor, standing up, but the shell fragments did injure a few people. By that time our nerves were so hardened we remained unfrightened by the roar of bombs, the din of the roof caving in, fire, the exploding shrapnel, and the shock wave that knocked us down a couple of steps. We merely picked ourselves up with great sangfroid, shook off the dust, and bandaged one another's wounds.

After the raid was over I went up to the apartment, where everything was covered with glass and rubble. I hastily cleaned off the bed, fell asleep, and slept like a log until morning, when I learned that a few of the surrounding houses had been partly destroyed. But that scarcely caused a stir, and there were no human casualties.

Around the beginning of September the deportations let up somewhat, at least during the day. The transports began leaving every few days instead of daily; for the umpteenth time the

optimists deluded themselves into believing the Aktion was near-
ing its end. A new pattern emerged. Whereas the early morning
hours (from five to seven) and evenings (from six to nine) had
hitherto been generally calm enough to allow some movement
about the ghetto, the evenings now became horribly fraught with
tension. Germans or Ukrainians went foraging on practically every
street, singly or in groups. They rounded up pedestrians, frequently searching and robbing them, and began taking random
shots at windows, particularly after dark. Columns of pedestrians
who had been hunted down and were being led to Umschlagplatz
by a single German or Ukrainian were a common sight. The
streets were practically devoid of movement. That same week,
groups of laborers returning from their worksites outside the
ghetto—who had until recently felt fairly secure—were stopped
and subjected to spot selections; those who were chosen—sometimes even the entire group—would be taken to Umschlagplatz. In
addition to such mass purges at the checkpoints, workers were also
subject to evening roundups on the streets. Previously they had felt
fairly safe once they had passed the sentries; they would move
about freely—some would even sell whatever food or supplies they
had brought in—but now they stole through the streets as if scouting enemy territory, peering around at every step and sending
pickets in advance.

In the evening, more and more gunfire was heard on the
streets as the Germans and Ukrainians went about murdering
pedestrians. When we ventured outside in the morning we would
see puddles of blood and often even the corpses lying on the
ground, although the funeral carts were generally very quick to
take them away. The undertakers were the only people who kept
working the whole time, and they were uncommonly active. Black
wagons circulated through the streets, frequently leaking streams of
blood as they passed. The wagons were furnished with two plat-
forms to hold the boxes that contained the corpses; occasionally a

single corpse would be resting on the very top. The undertakers' buildings were always fronted by a mass of bloody coffins.

Long bursts of machine-gun fire could also be heard in the night, coming from the direction of Pawiak. People said this meant they were killing Jews who had been caught on the Aryan side.

In the course of that week the Provisions Department undertook a registration of all consumers inside the ghetto. The Germans planned to use the information to decide how to proceed with the Aktion. An earlier decree had ordered all nonworkers and their families to report to Umschlagplatz under threat of losing their ration cards, so that workers were already registered separately from nonworkers. Now it was rumored that ration cards would be issued only to people who were actually working. Supposedly they learned that 105,000 Jews were still living in the ghetto. As the official ghetto population had been over 370,000 when the first Aktion began on 22 July, evidently over a quarter of a million Warsaw Jews had been liquidated in the space of those six weeks. In the wake of the new registration, a persistent rumor started making the rounds that no more than 30,000 people would remain inside the ghetto, all to be employed in German factories and worksites. The total combined staff of the other institutions, including the police, was to number no more than 1,000 and would be divided in the following manner: 500 for the police (out of 2,000); 400 for the Council, the JHK, the Provisions Department, and the Work Administration; and 100 so-called "redcap emergency services" maintained by the Jewish Gestapo (earlier known as the "Thirteen"). The news had a tremendously debilitating effect on the 100,000 left in the ghetto, who no longer believed they would be saved. Nerves were strained to the point of snapping. Every face was marked by physical and mental exhaustion. It was said that everyone had "death in his eyes" or "a skull instead of a face."

The number of people frantically inquiring about poison began to rise rapidly. On Thursday, 3 September, we were shaken by the deaths of two of our most valued youth activists, Józef Kapłan and Szmuel Bresław, who were murdered by the SS.* On Friday the anxiety reached its peak; by midafternoon the word was going around that the Germans had ordered the entire Jewish police force to assemble at 7 A.M. on Saturday morning. This included the so-called *Werkschutz,* policemen who had been assigned as factory guards and who for some time had not participated in the roundups. All other exemptions were similarly superseded by the order to assemble. Understandably, the decree set off a panic. Everyone understood the Aktion was about to enter its most drastic phase. Terrible things happened on the streets that evening. At seven I went next door to confer with Herman, one of the social activists; on my way back I had to wait a whole hour to cross the few steps to our building, so frightful were the scenes taking place. When I finally managed to dash across and inside our building, I could still hear the horrible cries of the murdered right outside our windows. This time the Germans did not content themselves with shooting; they tortured each victim for a long time before putting a bullet in his head. Four bodies were lying beneath our balcony. The Germans roamed the streets until after nine, shining spotlights and shooting at windows. No sooner did the moaning of the victims cease and the patrols quit the streets than the air-raid alarms began to sound, but this time it was only planes passing overhead. Even so, we spent a few hours in the dark on the stairs. After the all clear, we returned to our apartment and resolved to leave the ghetto the next morning.

ANONYMOUS WOMAN. Some time around 6 August a notice went up throughout the ghetto streets informing us that everyone who will-

---

*Józef Kapłan (b. 1913) and Szmuel Bresław (b. 1920) were leaders of Hashomer Hatzair, active members of the Antifascist Bloc, and co-organizers of the nascent (in July 1942) ŻOB—Jewish Fighting Organization.[4]

ingly reported for deportation would not be separated from their loved ones.* So great was the fear of separation, and so great the need to be with someone close until the end, that people responded. The new proclamation made it possible for them to meet their fate together, so families began to report to Umschlagplatz of their own free will. The numbers there increased: From 6 August on, approximately 15,000 people passed through Umschlagplatz, each day—in accordance with German demands.† Throngs of people were milling about the place with knapsacks and bundles. Each was clinging to the deluded hope that the journey might not end in death; consequently certain things would be needed. So they took the most essential items—warm clothes, shoes, a towel, some soap, a spoon. But even modest bags weighing only six or seven kilograms proved difficult to hold on to in the press of the crowd, so most people discarded what they had packed. Many tried to escape before the boxcars pulled up; instinctively they wanted to flee that cramped and noxious place, covered with feces and filth. As they waited for the freight cars, people took care of their bodily needs right where they stood, since it was impossible to move through the crowd. They told themselves they had to escape at all costs—but this was an unattainable fantasy with barbed wire everywhere and German guards on the alert on all sides, rifles ready to fire at any moment. A few people were released in exchange for money or valuables they offered to the Jewish henchman Szmerling;†† others had documents the Germans on duty decided to respect on that particular day, as a whim. There was no rule. Sometimes they released workers from the factory shops, while other times they

---

*The author is probably referring to the proclamation that appeared on the ghetto walls on 1 September 1942, signed by the chief of the SP.

†Many sources suggest the Germans demanded that between 6,000 and 10,000 people be brought to Umschlagplatz every day.

††Mieczysław Szmerling was an officer of the SP who served as commandant at Umschlagplatz.[5]

refused to honor any work papers whatsoever. Occasionally a simple request was enough, or else the intervention of a Jewish policeman or other official, and now and then someone managed to make it to the Jewish hospital adjacent to the yard.

There were cases where the hospital nurses or sanitation workers, who generally had free access to the loading area, were able to sneak someone out disguised as one of their own. Small children were occasionally carried out in knapsacks, after having been drugged so they would not give themselves away when passing near the Germans. A few people hid beneath the corpses in the collective hearses and managed to escape that way. All sought to save themselves as best they could.

As a rule, suicide was rare at Umschlagplatz—it was impossible in the crowd, the mass, the crush. There were those who waited for the last moment and then took cyanide right before being loaded onto the cars, when the rescue they had been counting on failed to materialize. But few were so fortunate. Jews who refused to board the cars were killed on the spot, but this was not common. Hope, the desire to live, and perhaps some insane curiosity about what would happen next left little room for resistance.

So they climbed aboard the freight cars, pushing their way inside, and when there was no more room a gendarme might fire into the crowd. People would instinctively recoil, and another several dozen would be shoved inside. They packed an average of a hundred people into each car, and on some days as many as 150 cars left Umschlagplatz. A contingent of Germans escorted the transports. After a while, the same cars returned empty (this was clear because of certain markings). The engineer was ordered to keep silent under pain of death. We eventually learned that, after the train had traveled a certain distance, the Polish engineer was replaced by a German.

By early September we knew that some of the transports went to Treblinka. But we didn't know what happened there.

At about the same time, an article on the deportations appeared in the German press, claiming that the Jews had requested German assistance in cleaning up the Warsaw Ghetto. Supposedly the Jews had suggested removing unproductive elements who were a burden to the community. According to the article, the Germans had agreed to help by providing the necessary transportation: in other words, the freight cars. What more telling evidence could there be of their lying and hypocrisy?

SAMUEL PUTERMAN. I looked in Kramsztyk's* room but didn't find anyone there or in the whole apartment. The building looked deserted. I kept calling for a long time before I glimpsed a living soul. Finally, some man stuck his head out of a basement window and told me to wait. It was the building caretaker, who knew me by sight. "You're looking for pan Kramsztyk; follow me." He led me along some twisted paths and down a long narrow tunnel into the basement, where I had to crawl on my stomach through a hole in the wall. Inside the large basement were several dozen people. Kramsztyk was lying on a pallet in the corner. His face was pale, nearly white. Seeing me, he tried to summon one of his charming smiles.

"I told them to let you in; the caretaker heard someone calling my name. They killed me today; I'm still alive, but I won't last very much longer."

Kramsztyk had gone to his apartment to fetch some pencils; at ten o'clock he was caught in a roundup with nowhere to hide. A random bullet pierced his lung; he fell unconscious, covered with

---

*Roman Kramsztyk was born in Warsaw. An outstanding painter and graphic artist, he painted landscapes, nudes, and still lifes and composed a cycle of drawings from the Warsaw Ghetto. Kramsztyk had been living abroad when his mother's illness caused him to return to Warsaw in the summer of 1939. He was shot during a roundup on 6 August 1942.[6]

blood. The Germans left him spread-eagled in the courtyard. It wasn't until hours later, after the shooting and screaming on the street had faded away, that people hiding in the shelters went out to the courtyard and took him back to the basement. A doctor who was on hand gave him a couple of shots but said there was no hope.

"I assured everyone it was all right to let you in, that you wouldn't give them away."

His words were more for the benefit of those present; he wanted to reassure them one more time that I could be trusted. He was running a high fever; one moment he was conscious, the next he was hallucinating. I didn't have the courage to leave; he stared at me with his burning gaze, clenching my hand.

"Tell them to go on painting, colleague. Tell them I said good-bye." I had to swear a solemn oath that I would urge our colleagues to paint scenes from the history of the ghetto, once the war was over. "Forget about nudes, portraits, and still lifes; the world has to learn about these crimes. Tell them that Kramsztyk asked them to paint scenes from the ghetto. Devote everything to this. Let the world find out about German bestiality."

He was already in his death throes; his mouth was spewing blood; he was suffering greatly but kept on speaking to me. Then he reached into his pocket, pulled out a few pastels of sanguine, and handed them to me solemnly, saying, "Here, you can give them these to remember Kramsztyk by; they're good pastels, original Lefranc."

He died within the hour. He had given me as a memento the gold watch he had won at an exhibition in France. The cover bore the engraving LIBERTÉ, EGALITÉ, FRATERNITÉ.

STEFANIA STASZEWSKA WAS BORN IN WARSAW; HER FATHER, Samuel Szochur, worked in a textile store on Gęsia Street. Active in Socialist youth groups, she had just finished her fourth year of Gym-

nasium *(secondary school) when the war broke out. Inside the ghetto she worked for the Polish Workers' Party (PPR) and participated in the resistance. In April 1943, Staszewska was deported to a labor camp but managed to escape and survived the war by obtaining false papers. After the war she settled in Warsaw, and became an actress in the National Yiddish Theater.*

The Jews march down the middle of the street four abreast, women and men, with rucksacks. Their gait is even, their heads held high, their backs erect; everyone is trying to look young and healthy. And everyone has just one thought: to get through the selection. A man in civilian dress—maybe Untersturmführer Brandt himself—is standing by the checkpoint, holding his riding crop, next to some other fat German. They use their crops to count off the ranks. Now and then they cry *"Halt!"* and bring everything to a standstill. One of the Germans searches someone's overly large knapsack or else removes a woman or an old man from the ranks. Then someone from the next group of four fills the gap and the command is given: *"Weiter!"*—Move on!

On this day the sobs, shouts, and despair reach their peak. Out of several hundred children they haven't let through much more than a dozen—all about ten years old—the rest were torn from their parents and left in the courtyard. Some German swine ripped a child away from its young mother. She seemed to hesitate, she reached out her arms, she had a chance to stay with her child. A split second of thought, the whip hanging in the air—and the mother turned away and went on alone. We all felt her pain and her despair, but we couldn't forgive her. Unfortunately there were many such mothers and fathers that day. We looked at the larger rucksacks with concern; these people were hiding their children, who had been drugged. How the fathers must have suffered when the whips fell on their backs, lashing their hearts. Many of the children never woke up; they did not survive the narcotic.

Brauer's workers had been beaten black and blue, but they had already made it through to the other side. Meanwhile Oschman's and Leszczyński's had yet to go, as well as a few worksite workers and some wild people who would never be allowed through. These included old or weak people, women, and children without parents. We waited until 12 noon, when Leszczyński was supposed to arrive and, along with Bauch, carry out the selection for his factory.

The square where we were waiting looked like an enormous bazaar: A few thousand people were milling about while hundreds of children with outstretched hands and eyes swollen from crying searched in vain for their parents. Whips and billy clubs whistled over people's heads. It was like a carnival of horrors; money had no value, and chance and fortune decided who would live and who would not. Masses of wild people were roaming about aimlessly and helplessly, and we too had no idea what was in store for us. Finally, at one o'clock Srulek gave the word to line up in rows of four. I clung tightly to Mama's hand as we took our places. We stood there for about an hour. It was crowded and chaotic beyond belief. Finally they marched us from the square toward the inter-section of Niska and Zamenhof. There a fence separated Dzika from Zamenhof, so that the only passage was through an opening where Leszczyński himself stood waiting to personally send people *links* or *rechts,* left or right, to die or to live.*

We had until four. Then the SS were to come and chase everyone not allowed to leave the square to Umschlagplatz.

There was a tremendous crush—several thousand, ten thou-sand, even more—everyone was trying to push forward. We were surrounded on all sides by Ukrainians. Masses of people were milling about on the street, dripping with sweat from the heat,

---

*The selection points were set up in different places, depending on where the roundups were being conducted, so the meanings of "left" and "right" could vary.—PB

loaded down with their heavy bundles. You couldn't hear over the Germans' shouting, screaming, shooting, and cursing. To make their "work" easier, the Germans ordered everyone to kneel or squat. Then the Ukrainians started screaming from all sides: *"Sadi, chalera, sadi yob twaya mat'"*—Sit down, damn it, sit down go fuck your mother. Rifle butts pounded the heads of anyone who lagged behind, and the Germans tore planks from the fence and beat anyone who attempted to stand up. We crouched and waited for the "party" to end. My hair was glued to my forehead; I wiped my eyes with filthy hands; my clothes were dirty and ragged from dragging myself across the cobblestones; my throat was parched; I had sand in my teeth and a stone weight inside my heart. At that moment I felt nothing except a fear of death, a fear of being gassed, and an animal instinct to survive. With dry eyes I looked at the bleeding heads, the young girls being sent to their deaths, the families being split apart, the mothers torn from their children, and the devoted ones who chose to die along with their babies. But I was indifferent, gazing at the sobbing victims and the sadistic Germans, who even then were flirting with the girls and teasing the children. All I could think of was my mother and myself, how to get us out of that hell. What kind of miracle did we need? I looked at my poor mama. She was barely alive. Her knees were in pain, she was reeling from exhaustion, her bundle was heavy, her forehead bathed in sweat. Our eyes met. Mama nodded. "Yes, Stefcia, you were right," she said. "All we needed was a backpack and some good shoes, and we could have saved ourselves back in 1939 and gone to Russia. But we stayed and took our chance in this terrible lottery."

"Mamusia, let's hope that Papa will survive Siberia."

We dragged ourselves forward, toward the gate. There were still about 500 people ahead of us. Suddenly Mama shook my arm. "Listen, child, if the Germans let you go and send me to the trains, don't come with me. You're young; you have to live. I'm already old, forty years old and sick, but you have to live."

Oh, Mama, Mama, why did you say those terrible words, why did you implant the idea of saving just myself? Because despite all my admiration and respect for you, and despite the fact that I definitely heard you say those words, I have this horrible feeling that I abandoned you, that I took advantage of your consent to leave. Oh, God! My conscience will never again be clean. I know now that *that* was the moment of my death, the death of my real self, my heart, my true life. Mama, everything that happened later took place outside of me; I was nothing but a spectator. To this very day, I don't know how to live. Yes, Mama, I should have died then and there, together with you. Papa, if you're still alive, if we ever find each other, you—and only you—shall be my judge.

It was a sweltering day, about four o'clock. We were getting closer and closer to the control point. There was a wagon behind us piled with bags and bundles. We looked uneasily at the luggage. Supposedly most of the suitcases contained children who had been drugged. Would they let the wagon through without inspecting it? The horses were restless; a few coachmen were trying to control them. Suddenly one of the Ukrainians fired a shot right next to the wagon; the horses reared up and jerked the cart forward, trampling the people underfoot. In the commotion a few suitcases fell, one landed on my head, and when I dug myself out from beneath the wagon and got back on my knees, my mother was no longer there. I stood on a suitcase and called out for her—"Mama!"—but she had disappeared. Just then, a Ukrainian roared in my ear, *"Sadi!"*—Sit! and threatened me with a plank. I knelt back down; I didn't know what to do. Every few seconds I would stick my head up and cry out "Mama!" but all sounds were lost in the general din. The crowd was pushing closer and closer to the fence.

Suddenly a German pointed at me. *"Du, Mädchen"*—You, girl. He ordered me to get up. I took my place in the line, a few steps away from the verdict, the final judgment, the border between life and death. A few young girls were ahead of me; they looked healthy, pretty. They stepped up boldly to Leszczyński. I watched his hand in horror: *"Links, links, links."* These tall beautiful girls were being sent to Umschlagplatz? My fate was sealed; my only consolation was the hope that I would meet my mother there. Still, despite everything I longed to hear the word *rechts,* I longed to survive, to live. My chances were slim: I was short and dirty, bowed from the bundle I was carrying on my back, my face swollen from crying.

Now it's my turn; my thighs are quivering. I hold out my Meldekarte, my heart pounding like a hammer, my gaze focused on the lips of the man who is my judge. It's all in the eyes, I know it; my eyes have to lock with his and summon from his lips the word *life.* Leszczyński inspects my pink Meldekarte, glances at the photo, asks where I work.

"Karmelicka twenty-five."

"Who's the head foreman?"

A smile lights up my face; now I'm sure he'll let me go. Without missing a beat I answer, "Winny, Srulek Winny."

Leszczyński returned my card. He slowly lifted his hand, his left hand. I was dying of fright. So, no, it's to the left after all? Once again I looked him in the eye, he looked at me, and his hand swung hard around to the right. The gendarme shoved me through the gate onto Zamenhof.

I was alive; I had survived. My heart was pounding, my legs were shaking. I was alive, alive! I ran for a few steps and suddenly my happiness dropped from me: What about Mama? Oh, Mama, can anyone understand the pain, the conflict that was tearing me apart? Here I was, happy to be alive, and meanwhile my mother was . . . over there, alone, abandoned. Poor Mama. For a moment I just stood there in the street; next I started running back and forth like a madwoman. Something was pushing me forward and something was holding me back. No, I'm not allowed to go back—to go back means to die. But Mama—the conflict was gnawing away at me—Mama! I burst into tears and stayed there sobbing on the empty street.

I dragged myself on. Where to go? I didn't know. Only then did I feel the weight of my knapsack, the pain in my knees, the stabbing thirst and hunger. I had no destination. I walked down Zamenhof Street, here and there tripping over a discarded bundle or stepping across a puddle of blood. At number 35 there was a corpse. Display windows without panes, streets full of tattered clothes and broken glass. Suddenly a gendarme stopped me. He ordered me to wait for some more people who had also been released. A few minutes later Pelc showed up with his wife and, amazingly, his child. I couldn't believe Leszczyński had let a child through. It was a miracle. A few tailors arrived, and then some others. Supposedly, this was the last group to be released. The Jewish policeman lined us up in ranks of four. "I'll escort you to the factory on Nalewki," he said, though it was all the same to me.

Pelc wondered whether to count the child as one of four or to keep him hidden between himself and his wife.

"Better hide him."

We set off. A car belonging to the Umsiedlungskommando—the SS squad overseeing the deportation—came down the street and stopped nearby. Handtke himself stepped out and inspected our ranks, crop in hand. He was on the verge of leaving when he noticed the child tucked between the adults. *"Was?"* he shouted. His face was twisted with rage; his eyes glowered red. "Whose child is that?"

Pelc spoke slowly and quietly. "Mine."

The crop came down on Pelc: once, twice, three times.

"Du Schwein!" Handtke shouted. "Don't you count your own child as a person? What kind of father are you? You want to lose him?"

What irony! Back on the square they were sending hundreds of children to their deaths; Herr Handtke himself was one of those who took special pleasure in hunting down children, and here he is concerned a Jewish child might have been wronged.

Pelc was shaking—we all were shaking for fear that Handtke would suddenly pull out his pistol and shoot somebody—but fortunately another SS man pointed to the time and pulled him back into the car. We walked to Gęsia Street and turned left onto Nalewki. The streets were deserted. We marched in silence, thinking about the ones we had lost that day.

The factory at Nalewki was already full; the tables and work stands had all been taken, and people were lying on the floor. I found a free windowsill and sat out the night while everyone slept; sleep helped soothe their swollen eyes and aching hearts. Some people were crying out the names of their loved ones in their sleep.

The morning came as gray and sad as we were. Our little group headed for the workshop on Karmelicka. The guards let us through fairly easily, and we soon arrived at our destination.

No one at Karmelicka was expecting us; they thought we had been deported. They received us so warmly we felt like one big family. The tailors laughed as they welcomed me— *"unzer maydele mit tsukerlakh,"* our little candy girl—since I had sold candy for a while. They all shook my hand, consoling me as best they could.

I don't know what happened during the next days; I felt I was in a dream. I moved about like a mannequin and spent most of the time asleep on the table that had served as my mother's and my workplace as well as our bed. I wanted to sleep through it all, to shed the memory, to forget.

One day in mid-September I learned from the tailors that we were moving to Többens's shop, because Leszczyński's Ausweise were only valid through November, while Többens's were good until January, and Leszczyński only wanted a staff of forty people while Többens could take seventy. So we simply made what seemed the better choice.

Walter C. Többens, omnipotent master of Leszno and Prosta streets, wanted to inspect his future slaves before taking them on. Four abreast, we marched to Leszno 42. In the courtyard we lined up in two long rows and listened to Többens's welcoming speech, which consisted of two words, *"Guten Tag."* Then pan Neifeld, the factory supervisor, took over, while Többens walked up and down, inspecting us up close, before crossing to the stairwell to survey the group from the window, just as if he were buying livestock. Többens looked like a cruel brute; he was tall and broadshouldered, with a crestfallen gaze and a slack lower jaw, of sloppy posture, always shifting his weight. His speech was slow and indistinct; he spoke through his teeth. He and his relative, Jahn, were notorious for their drinking bouts and orgies. And this was the person we were supposed to work for; this was the man to decide our "To be or not to be."

SAMUEL PUTERMAN. The wretched horses slowly haul the overloaded wagons, from which one can hear sobbing. At times an emaciated hand may reach out toward the people on foot and someone would shout "A piece of bread for the road!"—shout, not ask, demanding some bread from the ones who are staying. From all parts of the ghetto, the wagons roll along Zamenhof Street up to Umschlagplatz. They pass the guard post at Checkpoint Five. Then they turn sharply to the right, toward the wall along Niska, that runs a few meters away from the sidewalk. At the buildings used by the Transferstelle they turn left. Now they are a hundred meters outside the ghetto, outside the wall that runs from the checkpoint toward the ghetto. This same wall then breaks off at a right angle to enclose two huge modern buildings used as grade schools before the war, with beautiful halls and wide modern windows, that now house the hospital for infectious disease. Their courtyards are connected and adjoin the original wall of the rail yard. When the ghetto walls went up, these buildings were located in a no-man's-land just outside the boundary, a no-man's-land where Jews are collected and assembled. Next to these buildings is a small, unsightly public bathhouse—now used for forced

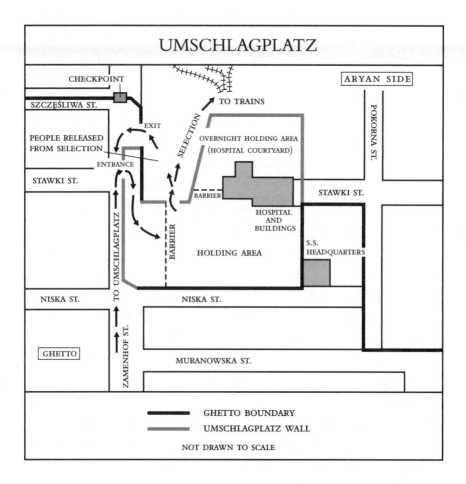

UMSCHLAGPLATZ

CHECKPOINT

ARYAN SIDE

SZCZEŚLIWA ST.

TO TRAINS

EXIT

PEOPLE RELEASED
FROM SELECTION

SELECTION

OVERNIGHT HOLDING AREA
(HOSPITAL COURTYARD)

POKORNA ST.

ENTRANCE

STAWKI ST.

BARRIER

STAWKI ST.

TO UMSCHLAGPLATZ

BARRIER

HOSPITAL
AND
BUILDINGS

HOLDING AREA

S.S.
HEADQUARTERS

NISKA ST.

NISKA ST.

ZAMENHOF ST.

GHETTO

MURANOWSKA ST.

━━━━━ GHETTO BOUNDARY

▨▨▨▨▨ UMSCHLAGPLATZ WALL

NOT DRAWN TO SCALE

communal baths—and a gateway leading to the spacious yard by the railroad siding: Umschlagplatz. The yard itself, which was enclosed before the war, has two gated entrances, one from Dzika Street and the other from Niska.

These grounds seemed perfectly suited for their current use, as if designed by some satanic architect. They were given the name Umschlagplatz, which acquired the permanent abbreviation "Umschlag," used with painful frequency by those who were left behind, whose loved ones had been taken away. Inside the ghetto, business appeared to go on as usual; life seemed to flow at its normal pace, although café and restaurant owners had closed their premises, which were glaringly empty for lack of clients. Meanwhile, small police patrols conducted roundups of street beggars and loaded them onto the slowly trailing wagons. The uninterrupted string of vehicles proceeded toward Umschlagplatz and arrived at the circular area in front of the buildings.

By order of the authorities, Mieczysław Szmerling of the SP was named commandant of Umschlagplatz. He selected a staff of five functionaries from the SP (from the epidemic disease group). The Health Department provided sanitation workers to unload the wagons and move the deportees into the buildings, where they were held until the next step: the cattle cars. Thirty SP men were assigned to watch the deportees and maintain order. Two additional functionaries were given the task of counting the arriving transports. Every evening Szmerling would report to SS Oberscharführer Mende, who would drive up in a green Mercedes and call out "Balbo!" by way of greeting, and "Balbo" would report—"Four thousand twenty people"—and one more day of the Aktion would draw to a close.

Ukrainians kept a constant watch day and night along the perimeters of Umschlagplatz—at the entrance and on the opposite side, along the wall that separated it from the Transferstelle. At night they were also posted on the yard in front of the buildings.

The yard was sectioned off by barbed wire to create a wide passageway leading to the building. This made it easier to count the incoming columns. It also made it impossible to escape or to smuggle anyone to the exit, since nearly half the yard was empty, not counting the detachments of SP, so that anyone dressed in civilian clothes would instantly attract attention. Different shifts of doctors and hospital staff entered several times a day in a tight column, always inspected by Szmerling or one of his deputies. Szmerling was responsible for the whole place. The Ukrainians just kept guard and were not allowed to intervene during the daytime operations.

The Aktion went on for three weeks, during which time the Jews learned to distinguish each SS man in the Lublin group.[*] No one knew them better than the SP, who were in contact with them several hours a day and soon came to know each man's habits, customs, and routines. Their bloody actions had already ensured these men a place in the ghetto's history; each had acquired a personal notoriety. Together they personified the menacing word Vernichtungskommando—extermination commando. Each gave the impression he was playing a role from some gruesome script written somewhere in Berlin. Copies of the script had been relayed to all corners of Europe that were groaning under the victorious German boot. In the Generalgouvernement, the leading man was SS Hauptsturmführer Hermann Höfle: He was handsome and tall and displayed that elusive elegance that military dress can help impart—despite the obvious lack of variety. He would show up in the ghetto and check on his underlings without leaving his car. He paid short visits to specific sectors, exchanging no more than a few words with his subordinates. He frequently stopped at Umschlagplatz—where he did leave his car—to inspect

---

[*]The group of Gestapo officers sent from the Lublin headquarters of Einsatz Reinhard to oversee the deportation of ghetto inhabitants to Treblinka.

the yard in the company of his chauffeur. At first he would enter the building there, but as the place became more and more filthy he began to forgo this. He would climb up to the top of the building and observe the people slated for deportation, calmly and nonchalantly. He stayed utterly impassive to tragic scenes worthy of great writers, film directors, or painters. His kindly handsome face never lost the hint of a sneer when he passed by an old man whose forehead had been split open by a whip; nor did he react when he entered a hall where small children and infants who had been snatched from their parents were lying on a dirty floor, covered with flies. With the same fixed expression he would order Szmerling to reinforce the guards, ask how many people were scheduled for transport, and watch—very briefly—as they were loaded into the cars.

His deputy, SS Obersturmführer Michalsen, was about forty-five years old, above-average height, with the flat pudgy face of a butcher and calm deliberate movements. He never used his pistol or the leather crop he usually carried. Always smiling and courteous to his men, he issued his orders quietly. He participated in the Aktion more than Höfle; he never got angry, never shouted, never shot or hit a single Jew. His dealings with the SP were correct in the extreme. He was especially partial to Lejkin* and obviously enjoyed watching him, a short man with an energetic voice, issuing commands to his SP subordinates. But Michalsen devoted most of his time and interest to watching the Ukrainians chase people from Umschlagplatz to the railroad cars. His visits there made little impression on the SP, but Germans of lower rank would snap to if they heard his name or caught sight of his jovial face, like regular enlisted men who have spotted a higher officer.

---

*Jakub Lejkin, a lawyer, was a commander of the SP. His zeal in office did much harm to the ghetto population, particularly during the deportations. On 29 October 1942, Lejkin was executed by Eliahu Różański on behalf of the ŻOB.[7]

And although he greeted them nearly as equals, they were clearly very afraid of him.

Geipel, whose name appeared on all the posters announcing the expropriation of pharmacies, small shops, and other stores, was very involved with the Aktion. After an exhausting day's work, he liked to drive around the ghetto. He often stopped in at Umschlagplatz, where he'd engage in conversation with Szmerling or lower SP functionaries, asking a few witty ironic questions as he fiddled with his pistol holder: "How do you like the Aktion?" Or "Where do you think this will all end up?"* Or else "How much did they make off the roundups today?" He didn't seem to mind if there was no response; sometimes he would answer himself, with a guttural, croaking laugh. Often he would interrupt these proceedings by singling out one person and calling him over. Once he selected a woman with a little child on her arm. He asked her some questions—whether she was happy to be going to work—then ordered that she be given a loaf of bread, for which the woman thanked him. He dismissed her, and she stepped away, her child's head resting on her shoulder. Geipel then drew his revolver, reveling in the long moment of terrified silence that gripped everyone in the vicinity. He took aim and fired. As he slowly lowered his revolver, a red stain blossomed from the mother's shoulder.

During one visit a ricksha pulled up, carrying an old man with a handsome face and imposing stature; he had a long white beard that reached his knees. The man climbed out of the ricksha, leaning heavily on his cane. Geipel was leaving Umschlagplatz, having just completed his visit and asked his witty questions. He'd also managed to shoot one young girl after suggesting she become his mistress. The girl, still a child, had responded with a stunned look in her blue eyes and simply stood for a long while, hypnotized by fear at the sight of his unholstered revolver. Not a word

---

*In all cases Geipel is quoted using the familiar *"du"* form when addressing Jews.—PB

crossed her lips. He shot her straight in the eyes; she collapsed at his feet without a moan. Her father had witnessed the whole scene from a distance; after the gunshot he ran to his daughter, held her in his arms, and sat beside the wall, rocking her rhythmically back and forth.

Geipel was on his way out when he caught sight of the old man and took a few steps in his direction. The man straightened himself; he was a head taller than the German. Once again, everyone within meters of the two men fell silent.

"How old are you?" Geipel asked.

The old man answered in beautifully accented German. "Eighty-nine."

"How do you know German so well?"

"I was a teacher in Frankfurt for many years." The eyes of the old Jew were sparkling with an energy far brighter than Geipel's.

"And how have you managed to survive until now?" As usual, Szmerling was listening. Geipel demanded that; he liked watching the huge man blanch at every new performance.

The old man waited a long time before answering this last question.

Geipel repeated it.

"At first I had eighty thousand zloty. I was hiding in an attic. The SP found me; I asked them to spare me and offered to pay them. Eight times they uncovered my hiding place; eight times I paid my ransom. The next two times they left me without taking any money, and today they found me for the eleventh time. This time I didn't ask for anything, and here I am."

"And here you are," Geipel repeated. "And you know that I can shoot you?"

"I know that you *will* shoot me," the old man replied, smiling. Geipel acted as if he hadn't heard the last response, and ordered that the Jew be escorted into the building. He turned to ask Szmerling a question; then, as two sanitation workers took the old man under the arms, Geipel shot him from behind, hitting him in his stooping neck.

The morning of 18 August arrived, followed by days full of yelling, shooting, and chaos. The Germans stepped up the Aktion. It was beyond all comprehension. Only one thing was certain: annihilation. The railroad cars took around five or six thousand people every day or, on rare occasions, every second day. What seemed safe and secure one day burst like a soap bubble the next. New announcements went up in the ghetto, calling on people to report voluntarily, and every day despair and hunger brought more volunteers to Umschlagplatz. Travel rations were lowered. Instead of 3 kilos of bread and 1 kilo of jam they received 1 kilo of bread and ¼ kilo of jam. One new change in particular added to the hopeless chaos: The Aktion was no longer confined to a few cordoned blocks, nor were the roundups restricted to a few hours on one street; rather, they skipped from one target to another, different blocks and factories. Now they rarely performed selections on the street. Instead, they chased people outside and drove them to Umschlagplatz. Gigantic factories were emptied in this manner. Then, just before the cars were loaded, one German accompanied by two auxiliaries would look over everyone's documents and release a few thousand. On occasion they would conduct the selection at the entrance to Umschlagplatz. There were days when 10,000 people were brought in, and 6,000 released. Or they would bring 12,000 and release 4,000. The system was erratic; no one could figure it out. At times the trains would leave every second or even every third day. Meanwhile, tens of thousands of people would pass through Umschlagplatz, where they were collected but not loaded. The place would be overflowing with crowds waiting for the selection, papers constantly at the ready. Then the freight cars would arrive and take four, five, or six thousand and leave the rest. New people would come, another selection would take place, and three days would go by with no cars and no one being loaded. All day long, column after column would enter the yard to be counted and then released at the selection—evidently one's Ausweis did make a difference, though some people were freed while others with the same documents were loaded onto the cars. Umschlagplatz was no longer emptied the way it had been, in groups of 5,000, or even twelve. Now even when 6,000 people were squeezed inside and 8,000 were freed, the place stayed full of people. The cars started taking only a fraction, as if the Germans wanted to show everyone left in the ghetto exactly what Umschlagplatz looked like. In many cases the same people were brought to Umschlagplatz several times over the course of a couple of weeks and then released.

People no longer knew what worked and what didn't, which documents were certain, which shops were safer, which were more likely to be respected. The groups being taken to Umschlagplatz changed their appearance. The columns being escorted went calmly now, without sobbing or crying; each person walked in step, documents in hand, looking for the place of selection, which was often set up a few hundred meters in front. After that they would check near the entrance to the yard; selections could also take place at any time on Umschlagplatz itself. They could happen before the march to the rail cars or right at the cars, just before they were loaded. People would climb inside the cars, gripping the same valuable document that had saved them two, three, or even five times before. From inside the cars they would still crane their necks to hear if someone was calling the name of their factory. Only the grating of metal, as the doors were barred, and the train's departing whistle would snap them back to reality and strip them of all hope as they were carried off into the unknown. The brave and daring would file away at the walls and floors of the railroad cars, open holes, and jump from the moving cars. Every train was escorted by a detachment of Ukrainians stationed in the last car. People would jump from the train, breaking their arms or legs, fracturing their skulls, and the Ukrainians would fire at them. Some would drop dead; others would get up, dragging their crippled limbs. They would go to nearby peasants, kind people who would give them food and drink and, more rarely, let them stay overnight. Courageous escapees returned to the ghetto. Doing this required a good deal of luck, to avoid falling into the hands of the blackmailers who, if they failed to obtain their ransom, would hand the poor souls over to the police.

The system of conducting the Aktion changed, the appearance of the groups being led away changed, and Umschlagplatz itself changed as well. On the outside, the central building still looked spic and span, but inside it was a gigantic cesspool. The toilets were stopped up; water ran unchecked from broken faucets and flowed from clogged sinks onto the floor, making puddles of thick, sticky mud trampled by several thousand people. The building emitted a nauseating stench that could be noticed hundreds of meters away. The situation worsened by the hour. Neither the specially assigned cleaning units nor the plumbers constantly called in to make repairs were able to help. The filth, stench, and mud increased with the number of victims passing through.

Earlier, people were glad if they managed to stay at Umschlagplatz overnight; they had to be forced out of the buildings with whips and guns. Now the hapless victims would leave en masse as soon as they were ordered out to the trains—if only to get some fresh air, just a few hundred steps' worth, before they were caged up inside the cattle cars. Eighty to 120 people were stuffed into cars that normally held a dozen cows. Umschlagplatz became even more unbearable once one building was declared a hospital. After all the people had been evacuated from the odd-numbered side of Leszno Street, the Jewish hospital in the Leszno Treasury building remained open only a few more days. Then the order was given to move the patients to one of the buildings at Umschlagplatz.

Over the course of two days nearly two thousand patients, along with the hospital equipment, were transported in wagons, trailers, handcarts, and rickshas. The rumor that the sick people were being deported aroused some fear; evidently the idea of hospital patients being moved to Umschlagplatz truly shocked people, probably because, despite everything, the remaining inhabitants of the ghetto still clung to the belief that the deportees were being shipped east to work. Whether they were entirely convinced or not, however, the optimists sighed with relief when they learned that one of the Umschlagplatz buildings had been assigned to the patients; within a few days it was officially converted into a hospital. But now the deportees suffered even more, having lost half their space. The buildings became so unbearably crowded and filthy that some people had to be left outside in the yard, which led the Germans to double the guards.

A backdrop of beautiful, stylish buildings: The Germans circle the entire area, then enter the courtyard where the miserable people are squatting. Everyone starts heading out. Fifteen armed Ukrainians have arrived and advance against the buildings, led by two commanders. Shots ring out; the air fills with the cries and sobs of the unfortunates as they are beaten with rifle butts. A column of living corpses moves out through the open gate leading to the railway siding; they drag sacks of red ticking stuffed with feather bedding. The path runs between a grassy lawn and some rounded flower beds, across a broad road, toward a wide opening in the wall. After several dozen meters they reach the true gate of the switching yard; this is the one they now pass through. Beyond this gate is an enormous yard containing a few buildings and sidings; the regular train tracks begin farther back. Two hundred policemen have lined up in a double row a few hundred meters long, forming an aisle that leads to the trains. The cattle cars have no steps. Lejkin has assigned two policemen to each car and ordered them to count off the people, some one hundred to a wagon. In less than an hour they manage to load sixty cars—to the clamor of beatings and the sobs of mothers who have lost their children. The doors creak as they are shoved shut; the rectangular maws of the moaning cars are closed. The chains grate and clash, the train begins to move. Through a little window covered with barbed wire come the last cries of despair from the people crammed inside. The train pulls out, headed for the unknown, while fifteen armed Ukrainians and two hundred SP men led by Lejkin head in the opposite direction. That's it for the day. The men are dismissed.

BER WARM *WAS A MEMBER OF THE JEWISH POLICE FORCE, and was first assigned to the* Befehlstelle, *the SS command post for the deportation, and later to the* Werterfassungstelle, *the Office for Value Assessment. In April 1943, Warm went into hiding on the Aryan side, where he wrote his account and ultimately died.*

I don't know what went on in the Befehlstelle during the Aktion from the end of July to the middle of August 1942; people just said that Germans were living in the building. I was assigned there as part of the Jewish Służba Porządkowa in early October 1942, so I know the Befehlstelle as it was between the first large operation and the second in January 1943. I presume that was when the building located at Żelazna 103 began living up to its name Befehlstelle—command post—for the SS inside the ghetto, since the earlier deportations had been directed from the KSP building at Ogrodowa 17. After this building was excluded from the ghetto at the end of September, the SS headquarters were moved to Żelazna 103. The KSP was permitted to stay on Ogrodowa a little longer, although the Jews had been cleared out from that street during the latter half of August.

The SS or, rather, the SD (Sicherheitsdienst) located at Szuch 23, had assumed command of the ghetto at the very beginning of the "deportation operation"—that is, at 8 A.M. on 22 July 1942. Until then the ghetto had been administered by civilian authorities, in the person of Commissar Auerswald,* plenipotentiary of the Governor of the Warsaw District, who implemented his policies through the President of the Jewish Council. The SS command post inside the ghetto was set up expressly for the Aktion. SS Oberscharführer Mende, the representative of Szuch Boulevard, administered the first stage of the Aktion from the offices of SP Chief Colonel Szeryński, on the second floor of the SP headquarters at Ogrodowa 17; a plate affixed to the door read SONDERKOMMANDO DER SICHERHEITSPOLIZEI UMSIEDLUNG—SPECIAL HEADQUARTERS OF THE SECURITY POLICE RESETTLEMENT. The adjacent office was shared by the brothers Stanisław and Jerzy Czapliński, district chiefs of the SP; group leader Mayzler; the daytime telephone operator; and officer Landau, the night operator. The wife of SP subdistrict commander Kornheim worked there as stenotypist.

The delegates from Szuch Boulevard and from Einsatz Reinhard† chose the KSP building precisely because it served as the assembly point for the SP, which had been ordered to take an active part in the operation by assisting in the forced removal of people to Umschlagplatz. The locale was probably chosen to facilitate contact with the SP leadership, as well as the rank and file, and to save time between the issuing of orders and their execution. During the operation, Obersturmführer Mende was evidently acting only as a delegate of Szuch Boulevard, while others represented Einsatz Reinhard, headquartered in Lublin. Because that

---

*His official title was Commissar of the Jewish Residential District.
†"Reinhard" was the cryptonym for the German plan to exterminate the Jews of Poland.—PB

office had sent only four or five officials, the deportation authorities had assigned certain local SD men to the Sonderkommando to share administrative duties.

The Befehlstelle had already assumed its final form by the time it moved, together with those Jews who, during the operation, had worked for individual Germans or else for the Sonderkommando in general. The new offices at Żelazna 103 were located at the end of the street, facing the cul-de-sac near the corner of Nowolipie. The three-story structure was recently built and considered contemporary; from the outside it looked quite attractive. The entranceway was paved, with tiled walls. Immediately to the right was a guardroom manned by *Junacy*—uniformed Poles in German service with a left armband saying SONDERDIENST (SPECIAL SERVICE).* This room was equipped with a small table, an armchair, three sofa beds, and a radio. Next door was the barber's room, containing one small table, two armchairs, and a medium-sized mirror; a white-smocked barber was permanently on call. Following the main corridor, the next room on the right was the Befehlstelle office, which housed the Czapliński brothers, Mayzler, SP section chief Mauer, the quartermaster, and pani Kornheim, the stenotypist. This office was equipped with a large table, a desk, a small table, and wall maps of the former and current ghetto as well as some nondescript pictures. On the left side of the corridor, opposite the guardroom, were the ricksha drivers and a shoeshine stand; the room had a small table and chair, as well as a sofa bed. Farther along was the SP guardroom, with a small table and chair, two sofa beds, and a small locker. At the end of the corridor was a glass door with the same plate I had seen in the KSP: SONDERKOMMANDO DER SICHERHEITSPOLIZEI UMSIEDLUNG. On the first door along the left inside this corridor was a sign

---

*The information is not entirely accurate; the Sonderdienst consisted exclusively of Volksdeutsche.

saying MENDE, SS OBERSCHARFÜHRER. This room had a desk, two armchairs, a closed set of shelves, a chair that folded out into a bed, a trunk on the floor, a radio set, two telephones with special hookups, a chandelier with five lamps, maps of the old and new ghettos, and portraits of Hitler and Himmler, as well as some nondescript pictures. The next two rooms on the left had no signs; I don't know what they were used for, just as I don't know the purpose of the three rooms on the right, of which only the middle had a nameplate saying KLOSTERMAYER—SS OBERFÜHRER; BECKER— SS OBERSCHARFÜHRER. I presume that the unmarked rooms belonged to Obersturmführer Witossek, Untersturmführer Brandt, Unterscharführer Miretschko, and SS men Blescher and Rizienschopf.*

Mende was the permanent on-duty officer at the Befehlstelle. Tall, heavyset, with a friendly face, he gave the impression of someone who had never harmed a soul in his life. He arrived by car—the well-known black limousine with the license plate POL 47525—at exactly eight every morning and left between four and six in the afternoon. Only on occasion would he stay late to work at night. Brandt came every day for several hours, usually in the afternoon and often in the same limousine, which would leave after bringing Mende. More often, however, Brandt drove his own car, a small green Opel with a license plate that said OST. Witossek also arrived in the black limousine, and they would all leave together.

Brandt had been the desk officer for Jewish affairs at Szuch Boulevard before the "deportation operation," and it was he who actually oversaw the Aktion in the field; after it was over he stayed

---

*"Blescher" is presumably Rottenführer Josef Blösche, known from the most famous photograph of the Warsaw Ghetto, which shows a little boy raising his hands at gunpoint. Blösche was identified, tried, and executed in East Germany in 1969. Karl Klaustermeyer was sentenced to life imprisonment by a West German court in 1965.—PB

on as chief spokesman for Jewish affairs as well as director of the Befehlstelle. Mende was merely the permanent on-duty officer. Witossek supervised operations from the office of Oberpolizei-führer Sammern:* He brought orders, evaluated reports, and decided on the more important matters. He frequently came with the Oberführer himself. Brandt was an overweight man of medium height, about forty-five years of age, with an extremely unpleasant face, always scowling, and permanent bulging folds under his eyes. Both he and Witossek had right eyes smaller than their left, or at least they both kept their right eyes in a permanent squint, as if straining to see something. Witossek resembled Brandt, but his face was smaller and paler, with regular features. I once caught sight of Witossek feeding the geese and chickens that wandered around the courtyard of the Befehlstelle. He had no cap; his head was completely bald; it was hot and he was sweating, but he was enjoying himself and giggling. A few minutes earlier he had decided that three Jews should be shot; that evening they were taken from the Befehlstelle and shot on Smocza Street. These were two smugglers accused of slaughtering a horse and a Befehlstelle ricksha driver. The driver had been turning off Leszno Street when he was stopped by a gendarme, who discovered the man was carrying 1,200 zloty. The driver replied haughtily that, as an employee of the Befehlstelle, he was allowed to possess such a sum. Brandt's subordinate Rizienschopf, together with the commander of the Sonderdienst unit, shot the driver three times, twice in the head and once in the back. Afterward the SS man shone his lantern and confirmed that the driver was dead. In fact, none of the bullets was lethal; all three made a clean pass—the first through his mouth, the

*Oberführer Ferdinand von Sammern-Frankenegg—head of the Warsaw SS and police from June 1942 to April 1943. Died in Croatia in 1944.—PB

second through his neck, and the third near his collarbone. A work squad coming back down Smocza Street several minutes later found him and took him to the hospital. I saw him there; he had grown a beard as a disguise. He recovered after three weeks.

Immediately before the first Aktion, Colonel Szeryński had been imprisoned in Pawiak and accused of collaborating with Lieutenant Michalski of the Polish Police to store fur coats, despite the order requiring all furs to be surrendered to the German authorities. Apparently there was quite a large cache, since Szeryński, like Czerniaków, had been allowed to keep and wear his own fur coat even after all other Jews were forced to give theirs up. Rumor had it that Szeryński had Brandt to thank for his sudden release from Pawiak on the first day of the operation, as well as for his return to favor as chief of the SP and especially for his additional appointment as plenipotentiary for resettlement. On the second floor of the police barracks at 10 Nowolipki Street, at the entrance to Szeryński's apartment, was a sign that read SZERYŃSKI JÓZEF, DER BEVOLLMÄCHTIGTE DER BEAUFTRAGTEN FÜR DIE UMSIEDLUNG—PLENIPOTENTIARY FOR THE RESETTLEMENT EXECUTIVES.

Whenever Brandt was expected at the Befehlstelle, there was always a flurry of activity, an urge to put things in order, even though everything was always spotlessly clean and in perfect order anyway. Brandt's first order of business at the Befehlstelle was to get a shave; the barber must have been a good one, though I don't remember his name. I only know that before the Aktion he was co-owner of a barber shop at Leszno 60. He still made some money from that shop even though he didn't work there himself—after all, he was now barber to the highest authorities in the ghetto. After his shave Brandt would call the shoeshine boy, Ajzyk, who would be waiting with his box in the hall, ready to be summoned. Ajzyk, to whom I'll return later, cleaned Brandt's shoes with particular care. At the Befehlstelle, Brandt often received visits from the well-known Zionist and literary figure, Professor Alfred Nossig, a

German Jew said to have been an Austrian diplomatic representative during the first World War.* About two weeks before the ghetto was liquidated, members of the ŻOB† shot Nossig in his own home, which suggests that he was a *kapuś,* or stool pigeon, providing Brandt with information from the ghetto. I just learned from reliable sources that, after Nossig was shot, a search uncovered a document that guaranteed his immunity as a Jew of proven merit, as well as a letter he had written to the authorities explaining that the Jews were organizing underground bunkers and other things in the event of a new deportation Aktion. The letter gave the locations of some of these shelters and described how they were equipped. I myself witnessed how cordially Brandt greeted Professor Nossig at the Befehlstelle and how they conversed at some length in the waiting room (this was the barber's room after the latter was moved to the second floor). Nossig possessed the so-called Brandt pass, which enabled him to move about the whole of the big ghetto, giving him unlimited access to all the factory shops. Upon learning that Nossig had been shot, Brandt is said to have declared, *"Ja, die Lumpen haben solch einen alten Mann nicht verschont"*—So, the scoundrels didn't even spare an old man like him.

How hypocritical that sounded coming from Brandt, a monster in human form who had on his conscience hundreds of thousands of Jews of both sexes and all ages! If Brandt was present, it usually meant there were interrogations going on in Mende's office. These were mostly of Poles who had been arrested—for trespassing or attempting to trespass the ghetto without a valid pass from the Transferstelle, for attempting to smuggle contraband

---

*Nossig, known before the war as a writer and active Zionist, did indeed serve in the ghetto as an agent of the Gestapo.—PB
†Żydowska Organizacja Bojowa, the Jewish Fighting Organization, came into being in late 1942 to mobilize the ghetto to armed resistance. Part of its mission included executing collaborators.

either over the walls or through the checkpoints, or for looting. Jews were also interrogated after being brought in by SS men, gendarmes, or Junacy for smuggling, trading, slaughtering animals, loitering during working hours, shirking duties, and a host of other offenses. But the majority of the cases involved Aryans arrested in connection with "looting"—which meant taking whatever they could from homes that had been inhabited by Jews. Occasionally Czapliński or Mayzler (both of the SP) were on hand to update the "criminal record" and take confessions, and one of Brandt's immediate subordinates—such as Rizienschopf or Blescher—was always available to function as torturer, though sometimes one of the Junacy filled in.

The reason there were relatively few cases involving Jews at the Befehlstelle was that Herren Klostermayer, Miretschko, Becker, and especially Blescher and Rizienschopf tended to sentence Jews summarily by shooting them on the spot. They only brought Jews in if they needed to extract further confessions.

The punishments meted out at the Befehlstelle varied. For Poles they ranged from an official reprimand and entry on the record, to flogging, transfer to the Arbeitsamt on Skaryszewska Street, deportation to a penal labor camp, or else the firing squad. Jews who were not released were either flogged (this was rare), transferred to Umschlagplatz (if it was operating), or else shot (this was most often the case). Poles were shot in the courtyard of the Befehlstelle; the Jewish undertaker service hauled the corpses to the Jewish cemetery and buried them there. Jews, on the other hand, were generally taken outside, before dusk, most often to Smocza Street, which was by then uninhabited. I know of only one case in which Jews were shot in the Befehlstelle courtyard. This involved the three Bucze brothers, who owned several horse-drawn carts used by the Provisions Department for transporting food to Umschlagplatz. One time their horse collapsed, and SA Untersturmführer Kerstenberg, the Transferstelle officer at

Umschlagplatz, accused the brothers of attempting to sabotage the operation by underfeeding their horse and sent them to the Befehlstelle. All three were sentenced to death.

The sentences were carried out by one of Brandt's subordinates, assisted by a guard from the Junacy. Oberscharführer Mende did not participate himself: That SS man in white gloves never beat or shot anyone. Oberscharführer Klostermayer also tended not to shoot people on the spot; he preferred to maintain a certain appearance. Klostermayer often stood in for Oberscharführer Orf or Oberscharführer Einert at the Leszno checkpoint; if he arrested anyone he would send them to the Befehlstelle, whereas Orf and Einert shot 90 percent of the Jews they detained right then and there. Klostermayer also beat the Jews less and the Poles more. There was little difference between Orf and Einert; they seemed to come from the same school. Orf, if he was drunk, would outdo even himself; he'd shoot for any reason at all—say, for smuggling a quarter kilogram of butter—or beat his victims unconscious. But when it came to beating, neither Orf nor Einert could compare with Scharführer Bogudt, a rather Semitic-looking SS man who was a master with the whip. He represented the Befehlstelle at the Nalewki checkpoint. Trying to smuggle anything past him was out of the question. If he detected the slightest offense, he would beat the person unconscious and permanently cripple him by poking out an eye, fracturing his skull, breaking ribs, and so on. For all that, he never shot anyone.

Some time after the first Aktion, the SS posts were removed from the checkpoints. Orf, Einert, and Bogudt went back to Szuch Boulevard and never had anything more to do with the ghetto, although Orf would show up now and then to visit his star pupil, SP group officer Józef Spira. This man had Orf to thank for being permanently assigned to the Leszno checkpoint, along with Einert's star pupil, SP group officer Klumb. Despite the potentially lucrative assignment, Spira was not a *grajek*—someone who specialized in smuggling goods past the guard post. Orf would come in to join Spira for bouts of drinking that lasted well into the night. Spira reported that Orf was a barber by profession, who proved himself sufficiently to win an important job as desk officer for foreign citizens, and he was mainly delegated to special cases of great importance. Indeed, at times when Brandt was absent, Orf oversaw the deportation in the field, despite the presence of other SS men of higher rank (such as Oberscharführer Diehm from Lublin and the local Oberscharführers Klostermayer, Becker, and Göscher). Orf at that time was only a Scharführer; he had apparently been demoted for running a motorcycle into a military car while on a drunken joyride. I saw Orf once last March, when I happened to be standing at the Nalewki checkpoint. It was immediately after a Polish underground attack on an SS car on Długa Street.* The Germans retaliated by sending all the Poles living in the adjacent building to Pawiak. I saw the police cars passing by, each with prisoners and guarded by SS men and German gendarmes, five or six for each car. One of them—a truck loaded with about forty people—was escorted solely by Orf. Unlike the other Germans, he wasn't holding his weapon ready; he had shouldered his rifle as if for a march and his head was bare. He had ordered the people in the truck to kneel and keep their hands folded behind their necks. Evidently the commanders at Szuch Boulevard knew their men and what they were worth. For instance, Oberscharführer Göscher, who was phlegmatic and indecisive and only carried his whip for the sake of form, could never have taken Orf's place. Once Göscher spent seven days on duty at the Leszno checkpoint, and I never saw him whip anyone; the one time he wanted to send a worker to the Befehlstelle for possessing too much lard, I was able to get him to change his mind. I explained that the man was poor,

---

*Probably the Arsenal operation of 26 March 1943, in which a Polish scouting unit freed prisoners being taken to Pawiak.—PB

he had to work hard all day long, and smuggling was his family's means of support. But perhaps Göscher knew that the fate of every Jew had already been decided.

Blescher and Rizienschopf struck terror wherever there were Jews, not just inside the ghetto proper but also at the factories. No sooner would they appear than the streets—which by day were pretty deserted anyway—would empty completely. If a street was already dead, it meant the "snipers" were out hunting. Rizienschopf typically carried his revolver unholstered in his pocket. Later, however, just before the final liquidation of the ghetto, the ŻOB carried out more and more executions of informers, and both Blescher and Rizienschopf left the sidewalks for the streets, which they would patrol on bicycle, guns in hand. Afraid of losing their own skin, they avoided chasing any Jews into the buildings. Supposedly they once ran away from a Jew who was defending himself with a knife. It seems they had gone into the basement at Franciszkańska 22, where some cows were being slaughtered. The Germans shot one of the two butchers present, but the other charged at them, wielding his knife. The SS men managed to escape, but they returned a few hours later with a cart, accompanied by two Junacy, ostensibly to confiscate the meat and take it to the Befehlstelle. At the entrance they ordered the Junacy to go in first, but by then the butchers had disappeared.

Hauptsturmführer Michalsen of the Lublin SS was a frequent guest at the Befehlstelle. He oversaw the operations in the Warsaw Ghetto on behalf of Einsatz Reinhard as the delegate of the SS police commandant in Lublin, the notorious monster Globocnik.

During the first Aktion, it was Michalsen who decided what size quotas should be granted to specific workshops and to the Jewish Council—particularly during the final phase of the operation, that is, on 6 September, when all Jews were forced into the so-called cauldron between Gęsia and Niska streets. Throughout the first Aktion, Michalsen stayed in Warsaw off and on, occasionally leaving for a day or two. People linked his departures with the end of the Aktion, but this hypothesis proved wrong: Both the second and last operations began before he actually returned to Warsaw—to participate as murderer-in-chief.

From January 1943 on, a detachment of gendarmes was stationed at the Befehlstelle, partly to increase the German police presence within the ghetto and partly to deter Poles from looting. Large numbers of Poles, mostly Aryan teenagers, would sneak inside the ghetto any way they could and break into apartments formerly inhabited by Jews. There they would take whatever had been left behind: clothing, pots, brushes, washbasins, clothes wringers, window frames, and even furniture, which they would pass back across the ghetto wall. Boys fourteen years or younger would be locked up at the Befehlstelle for a few days, flogged, and released. Older offenders received the usual punishment. Floggings ranged from five to fifty lashes to the naked body; repeat offenders received more than first-time delinquents. I once met some boys who bragged that they had been sent to the Befehlstelle eight times: "And soon as it stops hurting we'll be back."

A Junacy (Sonderdienst) unit guarded the Befehlstelle throughout the entire year of its existence, operating in two 24-hour shifts, from 1300 to 1300, with five men per shift. These men manned the entry post there as well as the jail (until the latter function was taken over by the Jewish SP). In addition, the Junacy escorted goods confiscated at the checkpoints to the Werterfassung (the collecting point for former Jewish property) at 20 Niska Street. They also escorted Poles to the Arbeitsamt on Skaryszewska Street, and Jews to the President of the Jewish Council or to Umschlagplatz, which between deportations became a *Durchgangslager,* or temporary transit camp for laborers. Frequently the Junacy administered floggings under SS supervision; they also assisted directly or indirectly with firing squads. Rarely did they help torture prisoners under interrogation. Generally speaking, the

Junacy faithfully followed SS orders; there were isolated instances when they would attempt to help someone, though only for material reward.

ANONYMOUS MAN. With the introduction of slavery, the policy toward Jews seems to have taken a new course. Maybe the awareness that the roundups are over and the trains are no longer running is enough to make people feel better, or maybe masters always show kindness to newly acquired slaves whose bondage has just been declared absolute—naturally, only insofar as these slaves blindly obey orders. Thus, while they shoot pedestrians who can't justify why they are out walking, Jewish workers—Jewish slaves— may still count on a certain consideration.

Children, however, are another matter. Evidently children are the most menacing enemy of the master race, since the mere existence of a child is sufficient reason to send the parents to Umschlagplatz. Certainly children are the most oppressed group in the ghetto, but still there are dozens of homeless orphans both in the ghetto proper and on factory grounds. What is to be done with them? With Brandt's permission—or even at his own initiative and behest!—the Council sets up an orphanage in the building at Zamenhof 50 (or 52).

Brandt attends the opening and gives a speech—essentially an appeal—to the assembled officials and volunteers: "For children we must do whatever can be done, make any sacrifice, give every ounce of strength and every last resource; no task is too difficult, because a child is a treasure, the future of the race." Over a dozen Jews listen, scarcely able to believe their ears, still resounding with the din of the deportations. Their eyes replay the scenes they witnessed on that very street, when every child, every woman tending a child, and every man who sought to save a child was sentenced to death. All the official proclamations and decrees made it clear that children had no right to exist. And now, just a few weeks later, the same man who had overseen the entire operation, the man who had given the orders and issued the commands—that same man is talking about children as the future of the race and its most precious treasure.

Is this mere cynicism? Sneering? Mockery? Irony? After all, it is hard to believe his words are genuine, that in pronouncing a few sentences on the occasion of the shelter's opening Brandt is speaking any more sincerely than he would have elsewhere in similar circumstances. Any "rotten liberal" or "Western democrat" so despised by the Nazis—anyone at all—could have spoken those sentences. The fact that his words are somewhat at odds with his recent role has nothing to do with it. The ability to reconcile such contradictions is a salient characteristic of the Herrenvolk, one very much in evidence here and now. Persecutions, murders, the hecatomb of millions—this is not unbridled hatred or a desire for blood or some murderous instinct. By no means! After all, we are a great people, civilized; even in the trenches we humbly acknowledge the profundity of Goethe's *Faust* and are inspired by the lofty idealism of Schiller's *Robbers*. We are deeply and truly cultural, we know what is proper, which words to choose to fit the occasion—and what to say at the dedication of an orphanage.

STANISŁAW SZNAPMAN. Infernal scenes were also taking place on Umschlagplatz. Each day about ten thousand people were herded there like cattle for slaughter. The exits were guarded by armed gendarmes or Ukrainians. Half crazed with despair, the victims ran around helplessly, sobbing and wailing. Intuitively they sensed they were being sent to their death, and they ran around in a panic, like mice in a cage, looking to save themselves. Deranged, terrified, they abandoned their children, discarded their packs, their packages, their suitcases. And the perpetrators goaded them on with mocking sneers, shouting and whipping, firing their rifles and revolvers at the crowds, driving them on toward the narrow alley that led to the trains. At every step someone was felled by a bullet. The sight was macabre beyond description.

Just before the exit leading to the platform with the waiting boxcars, several uniformed Germans with thick whips made the final decision as to the fate of those passing before them. To the left meant the victim was considered a worker and spared deportation for the time being. Straight ahead led to the cars. Anyone who didn't move quickly enough was beaten mercilessly on the head and in the face. No one was allowed to protest. Whoever so much as opened his mouth was immediately whipped on the head or else shot.

Those temporarily freed from being deported might find themselves back on Umschlagplatz, perhaps that very day, and this time be sent straight ahead.

The decision may have been strictly a matter of chance, or else it was related to the number of cars and people. If there were many cars and few people, everyone was subject to deportation. Conversely, few cars and many people meant more people would be freed.

Old people, children, and anyone looking feeble or sick were killed on the spot. The daily harvest at Umschlagplatz yielded several hundred corpses—and this does not include people killed where the roundup was being conducted. The bodies were immediately transported to the cemetery and buried in common graves. A few might still have been moving or groaning, but the Germans in charge would not let anyone check, so these people were buried alive.

HENRYK BRYSKIER. Selections in the workshops. At first people were unfamiliar with the SS methods being used, and so with little effort the Germans managed to reap substantial harvests.

Untersturmführer Brandt, who commanded the Aktion on behalf of the Befehlstelle, would drive up with several SS men and over a dozen Ukrainians and demand to review the entire workforce, in order personally to assess the quality of the shop personnel.

Everyone was made to gather in the courtyard or at the loading area and assemble in ranks of ten, one behind the other, facing forward. Brandt, an obese butcher, used his riding crop to conduct the review, which he did together with the notorious murderers Blescher and Klostermayer. Anyone who looked old or tired was eliminated, as well as a large percentage of the women. A blow to the head or shoulder was the cue to have the doomed person escorted away for deportation.

After several hours, the decimated workforce returned to the shop, deprived of their loved ones, unable even to say farewell. Sobs, outbursts, frayed nerves; the factories were paralyzed by the air of death. Scarcely had the pain begun to recede when there would be a second raid. This time Brandt would use a different pretext, claiming he was merely checking the Meldekarten and Ausweise. The workers assembled once again, while anyone without documents, as well as unemployed family members and children, ran to various hiding places.

Brandt's escort—SS and Ukrainians—searched the factory, the apartments, and the attics, looking for people. In earlier roundups they received the energetic assistance of the Jewish Werkschutz. Meanwhile, the leader checked all the documents according to profession and once again decimated the ranks, this time selecting those whose faces looked particularly intelligent or delicate.

Even though I had papers proving I belonged to group 26a (12)—as manager of an explosives factory, where I was the sole engineer, supervising a production that involved 700 workers—I was selected. Only the director's immediate intervention returned me to my place in the lineup, where I usually stood at the head, in keeping with professional and social protocol. They proceeded to lead out several very bloody women, children, and old men whom they'd dragged from their hiding places. Once again a shudder of distress ran through our thinned ranks as we returned to our workshops. A fresh wave of grief and lament prevented people from concentrating on their work. Everyone was completely bewildered. Even those not directly affected by the disaster were in a daze, shattered by the selection, by fear, by the peril that threatened them and their dear ones as they stood before the henchmen.

No sooner had our nerves begun to recover from the second terror when the murderers swooped down again like hawks for the kill.

There were few workers in the factories; they were worn out by the previous events and more wary, so that most had gone into hiding. This time the Germans didn't touch anyone inside, even feigning praise of their work, but went to round up the people outside.

The Aktion had been difficult but effective. The workshops felt the loss of experts; there hadn't been many to begin with, and these had not been spared. The managers were confronted with the possibility that the shops might falter.

Brandt, already so rich in experience, came up with a new idea. He telephoned the shop managers to say he was coming to carry out the final purge and warned that all those found at their places would be spared, while everyone else on the grounds would be found out and deported.

The German officer's assurances seemed plausible enough, so the German shop owners and managers followed the orders and urged the workers—perhaps even in good faith—to return to the shops and resume their work. They gave their word of honor—albeit a German one—that not a hair would be harmed.

Some of the workers, whose wives, children, or parents had thus far been spared by fate, trusted the manager's declarations and brought their families to the workshops, giving them some task so they would not be sitting idle. More careful people, who refused to believe the German assurances, and those who were not supposed to be there at all, went down to their well-masked hideouts in the basements or beneath the courtyards.

The detachment Brandt had announced by phone arrived. The Germans cordoned off the workshops and took away everyone who had been promised safety. The word of a German officer—a German word of honor—was binding, but not for Jews. They took everyone who had believed the Germans and didn't even search for those in hiding. Experience proved that anyone who trusted the Germans would regret it. In the end the best document, the best professional affiliation, the best stamp, and the best guarantee of immunity and protection from Brandt's summary verdict or from being deported was a well-camouflaged shelter. Whoever was well hidden survived the selection. The remaining factory workers, their numbers a fraction of what they had been, once more went back to work for a small bowl of soup and a slice of bread.

Threatened with their factories having to close, the interested parties held a conference with the authorities. The German entrepreneurs objected that their best professionals were being taken away; as a result, they claimed, they could not fulfill their orders for the military and they refused to be held responsible for missing deadlines. Consequently, the managers obtained certain concessions: They would issue new identity papers or numbers not to exceed 10 percent of their initial workforce, and workers with these papers or numbers would be spared. The managers also agreed to conduct their own selections.

The shop directors, wishing to divest themselves of any moral responsibility (after all, they had taken money in exchange for work papers), began to search out any wild people who were hiding on their factory's grounds and to remove them to Umschlagplatz with the help of the Werkschutz. They also ordered their managers to draw up lists of essential workers: Others deemed too old or unproductive were slated to be cut.

Fortunately I was not asked to prepare such a list, which was the equivalent of a death sentence. I might have had to do so, but the managers under me prepared lists in order to protect their own positions, which showed the minimum number of people required to keep a given workshop running, using no more than 10 percent of the initial workforce.

People began to plot and scheme, and the factory directors used their authority to take more money for negotiating various transactions behind the backs of the individual supervisors.

I had the more gracious role of intervening on behalf of this or that worker, whom the administration was threatening to take off the list in favor of someone who had paid. Out of the original 7,000 workers, about 700 were supposed to remain. After the various machinations, my own crew was further reduced from 700 to 270. And you who are reading these lines should not be surprised that I did not figure on a single list and might have easily been overlooked. The individual shop supervisors could not be expected to include me, their superior, on their lists; otherwise I would have appeared twelve times. And the factory directors only checked the numbers, not the names, while at the same time looking for ways to adjust them, for reasons already described. Although they placed 40 percent of the new reduced crew under my supervision, no one thought to list my name. I had no friends among the directors, since I didn't engage in any wheeling or dealing outside of my specific job, nor did I have any real connections. Besides, to make friends with that group you had to be witty and quick, you had to have a smooth tongue and a talent for intrigue, be a herald and a rumormonger—in short, a saint and a scoundrel in one and the same person.

At the last minute, one of the supervisors checking the general list noticed that my name was missing; he told me and then, in my presence, called the director's attention to the matter. The director then listed my wife, my daughter, and myself as permanent employees.

Meanwhile the SS men treated the lists very differently, despite all the changes and corrections. Despite the sheer number of selections, not everyone who was sent to Umschlagplatz was deported. The workshop directors were fairly successful at intervening on behalf of experts and irreplaceable co-workers who had been taken away, and even ordinary workers were occasionally called out by name and released from the loaded freight cars. Furthermore, the trains were not always ready, in which case the whole mass of people was herded into the municipal building attached to Umschlagplatz at Stawki 4. The SP functionaries, who avidly assisted the deportation, also smuggled many individuals back to the workshops, charging several thousand zloty per head for that civic service.

In this manner the reduced crews were reenlarged, if only by a fraction, but this did have an effect on the roundups' general statistics and confused the Germans about how many wild people were still at large.

ANONYMOUS MAN. During the deportations we studied these people closely. They were not bloodthirsty beasts or savage animals consumed with fury; they were systematic bureaucrats, eager field hands, hard-working tradesmen. Their faces showed no trace of rage or hatred that might have clouded their reason. Even hate would have been evidence of some human emotion, some human reaction—albeit a criminal one. But they showed none. They seemed mechanized to such an extreme they resembled robots more than people. At the end of a day's Aktion, after dozens of dead bodies had been hauled off to the cemetery and thousands of living corpses sealed in the freight cars, these men quietly went back to their everyday affairs; laughing and enjoying their small ordinary lives as if nothing whatsoever had happened. They showed off their new stamps—practically everyone was a philatelist—and kept each other abreast of the latest developments in the field: a special series or exhibition, a particular surcharge. One of them kept his desk full of illustrated magazines. After a day's work in the ghetto he would pore over them, absorbing himself in rebuses and crossword puzzles, at times systematically composing his own. He made an armband for himself out of some special paper he kept in another compartment of his desk and prepared a little packet of printed matter to send home to his wife and children. He didn't think about the other wives and children dying in the railroad cars. Now and then the commander of the gas chambers at Treblinka would visit the ghetto, during the summer deportation and, later, after 12 September. He would ride up to the Befehlstelle at Żelazna 103 and engage in polite conversation with the Jews employed there; he enjoyed literature and always carried an interesting novel. He was particularly fond of books about Jews and held the works of Joseph Roth in high esteem. And in front of Jews he didn't have to hide his admiration for those books that had been consigned to the flames—no, after all, he was a man of culture. As a rule these men did not dwell on the Jewish men and women, old people, and children being sent to a terrible death every day, every hour. Actually it would have been impossible for a man like him to think of those thousands of people in a normal, human way—even in the most hidden recess of his mind or for the most fleeting of moments—and maintain his unflappability. And this was not because these men were equipped with some grim sense of humor; they were simply carefree laborers, content after their long hours of work, farmers happy to have finished another day of harvest.

During the January Aktion the commandant at Umschlagplatz was an SS officer who was permanently drunk. He always kept a whip or a revolver in his hand and used either one to select his victims, whom he would "invite" into his little room, where he would torture them. One time he ordered a nice-looking young couple to be brought in; both spoke excellent German. He began a polite and sophisticated dialogue, after first promising to free them—obviously people like that shouldn't be sent to die. They discussed literature, art, and travel. Next he picked up his revolver and shot the man, calmly, slowly; he turned to the woman and shot her as well, even more calmly and slowly, taking time to enjoy her utter stupefaction. Yet this insane degenerate sadist was more "human," more comprehensible to us, than the others who, after the Aktion, would go back to their carefree conversations, their discussions of stamps, their illustrated magazines, their family's packages; their cigars, jokes, laughter, and telephone calls to the Aryan side; their evening rendezvous at the cinema, café, or club—after which they would drive out of the ghetto, only to return the next day to the same routine, the same Aktion, the same events, and the same evening. Their complete inner peace was amply demonstrated by their general composure and by numerous specific incidents, such as when SS man Becker waxed indignant at the Aryan women greedily exploiting the poor Jews, or when they showed respect to the yeshiva scholar Professor Majer Bałaban,* or when the Treblinka commandant discussed his literary interests. Inner peace and exemplary order: Everything was done pedantically, systematically. They would have been more human if they had behaved more insanely; it is their absolute order that was so astonishing.

Psychologists are undoubtedly familiar with similar syndromes. Just like a butcher in a Chicago slaughterhouse who plunges his knife into a different heart every three seconds does not see the

---

*Dr. Majer Bałaban (1877–1942), professor at the University of Warsaw and outstanding historian of the Jewish people, died in the Warsaw Ghetto and was buried in the Jewish cemetery at Okopowa Street.[8]

living sheep, cow, or calf but only some pulpy mass that he must pierce with great precision, so it must be that people engaged in analogous activities have to automatize themselves. But whatever has been concluded about such cases to date has been based on average individuals with average psyches who do not stand out from their group, race, or nation. The idea that these activities could be performed on such a massive scale by so many thousands of people—and with such inner peace—is something entirely different. This is a case of collective, not individual, psyche. It seems that nations do possess specific traits that leave a unique mark on people and events. And evidently the *genus Germaniae* may be found in their dispassion, the indifference with which the bloodiest murders are undertaken; the age-old practice of mass murder as the most effective stimulus for their own growth; the ordered calm with which everything from account books to gas chambers is maintained; the ease with which all labors are performed, even ones that are repulsive to some deeply hidden self—if such exists—and the alacrity with which an accountant transforms himself into a "warrior."

Finally, as can be seen in the systematic pedantry associated with the murders, incidents impossible to imagine outside the horrors of war, revolution, or raging passion are classified, filed in perfect order, and meticulously set into motion. And this is the most frightening thing about these people, the most monstrous feature of their cruel inhumanity.

STANISŁAW SZNAPMAN. Only about 40,000 Jews are left in Warsaw, out of the approximately 400,000 who were there before the deportation.

Once again there are dark clouds looming over us. Once again the Germans are planning to crush us. They never give us a moment's peace, never let us stay in one place. This is one of their special tactics, another way to torture us. And once again there is unrest; people sell off their last clothes, their sheets, so they can be ready to move at a moment's notice. We have nothing left but what we can carry—and, of course, our naked lives. But this is exactly what our oppressors are after, as they lie in wait and scheme. Now they tell us we're being moved to Poniatów or Trawniki* in the Lublin district, since Warsaw must be *"Judenrein."* They tell us to expect forests and fresh air; we'll sleep on bunks and live out the war there. But we already know there's nothing there for the deportees but empty countryside, heavily fenced with barbed wire and guarded by SS. The local population was deported some time back. Hunger and disease are rampant. So far they've starved about 20,000 Russian prisoners to death there, burying them in the nearby forests. We realize they're trying to tempt us to leave—it's much easier to get rid of everybody all at once, without commotion, without witnesses. That's why no one is eager to go. They prefer to die where they are. But the Germans force them to leave "voluntarily" by using armed thugs to surround the workshops and send people away on the spot.

From the papers it's clear that the situation on the front is getting better day by day: The Russians are bravely crushing this plague, and England and America are preparing to pounce, in order to free the world from this horrible monster. Hope is beginning to stir in our hearts. Perhaps we will live to see a miracle after all. We want to survive so much, to see the pogrom turned on the beast. We want to live to see light triumph over darkness, justice over tyranny, and freedom over oppression and terror. We yearn to live to build a better world. But will we make it? Is it not too late?

Until October 1942, the Jews didn't know where people were being deported. They held on to the illusion that at least some might survive, so they took their last savings, the last bits of jewelry

---

*The two camps mentioned functioned variously as training camps for the SS, prisoner of war camps for captured Soviets, and forced labor camps for Jews.

that even the poorest people keep stashed away for some bleak moment—such as their wedding bands—and hid everything, stitching it into the most secret folds inside their clothing, deluding themselves that these things would help them survive. But they were ordered to undress and shower, and after the shower they either went into the ground or into the ovens, and the clothes with the rings and wedding bands, the diamonds and money, wound up in the hands of the SS. It's no exaggeration to say that the booty taken from those 400,000 murdered Jews from Warsaw was worth tens of millions of dollars, and the value of the property and equipment left in their apartments—which also went to the SS— was similar. Moreover, the valuables, money, and other items that the Gestapo and the gendarmes took over the course of the previous year was worth the same amount. And what about the people murdered in other towns throughout Poland, or of those from France, Belgium, Holland, or Czecho-Slovakia? What about their possessions? And how many millions of dollars were in the warehouses that were plundered? The SS men, Gestapo officers, and gendarmes divvied up the booty, quietly and unofficially, lining their pockets with cash and jewelry and amassing huge fortunes, which they buried and hid. And after the war, the same SS men, Gestapo officers, and gendarmes will travel to America, Africa, or Australia and use that money to buy up plantations, where they will retire in comfort following their arduous labors.

You English and Americans! Know that, after the war, when the Germans come to your colonies and start buying up land, know that they murdered our mothers and wives, children, fathers, sisters, and brothers. They robbed them of their possessions, their money, their wedding bands, and their jewelry. Their money comes from theft and murder; it is stained with the blood of our dearest. Remember that every one of these Germans was once an SS man, Gestapo officer, or gendarme. Take the money away from them, and put it in the hands of the law. Let me repeat myself! You must do this, because what happened here was mass theft and murder, monstrous and horrible. They would have done the same to you and your children, to your wives and mothers, had you been under their rule. This is what justice demands, the justice currently being fought for, the justice for which so much blood is now being shed.

The deportation happened gradually, in spurts: The first group was sent off, and the people left behind deluded themselves into thinking there would be no more; some miracle might end the war. The deadline for the second transport approached relentlessly, and afterward those who had survived thought *they* would not be taken. But their date came too, and if not enough people showed up of their own accord, others were "volunteered" with the help of military cordons and pistols aimed at their heads. Then they herded whoever was left into a new location, packing them in even tighter so the workshop would take up less space. Everyone was ordered to move from Waliców Street to Prosta, so they began running around looking for apartments. The next moment a new order declared the reverse, so now everyone ran from Prosta to Waliców. Because the Germans were ordering everyone to move, people reasoned that they must be interested in decreasing the size of the factories but not in liquidating the shops completely—and they happily concluded that the transport to Poniatów must have been called off for the moment. Then, out of the blue, 800 people were ordered to the transport.

Sometimes people who already have a place to live don't want to take in others who need one, and the newcomers sometimes try to force themselves in, which leads to fights and quarrels. There are also those who simply break down in despair at the idea of being deported. As the factory grounds are reduced, new walls are built and old ones are torn down.

It's a vicious circle: walls built and torn down, relocation, deportation. Behold the twentieth century. Ordinary people, innocent and free, are placed behind walls, imprisoned, beaten, kicked, robbed, killed, enslaved, and freighted off to their destruction. Bravo, cultured, civilized Germany!

The Germans have conceived and planned the extermination with exactitude, precision, and devilish shrewdness. Now and then they seem to let up a little and pursue a gentler course, using propaganda to steer the masses to one particular spot. Then they surround the spot, capturing and liquidating everyone in their snare. They act like cats toying with a mouse—except cats are driven by instinct, while here everything is carefully thought out and planned in advance, because these particular beasts of prey are equipped with reason.

JAN MAWULT. Umschlagplatz: guards and shouting Germans. One after another, people move slowly into the center of the yard, past the barbed wire, and into the empty rooms of the school building. Some stay outside. There is no water, not a spoonful of food. Most people are alone, occasionally with their families. They wait, often more than twelve hours, sometimes a whole day or two. There aren't enough trains.

They wait. For what? Some for help from the outside: Maybe the ones they left behind will send a policeman; maybe they'll come up with some form of rescue. Many think like that, and they're often right. But the vast majority has no one and nothing to wait for.

Meanwhile, on the other side of the barbed wire on Umschlagplatz, some people are free to move around, and there's a good deal of commotion. Rickshas drive up with SP men or officials from various Council departments. Not everybody has permission to be there: An unauthorized presence on Umschlagplatz can have dire consequences; it's easy to move from one side of the barbed wire to the other. Whoever does show up has a pretext: The SP man is on "official business"; the Health Department official is there to help with sanitation—many health workers have been assigned to Umschlagplatz to maintain hygiene, deliver bread and water, carry the sick and the dead; Provisions Department personnel are checking on the distribution of food; and the Hospital Department has to staff the hospital located there. An ambulance drives up, and doctors and nurses scurry about amid a flash of white aprons.

Many pretexts—but they all have the same purpose: to rescue one more person from behind the barbed wire, to get someone released, to smuggle someone back. There are different methods of doing this; some involve exchanging money, others do not. One person may be disguised as a doctor coming off his shift and returning to the ghetto, another may be wearing the armband and cap of a Jewish policeman or the greatcoat, cap, and belt of a Polish policeman. Some crawl through a hole in the wall straight to the Aryan side; others sneak back into the ghetto, sometimes in a wagon or funeral cart. This is hardly a game; it's not an easy sport, ruthless Szmerling is watching. If the Germans uncover a ruse, it's either a bullet or the freight car—depending on the German's mood—for whoever used his privileged position "in a manner contrary to the law." And all the while the people behind the wire watch the others trying, talk with those who want to save them, count the long minutes, and wait. Will they make it or not? Will the train come today or not?

But most people, the vast majority with nothing and no one to wait for, have no illusions. They keep moving, always in motion. Some pace back and forth inside a room or corridor; others climb up and down stairs, passing from one hall to the next, switching floors. They cross the yard from one side to the other, from the outer courtyard to the one inside and then back again.

Then they're ready; the crowd sets out. This time they don't have far to go, only to the entrance to the switching yard: a few dozen steps, then about twenty more to the railway siding. Here, too, things are quiet. Occasionally there is one more selection along this last segment and a few more people go free. Sometimes this is the first selection, if everyone detained on the street was sent directly to Umschlagplatz; at other times they simply load everyone they've rounded up into the freight cars, without any selection. It varies. And here is the train: twenty-five to thirty freight cars, with heavy sliding doors, closed for the moment; SP men are standing next to the cars—that's the loading crew—as well as some Germans. The loading begins; it proceeds calmly—no moaning, no sobbing. Every head is carefully counted twice, once by a German and once by the loading supervisor, district deputy chief Brzeziński.* The numbers go in the report; this is important data, important numerical statistics! Very important, extremely important; after all, the report is being sent to Lublin, Kraków, and Berlin.

Now the car is loaded, its former application, so neatly labeled on every car—8 HORSES OR 40 PEOPLE—has been superseded by a new one; the latest scientific experiments have demonstrated that one car will hold 80 or even 100 people. So it's too cramped? So there's a danger people might be crushed to death, or suffocate inside the sealed cars, or bake to death in the scorching August heat? Well, they don't have that far to go; after all, it's a short trip. These are merely the temporary discomforts of summer travel. Slowly the train pulls away.

---

*Brzeziński, a member of the SP, was known for chasing Jews into the freight cars at Umschlagplatz. On 26 February 1943 he was shot by a member of the ŻOB.[9]

SAMUEL (SZMUL) ZYLBERSZTEJN, BORN IN WARSAW, OWNED A small hosiery workshop and store. Inside the ghetto, he was active in various social organizations and helped prepare the resistance at the Többens factory in the spring of 1943. Afterward he was deported, transferred from one labor camp to another, and finally liberated at Gusen. The account was originally written in Yiddish.

For hundreds of thousands of Jews, for our mothers and fathers, our sisters and brothers, the path that led through the buildings at Umschlagplatz was their last. Behind the buildings, to the left of Stawki Street, was a wide railroad yard, from where for many months the transports departed carrying our brothers to the gas chambers at Treblinka and elsewhere. The road that led up to Umschlagplatz was heavily guarded by gendarmes and SS soldiers equipped with all types of firearms, as well as detachments of Ukrainians and Lithuanians.

They led us inside the building, threw us in the basement, and left us there. The stench was unbearable. The floor was covered with refuse and human feces. The people were crammed in without food, water, or any kind of toilet or latrine. Women, men, children—all just took care of their needs on the spot, then sat or lay back down on the floor. Children cried out "Water, water," unaware they had no more than a few hours left to live. We formed a prostrate, inert mass, completely at the mercy of the Ukrainians, who harassed and tortured us. Every few minutes a different bandit would demand 5,000 to 10,000 zloty, saying, "I'm coming back in ten minutes, and if the money hasn't been collected by then I'm going to shoot ten Jews." In this way they squeezed the last pennies out of their unfortunate victims.

One of these bandits approached me as well. "I need ten thousand from the people you're with." Here he looked at his watch. "I'll be back in five minutes." He kept his word and showed up on time. Everyone had already been stripped of whatever money they had; the sum I collected turned out much smaller. Then the man demanded a pretty woman. I said I was alone and didn't know anyone, but my arguments were useless. He pulled an eighteen-year-old girl out of the crowd by force and dragged her into a corner to rape her. A fearsome struggle ensued. Promising to save her, the man ripped off her dress. As the struggle went on, the desperate girl cried out louder and louder. Then the murderer heard an SS man approaching. He was afraid he'd be accused of *Rassenschande,* defiling the race. The girl managed to tear herself out of his hands. Later he tried to find her but in vain; the girl had changed clothes and was impossible to recognize.

We spent two terrible days and nights in that basement. On 3 April, around 4 P.M., the order was given: "To the transport." All of a sudden a band of Ukrainians fell on us, snatching our bags and tearing the clothes off our bodies and the shoes off our feet. We heard shouting, *"Raus, raus!"* They led us to the train along the street, instead of taking a shorter way, as if to review the troops. Then we crossed the field to the side exit. The railroad cars were standing by. Before being loaded onto the cars we had to run a gauntlet of bandits, who were lined up along both sides of the way to the train, rifles in hand, ready to club us as we passed. I ran ducking, first to the right, then to the left. Finally I fell on the ground and crawled on all fours.

We waited beside the cars for nearly an hour. No excess was spared. The SS men kept choosing new victims; men over fifty, as well as youngsters and wounded people, were taken aside for immediate liquidation. Their torment was quickly over. They no longer had to wait for death to end the inhuman suffering; they were shot on the spot. Using their bayonets, the Ukrainians hauled the victims to a woodpile that was ready to be lit. The bodies were tossed onto the pile. We were loaded into the cars; I cast one last look at the slave hunter Többens, accomplice to the murderers, who was now openly collaborating with the SS as the Jews were driven into the filthy boxcars. I took my Ausweis out of my pocket and waved it at him. "Yes," he said, with a triumphant smile, "this train belongs to me. You're going to Poniatów."

One young man with an injured head tried to jump into the car. The wound was fresh, inflicted on the way to the train. An SS man pulled him back out and pointed the barrel of his machine gun straight at him, ready to fire. A dramatic struggle broke out as the youth attempted to wrest the gun from the villain's hands, and both men tried to shoot. Finally a fatal shot hit the youth in his wounded head and he fell. The SS man fired more rounds and then trampled the young man's blood with his filthy boots. Vile criminal, not fit to touch the blood of a young Jewish hero, blood that will always be holy for us, for all humanity.

They packed 120 people into a boxcar designed for 20 people or 10 horses. The doors were slid shut and sealed, the windows boarded up and covered with barbed wire. We stood crammed inside the closed box, each person glued to the next, forming a single mass. We could not raise our hands or make the slightest movement. Terrible scenes took place in the cars between people who had been condemned to death, people who had lost their wits. Everyone tried pushing through to the door or window, to find a crack, just to get a gulp of air. Some were sobbing, others fainted, but there was no room for them to fall. Their bodies simply stayed in place, pressed between our own. All desperate cries and sobs were in vain. No help was coming; no help could come. Human feelings disappeared; we were no longer human. The stronger tried to break away, to climb over the heads of the others, to win a little space so they could see outside. Some were shouting, "I have to look outside! I have to see where they're taking me! I know this road. I'm not going to the gas chamber! I'm going to jump from the train! Live or die by a bullet! No gas for me! It's the strongest who'll survive!"

The engines pulled slowly as the train rolled on toward the victims' doom. The cars were guarded on both sides. Ukrainians were lying on the roof. Sometime during the night people standing by the cracks in the window claimed they were taking us to Treblinka. The prisoners began to panic. Someone pried up a board and a few people tried to jump from the train, but unfortunately no one managed to escape. The murderers kept the entire route lit with spotlights, so they'd be sure not to miss anyone who attempted to get away. A friend of mine who was in the car asked me to hold his coat while he jumped and then throw the coat after him. I watched him: No sooner had he jumped than he was hit. His coat was riddled by bullets as well. Every time someone jumped, all the Ukrainians up and down the train started shooting at once. Occasionally the train would stop and start again, leaving behind a trail of corpses.

In the middle of the night they started shooting into the cars through the windows. The lucky ones were hit and killed. They were free. We could no longer stand it—the crowding, the stench, the unbearable thirst; we were covered with sweat and blood, the blood of our brothers. We did what we could to gain a little calm during our last hours. Our limbs had grown stiff; we couldn't straighten our arms. Our brothers' blood was drying on our clothes; we couldn't wipe it off and had to use our teeth to tear the garments off one another's body. Then we stood naked inside the crowded, stinking car. The thirst was indescribable; we tried using our tongues to wet each other's lips.

Toward dawn our car became less crowded: about 40 people were already dead, most killed by Ukrainian bullets fired through the walls. We tried to clean up so as not to trample their bodies. Now we were a little more "comfortable," at least able to sit down on the blood-covered floor, but with every passing kilometer our fear and despair grew. A panic broke out when we reached

Małkinia: "Listen! They're going to run us straight from the cars to the gas chambers! O God, O God, where are you!"

What they saw through the cracks took the last hope away from those who still had any illusions. People tore their hair, scratched at their faces, and broke their fingernails. That's what the last minutes are like before a gruesome death in the gas chamber.

But ten men in our car could count themselves happy; ten Jews were treated kindly by fate. "Now is the time, comrades," said Dr. Mantel. "We have a little more room." Ten young healthy people sat together on the blood-stained floor. They kissed one another, said their farewells, and then swallowed a dose of cyanide. One minute later nine more bodies were lying in the car. The tenth was not affected; his dose must have been insufficient. Oh, you happy people! You no longer have to suffer, no longer have to bear the terrible hell that we must face. They can poison you with gas and burn you all they want, but you will be numb to the suffering. Everyone envied those nine souls.

Of 120 people locked inside the car, 37 were still alive when the train arrived at the platform.

SAMUEL PUTERMAN. While the ghetto celebrated the end of the Aktion, and pious Jews gave thanks to God for reversing their misfortune, Oberscharführer Orf issued a command at Umschlagplatz. Over a dozen workers from the sanitation unit were to load the sick and the lame into four horse-drawn wagons from Kon and Heller; now and then a fifth cart from Pinkiert's showed up to collect the corpses. Once the "konheller wagons" had been loaded, they headed out of Umschlagplatz. Two SP men stood on the steps of each wagon to block any escape. Orf rode ahead on his bicycle. The wagons followed him past the checkpoint and down Dzika and Okopowa streets toward the Jewish cemetery. The cemetery administration kept large pits open for mass burials, and the gravediggers were ordered to take one hundred and two living

souls and throw them into one of these pits. Oberscharführer Orf
stood holding a pistol in his right hand, rhythmically tapping the
holster on his belt with his left. The gravediggers' faces were
flushed; their eyes popped out of their sockets as they proceeded to
fill the pit with broad shovels of dirt. It was then they began to
weaken, feeling they could no longer bear the ghastly cries of
people going mad. Every time they bent over the grave they grew
dizzy. The dreadful pit was drawing them in, swallowing them,
screaming out with a hideous voice that reverberated more and
more loudly. The last few to be thrown in kept shaking off the dirt,
struggling to their feet, and falling down. They trampled on the
bodies and faces of their brothers, beating them down, stepping on
their open crying mouths, stomping the earth raining thickly from
above. Oberscharführer Orf peered inside the grave with a look of
boredom on his long pale bony face. At a certain moment he
turned to the administrator assisting in the operation and gave the
command: "Lime." As the gravediggers continued tossing in the
heavy clods of earth, several wheelbarrows arrived full of lime. Orf
signaled to the gravediggers, who began scooping it out. With
each shovelful, the cries from the pit dropped by an octave, until
they finally ceased altogether. The bodies collapsed in a dense
tumble. Somebody tried to stand up one last time, a dark hole
emerging in the thick white mass. Then he fell down with a clap,
in time with the rhythm of the shovels. At Orf's signal, the lime
throwing came to a halt and the heavy clods of earth once again
began to fall into the pit, as people inside the ghetto began to fall
into each other's arms. The Aktion was over.

"The third front was finally broken after another few days' resistance…"

Chapter 4

PASSIVE AND ACTIVE RESISTANCE INSIDE THE GHETTO

The policy of appeasement pursued by the Judenrat met with little effective opposition before the death of President Czerniaków. Nevertheless, many people engaged in passive resistance, ranging from participation in secret schools, smuggling of contraband, and small acts of sabotage at the workplace to larger coordinated efforts, such as Emanuel Ringelblum's archival project Oneg Sabbath. In the spring of 1942, several parties joined in an Antifascist Bloc, which in the wake of the deportations promoted a course of active resistance: readying the ghetto for self-defense, training a cadre of armed fighters, executing Jewish collaborators, and negotiating help from friendly organizations in the Polish underground.* The surviving residents began building bunkers and shelters or looking for ways to escape to the Aryan side. By early December, the ŻOB or Jewish Fighting Organization had been formed; Mordechai Anielewicz, a young activist from Hashomer Hatzair, was named its commander in chief. Other groups, too, such as the Jewish Military Alliance (Yiddisher Militerisher Farband or Żydowski Związek Wojskowy) also stepped up the campaign to mobilize the ghetto.

---

*Primarily the Gwardia Ludowa (People's Guard), and—with some difficulty—the Armia Krajowa or Home Army.—PB

In January 1943, the Germans launched another intensified Aktion to liquidate the entire ghetto, but this time they met with organized armed resistance. Abandoning the large-scale operation, they changed their strategy, withdrew, and for several weeks resumed piecemeal roundups directed against the factory workshops. On Monday, 19 April, following Himmler's orders, the Germans launched a full assault with several battalions of Waffen SS, assisted by Ukrainian and Latvian auxiliaries and backed by Wehrmacht artillery and sappers. Large numbers of Polish police and German gendarmes patrolled outside the ghetto walls. With Molotov cocktails and the few arms they had been able to procure from Polish resistance organizations, the Jewish combatants fought against machine guns and tanks, drawing the SS into an unexpectedly long struggle. The Germans answered by razing and burning buildings; those dragged out of the bunkers were shot or sent to Umschlagplatz. The ŻOB leadership committed collective suicide rather than fall into the hands of the SS, although some managed to escape through the sewers with the help of the Polish underground. By mid-May, when SS Brigadeführer Jürgen Stroop celebrated the detonation of the Grand Synagogue on Tłomackie, the ghetto was one great field of rubble, which the Germans continued to use as a site for executions. Isolated fighters remained hidden in the ruins, however, and some survived to join the Warsaw Uprising of August 1944.

SAMUEL PUTERMAN. "Shortly before the war I left Palestine to go to Poland to visit my parents, whom I hadn't seen in ten years."

He spoke slowly, with his head hunched over his shoulders.

"Two weeks ago the SP caught me on the street. I had been hiding ever since the beginning of the Aktion, even though I had an Ausweis. I had a good hideout inside the ruins of a building that had been blown up. I was staying there with my wife and children and parents. I went out for a moment to get some bread; the streets were quiet, and I knew a baker who had a shop a few steps away. I was on my way back with the bread when the street was cut off.

The Germans hadn't arrived yet; it was the SP. Two of them grabbed me. I pleaded, I begged, I tried to break away, I offered them my watch—I didn't have any money to speak of—but they refused to let me go. They kept hitting me with their nightsticks as they chased me away off to Umschlagplatz as one of the first victims of the roundup. Then I tried to break away from there. I spent three days at Umschlagplatz. Twice I managed to hide overnight in the building basement. Then an SP man found me out. For three days I kept sending notes by way of the SP asking my relatives for money. For 3,000 zloty you could get away. The SP men took 30 or 50 zloty for the letter and never brought back an answer.

"It took two days to reach Treblinka. What happened in the rail cars is probably not worth going into. People fainted from the foul air, died of thirst.

"The train often stopped for hours in the middle of a field. On the second day, we stopped once again. This time several dozen Ukrainians surrounded the train, unsealed the doors, and leveled their heavy hand-held machine guns on the people getting off. It took a while to unload us. People helped each other off the higher cars. The train went on its way. The field had been fenced off; the Ukrainians lined up behind the barbed wire with their machine guns. There were a few measly workshops or barns on the same field, which was surrounded on all four sides by forest. We sat there for two hours; several handcarts were brought from the workshops, loaded with bread and large cans of water. Some Jews distributed the bread and water across the wire. I recognized one of them, a distant cousin; when he gave me some bread he whispered, "Stick close to the wires and don't leave this spot." After the bread and water had been distributed, a German came out of one of the buildings, handsome, elegant, and of charming appearance. He walked toward us casually, holding a lit cigarette. The Ukrainians separated the men from the women. Children stayed with the women. They led us toward the forest; the women and children went with us.

"The German stood on a platform made of two crates. Several dozen Jews came out of the nearest large workshop. Some were carrying rakes and shovels; a few stood beside the German. Those with rakes walked alongside us toward the forest. The German gave a sign with his hand and the camp quieted down. The German started to speak. He spoke loudly and slowly, in the most beautiful German accent I've ever heard. 'Your first step of the journey is over. You still have a long journey ahead of you. Today you will be traveling farther east to work. For all those who want to work, life will definitely be better than inside the ghetto; families will not be separated; you will receive a place to live and good food. You will wait here another few hours until a train is found for you and another transport arrives. For the time being you will go to the bathhouse. You are dirty and full of lice. After the bathhouse you will return here. You will be given new work clothes and you will leave the ones you are wearing behind. Whoever has any valuables should deposit them with me; you will be given a receipt. Women with no children of their own should take any children who are untended. Women should remove their shoes right away. The men should do the same. Tie the shoes in pairs so they will not get mixed up. After you come back from the bathhouse you will be given some soup.' The German finished. He stepped down from the platform. One of the Jews standing nearby took his place and translated the entire speech into Polish. When he finished, my cousin translated it into Yiddish. The German stood there the entire time, the kind smile never leaving his compassionate face.

"The camp began to stir. People tied their shoes together. Some placed little notes with their names. After a few minutes one of the Jews ordered the women to line up at the exit. A few Ukrainians led them toward the forest. After the women had left, the men were ordered to strip naked. Once again they reminded us not to mix up our shoes, as we would not be given any others. I was already halfway undressed when the German came over to me, in the company of my cousin, who pointed at me. The German nodded his head. 'Don't undress,' my cousin whispered and led me toward the exit. About six other young men, most of whom were large and well built, went with me. After all the men were undressed the Ukrainians led them off in the same direction as the women.

"The sympathetic German went away. A second one took his place. My cousin took command of us. They placed me and the other men in the first rank and the rest a step behind us. The German began to torture us. For half an hour he blindly beat away at us with his riding crop, which had little lead balls sewn into the whip end. When he had worn himself out and we were barely half alive, he stopped and ordered us to stand up. One of the men's eyes was covered with blood; the German shot him then and there.

"Our work consisted of sorting the clothing and things left behind by every group that had gone to 'bathe.' Two hundred young men were put to work, most big and strong. We separated and sorted the clothing, the shoes, the gold, the diamonds, every kind of currency. Small pieces of jewelry and valuables lay just under nearly every one of the piles of clothes strewn about the huge space. Every day our group was reduced by a couple of men. The work was hard; each day a few of the two hundred workers died from exhaustion or from being beaten. My job was to load the clothes onto the rail car. I had my cousin to thank for that; he was overseer of the entire yard. I worked there for five days. Every day, sometimes even twice on the same day, the identical comedy was performed. The sympathetic German held a speech, accompanied by those of us who looked most presentable. A few dozen would march off with shovels and rakes into the forest, where they would wait for about an hour until the new arrivals left to 'bathe.'

When the yard was emptied and the naked men had marched off to the 'bathhouse,' we went to work. Everyone dreamed of escaping, but the only ones who had a chance were those who worked loading the rail cars. Clothes from every transport were loaded onto the cars, but each time it was a different group. Only I worked there five days in a row, thanks to my cousin. It wasn't until the fifth day that I managed to jump into the car with no one noticing. I hid among the clothing. I had some excellent tools with me, which I had taken while sorting things. It was easy for me to hide them. The Ukrainians who were guarding us didn't care whether we were hiding gold or diamonds. Each one of the two hundred workers had on his person valuables worth a million. The Germans didn't worry about that. Every worker they killed or who died of exhaustion would leave his clothes, which were again inspected and sorted.

"Once I was inside the car and the train had started, I set about making some kind of opening in the wall of the car. It didn't take long for me to break off two boards and make an opening large enough for me to squeeze through. I made a fairly lucky jump from the train. It took me a few days to reach Warsaw.

"The peasants near Treblinka didn't want to shelter me even for just one night. They happily gave me food and even money, but they wouldn't hear of my spending the night, because the Ukrainians who were permanently stationed in Treblinka often showed up—their trade was making the locals unbelievably wealthy. For a few kilometers around Treblinka you could smell the gas and corpses. The local peasants told of things that were unbelievable but unfortunately true. Evidently when the naked Jews walk inside the building to bathe, they don't know what is waiting for them up to the last second. The doors are open; everyone goes calmly inside; when the building is full they close the doors and instead of water they turn on the gas. It lasts thirteen to twenty minutes. There are several such buildings. Some are constructed to tilt so the bodies can be dumped after the gassing; others only have trap doors. The Germans either burn the huge masses of bodies or bury them in gigantic pits; some are thrown into a kettle. The flesh is separated from the bones and made into soap. All over there are Jews working who are constantly being replaced. Giant cranes are operating everywhere, and machines for digging earth. A crematorium is being built. New ovens are always being added. In addition to all these installations there is a camp for a few thousand Jewish laborers. Every day a few hundred of these are lost, but they are replaced daily so that the number is maintained. This is what the peasants told me. Every one I talked to near Treblinka spoke of nothing else. They all told the same thing, in horror. Only the Germans know how many Jews have been executed in Treblinka. Jews are sent to Treblinka from other countries as well. In any event, what I saw was only a small part."

"Why did you come back to the ghetto?"

The man's face began to glower; he leaned over to Julian* and yelled through his clenched teeth. "I already said the peasants near Treblinka didn't want me to spend the night. The ones closer to Warsaw let me stay the night, but there was no question of staying there permanently. My most important reason for coming back was my wife and two-year-old son and my parents. But I didn't find anyone; your colleagues in the SP had already discovered them."

At that point he jumped up from the cot and stood there a moment, as if he wanted to throw himself at Julian. Julian stood up as well, took the man by both hands, sat him back on the cot, and in a calm quiet voice with just a quiver of emotion said, "Sit back down, please, sit down."

They smoked a cigarette.

---

*Julian is a member of the SP; there is no further identification.—PB

"I'd like to explain a few things," Julian began, in a measured voice, "to you and all those present. The entire ghetto is groaning from the blows the Germans are inflicting on us daily. Wherever I turn, I meet with threats and curses directed at the SP. But as far as I'm concerned the wisest and most moving are the requests I've heard from the unfortunate Jews who've been taken to Umschlagplatz. Don't think I'm out to defend the reputation of the SP. For three weeks we've been completely cut off from the world, and I'm your only link to the outside, your only source of information. From the beginning of the Aktion all my friends and everyone here have been telling me, 'Throw away your policeman's cap, throw it away, don't dirty your clean hands.' I didn't do that. I couldn't allow myself to throw my cap away and I probably won't, no matter what happens. Every day you ask me what's going on, and my answer is always the same, that things will turn out all right. I've earned the reputation of an incorrigible optimist, but that's not true; I lie to you daily. I'm not an optimist at all, I'm full of the worst presentiments, I'm almost certain it will all end in a great catastrophe, and I'm shaking with fear every minute of the day and hoping the catastrophe won't hit the people I care about the most. That's the way it is; I'm an egoist like everyone else. To get back to the police, the general opinion is that without the help of the SP the Germans wouldn't have been able to catch so many Jews. If the SP had refused to assist in the Aktion, the Germans wouldn't have managed. Nonsense. The SP in Mińsk Mazowiecki decided to be heroes like that: Four hundred policemen with the administration in the lead refused to assist. That same day within the space of one hour the Germans shot all their families, nearly one thousand people. Then they themselves carried out the Aktion with the help of a reinforced group of Ukrainians, as well as a few hundred *szaulisi*."*

---

*Szaulisi were Lithuanian units in the service of the Nazis. The name—from *śaulys* or sniper—was also used for a prewar paramilitary organization.—PB

LEON NAJBERG. At the morning assembly on my eighth day in the Durchgangslager (transit camp), Hauptsturmführer Nadolny (a Czech by origin) arrived along with engineer Jurinek (a German). Out of 800 people they chose 65 Jewish skilled workers—locksmiths, mechanics, drivers, and technicians—who were loaded into cars that sped through Warsaw in the direction of Bielany. I was in this group together with some comrades who had been taken from Umschlagplatz. We had no idea where they were taking us, and we resolved to make a run for it if we left the Warsaw city limits. In Żoliborz the cars turned onto Włościańska Street and drove onto the grounds of number 52.

These were the workshops that had belonged to the Municipal Transportation Agency until 1939, when they were taken over by Adam Oppel. He converted them into a repair and assembly works in the service of the Rüstungskommando, the armaments headquarters. We were housed in barracks on the factory grounds.

At first Jurinek tried to create decent conditions, promising our group that working for Oppel would help us regain our faith in people after our experience in the ghetto. We were given high-quality food products and promised a salary that amounted to 50 percent of the base earnings of Polish workers. After the constant hounding we had been through during the Aktion, we finally caught our breath, and we struggled with changing and contradictory feelings toward the Germans.

This calm didn't last long. A few days later Hauptsturmführer Nadolny returned from Lublin. He first decreed that all Jews had to surrender any money or valuables in their possession (except clothing); each person was allowed to keep only 100 zloty. We were also forbidden to have any contact with the Polish workers or to bring in or read Polish or German newspapers. Each of us was given two patches that we had to sew onto our work uniforms, one in back, the other above the knee—a six-pointed yellow star on a rectangular green background. From then on we had to report directly to the *Personalabteilung*—personnel department—headed by Hauptsturmführer Nadolny, while engineer Golc, a Pole, was to manage all administrative and technical matters for the Jewish workers.

From the day the new decrees took effect, the situation at the Oppel plant changed radically for the worse. Now there was no illusion concerning our relationship with the Germans and our future situation. Hauptsturmführer Nadolny took a car into the ghetto and returned with four SP men (along with their wives); they were supposed to implement Nadolny's orders. Their names were: Rotzajt, Rotbard, Domanowicz, and Szyffer.

Before Nadolny and Golc took over we had had more than enough good food to eat. Afterward they took away our rations of sugar, fats, and canned goods, and the bread we were given was specially baked with a dose of sawdust and marked with a letter *J* for *Jude*. Our daily ration was 200 grams.

We realized we wouldn't last long with that nourishment and the heavy labor. Each of us tried to make contact with the Poles in his department. At first they were very mistrustful of us, but this passed after we had worked together for some time, and we found a common language in our shared hatred of the Germans.

I was working in a warehouse along with six other Jewish boys. The building housed some offices where Poles were working supervised by German managers. Among the Poles employed in this office there was one who was especially friendly toward the Jewish workers: His name was Stefan Miller. He had been a member of the KPP, then of the PPR* during the war, and had been a captain in the Polish army. (In 1944 he was deputy commander of the Żoliborz district during the Warsaw Uprising; after the war he was placed in charge of the leather industry in Łódź.) Experienced

---

*KPP: Komunistyczna Partia Polski, or Communist Party of Poland; PPR: Polska Partia Robotnicza, or Polish Workers Party.—PB

in clandestine operations, this man very carefully sounded out the Jewish workers to determine their makeup. Both Szymon Fortajl—who also worked in the warehouse—and I managed to gain his trust.

Captain Miller began by bringing us Polish and German newspapers and after a while began adding underground PPR publications printed in Warsaw. Our material conditions also improved when we began exchanging with our Polish co-workers, trading clothes that were in very good condition for daily breakfast or bread. Poles and Jews undertook these contacts at the risk of severe punishment; for Poles it meant being sent to Auschwitz, and for Jews it meant death.

At the worksite we learned from the Poles, most of whom were members of the PPS—out of 650 Polish workers there were about a dozen Endecja men, of whom three, including Golc, were hostile toward Jews—that the transports of Jews sent from the ghetto were being shunted to Treblinka where supposedly all Jews were being killed in gas chambers. We didn't want to believe this, but the idea gnawed at our hearts. Our minds began to seethe as we wondered how we should react if this information proved true. Hauptsturmführer Nadolny noticed our unease and made our regimen even more severe. He would come by at night and wake everyone up to perform punitive exercises; once when it was icy cold he ordered us to scrub down the barracks all night long with cold water and then report for work at the regular time. A new order held everyone collectively responsible if a single Jewish worker escaped from the Oppel factory. Nadolny decreed that if anyone escaped the Jewish population would be decimated. The SP was given secret orders to keep their eyes on us—at work, outside of work, and during the night. In addition, as we were later able to determine, Nadolny recruited one of us to keep him informed of the general mood inside the Jewish barracks and what was being discussed there.

When the news of what was happening at Treblinka began to filter in, we reacted by creating a small group of Jewish saboteurs within the Oppel plant. At first we carried out small acts, such as destroying ball bearings, precision automotive parts, work tools. We also slowed our pace. That winter, when our workshops began assembling half-tracks to be sent to Stalingrad, we set about ruining the precision parts, together with the Polish workers. We also took advantage of the fact that we were housed on site. Some cars that couldn't fit inside the workshop were stored on the grounds; they were filled with *Frostschutz*—antifreeze—to protect them from bursting in the cold. During the night we drained the Frostschutz and poured in regular water, which caused the cylinders to crack.

Later, we decided to take revenge on the SP. During the night, when they were sleeping, four boys from the group of saboteurs sneaked inside and took their caps, armbands, and clubs. The same foursome overwhelmed Rotzajt, who was on night watch, undressed him, and took his club, armband, and cap. The next day when the SP reported at assembly without uniforms, the Hauptsturmführer threatened that if the uniforms and clubs didn't show up by ten he would send all Jews to Umschlagplatz. The items did not show up, but Nadolny didn't keep his word. At ten, he once again assembled all Jewish workers, and when the items did not appear he locked four people up for twenty-four hours in the detention cell. Those people were sent every few hours to the Personalabteilung, where Nadolny tortured them, but three of them didn't know anything so they had nothing to say, and Taub, who did know, didn't talk. Nadolny was forced to forget the incident. Other Jewish workers were also interrogated, but to no result. At Szyffer's request, Nadolny accompanied him to the ghetto and returned with new badges, clubs, and caps. All Jews had to give up their passes allowing them inside the ghetto, which as deserving workers they had been able to use whenever they had a day off, generally on Sunday. Now we were also given extra work: We had to unload the coal wagons whenever they arrived, no matter what the hour, day or night. After this incident we gained a great deal of sympathy from the Polish workers, who hated the SP as much as we did.

Some Jews working at the Ostbahn arrived at our worksite with a load of coal. They told us that everyone inside the ghetto (they were housed in the ghetto, went to work in the morning, and returned at night) was taking up arms. They said we should contact the Poles in order to buy weapons, ammunitions, and grenades. We heard the same thing at the Jewish Wehrmacht worksite in the Wola district, where we had gone to pick up some polished pistons.

In this way the time passed between the barracks and the factory until January 1943. On 18 January we heard shots coming from the ghetto, and during the night we saw fires. The next day Captain Miller told us that a new Aktion had started called *Warschau Judenrein*—Warsaw free of Jews—and that the Jews had resisted, using weapons. Other Poles told us rumors of Jewish tanks taking part. Everyone was full of sympathy for our fighting brothers. A few Poles claimed to have seen with their own eyes ambulances carrying wounded Germans out of the ghetto.

In light of the new development, we asked Captain Miller to direct us to partisan units of the AL* ("us" being the group of saboteurs consisting of Szymon Fortajl, Szymon Brawman, Zymry Taub, Leon Ajsler, Ganc, myself, and one more whose name I don't remember). Of all these men I am the only one still alive.

Szymon Fortajl, a member of the PPR, had studied in France, where he had belonged to the French Communist Party. The rest were members of Hashomer and other Zionist organizations.

---

*Armia Ludowa, People's Army, a resistance group formed in 1944 and affiliated with the PPR, or Polish Workers Party.—PB

Captain Miller promised that as soon as the order came to evacuate all Jews from Oppel, he would try to warn us in advance and give us an address where we should go. Then a female liaison would take us to the Lublin forests.

After three days, the fighting in the ghetto stopped. No order came to the Oppel factory, and the Poles maintained that the Germans had been forced to break off the Aktion because of the strong, well-organized Jewish resistance.

After this, things really heated up at our worksite. Everyone wanted to go back to the ghetto to participate in any future fighting. The enthusiasm was so great that most of us acquired copies of the key to the Oppel factory gate and to the railroad siding that led into the factory. Engineer Szymon Fortajl and Ganc used these to escape, which brought the full force of Nadolny's wrath on the SP. Under pressure from us and threats from the Poles that the Polish underground would punish them if there were any retaliation, the SP told Nadolny they weren't capable of watching us without help from the Werkschutz, the factory guard. That further annoyed Nadolny, who ordered them to clean up the grounds.

Szyffer and Rotzajt sensed we were making preparations to leave the Oppel plant. We invited them to cooperate with us, on condition that all Jewish workers receive improved rations. Because Szyffer had the key to the provisions warehouse, we demanded that he also let us steal from there. That way we also had the SP in our hands. Every day, the provisions warehouse was systematically robbed of vegetables, potatoes, and lard. The only thing we didn't take was bread, since the loaves were carefully counted. We also started constructing hiding places on the factory grounds, in case we were surprised by a German Aktion.

For three weeks we had no contact with Captain Miller, because he was being hunted by the Gestapo in conjunction with his sister, who lived on the outskirts of Warsaw (she now lives in Żoliborz at 18 Krasiński Street, Kolonia 8). Evidently word got out that she was hiding two Jews. In addition, Captain Miller's liaison, who ran communications between the AL and their partisans, was also found out.

We decided to try a new tactic, since we were so intent on leaving the factory. Ajsler, Taub, and I began to simulate being sick. Dr. Majer, a Pole who was the factory physician (people said he was Jewish, and judging from his looks he might have been), and whose attitude toward the Jews was exceptionally good and humane, saw that we were pretending and without knowing why gave us four days off and then extended the period. I also told him it was very important for me to see my family in the ghetto (by that point I had none). So Dr. Majer told Nadolny that I was utterly exhausted following an illness and needed proper care, and recommended I be sent back to the ghetto for a few days. Nadolny asked the director of the warehouse where I worked for his opinion, as well as Captain Miller, who testified that I was conscientious in fulfilling my duties, and I was granted the leave.

Sometime later, on 27 September 1943, after I made it out of the ghetto, I met Captain Miller, who told me what had happened to the Jewish workers employed at Oppel's.

By 2 P.M. on 1 May 1943, the Oppel factory had yet to receive any orders. At that time all the Polish workers left the workshop, and the Jewish workers went to the barracks to eat. After they had eaten, Golc came and ordered all Jewish workers to give the barracks a thorough cleaning. Nadolny had left Warsaw the day before, after promising the workers that they could go on working in peace and had nothing to fear. At 4 P.M. the entire Oppel factory was surrounded by Wehrmacht units and gendarmes; several cars drove up loaded with armed soldiers. The Jews were not particularly alarmed, since soldiers often drove up to the plant to pick up the vehicles. Suddenly an officer ordered all the Jews to line up. A few of the Jewish workers managed to hide: Taub and Ajsler hid in the pits used for repairing cars, Erenlib hid under a tarp inside the warehouse. Other activists ran to hideouts they had prepared in advance.

The Wehrmacht officer asked Golc how many Jewish workers were registered as of 1 May. When they counted the assembled workers it turned out that eight people were missing. The officer sent some soldiers to look for them. When the soldiers came back empty-handed, the officer was ready to leave with no more than the ones he had managed to catch, but this wasn't enough for Golc. He asked the officer to wait and set off on his own, searching with his dog. Golc managed to find everyone who was hiding except Erenlib. Those people weren't allowed to take anything with them. The Wehrmacht loaded everyone into the cars, and the cars set off toward the forest. There the Wehrmacht searched everyone and took their watches. Then the transport was directed to Umschlagplatz, from where the people were sent to Majdanek.

JEWISH WORKERS EMPLOYED AT THE ADAM OPPEL FACTORY (52 WŁOSCIAŃSKA STREET) FROM 28 AUGUST 1942 TO 1 MAY 1943[*]

	Name	Approx. Age
1	Angluster	19
2	Bekerman	24
3	Berlinerblau	24
4	Blat	24
5	Blusztejn	25
6	Brauman	46
7	Braumen Sz.	19
8	Brojman	22
9	Domanowicz[†]	28
10	Domanowiczowa	28
11	Erenlib	22
12	Elsner	21
13	Forteil	40
14	Fogelman	20
15	Fortajl	32

16	Frydman	18
17	Ganc	21
18	Gewiksman	22
19	Goldberg	34
20	Grynglas	24
21	Halpern	36
22	Harbsztajn	19
23	Kruszel	24
24	Meller	22
25	Naftaniel	46
26	Reisner	55
27	Rotrojd[†]	28
28	Rotrojdowa	25
29	Rotsztejn[†]	27
30	Rudolf	17
31	Ruzal	33
32	Stodolnicki	30
33	Stodolnicki Z.	32
34	Szyfer[†]	32
35	Szyferowa	25
36	Taub Z.	29
37	Werthajzer	46
38	Winograd	22
39	Ziółkiewicz	38
40	Ziskind	23
41	Żołądek	38

*List compiled by Leon Najberg. Note discrepancies compared with text: "Rotrojd" is presumably "Rotbart," and "Rotsztejn" is likely the "Rotzajt" described earlier. The decrease in number (41 instead of 60) probably reflects the fact that some died or escaped before 1 May 1943.—PB
[†]Indicates SP member.

NATAN ŻELICHOWER. A week before Christmas 1942 I learned that my brother was with the Raumkommando inside the walls. I attached myself to a group that was returning to the central ghetto and searched for several exhausting hours before we were finally able to sit down together and recount our experiences amid tears of joy and despair. He too had lost his wife and son and was living from one day to the next, with no thought of how he might defend or save himself. Despite the friendly atmosphere at the brush factory, I decided to move in with him. I wasn't fit to work; at his place I could count on getting some rest. Two days later I left the brush factory for good. I recovered at my brother's until New Year's, doing nothing except attending to the well-provided kitchen. The people there were more optimistic than elsewhere, since they had been subject to fewer selections. I gladly gave in to their mood, lapping up any bit of good news like a precious tonic to the soul.

Then, on 1 January 1943, the Germans sealed off the entire ghetto, intending to destroy any remaining hiding places. Army units in battle formation blocked off street after street, and groups of SS searched the buildings scrupulously from basement to attic; they moved every piece of furniture, tore down suspicious partitions, and used tear gas to flush people out of the darkest nooks and crannies. Large groups of Jews, including women and children, were beaten without mercy and chased to the resettlement area, their faces caked rusty with blood, their hair matted, their clothes in tatters.

The next day a large group of Raumkommando workers was taken into the emptied buildings to dispose of the Jewish property left in the apartments. I was part of that group. Our task was to sort the furniture, pictures, porcelain, and carpets and collect anything of value in one place, from which it would be transported to special depots outside the ghetto.

My first experience on the new job paralyzed me. I suddenly found myself in the homes of acquaintances and even close friends. More than once we found tables set for breakfast or dinner, pots in the kitchen full of food. The scent of life still lingered in these rooms, and the stench of death had not yet intruded, though their inhabitants had undoubtedly just perished in Treblinka or Majdanek. The apartments were still alive, but we had come to kill them, to shatter the lingering illusion of family life. The first time I had to tear a Jewish face out of the frame where it was pictured I couldn't bring myself to do it; I felt as if I were committing murder.

They assembled us in groups of twenty to thirty and sent us into several buildings, where we were further divided into smaller groups of five to six people assigned to particular floors. The people I ended up with made quite an impression on me: all tall well-built young men, full of youthful energy and unbridled vitality. They seemed utterly unafraid, both of the shouting overseers and of the potential consequences of some of their own unbelievably risky actions. While one of them kept an eye on the German *Vorarbeiter*, or foreman, the rest would look for whatever valuables we could stash away for ourselves. We would toss furniture out into the courtyard and so render it useless. We broke down doors, smashed mirrors, gouged polished surfaces, tore curtains into tatters, spilled ink onto carpets, and let lamps slip from our hands so they would break into tiny pieces. Of course such sabotage was an open invitation for a bullet to the head, but we felt emboldened by our first success and pursued our actions even further. We also built up a lively trade with the wagon drivers who were hauling furniture out of the ghetto. They would buy anything of use, particularly sewing machines, which they would smuggle into Warsaw hidden among loads of furniture. In return they brought us the best food and drink. This exchange evolved into an intensive barter in all manner of goods, under the very eyes of the Germans. It's impossible to describe all the curious ways we found to smuggle things. Every day people would gather outside the ghetto warehouses to take the goods—but we never knew where they came from or how they managed to get inside or who was protecting them. We worked at a hectic pace that kept us constantly on edge and led to brazen acts that happily had no unfortunate consequences. For instance, one day I found myself sending two Astrakhan coats into the city with none other than Captain Scholz, a local SS commander. Someone I knew who pulled the captain's ricksha laid the package under the carriage seat, the guard saluted the officer, and the furs rode into the city.

Another time our group was ordered to dismantle the tailor workshops at 14–16 Nowolipie Street. We found rooms full of sewing machines that had been taken from private apartments in the ghetto. We decided to sell most of the machines; they were in great demand. Our usual overseer had just been replaced, however, and the new one was an SS man who dogged us all day long. He would shout and goad us on, to the point of kicking us—all the time cursing us for moving too slowly. That didn't bother us too much, since we were well fed, well clothed, and in fairly good spirits. The next morning we fired up the stove in one of the rooms and set a table with wine, vodka, ham, cheese, sardines, and every delicacy we could get from town. I went looking for our supervisor, whose shrill voice was coming from one of the rooms downstairs, and asked him politely whether he had eaten breakfast. He just stared at me, wide-eyed, and it was only due to his extreme astonishment that my skull survived intact. For all that, he did not spare me a heap of vulgar abuse, but I didn't let this put me off track. I apologized for the "Jewish impudence" he had accused me of and explained that I had felt so emboldened because his colleagues had eaten breakfast with us all the time.

"What? They ate breakfast with you? You're lying, you scoundrel! No German would sit down to a table with Jews!"

"He certainly would to the kind of table we set. At least, the others always did."

"That would make them traitors! And we don't have any traitors!"

"Oh, well, too bad." I sighed and walked away with feigned resignation. The German followed, explaining that he was curious to see what Jews ate. When he saw our table, his appetite triumphed over his amazement. He sat down and asked where we got the money for so much food, all the while piling it on his plate. We said we could serve him breakfast like this every day, along with a certain amount of cash, if he gave us free run of the factory. He asked for specifics, and that was the beginning of our deal. I handed him an advance payment of 500 zloty for the first five machines. He quickly stashed the money and, after his plentiful breakfast, stretched out on the couch, leaving us to our own devices. The next day on his own initiative he led us to a bathroom where he had hidden two machines and demanded 200 zloty in payment.

During the four months I spent working under the SS, and later in the camps, I never met a single honest German. You could always figure out how to reach them by the way they looked at certain objects, the rapacity that would show in their faces. They were all thieves and burglars, who would break into other people's homes and steal whatever was worth the taking.

HENRYK BRYSKIER. The ongoing decimation created an urgent need for hiding places. The designs varied—some better, some worse; some people built according to their own ideas, in strict secrecy, while others consulted with engineers they knew and trusted.

The extreme caution toward the neighbors came less from a fear of betrayal, although one did have to be careful, than from the very small spaces chosen for shelters, which could house only a strictly limited number of people. Experience during the roundups showed that individuals who had nothing arranged would try to force their way into whatever hiding place they discovered. Too many occupants would use up the available fresh air and threaten to turn the shelter into a torture dungeon, uninhabitable for all. Mothers with little children would also demand to be let in, but in such conditions the terrified children would cry and involuntarily give away the hideout. Children were often given anesthetic to keep this from occurring.

To prevent similar incidents, groups of people pooled their funds and set about building collective shelters. They devised various ways to solve the difficult problems of water supply, sewage removal, electrical connections, and concealing the hideout. I am including a few of my own designs as examples. I am convinced that, by the time these words find their way into print, the Nazi inquisitors will be a thing of the past and the reader will no longer have any use for such plans.

Example No. 1: On every floor of a building, identical rooms or alcoves are blocked off by closing up the doors and wallpapering the entire adjoining room. Access to the closed room on the top story is through the attic; the other blocked-off rooms are connected through holes cut in the ceilings. An emergency exit on the ground floor leads to a windowless basement belonging to an adjacent property destroyed by bombs, from which a tunnel runs to a door built in the housing of a water meter inside a well.

Example No. 2: A tiled kitchen oven is mounted in a wall built to close off another room. The stove, which is connected to the flue system by means of a removable pipe, is on castors and can be moved aside to free a small door cut into the masonry.

Example No. 3: A water pipe is mounted to the wall of a blocked-off room and a mobile sink is installed with a high backsplash, which covers an entrance hidden in the wall.

Example No. 4: A trapdoor in a workshop floor leads to a windowless basement. To conceal the opening, a workbench is constructed from two sawhorses and some plywood. Here boards were piled loosely on top of the floor beneath the bench. One board was actually nailed to one of the sawhorses as a support, while the base of the second sawhorse was nailed to the trapdoor to make a handle for lifting. The opening was situated against a wall; two sides came out at right angles from under the molding nailed along the walls, and the fourth side ran parallel and tangent to the floorboards.

Example No. 5: Access to a windowless basement is through a sewage pipe running beneath an outside wall. The pipe is entered through a carbide drum hidden in the ground, which the person entering can cover with a lid. This lid in turn has a small opening along the rim with a small cap. Once the lid is in place, the person in the drum reaches through this opening to cover the lid with sand and rubble; then he masks the small cap in the same way. A handle affixed to the bottom of the lid made it easy to manipulate. This entire device was situated in a corner, behind a door leading into an adjoining basement. Thus whenever that door was opened it swung out above the hidden barrel, helping to keep it concealed.

Example No. 6: This hiding place is carved out of a cement well. An iron receptacle is affixed inside and supplied with water by means of a rubber hose. The receptacle has a drain hole that can be closed with a valve. To enter the hiding place, the receptacle is removed. Afterward it is replaced and refilled with water, and the person is pulled inside through a small opening. When someone wants to leave the hiding place, the water is let out through the drain hole and the receptacle cranked aloft on a winch. Whenever the receptacle is filled, the fresh surface of the water is immediately sprinkled with specially prepared dust in order to give the impression that the liquid is long stagnant.

People also built shelters below basement level. These involved considerable cost and effort and usually contained bunks or other bedding for ten, twenty, fifty . . . up to three hundred people.

Water was piped directly to a shelter's pumps and not from the filter station. Electricity was generally diverted from a transformer.

I knew of shelters built inside transformer housings, which are typically covered with metal-plated doors marked with warning signs featuring a skull and crossbones. The people inside would drape high-voltage cables over the iron doors, in front of which they would place wet leads—to frighten anyone thinking of entering. These shelters had the unique advantage of being completely dry and warm enough for someone to lie on the floor even during freezing weather.

The shelter where I stayed for two days had a small ventilation window facing the street, which I used to fashion a projector by draping a white screen across the dark doorway facing the window. This depicted reverse images of movements on the streets.

Under no circumstances would I accept payment for helping design and build such shelters; I also declined any special discounts I was offered and went so far as to pay the equivalent of one person's share in one of the above-mentioned bunkers. I considered this to be pro bono work, although not all my colleagues did the same; many took advantage of the situation and received high payments.

The governance, provision, and health care inside a shelter depended on the organization and resourcefulness of the given group.

The fear of exposing oneself on the street—even if the block belonged entirely to a given workshop—necessitated the creation of inside passageways. To this end, entrances had to be sealed off and holes opened in the walls to connect to adjoining buildings— which was at times quite complicated.

Entire streets were sometimes connected this way, by openings made in attic or basement walls. Such places were less conspicuous and remained hidden for longer from the Germans, despite their familiarity with the ghetto. These concealed passageways also provided additional income for the Jewish Werkschutze, the factory guards, who would watch the openings and prevent strangers from entering. Of course, when the coast was clear the passages stayed open.

ANONYMOUS WOMAN. For as long as I live I will never forget the few days I spent hiding from the German roundup, in a building that had been converted into a hospital. My child and I were waiting for my husband to return with a registration number for me, but he didn't get one. They placed him in some group and took them all away to a different street.

Almost everybody in our building was wearing a smock; their white figures kept floating back and forth across the small courtyard. Evidently they wanted to maintain the illusion to the last minute that they were on call, holding the fort. My child was very sick and stayed ill throughout the deportation. I resolved that when the Germans showed up I would disregard their orders and not go down to the courtyard. Still, we had to hide somewhere. There were many hiding places, but some were impossible for me to reach with my child and others wouldn't take both of us in. Another option was to go down to the basement and stand there in water up to my ankles or hide in a hole in the wall, behind a wardrobe, but that also was impossible with a child. Finally I decided to hide in a room concealed by a heavy cupboard. To get inside we had to crawl through the bottom part of the cupboard, which had a movable wall. The last person inside shoved the wall back in place, and when danger threatened we barricaded the entrance with iron bars.

Generally there were about two hundred people in the room. Everyone had decided to stay there to the end. During the whole deportation I never experienced anything else as nightmarish as that room: two hundred stifling, hot, dirty, stinking people; two cases of full-blown tuberculosis; one of measles. There was no place to take my child, no place to lie down, not even on the floor. It was impossible to cook anything. I begged for a little boiled water for my child—but there wasn't any. That was how the first day passed; the Germans didn't come. After dark, people went back to the apartments they had randomly taken over, since they expected things to be quiet and didn't have the strength to put up with the same crowded conditions at night. Since it was very hard to get my child through the hole in the cupboard, I was allowed to remain in the room. I slept on the floor beside my boy, a coat beneath his little head. During the night I could feel the bedbugs and lice crawling over me. I found lice in my child's head. During the night he woke up and cried. The others became angry and yelled at me. What could I do?

I debated with myself whether to leave the room or not, but I had no other place to go. I figured that this hiding place was safe from the Germans, and I believed that once the deportation was finally over my husband would come get me out of that house; he had a number and could move about freely. Whenever I could I managed to make some tea or a little soup for my child. One of the nurses looked after us. She gave me a little kasha; someone else gave me eggless noodles. I was amazed they were carrying all of that on their persons. I hardly had anything, because when I left my house on the morning of 6 September I was convinced we would no longer be alive that evening—since I had no intention of getting on the train. Besides, I was so upset that my child was sick I didn't think about anything else. I had brought a little rice, but there was no place to cook it. By some miracle even in those conditions my child's health started to improve a little bit. He asked for food, and I had no choice but to accept help from my fellow inmates.

We survived one roundup inside that room. One afternoon at five we heard shots in the courtyard. The Germans ordered everyone to come down. Almost everybody went down, assembled in ranks, and waited for what would happen next. A few minutes later the Germans dismissed them. The Jews deceived themselves that the spectacle of hospital workers in their white smocks had so impressed the Germans they had decided to show mercy and would not come back. That was a delusion. The Germans had left because they heard there was no more room at Umschlagplatz.

Night came once again, night and another day of waiting. The room filled up. Now there were more than two hundred people. My little boy caught cold and began to cough. People were upset. After all, in the event of a roundup, the slightest noise could attract the Germans and give us all away. I was finally told to leave the room.

In despair over losing the hiding place, I moved to a two-room apartment where we had to pass through one room to get to the second. Four families were living there, twelve people altogether; they all knew one another. They had decided that, in the event of a roundup, they would go down—no one was considering going into hiding. It was odd; they were afraid of being shot where they were, but they no longer had the strength to cope with the enormous strain of staying hidden, with children or sick people unable to control their reactions. There was one doctor, pani M, who believed the Jews who left would be sent to some distant province and escape the bombardment expected in Warsaw. She had decided to go down and had persuaded those around her not to hide; her words lifted their spirits and gave them peace. Talking people into hiding was evidently too much for her; she couldn't take on such responsibility. In those difficult moments everyone followed his or her own instincts.

For me, the only question was where to hide; there was no suitable place in the apartment. Finally, almost at the last minute, I decided to use a wardrobe to block off the second room and stay there with my child. The identical rooms on the other three floors had been blocked in the same way. On every floor, in each apartment there were people who hadn't decided whether to go or to stay. They would make their decision at the last minute. The people who chose to go shoved the wardrobes into place, leaving behind those who preferred to die where they were. In the room where I was hiding with my child were six other people, including two women and two children. My resolve not to go voluntarily probably influenced their decision.

The last roundup began at about three in the afternoon and lasted until six. For the second time people went down into the courtyard in their white smocks, but this time they were led straight out to the street. Then the Germans began searching the buildings. We could hear their heavy boots inside the stairwell. Now and then we heard cries, followed by shots. They killed anyone who hadn't assembled downstairs. We went through one moment of extreme tension and mortal terror. A German came into our apartment. Would he realize there was a second room? Would he move the wardrobe? We heard him open the wardrobe, looking for someone inside . . . then more steps and we heard him shout, *"Leo, komm!"* We were certain he was calling his comrade to help him move the wardrobe, but Leo didn't come. The German became impatient. He called out once again, and then left the apartment. We had been saved. All three children had passed the test. They didn't move a muscle the whole time the German was in the next room.

Some thirty people were shot in those three hours—in the courtyard, in the basements, and in the apartments. A heavy stream of blood flowed toward the entrance to our building and out onto the street. After the Germans had gone, the entire place was as silent as the grave. But we couldn't leave our hideout; we expected another search party at any moment. We couldn't light candles, start a fire, or do anything that might alert the Germans to the fact there were still people in the building. We had a little tea, some soup, and some bread for the children—we ourselves hadn't eaten for two days. When the hunger became unbearable, we decided to move the wardrobe and search the other rooms for something to eat, but we couldn't get it to budge. We tapped on the floor and on the ceiling, to signal to the other people in hiding. Finally, someone realized we needed help. We gathered some essentials from our modest apartment, but we couldn't find anything to eat. For the first time in my life, I resolved to steal. I went to the apartment of our neighbors, who had a fairly large supply of food and had refused to help us, and without asking I took a large pot of kasha from their kitchen. Our confinement was coming to a successful end. On the evening of the next day people started walking openly in the courtyard. The deportation was evidently drawing to a close.

I will never forget the moment when my husband appeared; friends had lent him two numbers—which we needed just to go outside. So we went out, utterly weak and exhausted. A Jewish policeman standing at the door demanded 300 zloty for letting me out with my child. He threatened to bring the Germans, but he didn't get his money. My head was spinning, I felt my legs giving way; after all this, we were together. My husband had gone through terrible things—for days he had had no idea whether we were still alive or not—and the torment and anxiety had left deep marks etched in his face. For the moment no one bothered to worry what would happen to the people without numbers. The most important thing was that we were still alive, and that the deportation was coming to an end.

NATAN ŻELICHOWER. On the night of 21 July posters went up announcing the compulsory deportation; they called upon all Jews to report to the "resettlement area" at Dzika and Stawki streets.* This did not apply to Jews employed in enterprises that produced exclusively for the Germans and who lived on the grounds of such

---

*The announcement by the Jewish Council concerning the deportation was dated 22 July 1942 and appeared on the ghetto walls 24 July.[1]

enterprises, nor did it apply to those Jews working outside the ghetto. All others were to comply with the order immediately.

The new regulations appeared on my daughter's birthday. I considered them a serious threat and decided to protect my child, whom I had reared and educated with the utmost care—my intelligent child, who had grown up believing in the goodness of life and in her parents' ability to protect her. My concern for my beautiful little daughter determined my course of action. Before finding a position at one of the firms exempt from deportation, my immediate task was to find a hiding place.

I quickly found one. At the end of the topmost hallway inside our building, someone had broken open a hole to the roof next door, which was about a half meter higher than the hole. It was possible to walk across that roof to the next building, which was one story taller than ours. That building had a very small attic, which I was able to enter by placing a board inside a hole in the wall. We fixed up the attic by equipping it with water, buckets, and an oil cooker and moved in. There were fifteen of us. The space was carefully allotted; when we all lay on our sides we completely covered the floor.

We spent the first night without sleep. Everyone was so nervous, we kept whispering back and forth about our new situation. We realized this hiding place was temporary, merely the first step down the difficult road of conspiracy. We saw before us a country teeming with uniformed German killers, whom we were opposing with no more than our determination and our will to live, like castaways struggling against the mighty ocean. It seemed foolish to expect salvation, but none of us in hiding yielded to despair. We refused to dwell on the immediate danger and, instead, discussed our future means of defense.

The manhunt began at dawn. The courtyards were swarming with SS men chasing people onto the street. Endless lines of Jews made their way to Umschlagplatz. There they were jammed onto freight trains, a hundred or more people to a car. It was clear from the way they were loaded onto the train that these people were doomed to annihilation. Rifle butts and SS boots worked mercilessly and without interruption, wounding whoever failed to keep up with the rapid pace of the orders. Death hovered over the ghetto, over the crowded mass at Umschlagplatz, and over the tiny handfuls of people in hiding.

Afterward a dead silence reigned in the ghetto. Streets that had been flowing with tears and despair during the day were deserted by evening, quiet except for the heavy tread of laborers returning from their places of work outside the walls. I left my hiding place and marched alongside them, to see if I could find someone who could help me. I was lucky. I met an acquaintance who worked in a safety-pin factory, one of Gustaw Zygmunt's firms. He promised me some work as soon as the other shops that had been shut down resumed operation, which was supposed to happen in eight days. Meanwhile I would have to stay in the hideout.

Although the little attic was well masked, it was terribly confined and stifling. The slightest rustle could give us away, so we sat absolutely still. We even gave up using the cooker; it hissed too loudly when we lit it. We spent our days listening to the frequent sounds coming from the streets and courtyard, the variety of voices. Every now and then groups of SS men showed up in the courtyard, accompanied by the Jewish police, who used their piercing whistles to call down everyone still inside. This was accompanied by repeated announcements that anyone who disobeyed would be found and shot on the spot. Minutes later they were running through the apartments, attics, and basements. We listened to the sounds of their searching, our hearts frozen with fear. A horrible racket filled the cavernous courtyard: doors being ripped from their frames, wardrobes overturned, windowpanes and mirrors shattered. From time to time this symphony of destruction would be pierced by the cry of a victim who had been hunted down, rending the air like a dagger. And above the cry we could hear the Germans' brutal curses, followed by a series of shots.

In the wee hours I would sneak out of the hideout into a store tucked away in one of the buildings, to gather some stocks for our hiding place. Once I made the mistake of eating some raw cabbage and washing it down with cold water. The result was horrible: I came down with a high temperature and bloody diarrhea. Half conscious by day, after dark I dragged myself around the streets in my efforts to find work and identification papers, without which you couldn't even set foot on the factory grounds. The matter was becoming increasingly urgent, because the searches were getting more and more thorough, and our hiding place might be undone at any moment. One day while I was keeping watch through a crack between the boards that concealed the entrance to our attic, I saw a hand come through the boards below and push up the tarpaper covering. The hand was followed by the head of an SS man. I began to choke with terror and with a feeble gesture tried to warn the others. Then I fell headlong into the people lying on the floor. I don't know whether it was fear that knocked me down or whether I collapsed because I was so wasted by my sickness. When I came to, my wife and daughter were leaning over me, calming me down, assuring me that the danger had passed.

I couldn't allow my illness to get in the way of finding somewhere to work and a different place to live. Finally, after one more week I managed to obtain papers that enabled me to move my family into a little room on the grounds of one of the factories. All I had managed to rescue from the pogrom was a little money and some jewelry. The rest of my possessions, the years of savings, my apartment, the dentist's office, our clothes—everything was lost. Even so, I didn't mourn these losses. But I could not suppress the guilt I felt toward my mother, who had stayed in the apartment, too old to manage the breakneck climb to the attic. She died in bed, shot by a German thug. I had returned to the apartment and seen her mutilated body. Before I left the building I swore to avenge her death. I felt my hatred of Germans was reaching its peak. If I manage to survive this terrible war, I thought, I'll devote the rest of my life to prosecuting the crimes committed by the most savage nation on the planet. Today, as I write these words, the Germans no longer rule the world; today I know that revenge is not a matter of one person's reckoning with another; it is the task of the International Tribunal to pass judgment on a nation that made murder a civic virtue.

While we were in hiding, the ghetto was completely emptied of its inhabitants. The streets that had once been bustling with life were quiet and deserted. Everything reeked of death. Plundered shops, broken doors and windows, piles of trash and papers littering the sidewalks, curtains swaying inside jagged window frames, piles of feathers rising and falling with every gust of wind, red pillowcasing torn to shreds and lying in the gutters like streaks of coagulated blood, pieces of ruthlessly crippled furniture stacked on the pavement or dangling from the windows through which they had been thrown—this is what a Jewish street looked like after the beast of the apocalypse had passed, the beast that had been nourished in the stable of German "culture"! Here and there, scurrying through this cemetery of Jewish life where everything was still warm with blood, human rats were on the prowl, in search of Jewish valuables.

The mood of the next two weeks was oppressive. The people in the factory wandered among the extinct houses of the city looking for surviving family members. Every thought was colored by the recent terrors. People were unable to break the ties between those who stayed and those who had gone. All conversations centered on worries about loved ones.

Little by little I regained my health. On 22 August I set off for the factory shop across the courtyard from where I was living.

Suddenly I heard whistles and shouts and running feet. The factory gate was slammed shut. We spent nearly two hours cut off from the world, full of dread. When the gates were finally opened, the courtyard was empty. The open doors of the apartments terrified me. There was no one at home. I refused to believe the terrible truth. Crazed with panic, I ran back to the gate, where I learned that several SS trucks had taken about 160 people from the factory grounds. As if through a fog I heard someone describe the factory manager's effort to intervene, how he had explained that all the people on the factory grounds were officially untouchable. But the reply left no doubt: The transport must be filled; it doesn't matter which Jews are used to fill it. I heard the words and understood what they meant; still, I could not believe it had happened to me, the most horrible thing that could possibly happen—and so quickly, too. I pushed my way outside, blinded by the despair welling up inside me, and ran in the direction of the resettlement area. I ran right through the German patrols surrounding the factory, past the piles of furniture stacked on the streets, completely dazed as I searched for my wife and daughter. Then a Jewish policeman stopped me, someone from our own factory. He started to tell me something, but seeing that I couldn't follow he handed me a piece of paper. I couldn't tear my eyes away from what was written there:

> Dear Papa!
> Save yourself! It looks like we are lost. I will do what I can to keep up Mother's spirits; maybe fate will bring us back together.
>
> Your Stella.

It took a long time for the meaning of my daughter's last letter to sink in. I sat down on the curb and wept bitterly. A needle of pain etched each of those words deep into my heart, those last words of my daughter, the only reason I had for living.

When I returned to the factory, I was all alone in the world—the most dreadful loneliness imaginable. For long hours I lay on my child's miserable little pallet, soaking her pillow with tears and with my unbounded longing. I kept thinking of suicide, but my daughter's words were like a commandment: *maybe fate will bring us back together*. Maybe, I fantasized—after all, Lublin isn't Treblinka—maybe there was a drop of truth to the Germans' proclamation. If so that was a drop I had to live for, so as not to bereave them of husband and father by escaping too soon, just when they would need my help the most! I decided to live.

For two weeks I was completely numb. I passed the time in a stupor, waiting for a miracle, waiting for the door to fly open and reveal my wife and daughter. I listened to the sounds from outside, straining my ears for familiar voices. The young people I was living with did everything they could to bring me back to matters at hand. They had lost their closest family as well and asked me to look after them, thinking the new responsibility would restore my energy.

Added to my boundless grief was a seething hatred of Germans; I spent entire days cursing them as a nation of sadists and murderers, a mob of humans turned beasts. For me the word *Nazi* came to mean the worst debasement of the human soul. I pictured myself trampling these monsters with my shoes, tearing their loathsome bodies to shreds, stamping on their hearts. I devised the most elaborate tortures to avenge the innocent blood they had spilled. Unfortunately, my revenge was confined to my imagination, as a new decree shook my vigilance from its stupor.

More new posters: All Jews are to gather at the resettlement area for a new selection! We were also informed that only a few of the nearly twenty factories still operating would remain open; the rest were to be liquidated, including the safety-pin shop. They were closing in. Once again I became a hunted animal, hiding in the burrows of the city of death. I sneaked into the building at Zamenhof

29, across from our factory, and there, in a corner on the second floor, I found a three-room apartment with an alcove located opposite the entrance to the courtyard. I fixed up our new hiding place, blocking the entrance with a large bookcase full of books, which I fastened to the wall. I cut an opening in the back of the bookcase and reattached the cutout with lightweight hinges. Then I covered the gap with bundles of books tied together. The hideout could be entered by removing three blocks of books. Everything was so carefully disguised that only an accident could give us away.

Twelve people crawled inside, bringing their provisions with them. We had furnished the hideout with buckets, bowls, and an electric hot plate. The wall had a window onto the hall, built at a right angle to the windows along the corridor. The one source of air was a little vent, which we opened only at night. We aired our cell at night, crawling back through the bookcase to rest in separate rooms. This also gave us a chance to exercise our limbs, which grew stiff from lying in the hiding place all day long. We never turned on the lights.

The first part of our forced imprisonment, which lasted from Sunday to Wednesday, passed relatively peacefully. The only sounds to break the silence were the occasional footsteps of someone in search of hidden Jewish "treasure." But these gold diggers were as scared as we were, so our noise frightened them away. Hidden behind the curtain of a window, I watched their catlike movements and wary glances as they entered and left the courtyard.

The roundups began on Wednesday. Bands of SS men burst into the courtyard with triumphant whoops, alarming the building with their whistles. A moment later they ran through the apartments. The thunder of the Germans, the harsh fury of their shouting, and the scrape of furniture on wooden floors reverberated throughout the empty rooms. Their voices carried across the silence with such clarity that we could hardly tell which direction they were coming from.

Minutes after the Germans broke into our building we froze in terror. From behind our wall of books we could hear furniture being dragged across the floor. We heard someone throwing glassware out of a cabinet. Suddenly the bookcase separating us from the Germans began to shake: Somebody was obviously going to some effort to move it. A moment later we heard footsteps in the doorway . . . and then in the stairwell. We wiped the sweat from our foreheads. Petrified, we didn't exchange a word. Through the curtain of the window onto the stairwell I saw an SS man hurrying a Jewish woman he had captured on one of the upper floors. He was shoving her ahead with his rifle butt, forcing her to take several steps at a time. The woman kept turning around, crying and begging the man to spare her life in return for some hidden valuables she would show him.

"*Gut, komm,*" answered the SS man. They walked back upstairs, and in the silence we could hear their conversation on the top floor. "And now run down to the basement, before my colleagues show up."

The woman raced downstairs, but when she reached the second-floor landing, a wrenching report from his rifle rent the air and the woman plunged head-first to the floor below. Her murderer jumped over her body and walked out into the courtyard.

We passed the next few hours in a state of extreme tension. At 10 A.M. nine beasts in human form burst into the courtyard, announcing their arrival with a great din of shouting and shooting. They rushed inside the three entryways to our building, and for half an hour we heard shouting and yelling, laughter and curses—and in our room: silence. We scarcely dared to breathe. One of the men, an electrician, stood over poor little Lilka holding a down cover. Then the mob left the building, spilling outside amid drunken shouts. And in our room—silence. Our breathing became a little freer. This time Lilka managed not to cough, but would she be able to stand it next time?

Twenty minutes later and all of a sudden Lilka started to cough: She was immediately muffled with the quilt. Then I heard a cheerful German voice coming from one of the entrances into the building: *"Hans, komm! Hier sind Juden!"* Beast number nine had hidden inside the entryway and waited. Weak with fear, I couldn't move a muscle. The pounding on the stairs shot through me like bullets from a rifle. One thought flashed through my brain— twelve of us! Then the sound of a child crying broke the terrifying silence, a pitiful wailing, full of inarticulate accusation, tearing at our hearts. The pounding stopped in front of our window. One of the Germans cursed brutally. *"Ein Kind! Verflucht noch einmal!"*— Goddammit! It's a child! A strong arm ripped open a window and the little thing was torn from its pillow and flung into the court-yard, where it somersaulted a few times before landing in a bloody heap on the cobblestones. The Germans ran downstairs. Soon they were stepping over their victim as they headed for the gate.

For an hour no one spoke. I stared numbly at the bloody stain on the cobblestones. All I felt was emptiness—no longer horror or despair, no desire to fight or even to live—just a terrible emptiness slowly welling up within me into a boundless sorrow.

It's two in the afternoon: We hear more steps, first in the entryway and then in the courtyard: Who could it be, a civilian? Yes, and a Jew at that. Look, he's been joined by a woman. They stand there, calling, in loud voices; they're headed for the vestibule. Another devilish trap? No, I can make out what they're saying; they're looking for their loved ones. Quietly I leave the hiding place and walk down to them.

"What's going on?"

"The roundup's over. They've driven away."

"Is it safe to go outside?"

"For the moment, but who knows for how long?"

I go back to the hideout to deliver the happy news. We begin to move about the building, at first slowly and carefully, then more and more boldly. We each go our separate way. Someone tends to the murdered child, wrapping the body in a pillow. Then they take it out to the garden to bury.

I go out on the street: an unforgettable moment and an unforgettable sight that nothing can erase. I've never seen a battlefield, but this is what it must look like after a hurricane of fire. The streets and sidewalks are littered with corpses: old people, women, children, lying in the strangest positions, evidence that death has caught them from all sides, that they suffered torments of fear and humiliation. Their clothes have been torn from their bodies and are heaped on the cobblestones in bloody piles. And strewn among the corpses that are crying out to heaven for vengeance are torn window frames, broken tables and chairs, pillows, down covers, pots, trodden mounds of linen, books torn to shreds. Here the human beast guzzled blood until its maw was full. The terrified faces of the murdered, emaciated and mutilated, and the silent, equally horrified faces of the living, sneaking through the shadows of the buildings—this is the unforgettable picture of the ghetto at the time of the grand Aktion.

STEFAN ERNEST. A few things are certain: First, this will turn out badly. Second, there's no choice but to hide—nobody's going to show up voluntarily anymore, believing that a registration number will provide immunity. There will clearly be passive resistance.

On 29 October, SP Jakub Lejkin is assassinated by a Jewish fighter. People speculate there will be active resistance. The fighting groups are beginning to make themselves known. Then one November morning, the Germans send mobile ricksha patrols onto the ghetto streets, who fire without mercy at anyone who happens to cross their path. People show their permits allowing them to be outside on business during work hours, but the SS beasts simply tear up the documents, turn their bearers toward the nearest wall, and finish them off right then and there with a pistol.

The same thing happens to workers carrying their pails toward the soup kitchens.

On the first day, the patrols claimed twenty-one victims; on the next, seven or eight. SS Unterscharführers Blescher and Klostermayer are primarily responsible for carrying out Brandt's order to shoot without warning. Klostermayer, who became notorious throughout the ghetto for hunting people down this way, would phone in his report from the Council Secretariat: *"Einundzwanzig Juden gemacht! Genug? Befehl!"*—Twenty-one Jews taken care of! Enough? Yes, sir!

Then with a smile he turns to President Lichtenbaum of the Jewish Council: *"Befehl ist Befehl!"*—Orders are orders!*

The Bloody Mass of that November morning resembled the "Saint Bartholomew's Day Massacre" of the previous April except in a few particulars. The earlier killings were intended to intimidate and frighten, whereas these new acts of sadism and "random" cruelty had little point—since we were no longer frightened by such terror. We knew we had all been sentenced to death, we just didn't know the date of execution. There was no need to frighten us anymore. The monsters just wanted to prove that each "legislative" caprice would be followed to the letter, that Brandt's district would be a model of obedience and compliance.

Whoever ventures outside doesn't know whether he'll come back—but that doesn't seem to matter; even the greatest fear can become routine. And in the meantime Klostermayer and Blescher go on hunting.

Rumors of an impending deportation are growing more and more persistent. The second Hoffmann factory is to be closed. The work crew scatters; nobody has any intention of being taken to Umschlagplatz to be transported to "work in Lublin." The new

---

*Marek Lichtenbaum, a largely despised figure, became president of the Judenrat after Czerniaków's suicide.—PB

Luftwaffe Okęcie worksite still has some places open; the truck from Rembertów is still picking up the workers. . . . But things are clearly turning more and more oppressive and gloomy.

On 18 January 1943, the fourth stage in the history of Warsaw's Jews begins with an Aktion lasting four days. The choice of the day and in particular the hour comes as a surprise. As late as Saturday afternoon, things are still relaxed. Then, for reasons unknown, one hospital prepares its people to go into hiding during the night. The workshops, too, appear to be making similar preparations. But the Jewish Council sleeps the sleep of the just and in the morning most of the officials find themselves dressing in the company of gendarmes. In a surprise tactic, the Germans have quietly fanned out through the entire ghetto, and now they enter different buildings nearly all at once. Anyone they find they chase downstairs and outside into an ever-growing column. Finally, all the people collected throughout the ghetto are driven en masse to Umschlagplatz, where they are hastily loaded onto the freight cars.

More than three thousand people, including hospital patients, are sent off in that first group. Next to go are the top officials of the Jewish Council. The buildings at 40, 42, and 44 Muranowska Street—the main housing for Council officials—are easily taken, since the occupants still believe in registration numbers and special papers. After all, they reason, there are still about ten thousand wild people left in the area around the Council, so there's no reason to hide. They are convinced they'll get their papers back at Umschlagplatz.

The wild people have a better sense of reality.

With the exception of certain places such as the Werterfassungstelle, by noon the entire ghetto, including the Council building itself, has been combed in the same manner. The prey is taken by surprise, virtually walking into the trap. So the actual roundups are conducted hastily and sloppily.

In fact, I owe my life to this sloppiness. I almost literally slept through the moment of my death. By the time I woke up, I learned that my building had already been worked over. It was easy enough to guess what was going on—my windows open onto the street, where you can see the guards marching with their prisoners—but I didn't realize they had already searched our building, so I spent nearly the entire day waiting with my household for them to take us away, until finally, in the evening, we set up a temporary hiding place.

And so we sit the whole next day, hardly moving a muscle, scarcely daring to breathe, afraid that the slightest sound might attract our persecutors. Our fear is heightened by our lack of news concerning the Aktion and by the surrounding quiet, which is broken only by frequent rifle shots. It's easy to imagine how terrible those first hours were for us. The surprise had been complete. It's one thing to discuss or brood or predict what is bound to happen, but it's something else to meet one's fate head on. That's only human.

Around noon they begin searching the homes they already checked that morning, this time with the help of the Jewish SP, which was mobilized earlier. Once again they ransack the entire district, running through apartments and breaking down all locked doors. Occasionally (less often than at other times) they go into the basements and attics. In this way they collect or kill about a thousand people. Since there aren't enough funeral wagons, they requisition all the Council transport wagons to haul away the corpses . . . just like earlier they mobilized vehicles to haul living people to Umschlagplatz.

We have no contact with the outside world. As darkness falls I watch through the window as the gendarmes and SS men march toward the checkpoint to quit the ghetto. We're not sure whether they've all left. The shooting has stopped. Just before evening I get up my courage and go outside. The streets are deserted. I enter the Health Department building. Utter silence. I see the torn-down doors that are so familiar from the previous Aktion. Through the gaping doorways and holes punched in the walls I see a ramshackle assortment of goods and equipment—evidently the looters have already moved in, quietly assisted by the Polish police. The object of my foray is a telephone on the fourth floor. I call up the hospital; the connection goes through. I receive a satisfactory report concerning the fates of specific people and then return home without incident. The streets are completely empty, apart from the occasional looter sneaking by with a bundle on his back. I only wish I had some cigarettes.

My brother is author, director, and star performer of our new hideout. A veteran of the Polish-German campaign and an officer to boot, albeit in the medical corps, he is unanimously chosen to be in command of everything. From a military point of view, though, everything is in the saddest possible shape. I'm the only one fit for active service. We have two old women (one is our mother), one young woman, one little girl, and one old man.

The day after the Aktion, Herr Brandt steps into the Council building and declares, *"Die weitere Umsiedlung kommt natürlich nicht mehr in Betracht!"*—Naturally any further resettlement is out of the question! The word *natürlich* is the best clue to his sadistic character, his perverse, monstrous deceit. But nobody believes him. Everyone expects the roundups to resume any day, any hour. Figures began emerging from the buildings, their sunken gray faces—the telltale mark of a hideout—bearing witness to the events of the previous four days.

After such an ordeal, the immediate reaction is to satisfy one's hunger; people's first thoughts are always of their stomachs. It's sheer animal survival instinct. So the Council hands out bread, honey, and jam, while the one remaining warehouse of the Provisions Department distributes products salvaged from stores that somehow survived the Aktion without being robbed. Soon people in the Council building are preparing meals and giving out soup. The survivors first must eat.

Meanwhile, patrols resume moving through the streets, shooting at anyone they encounter; after all, no one should be out during work hours! But even that doesn't scare away the looters. Nor do our fighters, who are organizing more and more openly.

Except for those that have been completely dismantled, the factory shops and worksites get on with their daily routine. But we expect the Aktion to be renewed any day. We keep watch throughout the night, on shifts, since we expect that's when they'll come; we hardly ever leave our clothes. We eat what we can and maintain our vigil. Many people work on improving their hideouts.

The Council building and its courtyard are mostly empty, coming to life only when soup and other provisions are distributed. Otherwise, small surviving groups of officials can be seen wandering idly back and forth, their faces contorted with the most recent suffering and loss, full of anxiety as to what will happen next.

Unlike the previous Aktion, this second roundup is unambiguous and undisguised. There is no longer any need for complicated tactics and carefully planned selections. The Aktion is mainly directed against the Council district, where it goes on for three days, and to a lesser extent against the factory workshop districts, which are mostly spared, as only one day is devoted to them.* The operation is carried out with the help of gendarmes and SS infantry; the Jewish SP plays an auxiliary role, breaking into doors and looking for hiding places.

On the first day the operation lasts from 5:30 A.M. to 4 P.M.; on the second day the same in both the big and little ghettos; on the third day, from 9 A.M. to 4 P.M. in both ghettos; on the fourth

*Following the deportations between July and September 1942, the Germans again reduced the size of the ghetto. Its southern boundary became Gęsia Street (currently Anielewicza Street). However, some factory workshops employing Jews were located farther south and east of that boundary. Hence the division into Council district and Workshop district. The three sectors of workshops that came into being were also referred to by the names of the factory owners.—PB

day from 10 A.M. to late in the evening. In our district the Aktion takes in essentially the entire quarter, where a large armed force has been assigned to cover a limited area.

Except for the first day, the Aktion reaps only meager harvests. People in the ghetto hide themselves as best they can, and in some places, especially at Muranowski Square and on Miła Street (No. 34) there is even armed resistance and the enemy suffers losses! Similar resistance is said to have occurred at the Schultz factory on the third day of the Aktion, i.e., 20 January. Altogether approximately 6,000 victims are deported or shot, 4,000 on the first day. The burial details report moving nearly 1,000 corpses. The enemy reportedly has suffered 21 killed or heavily wounded. Hardest hit is the Council administration—seven Councillors are deported and many employees of both sexes. The Jewish SP, who are still needed, are spared.

Warned by some miraculous intuition, the hospital on Gęsia Street and many of the people there manage to hide although the hospital is closed off early in the morning on the first day of the Aktion. Nearly all the sick people, however, are deported or shot (out of some four hundred patients, about twenty escaped), along with some of the technical staff and a few doctors who were on duty. The doctors at the Department of Health at 12–14 Majzels Street suffer heavy casualties, as most of them are caught by surprise. People working outside the ghetto and in the shops are allowed to pass through the checkpoints: They are kept at their places of work throughout the entire Aktion. Some of these workers who are caught inside the ghetto (the night shift of the Ostbahn, for example, which typically leaves at 4 P.M., and the Werterfassungstelle) are let out following a brief inspection.

The operation is obviously directed against the centers of "unproductive liberal elements"—meaning the Council district— the Council administration and the wild people. The Germans use hand grenades to blow up hiding places. This inflicts terrible losses

250 WORDS TO OUTLIVE US

among the workers at the Oschmann factory quartered at 13 Muranowska Street and elsewhere in the vicinity. The wild people rely on their experience from the previous Aktion and hide as best they can. The Halutz activists, mostly concentrated on Miła, are armed with revolvers; they show great prowess and courage fighting a hopeless struggle.* The workshops are hit less hard; some— including the large Többens factory, Von Schöne, and Hallmann— are not affected at all. Some groups are obviously meant to be spared: the Werterfassungstelle, the outside labor crews, the shops— the last either in whole or in part, although certain outside sites like Schmidt and Münstermann are evidently slated for liquidation.

The victims are chased away to Umschlagplatz, ruthlessly and relentlessly, or else finished off on the spot. Council members and their families are not spared; this includes higher officials, well-known doctors, and similar people. For those of us who work for the Council, the only recognized residents of the district, the Aktion is all-encompassing and merciless. The exceptions are random and few.

In this phase there are no negotiations on the battlefield, either individually or as groups. The only way to save oneself is to hide and hope for a lucky break—in other words, passive resistance, which is widespread.

In many places, though, the resistance is active. And even as the smoke rising over the city and the glow of fires proclaim the "victory" of the German troops against an unarmed populace and a handful of armed combatants, this time it also attests to a courageous if hopeless resistance—for the sake of honor.

Sporadic deportations will go on for three months—until 19 April 1943 and the beginning of the liquidation of the Jewish

---

*He-Halutz (Hebrew for Pioneer) was an umbrella for several organizations such as Hashomer Hatzair, Dror ("Freedom"), and Akiba. These groups always acted as one bloc inside the ghetto.

quarter, which on 24 April is declared nonexistent.* In theory the fifth phase is still going on and will continue until every last Jew hiding inside the cordoned area expires from thirst and starvation.

JAN MAWULT. In February 1943 the news starts making the rounds: The ghetto and all the shops are going to be liquidated, but not to Treblinka. Supposedly, all young men and women fit for work will be assigned to workshops relocated in the provinces. The rest will be eliminated. The brushmakers' shop is first in the line of fire, but it buys more time by "arranging" to be incorporated into the Többens enterprise.

By the end of February they begin implementing the new policy. Word gets out that Többens and Schultz, the two largest factories, are being relocated to the Lublin district: Többens's group to Poniatów, and Schultz's to Trawniki.†

Next comes the propaganda. Brandt, Többens, as "commissar for relocation," and the other factory owners try to assure, persuade, and convince the Jews they have nothing to fear; they'll be much better off in the country. Schultz, from Nowolipie—not a bad man, incidentally; sometimes his response to Jews is actually human—explains to his workers that resistance is hopeless, staying in Warsaw is out of the question, and they should go voluntarily, because otherwise they will be decimated and whoever is left will be sent by force . . . and then not to Trawniki but to Treblinka. He assures them they'll be fine; they'll have better working and living conditions far away from the big city. Together, with him, they will calmly live out the end of the war in the Lublin countryside.

---

*In fact, SS Brigadeführer Jürgen Stroop declared the Jewish district nonexistent as of 16 May 1943, when the Great Synagogue on Tłomackie Street was demolished with great fanfare.

†Himmler's order of 16 February 1943 to Pohl, Head of the Main Office for Accounting and Administration of the SS, called for the ghetto to be transformed into a concentration camp, which would then be relocated in the Lublin district.[2]

Többens addresses his workers, Brandt makes his rounds of the shops; others, too, urge, agitate, explain—to the point of entreating.

Többens opens a public discussion; he puts up posters listing his arguments, appeals, and threats. He speaks openly about everything: about the bunkers and hideouts, and how in the long run they'll either be discovered or else the people hiding will die of starvation and thirst; about the Jewish Fighting Organization, whose insane and senseless ideas lead nowhere but to certain death; and about how impossible it is to hide on the Aryan side— he cites as proof the fact that even wealthy Jews have been asking him to take them to Poniatów. Többens assures the Jews that they'll be well off in Trawniki and Poniatów, invoking the testimony of his Jewish manager Lipszyc as proof that life in Poniatów is much better than in the ghetto.

The Jews do not believe him and resolve not to leave. Moving dates are announced for specific workshops, and a handful of people report; the transport does not take place. Hallmann's shop is to be moved in March, but out of several hundred workers only three show up. Even so, some people succumb to the propaganda, the despair, and the helplessness and decide to go. The first and second transports leave, the considerate treatment arousing understandable suspicion. Then the news goes around that the last transport was unloaded outside Warsaw and gunned down with machine guns.

As Többens goes on agitating, the propaganda continues. Posters, speeches, arguments—the language is astounding. The Jews aren't accustomed to this new tone and the open talk of bunkers, of the Fighting Organization, of hiding on the Aryan side. Every possible argument is cited as proof that this really is a resettlement, not a deportation and not Treblinka. They are going all out to *persuade* the Jews, to win the Jews over. What's happened? Why are they doing this? Why the sudden consideration, the change of tone, the shift in attitude? After all, if they wanted they could just raise the curtain on the third and last act of the well-directed play entitled Deportation. So why this? Whatever the reasons, the idea of resistance is growing; people aren't going to let themselves be snared by words anymore. The Fighting Organization is on every-body's lips; people talk about it and think about it. By mentioning it in his polemic, Többens actually wins more adherents to the com-batants' cause than weeks of their own propaganda.

March and the first days of April pass in this way. Then the atmosphere again grows tense; people can sense the final decisive moment approaching. The general population doesn't know the details, they aren't party to the secret plans, but they do know that this time there will be resistance; the Jews won't simply walk off to the slaughter. They know everyone will perish, but the awareness that they'll die fighting gives them strength. A new spirit, new thoughts, animate the Jews.

In the second week of April the decision is made to finish off the ghetto. Where was it decided? Evidently in Berlin.* German shop owners later maintain that the decision came as a surprise not only to them but to everyone in the know in Warsaw.

On 8 April the Ostbahn starts moving its workers and billet-ing them on the worksite—one more proof that the showdown is at hand. A few last attempts are made to pressure people, and the Jewish Council is given an ultimatum: voluntary departure or liq-uidation. A meeting of the Jewish Council with representatives of the Jewish National Committee does not produce the intended results.† The Jewish Fighting Organization categorically rejects any program of cooperation.

---

*On 16 February 1943, Himmler issued orders to Friedrich Wilhelm Krüger, high com-mander of the SS and police in the Generalgouvernement, that the Warsaw Ghetto be completely destroyed after all articles of value had been removed.[3]

†The Jewish National Committee was an alliance formed after the deportations of July–September 1942, with members from various underground youth organizations except the Bund.[4]

On Saturday, 17 April, sentries are posted outside the ghetto.* Sunday night, units of German police enter the ghetto from Nalewki Street. Meeting with fire, they retreat. On Monday the siege begins. A new ultimatum: unconditional surrender, complete submission to German mercy. The ultimatum is categorically rejected. The Jews are not going to go to the trains. Their answer is *war*.

A significant number of shop workers don't see any way out. They have no weapons. Are they to fight with their bare hands? They have no choice; they give in. They go to Umschlagplatz and on to Trawniki and Poniatów, where they won't last more than six months. The rest decide to fight until the last Jew has the last shell in his pocket.

It will fall to others to describe the battle, to portray the fighters who resisted to their last breath: the children with rifles, the old men and young women with petrol bombs hurling themselves at the tanks, the mothers with their infants rushing into burning buildings to avoid capture. Others will tell about a dozen men charging an entire company, about the night raiders disguised as German soldiers, about the victories and defeats. And finally they will recount how one building after the next was bombed from the air and set alight, one point of resistance after another. They will praise the struggle and those who fought, their deeds and their exceptional heroism.

"Exceptional heroism?" It's true. Throughout history there have been acts of heroism that brought fame to the fighters— magnificent battles, charges, and defenses: Samosierra, Kircholm, Cecora, and Zbaraż.† But these were the exploits of soldiers. History knows strongholds that held out to the last man, cities that

---

*On Sunday, 18 April 1943, at 6 P.M. the German authorities ordered extra units of the PP to patrol outside the ghetto; at 2 P.M. the next day the ghetto was surrounded by heavy patrols of gendarmes as well as Latvian and Ukrainian auxiliaries.
†Famous Polish military achievements.[5]—PB

refused to surrender despite the heaviest of sieges. There was Jasna Góra, Saragossa, Warsaw in September 1939. But this was different. Think about it: A mere handful of people resolve to defend themselves. They have no weapons, no way of building bulwarks or barricades. They cannot obtain ammunition; every pistol must be smuggled in at enormous effort.

The fighters have chosen to die, to fall one after the other. That's their decision. But what about the others? Their wives will fight with them, shoulder to shoulder. But what about their mothers and fathers? What of their children? Shall they be left to their fate, which now no longer means the gas chambers but being burned alive? Abandon them to the flames? Inconceivable! What then? Kill them ourselves? Hardly—the few bullets left are too valuable, they can't be wasted; each one is marked for a German. What about gas? It's been cut off. There's cyanide—but how to find enough? And when to use it?

So don't be surprised when people compare this to other great historical examples and speak of "exemplary heroism." The decisions these people had to make, and the battle they fought, were by no means easy.

Warsaw, 19 April 1944: the first anniversary.

BER WARM. Just before the operation began, rifles and lighter weapons could be heard during the night, as the sentries fired warning salvos. On Tuesday afternoon, 20 April 1943, SS Obersturmführer Konrad* ordered all Werterfassung workers to assemble at 4 P.M. They were to proceed to the Jewish Council to obtain new registration numbers. Konrad's order applied to everyone regardless of age, including the elderly and even the workers' children. He claimed he had been granted a quota of 5,000, which was more than enough, so no one was in danger, no one would be

*Franz Konrad was sentenced to death by a Polish court in 1951.—PB

sent to Umschlagplatz. He also said that the warehouse buildings on Niska Street[6] would be searched at the same time, and anyone found there would be shot. But by now the Jews had learned not to believe anything they were told, so only 1,500 out of the 4,500 Werterfassungstelle employees, including about 15 children, actually assembled. The rest hid in shelters. The groups that did report marched off to the Jewish Council under supervision of their German bosses, with Obersturmführer Konrad riding in his car at the head of the entire procession.

On Konrad's orders, I remained at Niska Street along with nineteen other SP men to guard the building from being robbed by members of the Polish police stationed nearby. Meanwhile, the German search detachment arrived, consisting of one SS man (from the SD), six gendarmes, twelve Ukrainians, and three men from the SP. Their leader, a lieutenant of the gendarmes, assigned four men to each building and ordered a meticulous search, adding, *"Und wenn Ihr jemanden findet, wisst Ihr was zu tun"*—And if you find anyone, you know what to do. At that point SS Untersturmführer Scholtz from the Werterfassungstelle headquarters spoke up, saying that any workers found should be handed over to him. The lieutenant then corrected himself and ordered that anyone discovered should be brought out to the street, not shot.

At one point the lieutenant asked why there were SP men posted outside certain buildings, and when Scholtz explained we were guarding them against being robbed while the workers were away, he shouted, *"Wenn zu meinen Leuten in den Häusern geschossen wird, mach ich die alle kalt"*—If anyone starts shooting at my people inside the buildings, I'll wipe them all out. The detachments entered the buildings while we set about sizing up this unknown lieutenant.

Less than ten minutes later we had him inside the bathroom at 20 Niska Street, eating to his heart's content and sipping some liqueur. We gave him a bottle to stash in his pocket and a large

piece of ham, and he left satisfied. Soon he started shouting at his
people that they were taking too long inside and should come back
down. They hadn't found anyone. The lieutenant wanted to send
the men on to the remaining buildings, but Untersturmführer
Scholtz explained there was no point searching because all the
workers had gone to the assembly. The lieutenant ordered everyone to fall in and marched off. Meanwhile, Werterfassungstelle
workers began returning from the selection—everyone looked
happy; no one was missing. Leading the procession was the Jewish
manager, Gutgold, with his wife and their small daughter, a look
of triumph on his face.

People emerged from their bunkers, and everyone started
asking whether anyone had been discovered or taken away. The
answer to both questions was "No one is missing." We kissed one
another; our joy was unbounded. Overcome with emotion, even
the grocers began selling off food—albeit at gouged prices—but
that didn't last long. We told the people coming back what had
happened on Niska Street, and they told us what happened at the
Jewish Council.

Groups of workers had been lined up in the courtyard of
Zamenhof 19. Eventually Walter Caspar Többens showed up, as
commissioner in charge of factory shop resettlement. He and
Konrad greeted each other warmly and conferred for some time.
At one point Többens demanded 500 people. Konrad said he
couldn't possibly agree because he didn't have enough people as it
was. A fracas ensued and the two men started shouting at each
other. Többens said that if the Werterfassungstelle was short-
handed, he would provide Jews from his own shop. Konrad replied
that he didn't want new people; he preferred the old ones who
were already qualified. When the two men couldn't reach an
agreement, Konrad climbed in his car and drove off. Twenty minutes later he came back, said something to Többens, and ordered
his entire group to return to Niska Street. He had been to see the

SS Brigadeführer, the Police Commandant in charge of the Aktion, and had evidently won his duel with Többens, since the SS commandant had decided in his favor.*

And so on Tuesday, 20 April 1943, the residents of Niska Street went peacefully to bed in the belief that they had been saved.

After this, more and more Jews began showing up at Niska. Two wagonloads of people managed to leave the Oxaco shop on Szczęsliwa Street—the gendarme at the Niska checkpoint pocketed 10,000 zloty. For a fee, Germans stationed on Niska 20 would accompany individuals to bunkers inside the ghetto and provide an escort for those who wanted to move back to Niska; some managed to make it there on their own by crawling through openings in the buildings. The SS men assigned to the laundry at Nowolipie 18 escorted forty-five of their workers. An educated guess would be that the number of people on Niska Street immediately rose from 4,000 to 6,000.

At dusk on Wednesday, a forty-man SP detachment marched onto Niska. Several among them were no longer actual members; they were just wearing their caps for protection—a practice that had become widespread since the first deportation operation. The new chief Piżyc (who had taken over after Szeryński committed suicide) and his deputy, Kac, were leading the detachment. Piżyc ordered the group to report at 6:15 A.M. the next morning, reminding them that sanctions would be taken if anyone failed to appear. Then he gave the command to disperse.

Evidently the SP appearance on Niska came about in the following manner: On Monday morning, 19 April, SS Untersturmführer Brandt had ordered an emergency meeting of the entire SP in the courtyard of the Jewish Council. But since few people

---

*Presumably SS Brigadeführer Jürgen Stroop, newly arrived to command the Aktion. —PB

showed up voluntarily, their numbers were augmented by others caught attempting to move out of the police barracks onto Niska Street. Each German detachment was then given several SP men, whose job was to force their way into apartments ahead of the Germans. This went on for three days. At night the SP were taken to the Befehlstelle, where they received a modest meal and a place to sleep. On the Wednesday after the Aktion, Brandt—now acting on orders from the Brigadeführer—ordered Blescher to take a group of SS men and escort the entire SP detachment to Umschlagplatz. On the way, Piżyc asked Blescher to intervene on their behalf. When they reached their destination, Blescher ordered the commander at Umschlagplatz to keep the detachment separate and refrain from loading them onto the cars. This is exactly what happened, and two hours later Blescher came back with orders from Brandt to free the group and escort them to Niska—hence their sudden appearance there. At the same time, Blescher took down each policeman's name and ordered the entire group to report as usual the next day on pain of death.

It seems that the entire group actually did show up, with the exception of Józef Fels. Brewda, the lawyer in charge of the SP detail assigned to the Werterfassungstelle, delegated him to one of the work camps on Leszno, thereby enabling Fels to escape to the Aryan side.*

The SP assigned to the Werterfassungstelle normally escorted the carts hauling Jewish property taken from the empty apartments—such as furniture, pictures, and books—to the special depots created for that purpose. They also guarded these warehouses around the clock to prevent anything from being stolen—a service they continued to perform during the April Aktion. Each

*As the area of the ghetto was reduced, certain sites were designated as forced-labor camps.—PB

day they received assignments from either Konrad, some other SS man from the Werterfassungstelle, or a gendarme. If the depots were outside the ghetto boundaries, for example the warehouses at Leszno 13, 15, 18, and 24, the SP man had to be escorted to his post. (The depot in the Great Synagogue at Tłomackie 5 was guarded by the Polish police.) As the Aktion proceeded, these SP men generally did not return to the ghetto but stayed on the Aryan side although a few went back to be with their families. Some of them had good connections on the Aryan side and took advantage of being unguarded to sneak off, while others simply spent the night inside the work camp.

But on Thursday afternoon, Obersturmführer Konrad suddenly ordered that all people be brought back from these camps and that sentries no longer be assigned there. Clearly, Tuesday's decision in the courtyard of the Jewish Council was not final.

By Thursday evening, Niska was the only street in the ghetto that wasn't in flames: Every surrounding street was at least partially on fire, and the flames threatened to spread from Muranowska onto Niska. But Konrad alerted the fire brigade, which was able to contain the blaze and protect the Werterfassungstelle buildings, although the Germans would not allow them to put the fires out completely. Before the fire brigade arrived, however, people managed to extinguish the one at Niska 7; they also saved the buildings on the even-numbered side of the street by keeping the rooftops wet and removing wooden boxes from the balconies.

Throughout that Thursday, many groups of Jews were taken to Umschlagplatz. They weren't loaded down with packages, which indicated that they had escaped the burning buildings without saving anything.

On Friday morning, the news went around Niska that Konrad had ordered all Werterfassungstelle workers to assemble at 10 A.M., and proceed to Umschlagplatz for a selection. We were told to take our most essential items, since we were going to be quartered on Prosta Street for a few days instead of returning straight to Niska. Konrad once again urged us not to hide, since the Werter-fassungstelle had an allotment of 5,000 people, and all those currently employed were bound to receive new numbers.

This time nearly everyone complied, since Konrad had unlimited credit after winning his match on Tuesday. Only a few older workers moved into the bunkers, along with some new arrivals who still didn't have "Konradian" registration numbers. Everyone else—about 4,300 people—showed up at the roll call with bundles on their backs (including some who had paid the Jewish group leaders a large sum in exchange for a place on the rosters).

About an hour before the official assembly, eighty or so Jewish wagons drove onto Niska. There was no room for them to stand. However, shortly thereafter SS Untersturmführer Faters arrived, the supervisor of the Jewish cobbler and carpenter shops that operated under the aegis of the "SS und Polizeiführer in Distrikt Warschau." Faters had brought along several dozen Poles. He looked over the horses and wagons, picked out the best ones, removed the Jewish drivers, and ordered the Poles to drive the wagons to the Aryan side. Supposedly the wagons had been requisitioned for Faters's German estate, "Falenty."

At ten-thirty, Konrad ordered the group to head for Umschlagplatz, along with the remaining wagons. More than 4,000 Jews marched to Umschlagplatz of their own free will, full of hope that they'd be back a little later, armed with new numbers, new permits for living. Only one wagon went along with them; it was piled a whole story high with packages and suitcases belonging to the Werterfassungstelle's Jewish managers. The other wagons stood lined along the street, one driver for every wagon. The short distance from Niska to Umschlagplatz—barely 50 meters—was guarded by about ten SS men; several gendarmes were milling about the Dzika checkpoint just by the entrance to Umschlagplatz; a few SS men with bayonets affixed to their rifles were stationed at the entrance ramp. Over a dozen SS men were posted in the yard itself, four of them manning a light artillery battery on the roof of one of the buildings.

The yard of Umschlagplatz was empty; only the former elementary school was filled with people under separate guard. The groups of workers took their places on the large square (80 by 150 meters), and Konrad ordered the group leaders to give an exact count. That done, he made some calculations, assisted by his cohorts: Untersturmführers Kutscha, Scholtz, and Hagen and the Jews Gutgold, Fogiel, and Ring.

Two hours later a car drove up, and out stepped W. C. Többens and his chauffeur, who had a rifle on his shoulder. Többens greeted Konrad and the other SS men. The Jewish managers withdrew while the Germans conferred, and the word was passed from one group to the next: "Everything's fine." All had their eyes fixed on the small cluster of men who were deciding the fate of the several thousand assembled Jews. People tried to read their faces. I would have guessed they were talking about a successful business move or an interesting sports event, since they were laughing heartily and patting one another on the back.

At one point Többens and his chauffeur walked back to their car. They took out two signs, written in Polish, and attached them to posts. One said, WORKERS OF THE O. SCHILLING COMPANY REPORT HERE WITH DOCUMENTS,* while the other announced WORKERS OF THE B. HALLMANN COMPANY REPORT HERE WITH DOCU-MENTS.† Többens held one sign himself and gave the other to someone else, to hold a little distance away. As it happened, several weeks before the Aktion, workers at the above-mentioned

---

*O. Schilling's workshop was located on Nowolipie Street and employed approximately 500 workers.
†B. Hallmann's workshop was located on Nowolipki Street. Initially the firm employed approximately 200 workers; in August 1942 it had about 900.

woodworking firms had been slated for transferral to the Flugplatz camp at Lublin, but in order to avoid the forced deportation they had escaped to other shops or else hidden inside the ghetto. At that time only 35 out of B. Hallmann's 800 workers had reported voluntarily, and not a single one of the 500 working for O. Schilling.

STEFANIA STASZEWSKA.[8]

19 APRIL

It's already started inside the big ghetto. We can hear the sound of fighting. Here on Leszno Street things are still quiet. It's warm; the sky is clear, studded with stars. I'm standing in the courtyard, listening. The shooting intensifies, then grows quiet. When will it be our turn?

The authorities posted their decrees all over the streets early in the morning: The last transports for the Többens and Schultz factories (Leszno—Nowolipie—Nowolipki) will take place tomorrow at 7 A.M. Anyone who stays will be shot.

Outside the ghetto, army units are cordoning off the walls. Gendarmes have been called in to reinforce the sentries. We make our final preparations and set up our chain of contacts. Lots of running around. On the street I meet up with Bernard—he's in the bunker with Różka. We talk for a minute, then shake hands with heartfelt emotion. I ask myself whether we'll ever see each other again. Before evening I make the rounds of my friends. We say our farewells; they have decided to report for deportation.

Today no one will be able to get out. Suddenly the streets are empty but for the sound of the gendarmes' boots beating the cobblestones. I turn around. They're marching straight toward us, and the way back has been cut off. The Germans are rounding up everyone waiting to pass through the checkpoint, including me. They aren't letting any of the off-site workers through. I'm furious at myself for not making it back to my people in time.

The Germans shout, "You're trying to escape! We'll take care of you bandits right this minute." They line us up—thirty to forty people—in ranks of four. They lead us outside the ghetto and herd us down Żelazna Street to the Befehlstelle. That's bad. We know what they do to people there. I'm too mad at myself for getting caught to be afraid. How could I be so stupid? One boy tries to escape and takes a series of bullets in the stomach. He runs a few more meters, curling up like a cat. He's writhing with pain; the Germans order us to carry him by his arms and legs to the Befehlstelle. We wait next to the wall for the end, men on one side, women on the other. The wounded boy is howling with pain; his brother asks the Germans to put him out of his misery but they just laugh. "You'll all look like that in a minute."

The day is hot, the sunlight stings our eyes. I stare at the walls and listen. I can make out shots from around Nowolipie. There are only a few dozen meters between me and the wall, but they are insurmountable. Some armored cars drive up. The Germans unload ammunition, set up their heavy guns, ready themselves for the siege. All these tanks and cannons, their whole army armed to the teeth—all mobilized against our pistols, grenades, and fire bombs.

I know our side won't give up easily; our people are ready to fight to the last, their only thought is to fell as many Germans as possible, to do their little part in the struggle for freedom, for human dignity.

I'm standing on Żelazna waiting to be executed, completely numb, surrounded by barking Germans. Some are yelling to shoot us right away; others want to take us to the transport. I hear the words *Lager Poniatów*. And all of a sudden we're marching in double step along the walls, down the Aryan side of Leszno and Karmelicka. I see the Poles' horrified faces; the Germans chase them away.

We pass through the space between the ghettos and finally we're in the big ghetto, which is full of army troops, gendarmes, shooting, and, in some places, fires. Near Niska Street we see a burned-out German tank. Hurrah! It's worth being alive just to see that. The Germans are cowering, they're creeping along the walls; they're afraid, afraid of the "Jewish bandits." Angrily they prod us on with their rifle butts, shouting *"Schnell, schnell!"* We're already at Umschlagplatz. The freight cars are packed, they load us on. We stand, jammed together, and listen. The sound of the fighting grows louder and louder.

Later, during the night, as the train carries us into the unknown, we see a light above Warsaw, a great bloody glow. The ghetto is fighting; the ghetto is burning. Does the world see that glow?

SAMUEL ZYLBERSZTEJN. Finally the Nazis decided Warsaw must be *Judenrein;* all Jews had to leave. They devised a perfidiously clever tactic of murder, securing the help of the shop owners. The slave dealer Schultz went from house to house delivering his pre-planned "sermons." "My workers! Come out to the country with me and we'll work there. I will take care of you. From now on you will no longer be considered Jews but workers in a German armament plant. Stick with me and you'll survive the war."

His colleague Többens gave a solemn speech at 72 Leszno Street: "Workers! I swear by the life of my child, who is very dear to me, that if you go with me to Poniatów you will not be going to your deaths. You will be leaving to work there and to live. I want it inscribed in your history that my Jews survived this terrible war by staying with me." His partner—who happened to be his brother-in-law—picked up where his accomplice in murder left off. "We have also set up a nursery school for your children who have survived and hired teachers to look after them." He further promised to organize an orchestra.

Next they took Jewish envoys to Poniatów and Trawniki to verify the Nazi promises. The Nazis were overjoyed when the envoys came back and made speeches in the workshops, pitching their propaganda to the more naive and simpleminded among the slaves: "Let us leave, let us leave to live and to work." But all these agitators who called on people to leave for Poniatów had long before secured a hiding place on the Polish side, where their families were waiting for them. Every one of them knew when he had to disappear. *Jews, let us leave*—indeed!

At tremendous risk, Jewish resistance groups tore down the SS posters calling on Jews to leave and distributed flyers to the shop workers: "To those of our brothers still alive! We warn you, do not deliver yourselves into the hands of the murderers! Do not offer yourselves voluntarily to the Nazis. Do not believe the slave-trader accomplices of the SS." A genuine debate commenced on the walls between the SS appeals and the Jewish flyers.

Meanwhile the roundup was beginning in the Többens factories on Leszno Street and inside the little ghetto. At that point the majority of workers were still being sent to Poniatów instead of to Treblinka. The murderers weighed their options: "How long will we have to deal with the Jews before they're all deported? There's still plenty of time. They're caught in a net and will fall into our hands sooner or later. First we should delude as many as we can, then move in and sweep up any trash left behind."

Until then Jews had been prohibited, under pain of death, from sending letters outside or receiving them, but now the Nazis Steinmann and Bauch brought letters—unstamped, at that—from Poniatów into the Warsaw Ghetto. The people from Poniatów wrote that they were in paradise. Unfortunately, this convinced most of the Jews still alive to leave for Poniatów and Trawniki. And so every few days a new group was sent to be "taken care of." They were given special permission to take their belongings with them, and packed up the little they had. Others would say to themselves, "Those people are leaving in order to live," and join the transport.

My comrades and I, on the other hand, decided not to leave under any circumstances. We preferred to die fighting in the ghetto,

armed with a few revolvers, than fall victim to Nazi sadism in Poniatów. Since we felt the decisive day was drawing close, we began to
prepare for armed resistance. First I made my way to the brushmakers' shop on Świętojerska Street to say farewell to my family and
friends. I wanted to see my sister's wonderful little boy, five-year-
old Mietek, one last time. On 7 September, his father had saved
him by hiding him in a sack and carrying him out of a group
already selected for deportation. My heart ached as I looked at him,
a child who at the age of five was as mature as a thirty-year-old
man. "What can I do with my papa?" he asked me. "He thinks we
should both go to Poniatów. But they'll just shoot us there. They
promised Mama work there too. And she rode right off to the gas,
my beautiful dear mama. Why was I even born!" I hugged and
caressed the little boy and said to him, "You'll see, it'll all end well."
The child started crying, "No, no!" When I kissed him for the last
time, his eyes were flooded with tears. I closed the door behind me.

The next morning I went to work. An hour after I arrived,
the factory was blocked off by a detachment of SS. The work that
day turned out to be a little different. Instead of overseeing production, they compiled lists of people who could stay and those
who had to leave. They announced the order of transport for all
the workers on the second floor; I'm safe for the moment. So I
decided to save my comrades who were already lined up in the factory courtyard. I quickly threw on a Werkschutz uniform and ran
to the comrades at 76 Leszno Street. There I managed to obtain
four additional uniforms for men from the Schultz factory. Unfortunately, I couldn't get hold of any more.

The definitive order came on 19 April 1943. In every shop,
the Werkschutz men were told to order all workers to report—
with baggage—at 72 Leszno Street by 9 A.M. for the final transport. Whoever failed to appear on time would be shot. A few
prominent figures and shop managers were allowed to stay behind
for several days to dismantle the factories. The news spread like

lightning. The next day everyone ran with their bundles to Leszno Street. They arrived punctually at nine o'clock. God forbid they should be late.

Our group consisted of seventeen men; we had seven revolvers and four grenades. We stationed ourselves in three separate hiding places. All was quiet once everyone had left. Just before sunrise, Czarny had come to deliver the news: "Get ready, comrades! This is where it's going to start—here, in our building, with us! It's going to start with us! Rufinow is still inside the factory; he has a permit from the SS." I ran up to the attic where I could watch. I had to be there, I had to witness the Jewish fighters avenging their nation, avenging the blood that had been shed.

I wait at my post anxiously, but not for long. I cock my ears and hear the heavy tread of the uniformed killers. A detachment of murderers is marching down Żelazna toward Leszno, into the ghetto: one two, one-two, more blood, more blood. But then comes the most beautiful moment in my life. A tremendous explosion rends the air. *Crash!* They're falling to the ground. Again, *crash!* All of a sudden the Ukrainians are rolling in puddles of blood. Blood for blood! The murderers disperse in a wild panic, seeking shelter in the entranceways. Shots and flames, on the right and on the left, start spewing from buildings on both sides of the street, Aryan as well as Jewish. Bullets go whizzing over my head. I have to retreat. I race through the secret attic corridor that runs from house to house down the entire length of the street, an emergency lane for saving Jewish lives. I want to make it back to the shelter, but the stairs seem to snake on a long way ahead of me. More bullets whiz by. I feel hot, my leg is bleeding, I have been wounded.

At last I make it to the darkness of a bunker, then cross to the Aryan side of Leszno, where I manage to stay for several days. I telephone my comrade at the brush factory to learn what's going on there. He yells into the telephone, "It's horrible!"

They're fighting in the ghetto; our boys are fighting like heroes. The area around Muranowski Square has become a fortress that the Waffen SS can't take. And two flags are flying over the building at number 19, one blue and white, the other white and red.*

"I can't go on any longer. Our building's on fire. My apartment's going up in flames. There are SS men outside with their rifles trained on the exits, shooting the Jews as they run from the building. I can't go on!" he shouts. His voice is filled with horror. "The door's caught fire. I'm going to stay here in the flames. Take care, farewell."

I took one more look outside. There, next to the building at 76 Leszno, the bodies of my murdered comrades were lying in their blood. Over the city I saw a sea of fire. The Jewish ghetto was burning, and with it the heroes of my nation. I felt as if my blood were flowing straight into that fire. O twentieth century! Behold your disgrace.

LEON NAJBERG. The commander of the courtyard at Świętojerska 38 was Sławek Mirski, the engineer. When I asked to be assigned to a fighting group, he said there were no weapons and explained that unless I was armed no one would take me. But he promised to send me to the appropriate group in a few days, when it was time to relieve the fighters at their stations.

That day the Jewish managers of the brush factory had met with the German director Laus, who demanded that all resident workers be evacuated to Trawniki and Poniatów. The brushmakers passed the word along that everyone should be directed to the shelters. Sławek Mirski sent me to the so-called general shelter,

---

*This appearance of the Zionist and Polish flags was immediately reported in the Polish underground press.[9]

which had been prepared for the poorer people living at Święto-jerska 38.

On my way to the shelter (in the same courtyard as my building), I saw a few young people milling about, carrying arms. Aside from them the whole courtyard seemed completely dead. Beyond the walls we could hear the heavy tramping of the German patrols. Machine-gun fire from the Krasiński Garden frequently hit the front windows of the apartments, and grenades kept landing in the courtyard.

I entered the shelter at two on Tuesday, 20 April. Mirski summoned everyone there to the largest storage vault in the basement, where he spoke frankly and powerfully. He said that each Jewish shelter would now have to become a fortress, that we would no longer allow children to be separated from their mothers and husbands from their wives. He told us to be ready to spend days, weeks, or possibly even months together in the shelter; it could become our common grave. But whatever might befall us, he said, we must no longer be passive. At the end of his speech he declared, "The July Aktion cannot be repeated." Mirski took his leave amid much wailing and weeping from the women. (It seems that Mirski belonged to the PPR; Edelman knew him well.*) On his way out he camouflaged the trapdoor that led to the shelter, as well as the corridor inside the basement. He shoved a machine over the trapdoor and sprinkled feather down all around the entrance.

Our shelter consisted of five basement vaults, located on either side of a central corridor. The corridor had been walled off where the shelter began: The new wall looked exactly like the others. The actual entrance was masked by a so-called "rolling cart," a section of wall made of reinforced concrete and faced with brick. The section stood on small wheels that rested on a two-

---

*Marek Edelman, a Bundist leader of the ŻOB, currently lives in Warsaw.—PB meter track. Once everyone was inside the shelter, the cart was rolled into the opening (70 centimeters long by 80 centimeters tall) located just above floor level, effectively masking the entrance. From the inside, the cart was latched with heavy bars. The basement windows were covered on the outside with piles of trash—large pieces had purposely been left in the courtyard.

One vault was designated as storage for provisions; unfortunately, it was glaringly empty. A second vault was lined with cots on three of the four walls—these belonged to the lucky ones who had first moved into the shelter; they stored their possessions beneath the cots. The third vault had running water, electric light, gas, and a special stove with a large built-in kettle. Here too the room was lined with cots. The fourth vault served as an isolation area for the sick and aged. The fifth contained a well, six meters deep, as well as a partitioned toilet. All the walls were lined with cots.

On 20 April, the shelter that had been built for 60 people contained 120. At first it was difficult to figure out who had taken refuge here. Later I learned that the majority were people who couldn't afford a space in smaller multifamily shelters, as well as some who happened to be on the factory grounds that day. All the other Jews who had been living on the grounds were hiding in whatever places they had arranged.

This situation grew even worse the next morning, on 21 April. The children (there were between ten and twenty) were crying terribly; the mothers were afraid the Germans would hear them and tried to muffle the sound with pillows. But that didn't work, since the women beneath the pillows began to faint for lack of air. Then during the afternoon the light suddenly went out, and the anxiety began to build. The women started screaming: "Open up, we want to leave, we don't want to suffocate with our children." The young people used crowbars to make some holes in the flue, to let in some air. But then flames began flaring in through the open hole. The vent was again closed up and filled in with clay.

The women began to faint, and the children started crying. At first the young people went around the shelter with water, trying to save people, but then decided to leave, myself among them. To our great despair, though, after we rolled away the cart we found we couldn't open the trapdoor. We set about knocking a hole in the wall that separated the shelter from the rest of the basement. The job was backbreaking—the wall was eighteen inches thick—and the men kept fainting. We worked in complete darkness because the electricity had gone out and the candles refused to light.

After nearly an hour and a half we managed to open a hole. First to crawl out was young Szyja Szyjer, who shouted to us not to follow him, since the stairwell on that side—which led to another courtyard belonging to Świętojerska 38—was on fire, and he couldn't make his way out through the soot, smoke, fire, and rubble. Clouds of smoke and soot burst inside the shelter, causing nearly everyone to lose consciousness. The few who remained conscious went around pouring water on those who had blacked out.

We plugged up the opening with bedding and began digging beneath the foundations to create a direct escape to the courtyard. But that didn't work either. The adjacent basements were full of soot. After several more hours of work, when the situation seemed hopeless, we decided to force open the trapdoor behind the cart. Using the little strength they had left, several men succeeded in prying it open, only to find dense smoke there as well, and the stairwell on fire. There was not a moment to lose if we were to escape. The order was given to wet our clothes and wrap wet rags around our hands and faces before pushing through. Otherwise we were likely to die in the raging fire, which was bound to reach our shelter. A few lost their heads and ran out barefoot. Some women didn't manage to cover their hair, which burst into flames the minute they stepped into the corridor that led to the shelter. It was only because the young people kept their presence of mind that we were able to drag everyone through the burning corridor into the courtyard . . . but there, too, all the buildings were on fire. Instinctively we made a run for the entrance to Świętojerska 38, which opened onto the street toward the small wall that separated the brushmakers from the Polish district.* We were greeted by salvos of shots from behind the walls, as well as grenades thrown by the Ukrainians, who were milling about just inside the wall: A few people were wounded. We ran to the courtyard of Świętojerska 38. From there we traveled underground through holes that had been made in the basement walls. We reached Świętojerska 36 (the front of the building had been blown up in the 1939 bombing), where we intended to hide. But well-aimed fire from the Krasiński Garden forced us to leave that place as well. We ran to the basements in the left annex and hid in rooms that were flooded with water from broken pipes. There we found people from Mietek Rozenberg's shelter—used by the top people in the brush factory—who had survived the fire. The shelter had burned completely, and the eighteen-meter tunnel leading to the Krasiński Garden couldn't be used because of the machine-gun battery stationed at the tunnel exit. We also ran into a group of fighters from the Chamer group.† People stood in the water as the heat came beating down from the ceilings of the basement vault; the annex (where we had hidden) was still smoldering, all around us a sea of flames, thick clouds of smoke. I had the impression of being inside a red-hot bread oven. The din of the buildings on fire mixed with the cries of the wounded and the wailing of the women.

We hadn't been in the basement very long when the Ukrainians marched into the courtyard, accompanied by German gendarmes. The Chamer fighters received them with a hail of bullets. The Germans threw a few grenades and retreated. More clouds of

*Presumably areas in the former ghetto that had been cleared and reassigned to Poles. —PB

†An armed group not affiliated with the ŻOB, evidently named after its leader.

smoke settled in our basement. A grenade fell close to the Braun family from Mietek's shelter (Braun had owned the Olza plywood factory before the war). Braun's wife later told us that she saw a flash of fire before she and her daughter were deafened by the blast and covered with dust. Her husband, however—who had a heart condition—had an attack and died. A few days later at his wife's request we buried him in the basement.

After the German attack, many people withdrew through the basements to Wałowa 4; we went with them. As it later turned out, that was where Szymon Melon's unit was fighting. At Wałowa 2a a group of carriage drivers was fighting off the Ukrainians trying to take their courtyard. More than one person in the basement suffered an attack of hysteria at the sight of the raging fire, now certain they would either be burned alive or crushed beneath the falling buildings.

Several times people tried to make it to the wall. Some escaped death in the flames only to be shot down by heavy German gunfire or blown up by grenades. The people in the basement transformed before our eyes. Some were dazed, others wide-eyed. The women gripped their children tightly and tore at their hair; the men paced, waiting for night to fall, completely at a loss. In the evening Szymek Kac (from the brushworkers), Heniek Zemsz from the Chamer group, and Fugman from the brush factory's metal mill showed up. Some of the Chamer people and the carriage drivers helped the fire victims, assigning them to remaining shelters. From that moment the only fighting at the brush factory involved battling the raging fire.

I went back to Świętojerska 36 and this time made it to Szymek Kac's bunker in the basement at the front of the building. There I met Festinger, who told me that, along with a group of more than twenty people, he had tried to break through to no-man's-land after escaping from our burning shelter at Świętojerska 38. They were running in the direction of Wałowa Street when a strong German guard force drove them back, wounding several and killing some. The rest of the group sought shelter at Wałowa 2, but the Ukrainians followed them into the courtyard and began throwing grenades down the stairwells and vaults where people were hiding. A few of the group were armed and took positions behind the breaches in the walls to fire on the Ukrainians, forcing them to retreat. The Ukrainians did not come back to that courtyard that day.

I also heard about a mine set by the ŻOB fighters at the entrance to the brushworks that went off and killed or wounded an SS detachment marching onto the factory grounds.*

The poet Władysław Szlengel† was also there and continued to compose verses to honor ghetto fighters. He described the heroism of the soldiers without arms, the Jews hiding in the shelters. But in fact none of us could shake off our despair after the whole area of the brush factory had been burned down. We couldn't imagine the Germans could be so bestial as to set fire to a whole district in the heart of Warsaw and burn the residents alive. The reality was too terrible to be believed. When the children heard that the houses were burning, they naively asked their parents, "Where are we going to live now?" The children thought that the shelters were places to hide in during the day, while the Germans might come to take away their parents, but they were used to going back to their homes to sleep at night.

Many people in the shelter had Aryan documents. Some even had apartments waiting for them in the Polish district. Szymek Kac had an apartment ready in Otwock, outside Warsaw: His brother had signed the *Volksliste*‡ and had a job as a railway worker at the Ostbahn. All these people made desperate attempts to get in touch with

---

*Twenty-two Nazis evidently perished in the explosion.[10]
†Szlengel (1914–1944) was a well-known cabaret artist and poet.—PB
‡A list confirming the German ethnicity of Polish Volksdeutsche.—PB

the Polish district, to contact someone from outside who would come and save them (they had money and jewelry). But all communication with the Polish district had been cut off since the beginning of the uprising. The shelter was equipped with a secret cable and a phone line that could connect to the Polish district, but no one wanted to try it; they were afraid it might give the shelter away.

So they tried to reach the Polish district by digging another tunnel through to the Krasiński Garden (18 meters). People thought they would be able to dig through to the other side using weapons stored in the bunker. But once again, fate was unkind. The earth was very crumbly, and there was nothing to use to prop up the walls. The makeshift supports kept caving in under the weight of the falling sand. It was also very difficult to haul the sand away and hide it. Whenever a newly propped section of tunnel collapsed, there was a large cave-in, and huge amounts of sand would cover the tunnel floor, all of which had to be removed.

The sand was taken out by a relay system, but this was tedious. There was not enough room to work, since every free bit of space was occupied by someone. Many people whose shelters had burned down were forced to stay in the tunnel itself. (We had approximately 160 people in a shelter built for 70 at most.) During the day the sand was dumped in the corners of the small shelter; at night it was hauled out to the ruins and deposited among the fallen bricks. Ultimately we reached a section where the sand just kept falling, and where each move of the spade set off huge cave-ins, and we were forced to break off our efforts. And so our last hope of being saved slipped through our fingers.

The bunker was also equipped with a radio, which unfortunately had no encouraging messages for us. We had over 4,000 kilos of provisions: flour, beans, sugar, lard, macaroni, hardtack, and many other things. These were packed in special tin containers, hermetically sealed for lengthy storage. Fans had been installed, so the air in this shelter was better. When all chances of making it to the Polish district proved futile, the rightful owners of the shelter decided to relocate all the fire victims they had taken in. It turned out that the shelter for poor people on Świętojerska 36 (where I had been) had burned down.

On 27 April we decided that from then on each day one of the young men would venture out to the ruins to keep a watch on the surrounding area and observe how the Germans were proceeding. When the first lookout returned in the evening, he reported that nothing of note had happened, except he had been troubled by an older woman standing in one of the outbuildings, her dazed eyes fixed on the stairwell. At sunset she moved to the middle of the courtyard where a handcart was standing, in which she lay down to sleep. She was cursing and calling out some names.

At the time people in the shelters were extremely paranoid: They considered every unknown Jew a potential informer in the service of the Germans, or at best an "uncertain." Similar suspicions fell on the old woman lying in the handcart, and it was decided to bring her into the shelter. But the woman resisted, putting up a desperate defense: She refused to budge. Dr. Krukowski said she had suffered a nervous breakdown and lost her mind. Some people in the shelter recognized her from the names she kept repeating; they explained that these were her two children, who had been burned alive in the hiding place they had built in their own second-story apartment. On the day of the fire, the mother had been unable to make it inside the shelter. For several days the woman stood in the outbuilding, resting by night in the handcart. Until one night—the night of 1 May—we went outside to discover the woman's remains in the courtyard, a coagulated puddle of blood beside the corpse, clear proof that the Germans had been on the prowl in the courtyard that day.

On 28 April, Pierocki told us that the Germans had just uncovered little Leonek's shelter at Wałowa 2a, where Pierocki had been staying along with several dozen other people. The shelter was a makeshift construction with only one exit; some children crying had evidently given it away. There had been three pistols inside the shelter, but the inhabitants wouldn't allow them to be used; they were afraid of being shot on the spot. They still deluded themselves into thinking that Umschlagplatz and the camps near Lublin would extend their lives and bring them closer to liberation. Having heard the crying, the Germans set about trying to locate the actual shelter by drilling a hole through the basement wall. They hit one of the vaults that formed the shelter; a blast of hot air told them people were inside. When they shouted *"Alle Juden heraus,"* no one appeared. Then the Germans used dynamite to blow up the entire storage area, and with the help of Ukrainian flunkies chased everyone out through the opening. Pierocki crawled under some cots and covered himself with sand. The Ukrainians quickly hounded the others out and left. The people were searched and sent to Umschlagplatz. That evening Pierocki came to us. He suggested we go to his shelter to take the provisions the Germans hadn't touched. That was our first looting expedition, and it improved our stocks. But after that our rules about keeping quiet were even more strictly enforced.

At night, the sky is filled with the glow of fires from no-man's-land. Some in our shelter say the fires were lit by Poles trying to come to our aid, that it's only a matter of hours before the walls that separate the ghetto from the Polish district are stormed. People have found faith; hope is brightening the faces of our cave dwellers. They hatch various plans, how to escape and where. Some have even suggested that people will drive up in cars to take us away. Others have it on good authority from acquaintances in the Polish district who have vowed that, after the uprising in the ghetto, the people would rise up there as well, so that together we will free ourselves from the German occupation. But these illusions, too, burst like soap bubbles. We've learned it's the Germans who are setting fires in no-man's-land—just like they have in the ghetto. The people in the shelters are once again overcome with despair, depression, and apathy. The enormous physical and moral exhaustion has taken its psychological toll. People forecast the worst possible horoscopes. At best, they say, after wrestling so long with death, we will succumb as tragically as the bakers did.

But the idea of escaping to the Polish district again becomes a possibility. A few people leave the shelter one at a time, in an attempt to make it through to the central ghetto, where their friends have shelters with tunnels leading to the Polish district. But the young people, along with Klojski and Heniek Zemsz, decide to open a manhole on Wałowa Street, enter the sewage canal, and scout it out. While keeping the strictest guard possible, we manage to reach the canal. Lacking a map of the sewage system, some of us tie ourselves together using long ropes, with the free end aboveground where others are waiting. In this way we wade through the sewer until we reach a segment that is completely walled off, and from which we can smell sewer gas. We can go no further. Despairing but resigned, we leave the sewer and resolve to try other canals the following day.

STANISŁAW SZNAPMAN. On 19 April 1943, German army units accompanied by SS gendarmes suddenly surrounded the ghetto and began bombarding it with cannon, machine guns, and incendiary bombs. For several days people in the city could hear the din of exploding buildings. Clouds of smoke rose above the ghetto, and at night the glow of fires lit the so-called battlefield. The "heroic conquest of the ghetto" lasted four weeks, with the Germans spreading rumors that the Polish population was carrying out a pogrom against the Jews. When it was all over, the deed was crowned by blowing up the magnificent synagogue at Tłomackie Street and the mortuary at the cemetery.

So ended the deportation that began on 22 July 1942, the premeditated and organized extermination of the Jews of Warsaw. Decrees had proclaimed that people who were not working were to be deported, while those capable of work were to be employed.

But gradually, under the guise of repeated "inspections," more and more working families were deported. Next they carried out systematic selections to reduce the number of workers in the factories. And even though they worked efficiently and productively, these people were removed regardless of the economic loss. During the most recent Aktion that began on 19 April they sent more than 12,000 people to the concentration camp at Majdanek, to be killed by hunger, gas, electricity, or a bullet, while about 10,000 were murdered on the "battlefield." Their dead bodies were doused with gasoline and burned in a pyre at the square on Gęsia Street. Brandt and Witossek, the bloody leaders of that particular Aktion, watched as the execution was carried out. The beasts bared their teeth in satisfaction; their goal had been accomplished: Warsaw now was Judenrein.

The ghetto has been liquidated. The dynamited buildings lie in ruins. All that remains are their charred walls. For any Jews who may still be hiding underground, they have channeled gas into the basements, to poison people like rats. They go about the extermination with pedantic precision.

Is it possible that some have survived undergound? Will some save themselves and live to see the end? A handful of Jews is hiding with Polish families on the Aryan side. Life there is hard. With every knock, every ringing of the doorbell, their hearts freeze in fear as they crawl inside their hiding places. They tiptoe around the apartment, speak in whispers, and avoid the windows so as not to be noticed by the neighbors. Despite this many are found out, as there are always some obliging individuals ready to snitch.

LEON NAJBERG. Wednesday, 30 June 1943. At five in the morning our sentry observed a group of bandits marching down Gęsia Street accompanied by two Jewish stool pigeons from the Befehlstelle. Suddenly the whole horde stopped in front of the rubble at Gęsia 3. You could hear someone shouting in Yiddish, calling on the Jews to come out of the bunker, using the same old ploy: "Jews, come out, the war is over." But no one came out. The German bandits started to clear the rubble and drill holes in the ruins. They worked for four hours but did not give up, and by 10 A.M. they had drilled an opening. We heard a general commotion followed by shouts of "Juden-Bunko" that ran like lightning among all the participants in the operation. We all stood by the window that looked out to Gęsia 5; the whole block from 1 to 5 had been burned, so the area was completely empty. The wall of our building was broken off at that point and no longer connected to any other building. The bandits had spread out, blocking the other side of Gęsia (the wall ran down the middle of the street), and posted troops along Gęsia from Nalewki to Zamenhof. One gendarme was assigned to each of the courtyards: One of them took his position right beneath our window, so we had to reduce our observation post to two people. The bandit was wearing white overalls and carrying an automatic rifle; Festinger and I were so close to him we could smell his breath. We had to take care not to accidentally cough or sneeze, or even breathe too heavily, or else the whole shindig would soon be over; our hideout would be dis-covered and a firing squad would teach us what it meant to die. But our priceless field glasses proved enormously helpful; through them we could watch the smallest move the bandits made from the distance of our window, and our ears were so well trained we could hear the smallest sounds coming from the scene of the tragedy at Gęsia 3.

A minute later we heard some SS man order, *"Schmeiss ran das Gift"*—Start in with the poison. The results weren't long in com-ing. At ten the first skeletal figures began crawling out of the earth, coughing horribly, gasping, literally rattling, which meant some kind of gas was being used. The murderers themselves were merry; splitting their sides with fifteen-minute fits of laughter punctuated with cries of *"Jude, halt!"*

Twenty-five people emerged from the underground den: men, women, and children. The bandits surrounded them in a tight circle and lined them up in a double rank near the wall. When their furious merriment had subsided, and the Jews were able to breathe, one of the SS men approached the circle and spoke to the Jewish victims: *"Ihr alle Männer kommt zur Arbeit nach Poniatowa in ein Metallwerk von W. C. Többens."*—All you men are going to Poniatów to work in a metal shop belonging to W. C. Többens.

After this pleasant speech the bandits led everyone out of the bunker in groups of three. Most of them came out empty-handed or carrying a small bag or travel case. A few were dragging suitcases. Evidently the speech worked like a charm; these people had started giving in to thoughts such as Maybe it's true? They stood there spellbound like a herd of cattle, waiting to see what would happen next. But the herdsman had now gained control over his herd and, feeling in complete power, went swishing his whip wherever he wanted, while the herd danced around the powerful blows just as he commanded, still deluded into wondering, Maybe it's true? Maybe they're just trying to scare us? To see how much we can take? After all, there's no way the Germans are going to kill *me,* little Abramek, alive and well, thinks six-year-old Abramek, or Sura, or Jakub, up to the last minute.

The people pulled from the bunker are subjected to the tyranny of the bandits and their sadistic pranks and put through a huge range of physical and mental tortures; some go on believing everything they're told, that they'll be spared; they keep deluding themselves right up to the last minute, when the bullets rip apart their bodies and they start spewing blood and give up the ghost. Even at the place of execution, they watch the preparations being made and think, That's probably not for us, They can't possibly mean to kill *me,* Maybe we'll survive after all—until the first bullets hit their body and shock them into awareness: They're killing me because I am a Jew!

Again the victims were lined up, this time in one row. In German they were ordered to place all baggage in one pile and undress within five minutes. At first they took their clothes off slowly, but rifle butts and bayonets urged them to hurry. The men stood there in their long underwear, and the women in their slips, without realizing what an opportunity they were providing. One SS man moved in on one of the men and with one powerful kick ripped off his underwear; another (wearing gloves) grabbed him by his privates and pulled. When the man cried out to high heaven the SS man started croaking in laughter. The Jew fainted, most likely from the pain, but a few blows from a knout soon brought him back to consciousness, and he stood back up in the rank completely naked. Next they picked one of the women and tore off her slip, without sparing her any of their blows. And then they manhandled each person, one at a time, pounding them repeatedly between the eyes with their fists, or using their whips, or prodding them with bayonets, wounding and mutilating their faces, from which the blood was streaming. One young girl was ashamed to show her innocence in front of the barbarians. She was a schoolgirl raised in Warsaw, evidently unfamiliar with the new western morality brought by the Nazis straight from Berlin itself. When an SS man approached to tear off her underclothes, the girl reacted impulsively, desperately reaching for a brick. But before she could throw it at the sadist she was stopped by a series of shots from an automatic rifle. Afterward everyone stood there stark naked, with none of the proverbial fig leaves.

But that was only the sadistic introduction, prologue to a grand performance entitled "Prelude to a New Mass Murder," starring the brutal thugs, sadists, murderers, degenerates, and barbarians of the twentieth century and directed by Hitler himself. The bandits had obviously been through more than one training school and had acquired a thorough education in how to murder innocent naive people with perfidious sophistication. Four SS men (evidently the only ones allowed to conduct body searches) ordered all clothing to be placed three meters away, after which the victims were bodily searched.

At four, after the general search had been completed, they ordered the Jews to shake out their clothes, stand up (they had been sitting naked on the cobblestones, leaning against the ghetto wall), and get dressed, after which, they were told, they would march without their bags to Umschlagplatz, from where they would be sent to work at Poniatów. They were warned, "If anyone dares take one step out of line during the march, he will be killed like a dog!" The Germans said their luggage would be hauled to Umschlagplatz on carts. I forgot to mention that the victims were also interrogated about the "Juden-Bunko" but all gave evasive answers. At 4:30 P.M. one more group marched down the path of executions. In all, twenty-four Jews walked down their last road to the place of slaughter. One more link was added to the historic chain of the bestial collective murder of Israel. Then some civilians came wheeling handcarts, loaded the baggage, and left.

Half an hour later we heard some shots from the little garden on Zamenhof Street, several series in rapid succession that didn't stop for fifteen minutes. They were undoubtedly executing the twenty-four fresh victims. An hour later our nostrils caught wind of something burning—the bodies were already being converted into ashes. Only their pure immaculate souls flew away and hovered above us living Jews, their blood-caked lips frozen in a mute complaint: *Why?*

In our hideout, thirty-nine people finally let out the weeping they had been holding in so long: The walls of the hideout shook from the sobbing, a sea of tears flowed down faces that were covered with sweat from toil and tension, and our lips repeated after the souls of our brothers: *"Why?"* We concentrated all the power of our common suffering in that one word. We no longer paid any heed to the danger that threatened us, we all cried together, and the lament was so strong, so genuine, it would have moved the hardest heart of stone. And then the beautiful sun left the sky, unable to bear the sight of such bestiality, and nature, shaken to its depths, opened its eyelids and shed its own dewy tears on the sacred ground. Weeping and sobbing, we joined to say Kaddish for the souls of those who had been murdered.

This outpouring of long-pent-up bitterness was interrupted by the sound of crunching glass coming from the courtyard; someone was moving. The sentry alerted us that someone was approaching our stairwell. A stool pigeon! everyone thought at once. The bandits must have noticed us while we were watching from the window, must have sent someone over to look for a way in.

These suspicions sliced through our bleeding hearts like a blade. In a second we became all ears, alert tigers ready to strangle and defeat our prey before it could manage a squeak. The grating sound of locking and loading could be heard, and our boys' broken souls transformed into tough, strong, inflexible defenders. We stood at the window overlooking the courtyard of Nalewki 27 and secretly watched the man walking our way.

The man was moving about uncertainly; he looked extremely upset. His hair was standing on end; he was wearing only pants, a shirt, and shoes and was covered with blood. At every step he looked around; he went into the stairwell of the opposite house, either searching for the entrance to our hideout or else looking for a place to hide. Amid all the burned buildings and rubble he looked like the madman from the film *Year 2000* who by some miracle had survived an enormous historic cataclysm but had no hope of aid or shelter while the devastation was raging all around. He stood in the stairwell, looking resigned and tired of life, leaned against the charred wall, and sobbed heavily. His head was hanging down and he stayed there motionless.

What an actor, we thought; probably an informer. But one way or the other we had to capture him alive and bring him to the

basement. Festinger, Trynke, and Z. Asenheim decided to undertake this task; they crept down the stairs as quietly as cats and surprised the mysterious man from three sides. We could hear them
shout *"Stój"*—Stop! The mysterious man tried to get away, but
three pistol barrels showed him it was senseless. He stood up and
passively submitted to my comrades. Some special boards (like
masons' planks) were let down; the four people entered the hideout, and the planks were again stowed. Imagine our confusion
when that man threw himself onto Z. Grynbaum . . . and greeted
him with cries of joy! It turned out he was Grynbaum's brother-
in-law, pan Lipski, who at our request started telling his experiences from the beginning of the Aktion to the present. He had left
the Wehrmacht firm where he had been living on 30 April; during
the night he sneaked into the no-man's-land at Nalewki 27, where
his family had a bunker that had been prepared earlier. But that
bunker was discovered in the middle of May, so he and Grynbaum
escaped to Zamenhof 24, where Lipski stayed until dark. Then he
went out to look for the doctors' bunker at Gęsia 6, where he was
detained as a potential stool pigeon and placed under strict watch;
he was not allowed to set foot out of the bunker.

There he also experienced the end of that bunker. The place
had twenty-two basement storage vaults, which stretched beneath
the building at Gęsia 6 and continued underneath the demolished
buildings at Gęsia 1 and 3, the whole shelter connected by a little
tunnel that ran below the street. When the bandits discovered the
bunker at number 6, they blew it up without realizing there was a
second part. Thirty-one people survived. Some critical days passed
as people waited to see whether one of the people who had been
captured would give them away, and all the time hunger and thirst
were leaving their mark. There was no time to reflect on things or
complain. Evidently no one gave them away, so they had to get
busy again. The Klajnbajer brothers—two boys sixteen and eighteen years old who had been in school before the war—went out-

side. There's no sense in despairing, they said, we just have to grab some shovels and spades and work hard to make things livable. They enlisted the others, devised a plan, and built a special tunnel underneath the provisions stores, where they took out 1500 kilos of products. Working at night without rest, they also managed to dig a well for water six meters deep. And once they found food and water, they started to make the bunker secure. They made three exits by digging 80 meters of tunnel in three directions. One led to Gęsia 1, a second to Gęsia 3, and a third to Nalewki 27, to Grynbaum's former bunker. There were seventeen doctors, men and women, from the Czyste hospital in the bunker: No one was allowed to leave. Only the Klajnbajer brothers occasionally went out at night to fetch boards for shoring up the tunnel or to see whether the Aktion was still going on. But they knew from the hellish sound of shots coming from the ghetto that Jews were still being hunted. They lived inside the bunker quietly, calmly, doing their chores at night and working by the light of a kerosene lantern. During the day they rested or slept. The bunker was hot, there was not enough air, they sweated constantly and were being drained of their remaining strength. But they went on in the belief that they were destined to live out the war inside that bunker. Any discomfort was happily borne with the thought that, if they survived, life after the war would reward their toils. They abandoned two of the basement vaults and nested inside the remaining three, constructing little safety tunnels. They hauled away many cubic meters of earth—nearly six boxcars' worth. Everything they did was with the thought of surviving. But then came the tragic day of 30 June 1943. That day their stove was cooking until 5 A.M. It was connected to a narrow one-story chimney, which had remained intact when the building had been demolished. Fate had it that on that day the bandits started the Aktion earlier than usual and spotted the smoke coming out of Gęsia 3. Their sentry heard steps above them and German voices saying that since there was smoke coming out of the chimney it had to be a Juden-Bunko. The residents of the bunker were informed of this at 5 A.M.; they put out the fire and waited. When they heard the drilling over-head, they started to escape through the little tunnel that led to Gęsia 1. Imagine their disappointment—that is to say, their terror—when they saw a patrol of Germans nearby. So they went back inside the bunker and decided to see how things developed. Up to the moment when the gas started to reach them they were fully conscious, but then they started suffocating. They lost their self-control and clear-headedness and broke down, saying, "It's no use anyway" and crawled out of the bunker, coughing. Pan Lipski, however, had already lived through one bunker's being discovered; he did not lose his presence of mind but immediately wet some rags, used them to breathe through, and when everyone else left the bunker, he buried himself in rubble and waited. He heard the Germans taking people in and out, and searching the basement. Finally they set the place on fire, using all the bedding and cloth-ing, and poisoned the well. He started choking on the smoke that had no outlet. Fortunately the bandits didn't go back inside. Lipski stayed until he heard bandits marching away. Half an hour later he decided to leave the bunker. In two bounds he reached the nearest building. And since he knew of the opening in the wall between Gęsia 5 and Nalewki 27, he went through it and wound up on the lot where we were hiding. Lipski told us we might find a decent stash of food and clothing that had survived inside one of the little tunnels. As it was already ten in the evening, Heniek Zemsz and some others went over to the second doctors' bunker. When we went inside we saw that the place had not been burned down (that was his imagination), but pan Kłoński and pan Zemsz deter-mined the presence of phosgene gas, which meant we couldn't stay there.

We went to the little garden on Zamenhof to examine the bodies from the doctors' bunker, but all we found was a pile of human bones and ashes. The sobs from our broken hearts shattered the nighttime quiet, and our tears rained on the ashes of our brothers. I looked at Lipski. Far from rejoicing at his own salvation, he was walking in the makeshift cemetery and mourning the brave Jews, the doctors, the recently murdered victims. He was right: One does not enter a cemetery with laughter in one's soul or with joy at one's existence. One is only allowed to tread the historical sacred ground with sobs.

STEFAN ERNEST. The war's "third front" was finally broken after another few days' resistance, from Monday to Saturday (19–24 April). The cleanup action is still going on; anyone caught is sent to the Befehlstelle or to Umschlagplatz.

The final act of this tragedy is coming to a close, behind a curtain that was never raised, a thick cordon of army and police at a distance from the walls. According to the decree of 24 April, trespassing in the former Jewish district is punishable by shooting. The liquidation of the ghetto is to be kept shrouded in secrecy. Only the din, the smoke, and the fires attest that it's still not over.

There are stories going around about Jewish fighters wearing German uniforms and helmets, about a decisive battle at Muranów, about the Germans storming the hospital on Gęsia Street and massacring all inside, about the Polish flag flying from the Carmelite Church—exaggerated enemy losses numbering in the hundreds.

A thick cordon of police and army units are strictly guarding the secret of what has actually happened. But even now we know for a fact there are some who, armed only with a revolver or a grenade, or perhaps with nothing at all, managed to break through the columns of fire and smoke, through the walls, through the cordon of police and soldiers. And they will tell what happened. They will preserve the memory of the last days of the Warsaw Ghetto, when resistance atoned for previous submissiveness. They will testify to the heroism of those who fell and of those who are dying still—the last of the last—to salvage the honor, courage, and dignity of all who died earlier, without fighting, and of all who were saved earlier, also without fighting, on the other side of the wall.

They died in glory for those who yet survive, who are being hunted down like animals, who are hiding and waiting for the war to end or plodding along from day to day pretending to be Aryans. May these people remember what they owe to those who died, so that those fortunate enough to spend the war in Allied or neutral countries will know what happened. May they remember what they owe. And may they fight on.

They died for other nations, as a testimony of their own right to exist. They died for Poland, whose banner they raised in their last battle, in honor of a shared tragedy of enslavement and persecution and in the hope of a better coexistence in the future. They died to bridle the Nazi beast.

On 19 April, at five in the morning, the same beast commences the final liquidation. Because they're expecting resistance, the Germans are employing special equipment: tanks, light artillery, flamethrowers, howitzers, grenades, and machine guns—even reconnaissance planes.

The main points of defense are Muranowski Square and Muranowska Street itself, the hospital on Gęsia, and the brush-makers shop. The district is bombarded, the buildings burned or reduced to rubble. The organized resistance breaks, with smaller pockets remaining. The soldiers move in to ferret out those in hiding. With tried and true methods they finish off anyone they find. Supposedly the beast is avenging the loss of some hundred soldiers—as well as a tannery, burned down inside the ghetto, and a few other places producing for the German war effort. People talk about prisoners escaping from Pawiak.

To this day the former Jewish District is heavily cordoned off, and trespassing is still punishable by death. News comes by way of the firefighters or occasional escapees. The fact that SS men and Ukrainians continue to hunt them down proves beyond doubt that there are some Jews left hiding in the ghetto, fated to die of starvation.

KAROL ROTGEBER, FIFTY YEARS OLD WHEN THE WAR BROKE out, was working in Warsaw as a factory clerk. In the ghetto, he, his wife, and their ten-year-old son, Paweł, eventually found employment at the brushworks. In August 1942 he lost his son during a selection at Umschlagplatz; a few months later he and his wife escaped to the Aryan side and hid in the Praga suburb. When fighting broke out in the ghetto, Rotgeber—in despair at his own inability to help—wrote to the head of the Roman Catholic Church in Poland, in care of the Polish Red Cross. He signed the letter Lewap, his dead son's name spelled backwards.

Nothing further is known about Karol Rotgeber.

WARSAW, 29 APRIL 1943

To His Eminence, the Archbishop of the Polish Lands:*

I am turning to you, Reverend Father, despite the fact that I do not know you and have never seen you. I only know you represent the church of the nation of which I consider myself an eternal son. Though I am of the Mosaic faith, I am not unfamiliar with the teachings of the Lord Jesus, who suffered for millions to sow love among all mankind. Today the Son of God is looking down upon our sinful world, aggrieved by the sight of so much bloodshed, searching in vain for charity and compassion. Let us show Him that the spirit of mercy has not vanished

---

*Adam Sapieha (1867–1951) filled this office in the absence of Cardinal August Hlond.—PB

completely from the earth; let us cause the Lord of the world to rejoice. Today, amid the thunder of cannon, the rattle of machine guns, the rumble of tanks, and the exploding of bombs and grenades, a crime of unprecedented scope is being perpetrated: the mass murder of millions of innocent children, women, and old people. The evildoers show arrogant disregard of all conscience and compassion. The heavens run purple with innocent blood. The sobs of the murdered children make the earth tremble and shake the very foundations of heaven. O God, where art Thou? Where art Thou, Savior? Do you not see, do you not hear? Make yourself heard too, Servant of God! Summon your strength and, while there is time, save the few who are left—innocent, loyal citizens all. Do not tempt God's wrath by inaction, by failing even to attempt to save the lives of the innocent. The conscience of the world demands it! Do not give the mighty cause to mock you for neglecting to assist in the struggle against evil—even if only with moral support given in the name of love. Let no one succumb to fear. The whole civilized world is behind you, faith in divine power and justice. The ancient Christians, professing their faith in the Redeemer, feared neither fire nor ravenous beasts: In the name of God and the love of one's neighbor they forged ahead in their faith and conquered the entire world!

Thus I turn to you, Reverend Father—I, one of the gray masses whose soul is suffering beyond measure. All around is forsaken, there is no voice of comfort, no salvation for us unfortunate brothers of those who have been murdered, tortured, gassed by the latest scientific methods, cremated, and, according to rumor, converted into soap. And what about you, Reverend Father? Are we indeed surrounded by wilderness? Do you not hear their voices, their moans? Forgive me, Reverend Father, but did not the Savior charge you with raising a mighty voice to testify to these unheard-of, infamous crimes! What will the Savior say? The fiery writing is already inscribed in the firmament, the ominous memento—Mene, Tekel, Upharsin—and the crime will not escape the punishment it deserves.

But the dying women and children are calling for help; the cries of the murdered reach to the heavens and beg for revenge; the slain husbands appear before the Everlasting with the terrible accusation that they were deprived not only of life but of successors in the world! What happened to the teachings of Jesus Christ? Forgive me, Reverend Father, but how can you, a Servant of God, remain silent? You spend your days in peace and quiet. Do you not think it is time, Reverend Father, to speak out, to harbor and defend the survivors of our oppressed people, loyal citizens who have shed their blood for Poland now and in ages past? Who fought under the banner FOR YOUR FREEDOM AND OURS, sacrificing their blood, sending their sons into battle during the uprising in 1863 against the oppressor, as well as in many other instances.* Know, Reverend Father, that mine is not an isolated voice of protest. Even now my brothers are engaged in a fierce battle. They are struggling in silence, with utter disregard for death—a handful of unarmed men on foot against legions with tanks. Deprived of gas, electricity, water, and provisions, they are fighting a well-fed bloodthirsty enemy who is aided by criminals let out of prison, bandits, Ukrainians. Sadly and sternly they look across at you on the other side of the walls. They are not calling you; they are waiting to see whether your conscience will do so. Shall they be left to perish unaided? Poland, wake up before it's too late. Reach out a helping hand. You will not regret it; the Savior will pay you back one hundredfold. People will preserve their gratitude for you and never fail to speak in your defense. Reverend Father, as a Shepherd of the Lord, call upon the faithful to reach out to their fellow citizens so that they might survive, on this side of the walls or that. We are waiting. Poland is resounding with my words. My cry, and that of my people, will reach the foot of the Everlasting and will never fade. The mighty echoes shall ring across vast lands and encompass the entire globe. For the whole world will be witness to your deed!

---

*"For your freedom and ours" refers to the slogan of those fighting under Kościuszko; the January Uprising in 1863 was an insurrection against the Russian occupying power.—PB

Full of pain, with the greatest respect for you, Reverend Father, I bow my head in quiet and fervent prayer.

Karol Lewap

Polish Red Cross
To the General Secretary of the Polish Red Cross in Warsaw,
His Excellency Count Skarżyński:

As the Red Cross is our country's most humanitarian institution, I am entrusting to it this open letter to His Eminence, the Archbishop of the Polish Lands. After it has been read I kindly request it be forwarded to the addressee.

It is now also up to you, O noble institution, to tell the civilized world about the horrible, unprecedented mass crime being perpetrated against an innocent branch of your nation: the murder of millions of this country's sons, who for centuries have sealed their loyalty to this land with their blood—millions of innocent children, women, old people, and men in the prime of life, who were murdered in bestial fashion and amid terrible suffering at Treblinka. Those who are left are also awaiting annihilation, but now they recognize the enemy's perfidy and for ten days have been defending themselves resolutely, heroically, but also hopelessly.

Summon an international commission of the Red Cross for these martyrs and reveal to the world the horrible secrets taking place in the remote reaches of our country. All other crimes pale beside these; they freeze the blood and shake the conscience of the world.

Let no suspicion fall upon you, noble institution, that you are biased, that you are the tool of those in power, that you have forgotten your sacred obligations.

You may not ignore this mass murder committed in broad daylight and of a monstrosity never before seen, perpetrated against an innocent people; you are a witness to the bestial crime, the scope of which exceeds even the boldest fantasy, and you . . . say nothing?

Defend the innocent while there is still time! The dead will not rise from their graves. Sound the alarm! To action! To the rescue! God is with you!

Please accept, esteemed Count, my deepest deference and respect.

Karol Lewap

P.S. In the name of this holy cause I place my blood, my life, at your disposition. You may summon me, . . . and I will appear at once.

ARON CZECHOWICZ AND GURMAN. We planned our escape for the second night of the Easter holidays. We purposely chose that date because fewer Germans would be at Pawiak. Some would be gone on furlough, and those who stayed would be in holiday spirits abundantly boosted by alcohol. The Ukrainians would be the first to get drunk, and the guards patrolling the prison generally weren't sober at such times either. So we foresaw that that night would be the most suitable for our escape.

We prepared all the necessary accessories, as well as a sufficient amount of the sedative Luminal. We found a way to extinguish the searchlights. We were promised two revolvers and three hand grenades for self-defense during the escape. We obtained the key to the workshop and the money we needed for our escape. We secured a suitable shelter. In short all the preparations were successfully carried out. The only obstacle that remained was how to avoid being seen by the guards as we let ourselves down a rope from the third story. Aside from that there was the difficult journey through the ghetto in the darkness of night, the task of reaching the wall without running into any gendarmes, and the problem of finding any shelter at all on the Aryan side until 5 A.M.

It was just before the holidays, so we had a great deal of work. Our Polish comrades started receiving holiday parcels from home, and packages also began arriving from the prisoners aid society, which meant the holiday season was at its peak.

At that time two new Jewish prisoners arrived—one from Kraków and the other a Warsaw tailor from Świętojerska Street. I should mention that the last days seemed like an eternity to us. We couldn't wait for the decisive night, the moment that would decide whether we would live or die. The preparations had cost us a great deal of effort and nerves, and we were utterly worn out physically. We looked like shadows, since all our energy and attention had been focused in one direction. We spent the last evenings discussing the final details with two or three comrades from our group, trying not to attract anyone's attention.

On the day before the escape we divided the tasks among ourselves. There were ten men. That's right! Ten men who decided to escape from Pawiak. We set the time for our escape at 1:30 A.M. The ropes were already hidden in the workshop, and our "district attorney" was supposed to bring scissors from the bathhouse, where they were stored, since we weren't allowed to have scissors in the cells and they occasionally conducted inspections. We had to pray that the scissors would be brought from the bathhouse without difficulty. Each of us had a task. The comrade who had been assigned to deliver the coffee was to pour some Luminal into the vat, and then add extra sugar to mask the taste. Sweetened coffee was an exceptional event inside the prison, so it would be quickly portioned out. Once the others fell asleep, we would be able to leave our cells unnoticed. The same powder was to be poured into the pot used by the Scharführer and the Ukrainian assigned on duty the next day. No one should see or hear that anyone was going inside workshop number 2. The three most physically fit men (including my brother-in-law) were supposed to go inside the workshop ten minutes ahead of us; they would open the door, file away the bar, and fasten the rope in such a way that we could pull it down and take it with us afterward. We didn't want to leave behind any traces that might be noticed by a passing patrol. The next two comrades were given a different assignment. One was to quietly sneak over to the duty-office on the first floor, where he would switch off the lamp that lit the street; the other was to check to make sure the light was out.

That was the sign to leave the cell, which had to be done without making any noise. At first we tried oiling the hinges, but that didn't produce the desired result. Then we decided one of us would keep watch in the corridor: When the clock there showed twenty past one he would flush the toilet as a signal to move. We agreed to go to bed in our clothes without letting anyone notice we were doing so. We also had to walk in our socks or else wrap our feet in rags in order to muffle our steps; our shoes would be tied and draped around our necks. We had to leave the cell one at a time, and each person leaving had to check that the corridor was empty, that no one was going to the bathroom, which might easily happen among 150 prisoners. We had to climb the stairs as quietly as possible, then sneak inside the workshop with the utmost care, and check through a window on the stairwell that no Ukrainians were roaming about the courtyard. All talking or whispering was forbidden on the way to or inside the workshop. We determined the order by which we would let ourselves down so as to avoid any mixup. The first one down would stay and hold the rope to make the descent easier for the next person, and to make sure none of the windows were broken on the second story. As soon as the second person reached the ground, the first would cross the street and hide among the rubble in a predetermined spot. Then the second one would hold the rope for the third person, and so on. The last one down was responsible for tearing down the rope, and taking it with him as he joined the group. When all this was successfully accomplished we would have to check that things were quiet inside the ghetto, and then head for the wall that separated the ghetto from the Aryan side.

The group would be led by whoever knew his way around the best, who could best guide us through the streets to the wall. We would move in single file, one right after the other, so as not to lose each other or lose our way, and in order to give the impression that it was only one person. If we heard footsteps we would lie down on the ground without panicking or making noise, and if danger threatened we would defend ourselves with whatever means we could. (We were supposed to receive a rifle, but unfortunately we didn't.) If things went wrong we were not allowed to give ourselves up alive to the Germans. When we reached the wall, if things were quiet, one of us would climb up and look around carefully to make sure there was no one on the other side. If a Polish policeman was standing guard then we would enter into an agreement with him. For this we chose a boy with good Aryan looks—a sly devil who was an old hand at smuggling and dealing with looters. He knew how to work out deals with policemen and even with gendarmes. He looked and behaved like a kid off the streets. If necessary he could convince someone that the rest of the group wasn't Jewish. If there wasn't anyone on the other side we would jump over one at a time. Then we had to find a hiding place, all the while keeping quiet and moving in single file. As the day went on we would be able to leave the hiding place. The first one out would be the one with the Aryan looks who would signal whether the others could leave. Then, if everything went well, each would go his own way.

We thought about what would happen to the 140 prisoners we were leaving behind and whether our escape might lead the prison administration to toughen the regimen or even execute some people. But we came to the conclusion that there was little threat of reprisal. It was safe to assume that some sanctions would be applied, such as strengthening the guards, locking the cells, doubling the bars in the window, et cetera. We figured that the administration would feel responsible for its own negligence, and would try to hush up the matter and not make a big fuss in order to escape any unpleasant consequences for itself. In a word I think the whole undertaking was well planned and organized down to the tiniest detail; our resolve was strong and our will unshakable. After all, what can be stronger than the will to survive, and that's why we believed our plan of escape would succeed. At the same time, we also realized that we would pay with our lives for the slightest negligence. So we discussed everything down to the smallest detail, then we said good night to one another and went our ways. Each of us was convinced our fate would be decided that next night; each was wondering whether the escape would succeed or whether we had only a few hours left to live. We noticed that the number of guards gradually decreased toward evening. The single, biggest obstacle was the guard on duty in the watchtower. And this became the source of disagreement within the group. Four of the men, including the "district attorney," wanted to postpone the escape, but the remaining six, including me, thought that we shouldn't change the plan that had already been agreed upon.

It was still too early to escape right then. For one thing, sawing through one bar wasn't enough, and for another, we had to try at all costs to get rid of the guard at the Więzienna Street* gate; otherwise we would be risking certain death. The "bathhouse" group realized that we wanted to hurry and tried to get us to postpone things. Our group, on the other hand, was worried that the others might leave without us, so we kept our eyes and ears open. Now came the last sleepless nights, when each group was watching the other. Moreover a few of our people began to suspect that some of the other prisoners were meeting in secret. We had to be on guard against anyone possibly interfering with our plans. There were also some older people in our cell who were waiting for a "miracle," and some who had no place to escape and did not

---

*No longer in existence.

believe such an escape could succeed. They expected that our attempt might make things worse for them.

After a while even those from the "bathhouse" group who were critically inclined came to the conclusion that the time had come to put the plans into action, and they resolved not to put things off any longer. We agreed and decided to leave that very week. Finally everything was prepared, and all the obstacles were overcome with the exception of the guard at Więzienna Street. This seemed to pose an insurmountable difficulty, but our will to get out of that hell helped us clear this hurdle. It should be stressed that this was cleverly and adroitly accomplished with the help of a certain sergeant of the watch with whom we had been cultivating good relations for some time. As it turned out, this watchman was a decent man and kindly disposed to us. We had been observing him for some time and finally started up a conversation with him. It turned out he was opposed to the Nazi regime. He spoke out with great indignation against the cruelties perpetrated by the Germans and severely criticized the Nazis. Hearing this we very carefully steered the conversation toward the possibility of being saved from the oppression. The Wachmeister consoled us, encouraged us, and even began urging us to escape. He won our trust and we told him about our plans. We told him that the biggest difficulty in putting the plan into practice was the watchtower guard overlooking Więzienna Street. To our astonishment he promised to help. Hearing him talk made us more optimistic that things might work out. We suggested to the watchman that he invite the guards out for vodka on the designated night. Once the inebriated guard fell asleep we could let ourselves safely down the rope. The man agreed, and we gave him money for vodka. We agreed that on a night when he was on duty at Pawiak, he would invite the guard into the orderly room between 1 and 2 A.M. for a libation. That was the moment we had chosen to escape at the prearranged signal. We gave the watchman more money to buy vodka on three different occasions.

During the next two nights the guards on duty at the watchtower were ones the watchman didn't know, so he couldn't invite them for vodka without arousing suspicions. He had to wait until one of the ones he was friendly with took the 12:30–3:00 shift.

Finally a week later—it was 30 May at 6 P.M.—we received the long-awaited word. That night our Wachmeister came over to our fence and tossed a cigarette butt on the ground. Inside was a secret message: "You can leave today between 12:30 and 3:00." That meant one of our man's acquaintances was going to be on duty at the watchtower—someone he could invite to join him for some vodka. Here we should state that apart from several hundred zloty for buying vodka he refused to take any other payment from us. Everything he did for us he did unselfishly, guided by a human sense of obligation to help.

Our group held a brief council in which we decided to leave that night at 1:30. We assigned tasks as previously planned. We also warned that anyone who failed to wake up at the designated time would have to bear the consequences. Those who made it down to the workshop in time would have the possibility of escaping. I won't describe all the difficulties that came up trying to secure a safe passage to the workshop.

Finally, the decisive night arrived. We went to bed in our clothes. As we lay on our mattresses we wrestled with sleep, our heads were ringing, our nerves were taut, each person evaluated the current situation, each searched his conscience as he waited for the hour that would bring freedom or death. Each begged providence to protect him from any unforeseen trouble that might foil our escape. The hours seemed like years. As we waited for the prearranged signal, our heads filled with fantastic notions. We knew that if we didn't succeed that night we would be lost. We would not find an equally suitable occasion. That night was our only chance.

After a long, torturous wait, we finally heard the signal. We rose from our beds. Three men from my cell left together with me:

Lipszyc, Zylberman—who had recently arrived—and Zaremski, a boy of twenty-two, whom we had invited to join the last day. We liked that energetic boy, so much craving life and freedom. We were genuinely pained to think that he would perish at such a young age, and so we decided to take him along.

We crept out of the cell as soundlessly as shadows. The guard in the corridor was deep asleep. In our sock feet we went down to the workshop on the third story. There I met my brother-in-law. Each person immediately set about his assigned task. Two began filing away the second bar (the first had already been taken care of). With bated breath we waited for events to unfold, aware of the danger that threatened. Finally the bars were filed away. Now we had to leave, without looking back; so we bent open the bars and unlatched the window, the road to freedom, then tied down the rope and secured it from breaking.

Ten men, ten human beings instinctively held hands in collective self-defense. We listened for a moment to make sure no one had noticed us, then someone checked the street to make sure a patrol wasn't passing just by chance, that things were quiet. Then with what strength we had left we began lowering ourselves down the rope. Zylberman was the first to go, quick and nimble as a cat; in the blink of an eye he was standing on the street. When the next one dropped down we heard the footsteps of the first person moving into the ruins, and the sound of bricks falling as he did so. We stopped for a moment even though the ground was burning our feet, but there was no turning back, so the third one went on down. We hadn't foreseen that our steps would make noise in the rubble. For one terribly anxious moment we thought our cause was lost. But some secret internal force was guiding us, keeping our spirit of resistance unbroken. Finally we all managed to go down one after the other. Thus the first step was complete; we were outside the prison walls—but we were still not safe, we were still surrounded by great dangers. For some unknown reason the last person out, who was supposed to pull the rope down from the window, was unable to do so. Maybe it was because of nerves, although he tried three times. This took precious minutes, but we signaled to him that the rope had to be removed. Unfortunately he couldn't manage. We couldn't wait any longer; each second had enormous meaning, the danger was growing by the moment.

Guided by our instinct, we headed for the wall that enclosed the ghetto. Everywhere was a deep silence. Everything created an atmosphere of secrecy and uncertainty. The way led up and down through hills and valleys of rubble and ruins. We walked barefoot, cutting up the soles of our feet. We proceeded slowly, our eyes wide open in the darkness, peering ahead, our ears cocked for the military tread of a chance patrol.

We went on like this, stopping every few careful steps to listen, anxiously, to the nighttime quiet. Finally we reached the wall we had to cross without attracting the attention of the gendarmes posted on the other side. Then we would be in the Aryan district.

It's difficult to describe what we sensed in the darkness. Soaked in sweat, we groped at the wall. We discussed the consequences of our escape. In our imagination we saw a patrol passing by Pawiak and gendarmes spotting the rope dangling from the window. So we stood beside the wall seized with fear, expecting the Germans and Ukrainians to catch up with us there. But there was no time for reflection. One of our group was boosted by two others onto the wall; he looked around diligently to make sure things were quiet on the other side, then gave the signal. Then one at a time, we helped each cross over the wall and found ourselves on the Aryan side.

"One night, toward the end of February 1943, I crossed to the Aryan side."

Chapter 5

ON THE OTHER SIDE
OF THE WALLS

*Soon after invading Poland in 1939, the German forces imposed the Nurem-
berg race laws, which stipulated who should be considered Aryan, Jewish,
and so on, regardless of religious or ethnic affiliation. To escape persecution,
many Polish citizens of Jewish background procured false papers that identified the bearers as non-Jewish Poles or even Volksdeutsche. Some lived quite
openly under their assumed identities; others went into hiding with friends,
relatives, or total strangers. The difficulty in arranging hiding places increased
with the severity of Nazi persecution, especially as the punishment for aiding
Jews in hiding was death. Gestapo agents, paid informers, and professional
extortionists and blackmailers (szmalcowniki) were a constant danger.*

*As the documents in this chapter testify, the response of non-Jewish
Poles ranged from active aid at the risk of life to open collaboration with the
Nazis. Within the organized resistance there were only a few groups able
and willing to offer programmatic assistance. One such group, the Council
for Jewish Aid (cryptonym Żegota), was established under the aegis of the
government in exile, and appealed to Poles to help Jewish fellow citizens.
The resistance movement in Warsaw also carried out several death sentences
on suspected blackmailers. Certain groups, however, even among those resist-
ing the Nazis, were indifferent or openly anti-Semitic.*

Some 50,000 Jews are thought to have stayed on the Aryan side,
masking their identity or concealing themselves fully. Of these, an unknown
number died at the hands of the Nazis or their collaborators. During the
Warsaw Uprising of 1944, many Jews came out of hiding to fight alongside
the insurgents; survivors were later evacuated along with the entire civilian
population and relocated in the province or dispersed among various camps.
A few resumed hiding in underground bunkers while the Germans set
about systematically demolishing the city, which was not liberated until
January 1945.

STEFAN ERNEST. The Germans break off the January Aktion after
four days, and people immediately look for ways to save themselves.
The few telephones inside the ghetto are constantly besieged; anyone who is able, anyone with the slightest chance, crosses over.
With every passing day, more and more people move out of the
ghetto. Still, this is only a small percentage of the whole. Others
resort to halfway measures—not without good reason—and move
to the workshops in the big ghetto. Finally, there is the vast majority, for whom neither of these solutions—particularly the first
one—is an option. These people are waiting for the final alarm;
they stay put and dig in, building shelters, safe places, and hideouts.
Only a minority waits passively for a miracle or else for death.

At home we discuss the family's chance of being saved and
come to a decision: We will cross the wall. Hiding in a shelter
would at best mean a slow painful death by hunger, thirst, and
exhaustion. And we don't believe the workshops are a sure bet
either, at least not in the long run, since we don't share the opinion
that the war will end soon. I decide to cross over, make arrangements, and come back for the others.

On 29 January 1943, at 5:15 A.M., I leave that cursed city of
insult and humiliation, of misery, pestilence, hunger, blood, and
death, that hellish home to every conceivable torture and suffering
that can be devised by human beings: *the beast*. At about 7:30 A.M.

I arrive at the worksite Ostbahn-Praga. At 5 P.M., in the twilight, I break away from the returning column. For three years I've been wearing an armband; I now remove this badge of shame and slip away, alone, into the evening darkness and the traffic of the city. I am free.

Of course, those of us hiding here on the Aryan side are not organized in any way; we live separately and in isolation. Our lives are full of emotion, stress, and surprises—often tragic—but apart from that our situations are all so diverse, the specific circumstances so varied, that any generalization is impossible.

Simply put, anyone with "good looks"—who can pass as an Aryan—lives completely differently than someone without them. Men live in different circumstances from women. People with family, relations, friends, or acquaintances have situations far unlike those who sadly lack such blessings; people with money live differently from those without, as do those who have work, those with good papers, and so on. But they do not form a whole; they live alone, truly dispersed. The only thing they share is a fear of informers, an anxious anticipation of the end—and the fact that they are Jewish.

But now to return behind the walls, where the community under discussion will go on existing for another three months, even though my own story there actually ends on 29 January 1943.

In fact, I know a lot less about what went on there between 29 January and 19 April, and what is going on to this day, than the average Aryan citizen of Warsaw, simply because of my "looks."

Up until the April Aktion I maintained a fairly lively exchange with my brother, by letters and telephone; at that time it was possible for me to do so.

During the so-called Mexican* period, the Council became increasingly idle and helpless; the general anarchy grew to the

*Refers to the chaos that ensued as the authority of the Judenrat eroded.—PB

point where armed bands of robbers were roaming the ghetto streets, while SS snipers took sport in hunting down any two-legged animals marked with a band on the upper right arm. Finally, there was the beast's ongoing liquidation of the shops and worksites in both districts of the ghetto.

The general exodus across the wall is on the rise. Whoever still can is looking that way for salvation.

ANONYMOUS WOMAN. One night toward the end of February 1943 I crossed over the wall to the Aryan side. My four-year-old son was handed over to me at the same place on Franciszkańska Street, while I stood on the shoulders of an unknown Aryan friend. From that day on I began a new struggle for the life of my child and myself. The struggle on this side of the wall has been different, occasionally desperate; our lives have often been hanging in the balance. More than once I've broken down. I think increasingly about taking my child's life and my own. I see no way of surviving. For that reason I've decided to write down what I've experienced. At the moment I am living in an attic. I'm using a turned-over bucket as a table and a small crate as a chair. I'm writing hurriedly with the idea that some day these pages will be found in a liberated Warsaw.

As I finish this writing, it is 21 June 1943, a day swollen with despair and pain. The only person close to me—the father of my child—is still on the other side of the ghetto walls. I will never see him again.

MARYSIA SZPIRO WAS ELEVEN IN 1946, WHEN SHE WROTE HER account. Before the war, her parents sold stationery and kitchen implements at their home on Wolska Street. Inside the ghetto, her parents and two of her five siblings died of hunger. In July 1942, when she was seven, Marysia and her brother Josek managed to escape from the ghetto. Marysia Szpiro survived the war. She eventually joined a kibbutz in Łódź and presumably emigrated to Israel.

The day after we left—it was the summer of 1942—my sister Estera came over to the barbed wire and used her hands to tell us she was volunteering to go to Treblinka. She was inside the ghetto, and we were on the Polish side. We were separated by barbed wire guarded by Ukrainians who watched every move you made, so we couldn't really talk with my sister even with our hands. Only Estera managed to show us that she was going away forever. That's how we said good-bye. She volunteered to go to Treblinka because she didn't have anything left to eat.

I stayed with Dora and Josek on the Polish side. For a while we wandered about without a home, just walking around on the streets. We started wishing we had died in the ghetto along with everyone else. Sometimes, late at night, when we were looking for a place to hide, we were stopped by policemen and Germans who asked us where we were going so late at night. I was most afraid when a German asked me my name, because I knew he suspected I was Jewish. We agreed to use Polish first and last names. We called Dora "Mira Wójtowicz," Josek, "Józiek Wójtowicz" and I was named "Marysia Wójtowicz."

Policemen often stopped me and asked what my name was and where I was from. I had to stay alert and answer everything very sure of myself, so they wouldn't figure anything out. Once when I was walking down the street, a policeman grabbed me and ordered me to go to the ghetto. I didn't want to go, because I knew I would never get out of there again. I screamed at the top of my lungs, "What am I supposed to go there for? I'm Polish!" People who were passing by stopped and listened to what was going on. And since I didn't look very Jewish, some of them yelled at the policeman to let me go, that I was Polish. But others shouted, "Shove her in the ghetto, she's a Jew." At first the policeman didn't know what to do, whether to let me go or not. Most of the people were shouting for him to let me go, and one lady called out that if he let me go, she would walk me home. The policeman handed me over to her and told her to check whether I really was Polish. She said she would and took me away. When we had gone far enough from the policeman, the lady said to me, "I know you're Jewish; go wherever it is you have to go." I thanked her and went on.

One time we met a girl who was staying on the Polish side just like us. We asked her where she was spending the night, and she said she was paying a certain Polish lady to sleep at her place. We asked her to take us to there. She said the lady had already taken in one other boy and she would ask about us. The lady agreed; we paid her to spend the night, but we had to leave the house early in the morning and stay out until it was completely dark. That lady had a fifteen-year-old daughter.

We started going back into the ghetto. By then everybody had been murdered, and the Poles were taking clothes or whatever they wanted from the Jewish homes. The Germans drove up in cars as well and also took everything they wanted. We were struggling hard just to survive, so we broke in and took clothes too. Then we'd sell them so we'd have money for food and everything. The Germans didn't let the Poles take things; they wanted everything for themselves. But we didn't care that it wasn't allowed. We didn't care about anything. When a German caught us, we said we were Poles. Even though the Poles weren't allowed in the ghetto either, if they caught a Pole they'd just take what he had and tell him to go home, or else they'd say, Go on and take what you have there but don't ever come back. When they caught us we begged them to let us keep what we had. Sometimes they did, and sometimes they didn't. We took everything to the lady, and she took whatever she wanted for her fifteen-year-old daughter. If we didn't want to give her something, she'd start yelling that we were staying in her house, she was keeping us, and now we didn't want to share. We had to give her things whether we wanted to or not, because what would happen if she threw us out?

The boy who was staying there was seventeen years old. The lady didn't allow us to talk in Yiddish, because she couldn't understand; she was afraid we might be saying something about her. Whenever the boy did want to talk about her, he'd speak in Yiddish. She had this long stick, and right away she'd hit him with the stick. He mostly talked late at night, and every evening she put that stick next to her bed, and it was long enough to reach the boy. The boy's Polish name was Mietek. Whenever she started to hit him with the stick he would holler that he was going to stop talking.

My sister had a friend named Blima; she had two sisters in the ghetto. She escaped from the ghetto along with us.

One time we came home, everything was fine, we went to bed, and then somebody knocked on the door. The Polish lady could tell they were Germans from the way they knocked, for a moment she didn't know what to do. She wasn't so much afraid for us as for that Mietek. Then she had an idea and told him to crawl in bed next to her daughter so he was completely hidden under the down cover. That was a good idea. The Germans came into the room and started shining their flashlights; they saw children sleeping, but nobody older. They searched everywhere and didn't find anybody. Naturally they didn't look under the down cover, they didn't expect anyone would be hiding there. They looked around and left. The Polish lady told us she had two cousins and she could give some torn pieces of their registration cards to my sister Dora and her friend Blima. In case something happened, they would have something to prove they were Polish. At least we still had some good clothes. Dora and Blima had real winter coats.

One day when we left the house, it was very warm. We were wearing summer dresses, with no stockings. We had left everything at the lady's. We came back in the evening, and the lady didn't open the door. We started to knock louder, and she came to the door and said we should sleep somewhere else, because Mietek hadn't come back home and he might give us away. We had to find some place to sleep whether we wanted to or not. We went up to the attic of that building. It was cold, but what could we do? Early the next morning, while it was still a little dark, we went out where we did every morning. That evening we came back, knocked on the door, and the lady screamed at the top of her lungs, "What are you looking for here, you Jew-girls? There's nobody here who knows you." We saw that things were bad, so we walked away a little. After a while I went to the door and asked her to at least give me my slippers, because I was barefoot, but she shouted, "You better run away, because I'm going to hand you over to the gendarmes, you Jew-girl!" We left the building and spent the night in some stairwell.

The next day we went outside and saw that two boys were leading away my brother Josek (he was staying somewhere else). Right away we suspected something was wrong. We started walking toward him, but he held his hand behind the boys' backs and signaled not to come his way and not to look. Well, we already knew what they were after. They stepped inside some entryway and told him to hand over his shoes; he had good shoes at the time that he had brought from the ghetto. He took off his shoes and handed them over, because if he didn't they would have turned him in to the Germans, and they gave him a pair of old worn-out ones instead. Next they told him to give them 500 zloty. He didn't have any money, so he went to the lady he was staying with and borrowed 500 zloty. They wouldn't let him leave until he handed over the money. Then the boys wanted to know where Josek's friend was. If Josek didn't tell them, they'd catch up with him and kill him. Josek didn't want to betray that other boy, so he decided to leave Warsaw. We couldn't meet because he didn't have time; he had to leave Warsaw right away, because otherwise they might turn him in to the Germans. It turns out that before he left those boys caught him again and took everything—even his jacket and his sweater. The only things he had left were his pants and his shirt. And then I heard he went to the country and I haven't seen him since.

FRANCISZKA GRÜNBERG WAS BORN IN WARSAW, WHERE SHE lived with her husband, Stefan, and their two children on Chłodna Street. Before the war she was a dentist.

Inside the ghetto, she lost her sixteen-year-old daughter Liliana during the deportations of 1942; the following spring the rest of the family moved to the Aryan district. For some time they lived with Józefa (Ziuta) Turska at 21 Chełmska Street, until a blackmailer forced them to leave. Pani Turska helped them find someone else who sheltered them through the Warsaw Uprising of 1944, after which they moved to a village in the country. After liberation, the family emigrated from Poland. The account was written shortly after the war.

The car pushed through toward the sentry post at the corner of Nowolipie and Karmelicka. Several Jewish policemen were milling about, and a few gendarmes were standing by the gate. All of a sudden the car stopped directly in front of the gate. "My" agent came running up, all out of breath, and started arguing with someone else who represented the car. My agent said he wasn't going to let anyone steal his clients and he wouldn't let the car through, since it was his client sitting inside. The man from the car didn't want to lose his client either. Right away the "players" (policemen who made deals with the sentries) started to intervene, and the argument grew even worse. Finally the man in charge of the cars gave my agent something and the car started. The gendarme calmly opened the gate. I felt as if the angel of death were releasing me from the depths of hell. One moment later, instead of throngs of miserable beggars with swollen yellow faces, instead of the desperate clamor, the terrified mob, instead of dirty streets full of trash, I saw clean, empty streets with an occasional figure passing by. I felt hypnotized: completely disoriented by the new sights, and by a new kind of fear; everything seemed strange and unfamiliar. I was in a thick fog and couldn't see a thing ahead of me. I was like someone who's been sitting in the dark for a long time and who then goes outside to discover that he can't see: The sunlight makes him squint; the blinding brightness hurts. I felt blinded as well.

As if in a dream, I heard Cyla say that she and Erna were going to spend the day with Basia. A few houses away from the Ps, I asked the driver to pull over. When the car stopped I jumped out and started walking straight ahead. I was so mesmerized I left without saying good-bye to my companions: I just heard the rumble of the car as it drove away. My heart was pounding as I walked through streets that seemed utterly foreign, even though I was born in Warsaw. Within minutes I was standing outside an apartment on the third story. One second later I was embraced by several pairs of arms: my husband's, my son's, and pani P's. I was intoxicated by the change in my circumstances. To this day I don't understand why I was so benumbed. But that's how it was. I couldn't get enough of the sight of Rysiek, my son. I hadn't seen him in his new school uniform; when he left the ghetto he was wearing old pants and an overcoat like a child from the working class. Now he was a spotlessly clean schoolboy; his uniform made him look no older than ten or eleven. I smothered him with hugs, holding and kissing him. My husband wept with joy that we were again together. Pani Maria P said she was happy there was no more worrying, no more waiting by the telephone. There was a young man as well, Michał, a student twenty-two or twenty-three years old. We were supposed to stay at his father's apartment.

We were in a beautifully furnished study with a desk, a sofa bed, an armchair, several chairs, beautiful curtains, and many lovely knickknacks. I felt a little uncomfortable; I'd grown unused to such luxuries. This was a new world to me. Pani P cooked dinner for us—the first such meal I'd had in almost a year. After all, what could I cook, hiding in dark holes and shelters? Even when things were relatively calm I had nothing to cook with—no household items and no utensils other than a broken pot and a scratched-up spoon. We all ate straight from the same pot and shared that one spoon. Of course, the abandoned apartments were full of plates, pots, spoons—often very nice ones, if you dared go right in after an Aktion. I use the word "dare" in a strictly moral sense; it was easy enough to get inside the apartments once the Jewish police, the Germans, and the szaulisi had left. But the only people who did so were marauders and hyenas who wouldn't think twice about robbing a corpse. The looters often ran into a szaulis or a Ukrainian who'd sneaked back to steal things. I say "sneak" not because they were forbidden to steal but because if anyone saw them they'd have to share their booty. Sometimes they'd roam about in groups of three, just so things would be more fun.

Over dinner we discussed what pani Maria had arranged. We would be living in the Rybaki district, in the Old Town, in an apartment consisting of a room, a kitchen, an alcove, and a bathroom. Pan Michał's father and brother lived there as well. The father was a railroad worker. Pan Michał had his own room somewhere on Długa. When we explained we had no intention of going out or of registering ourselves, he promised to buy our food and stop in every day. There would be a one-time payment of several thousand zloty and a minimal monthly fee, long before agreed on by pani Maria. We paid right then and there.

I sat in a corner with my child to find out how he was getting on and learn what he had been doing. It turned out he was well cared for, with more than enough good food; the Ps treated him very well, taking him to the theater and the movies. Pani P also took him shopping. However, the couple was often drunk, particularly pani Maria, who liked to have a glass now and then. That was a tremendous flaw in anyone hiding people, since alcohol is a sure inducement to blabbing, and I hardly need explain the consequences. Moreover, the Ps had frequent visitors, including two police inspectors, one of whom had a German last name and was most likely Volksdeutsch. The Ps maintained that both inspectors were their friends, but I was nervous. A policeman is a policeman. Worse, when I asked my child what he did all day, he said, "I take out books from the library and read," whereupon pani Maria added, "And he helps me too."

"With what?" I asked.

"He boils my operating instruments."

"What operations?"

"You mean you don't know?" she said. "Do I have to explain it to you? I'm a midwife."

She didn't have to say any more. My thirteen-year-old child was helping the woman prepare the tools for abortions! My child, who had never laid his innocent cornflower-blue eyes on anything sordid, had repeatedly witnessed this criminal act; his child's hands had even taken part! Was this his moral education? Was this how my only child's soul was expected to develop, warped and disgusted by age thirteen?

I took pani Maria aside and expressed my indignation at her having involved him in her work, which wasn't really any of my business, but what was my child doing there? To which she said, "Let him learn what life's about. Besides, I can't hide it; he sees the patients coming in, and the instruments being carried to the office. A few minutes later the pans come out full of blood, sometimes you can hear groaning, and then the patient usually leaves right away, so he'd probably catch on sooner or later. I can't hide it from him, since it happens all the time, and I can't change the way I live on his account, so there's no other way. Besides, he's doing well and that's that. That's the most important thing."

I was crushed, but what could I do? Where could I move him? There was no point in wasting words. I kept my worries to myself and rejoined my husband, my son Rysiek, and pan Michał. We agreed that my husband, pan Michał, and I would spend the night at the Ps', wake up at five, and leave at six to move to Rybaki.

Early the next morning I covered my head with a large woolen shawl I had brought from the ghetto and left with my husband and pan Michał for our new apartment. I felt as if I were in some strange German city, where I should feel afraid of the stones under my feet, afraid of the air and afraid of the sky. I crossed Kredytowa by the gas works and the Zachęta Museum, past Piłsudski Square toward Senatorska Street and the Old Town. The streets were fairly empty of civilians (or maybe it just seemed that way to me after the unbearable din of the ghetto), but they were full of Gestapo men wearing yellow coats with swastikas on their arms. Military personnel were milling about everywhere, stiff and wooden. I gazed off into the distance. I was afraid to look anyone in the face; I felt that every glance would betray me. After an hour's brisk walk we reached the building in Rybaki (I don't remember which entrance). I had covered nearly all of my face with the shawl, as if I had a toothache, and I kept wiping my nose with my handkerchief, so that I crossed the courtyard almost completely concealed, with my eyes downcast. I had the feeling that everyone was staring at me, that I looked peculiar, and that everyone recognized the fact that I was Jewish. At one point I imagined I was wearing my armband with the Star of David, and instinctively reached for my right arm; the next moment I was terrified that I had left home without it. I was shaking with fear; I struggled to control myself and not break into a run. Finally we reached the third floor, Michał unlocked the door, and we went inside.

STANISŁAW SZNAPMAN. April inside the ghetto: The golden rays of the life-giving springtime sun are peeping through the windows. The tranquil air is filled with the aroma of the nearby fields; it soothes the frazzled nerves. Far beyond the ghetto walls you can see treetops covered with a vernal green. Fields and gardens are bustling with springtime chores. The world is so beautiful, but we aren't allowed to see it; we aren't allowed to be in a field or garden. Everything in our world is gray, covered with dust, littered with trash, because each of us is thinking about only one thing: escape. We have to sit behind the walls and toil under the whip for twelve hours a day for a little soup and 16 dekagrams of bread, and now they're taking even that away from us. They are supposed to send us to some camp in the Lublin district. We know what their camps are like and what we can expect there. The only fate that awaits us there is inevitable annihilation.

Looking out the window, beyond the wall, there are so many empty buildings, so many rooms, and so many hiding places. How nice it would be simply to sit things out there, unnoticed, until summer, and then go somewhere far away into the woods. The world is such a big place—except there's no room in it for us.

On the Polish side there are nice stores with beautiful displays. People are decently dressed; the women in particular are elegant. They can wear furs, watches, rings, and jewelry and have carpets at home. There are streetcars and carriages. People have attractively furnished apartments with bathrooms. They take outings to the countryside. There's plenty of greenery and flowers. The streets are full of children.

We were chased into miserable filthy holes. They took away our furniture and household possessions. We were prohibited from having jewelry or furs or carpets. They removed us from our businesses, our workshops, and our positions. And, most terrible of all, they murdered our dearest—our wives, children, mothers, fathers.

They destroyed that which any animal is able to respect, our families. They even aimed their rifles at our pregnant women and shot them in the stomach. All we have left is what we can carry on our persons and our bare lives, although who knows for how long. We are not allowed to venture outside. A dog can cross the street freely, but Jews are forbidden to do this. Jews aren't even granted the same rights as animals. One can show pity for a dog or a horse. But these feelings do not exist in relation to Jews.

And this is unfortunate. For taking in a Jew on the Aryan side, horrendous fees are demanded, payable months in advance. Occasionally the payment is made and then people pretend the hiding place has been "discovered," which means the Jew loses his money and anything else he's stored there and is sent back outside or else taken to the wall to be shot. Sadly, this happens often. And Jews in hiding are routinely blackmailed, even as Polish friends are risking their lives to save them.

As they set about liquidating the ghetto they launched a vicious campaign against Jews, which they blew up to monstrous proportions. Every crime anywhere in the city—every murder, fire, and robbery—was blamed on Jews, to convince the Poles who their worst enemy was and to persuade anyone who was hiding a Jew to hand him over to the Germans. In the papers, over the radio, on wall posters—everywhere they warned against the Jewish fiend. The streets became a genuine hunting ground, with Jews as the quarry. Various shady characters roamed the streets, maniacally searching for anyone who looked Semitic. The Gestapo rewarded successful hunters with money and valuables taken from Jewish homes, so the rabble ran riot. Some of the Blue Police, too, the PP, worked with particular zeal, scrutinizing pedestrians and demanding to see their papers. Civilians were dragged out of carriages and streetcars. At the slightest suspicion men were taken into some entryway, where their pants were unbuttoned in a cursory inspection. In case of doubt, people were killed on the street regardless of their papers. It was enough for a woman to look Jewish for her to be shot on sight. In this way many Polish women fell victim as well. In the search for Jews hiding on the Aryan side, whole buildings were raked over, including basements and attics. Hiding Jews was punishable by death, and all the people living in a given building were collectively responsible. Thus anyone with good intentions who wanted to take in a Jew had to act in strict secrecy, as the tenants were always keeping an eye on one another.

People told of macabre scenes they witnessed as Jews were being hunted. For example, a gendarme noticed a Jewish woman nursing an infant. The child was nursing. The gendarme shot the woman dead, while the child kept on suckling. The gendarme suggested to a Blue Policeman who was present that he shoot the child; the policeman refused, so the gendarme shot the infant himself. Another witness told of a man walking down Ceglana Street with a woman and a small child. Suddenly someone pointed at them and said they were Jewish. The man ran into a nearby building and up into the attic. The woman ran to the nearest entryway, while someone grabbed the child to save it. Some Germans drove up in a car and one zealous individual found the child. One of the Germans lifted it up by the head and aimed his pistol. The mother, watching from the entryway, ran out, oblivious to everything around her, wrenched the child back, and held it close. At that sight people in the crowd started sobbing, so the German placed both mother and child in the car, to deal with them later, out of view of the shocked crowd. Then the others went to the attic to shoot the man.

A woman was walking down the street with a four- or five-year-old girl; someone pointed her out as being Jewish. A gendarme took out his revolver. The woman prostrated herself in front of him and begged him to shoot her and leave the child. That evil beast refused to spare the woman the terrible sight. The child fell first, then the mother.

One gendarme noticed a five-year-old boy riding the streetcar and became suspicious. The boy's guardian vanished. The gendarme unbuttoned the boy's pants and then led him off the tram. A moment later a pistol shot rang out.

An armed gendarme boarded another streetcar with a four-year-old boy who was calmly eating bread and jam. The conductor asked where the man was taking the child. The gendarme smiled and ran his finger in a slit across his throat. The conductor understood; she was the one who told the story.

One Polish family regularly fed a Jewish boy leftovers after dinner. Some obliging individual reported this to the Germans. One day as the boy was leaving the building, a gendarme lurking nearby started running after him. The boy fled like a hunted animal, sobbing in terror, trying to save himself. But he was caught and shot before the eyes of the passersby.

Unfortunately, these were far from isolated incidents. The sight of armed gendarmes escorting Jews who had been found out, and the earthen-gray faces of the latter, already bearing the imprint of death, made people feel faint.

Jews who were found out were exterminated as entire families; people saw murdered couples gripping each other in a final embrace, often together with a child, or else daughters pressed tight against their mothers. These were heartrending sights.

Reader! Perhaps while reading these descriptions you might have certain doubts, thinking they contain a dose of exaggeration. Therefore know that the horrors that happened here are beyond even the wildest imagination. I want to stress that the incidents described constitute only a small and by no means extreme portion of the events, since they took place within a limited area, namely the city of Warsaw and its environs, where German behavior was regarded as relatively mild.

22 July 1943—The first anniversary of the deportation in Warsaw. The war is still going on. The crushing superiority of the Allies is already in sight. They are on the offensive. They are delivering powerful blows to the German beast, which is being routed in the east by mighty Russia. In the south, England and America are taking Sicily. They are also bombarding German cities without mercy. Now the Germans are getting a taste of what it is like to be bombarded. Their own cruel barbarian methods are coming to haunt them with a vengeance.

As I begin this final, most tragic chapter of my chronicle of Jewish martyrdom, I would like to note a rumor that reached me in July 1942. I don't know how much truth it contains, but I imagine that someday it will be researched and explained.

A certain German periodical carried an ad calling for an agronomist, which was answered by a female specialist in that field. During the interview that followed, the manager of the institution explained that the task at hand was to increase poultry production in the east, by using meat as fodder. When the specialist noted that such a program would require vast amounts of meat, the director answered that there would be enough *"Judenfleisch."* After that gruesome answer the specialist declined the position.*

ADOLF BERMAN. Smocza Street was bustling with activity: People were buying and selling sweaters, overcoats, and dresses for pennies. The worksite laborers take things across to the other side. My wife and I made our way toward Ogrodowa Street—which was actually off limits under pain of death—frantically searching for our acquaintance. We didn't recognize a soul. We began to wonder if we shouldn't go back home and try to find someone to help arrange a semi-legal crossing, but we sensed it might be too late for that. So we approached the first Jewish policeman we met

---

*This report was not confirmed.

and asked whether we could cross. He said we could, but it would cost 600 zloty per head. We made our decision right then and there and handed him the money. The man disappeared, and for a minute we feared that our money might have evaporated. A few minutes later he came back, wincing when he heard we had no documents. Then he led us to a Polish policeman. At the crossing he told us to remove our armbands; then he stepped aside and waved us on toward the Polish policeman, who asked, "Where are you going?" and his Jewish counterpart signaled to him from the side that things had been taken care of. We crossed and immediately found ourselves on an empty street on the Aryan side.

We felt a strange sense of triumph that it had gone so well, and at the same time a great fear for what would happen next. We tried not to walk too quickly, to avoid attracting attention, but we were aware that we made a rather bizarre sight. Flushed and out of breath, hatless, carrying our coats, we could feel our veins pulsing in our temples and sensed we were being observed. We would have liked to crawl inside a mouse hole, anywhere, just to relax for a minute and regain our composure, but we were afraid to step inside an entryway; we wanted to get as far away as possible from that damned guard post. We considered taking a streetcar but were afraid of that as well.

After a moment of hesitation we finally turned onto Wronia Street, then crossed over to Chłodna, when suddenly we felt we were being followed. Thrown off balance, we made the mistake of heading toward Żelazna, where the guard post is located. Suddenly we were surrounded by a swarm of young scoundrels fourteen to sixteen years old. There were about ten of them, snatching at us from all sides, shouting that they were going to the guard post to hand us over to the Germans if we didn't pay what they asked. Their faces were disgusting, typical *bezprizorniye*—homeless waifs. The majority were girls; they shouted the loudest and were the most aggressive. The boldest among them grabbed our bags, while the others, feeling shortchanged, called out, "Why did you give everything to them? Give us some money too or else we'll go fetch the Germans." They pulled us into an entryway; we fished out some money (a few hundred zloty) and began dividing it. There wasn't enough for everyone because new urchins kept appearing. They wanted to take my wife's purse, but we assured them it was empty and they let it be. However, they snatched her coat out of her hands and one girl pulled a ring off my wife's finger. We tried to stop her, saying it was only a keepsake and not worth much, but to no avail. Then one of the boys started squawking that he didn't get anything, but we didn't have any more money within reach and somehow we managed to break away. They ran after us a little bit but then gave up. There was almost no reaction from the pedestrians; perhaps they were afraid to say anything so close to the guard post. One little old woman did start yelling at them to leave us alone: She came over and asked us what they took and where we'd like to go. She obviously sympathized with our plight and might even have been willing to hide us, but we didn't want to put her in danger; besides, we wanted to get as far away as possible. Her sympathy gave us heart, however, and made the whole event seem a little less horrible.

We went back to Wronia Street and crossed Kazimierz Square over to Złota. For a few minutes things were relatively calm, but then the traffic on the street increased. It was already after seven; we weighed whether to go inside somewhere. Then once again we had this horrible feeling we were being watched; we could feel someone's eyes on our backs. We heard steps behind us. We turned onto Zielna, and two youngsters with suspicious-looking faces caught up to us and whispered, "Get inside the entryway!" We stepped inside the entryway; some more youths showed up and the first one demanded 500 zloty. We walked up to the first landing, where we could hear the caretaker sweeping the stairs; the gang told us to hurry. I took several hundred zloty out of my pocket. Then we went downstairs, where we ran into a new gentleman. He was a little older than the others and carried a satchel; he looked like an informer. He claimed he had come to check what was going on. We were more afraid of him than the others. Naturally the pot had to be increased now that he was in on it. Finally some other shady characters showed up, and in the end the whole band managed to extort a substantial sum of money. In exchange they proposed to escort us wherever we wanted to go, but we were afraid they might blackmail us again. We wanted to get away from them as quickly as possible and shake them off our trail.

We ran out of the building. A moment later a different boy came up to us and said, "Mister, there's somebody picked up your scent." We followed Marszałkowska Street across Świętokrzyska down to Jasna and there at the corner were joined by two juveniles. One of them, an obvious alcoholic with criminal features, whispered, "Please follow me to number one Królewska Street."

At first we thought it was one of the group we had just paid off, warning us to go in a better direction, so we asked, "Didn't we meet you a little while ago, in the entryway?" But a moment later we realized this was yet another case of blackmail, all the more threatening since there was no talk of money; they were just taking us to some building on Królewska, which we assumed housed a branch of the Gestapo or something similar. This time we ourselves suggested going inside one of the entryways. At first they pretended to object, then finally presented their demand: "Two thousand zloty, and not a penny less."

We explained we no longer had that much. One of the boys became agitated; the other tried to quiet him down. We pulled out the rest of our money (over 100 zloty) and bargained with the juveniles a few minutes. They kept threatening to take us to Królewska, but finally they accepted the money and calmed down. We asked them whether we'd seen the last of the blackmail, whether we'd be left alone now. They gave us their word of honor that no one would follow us; even the one with the alcoholic face tried to reassure us. He struck us as the type of scoundrel one could talk to after the "business" had been transacted. So we proposed that he accompany us for a while, to protect us from any further attempts at blackmail. He was flattered by our confidence. We walked out onto the street in two pairs. The two explained that they had been watching us from the moment we left the ghetto, but couldn't approach us right away because "those kids got in the way."

The one with the alcoholic face proudly admitted to being an informer and said he knew what was in store for him once the war was over. He was a little drunk and didn't really know where we were. We asked him to escort us down Krakowskie Przedmieście toward Powiśle; we wanted to get away from the center of town to a quieter district, where we could rest. The youths accompanied us politely all the way to Powiśle; finally we said good-bye and watched them walk off. We went on a little bit and stepped inside a pastry shop, horribly shaken by the triple blackmail. We were convinced that we were in for more, that someone else was waiting to pounce on us. We felt as though every passerby was eyeing us suspiciously. It took us hours to calm down, and for a long time afterward we were haunted by memories of being blackmailed.

STEFANIA STASZEWSKA.[1] It's just before curfew hour. I walk to Madaliński Street and knock on Marysia's door. Luckily she still has the key to the attic; she signals for me to run upstairs. I can hear her explaining something to her brother, and then she steps out of her apartment carrying a down cover, jangling keys, and mumbling something about bedbugs.

To me she says, "Jadwiga, I told my brother we have bedbugs and that's why I'm taking the down up to the attic. But listen: Our neighbor's doing laundry tomorrow and has already requested the key to the attic."

I understand: I better not show up tomorrow. But for the moment I can sleep! And that's what I do, no matter how much the iron bed grate pinches my skin. But before lying down I have to rub the unguent on my hands so the damn scabies will finally go away.

In the morning Marysia comes to the attic using the pretext of laundry. She takes me downstairs; her brother has already left for work, so I can wash up. All of a sudden her neighbor knocks at the door. There's no place to hide, so I grab my purse and coat and crawl into the bed; Marysia throws the down blanket over me. I huddle underneath, next to the wall, and make a little opening to keep from suffocating; I lie still and try to breathe as quietly as possible. I listen to Marysia trying in vain to get the neighbor to leave.

It's hot underneath the down. My poor mama sweated the same way when I hid her in a bed during a roundup inside our building in the summer of 1942. I myself hid in the pantry beneath some coal sacks; when I pulled her out after the Germans and the Jewish police had left she was barely alive. And what's become of her now? No doubt she died at Treblinka. They took her away during the huge Aktion, when they were sending everyone to Treblinka. Or maybe she died during the transport; the railcars were always so packed that people suffocated from lack of air. My poor delicate weak Mama might not have survived.

"Jadwiga, you can get up—she finally left," Marysia said.

I clamber out of the bed, wash up, and comb my hair. I put my treasure, a fine-toothed comb, back into my purse. I had bought it in the camp at Poniatów for a kilogram of bread, paid out over several days. I preferred starving to having fleas. There were many nights when instead of sleeping I would stand in line at the bathhouse to scrub myself and have my clothes disinfected.

Now my head is clean, but these damned scabies! It's getting a little better, but I have to keep rubbing on the unguent for another several days. Not too thickly, though, since it smells so awful.

I run into town to telephone pan Ludomir. It's not that simple. First I have to find an out-of-the way little store. I'm afraid of calling from the post office; the place is full of Germans, police, various officials. But I can't call from just any store either: In one the telephone is on the counter next to the cash register and the cashier can hear every conversation; another shop is so empty that anyone coming in would hear my voice. I walk through several streets, passing a number of stores and pubs, but none of them have telephones I can use; I'm just too afraid if someone decides to listen in he might become suspicious. Finally I find what I'm looking for at a grocer's on Grójecka Street. A few old women are buying some things in the front of the store; the telephone is on the sill by the display window, the shopkeeper is constantly running outside to the crates of vegetables. I ask whether I can make a call. She nods her head and rushes out again. My heart is pounding as I dial. I hear the phone ringing, and a moment later a quiet male voice. "Hello?"

"May I speak with pan Ludomir?"

"Speaking."

I try to speak calmly, briefly, and concisely. "I need to see pani Bogusława as soon as possible.* She knows me from the Kalicka School, my name is Stefa Szochur, I'm coming from Poniatów."

For a moment the receiver is silent. I'm careful not to mention I escaped from the camp, but he can probably figure that out. Pan Ludomir tells me to call back tomorrow at noon. I hang up the receiver, pay, and go outside. What now? Once again the

---

*Alias of Klima Fuswerk of the Jewish National Committee, who worked on the Aryan side of the city.[2]

streetcar, Dreszer Park, and Ania's—where else is there? Where will I sleep? I don't want to go back to the camp! I know Klima will help me; I have to survive, to hold on somehow.

I tell Ania to be patient just a little longer, I'll get situated soon. Ania wishes me well but she is afraid. Little Jerzyk's black hair is growing back quickly; the neighbor women have really taken an interest in that child. Ania never lets him out of her sight. He cries often. Ania says, "He's wild." He's not wild, just poor and afraid. The night passes quietly.

In the morning the Germans are rounding up people off the street in the Mokotów district; I have to watch out. I hide as well as I can inside the entranceways, and at noon I ring up pan Ludomir. Pani Bogusława tells me to meet her at noon tomorrow at Dąbrowski Square, in the little plaza off Marszałkowska. I'm giddy with happiness. Tomorrow I'm going to see Klima! I run to Ania's. I have to ask my "uncle" to hold a *Kennkarte* for me, since now I'll be able to pay for one. Jerzyk's mother is at Ania's; she asks me when I can give back the documents. I beg her to hold out just a little longer; things are finally beginning to look up for me. I'm too full of joy and faith in the future to sit around idly, so I go into town. I have to see where I am going tomorrow, so that I'll act naturally and not get lost or have to look around. The square is pretty, and close to the Saxon Garden and the beautiful streets Krakowskie Przedmieście and Nowy Świat.

But I'm afraid to go there. In my rags I feel better in Mokotów or Praga or Grochów. I walk down the side streets, as usual pausing in front of the display windows to see how I look. I go inside a pharmacy to buy some more unguent. When will it heal? Lost in thought, I wander over to Theater Square and suddenly feel a heavy male hand on my shoulder. I turn around and freeze in horror. Right in front of me is a Blue Policeman, wearing the armband that says GENERALGOUVERNEMENT. There's no escape, that much is clear; the only thing that might save me is calm. Ready to feign indignation, I lift my head—and suddenly my mouth speaks of its own accord. "Rysiek?"

There's Rysiek's kind, smiling face—and that awful uniform. "You see it's the same old me, right?" he says. "You're not going to disown me, are you?"

"Of course I see it's you, and why should I disown you? What's this all about?"

"Do you trust me?"

"I trust you."

"I've met some of your boys who pretended not to know me and ran away. I told myself the next time someone does that I'll take revenge!"

"Rysiek, you have to understand, they were afraid!"

Rysiek can't understand. Good-looking Rysiek, the most popular boy on the block—probably the only goyishe child who played with the Jewish boys in the courtyard—Rysiek, whom all the Jewish girls were wild about—and he can't understand why his friends might be afraid of his being a policeman. We walk around the streets of Warsaw, Rysiek leading me by the arm. I feel safe, but I can't understand why he is a policeman. We lived on the same street. His father was a policeman before the war, supposedly harmless. Rysiek's mother was pretty and extremely nice. Everyone liked them; once my mother took me along because she had some business with "the policeman's wife." I was happy because I got to go inside Rysiek's house. I really liked him; he used to tease me—pelting me with pebbles, the rascal—and I would turn red and run away.

When I grew older the teasing stopped and we would discuss and debate this and that. Still, I had to be careful, since I was in the ZMS,* and his father—while a very nice man—was nevertheless a

*ZMS: Związek Młodzieży Szkolnej—School Youth Association, a Socialist group.

policeman. I remember that Rysiek didn't want to become a policeman; he had other plans—and there you have it! Now we're under occupation and I run into him wearing this disgusting uniform! It's terrible! Rysiek explains: His father is old and retired, he couldn't find work, they came to persuade him to join, and he finally agreed. He's married; his wife Halinka is expecting; her father is also a former policeman.

"But don't think we're 'that kind' of people—I don't do any dirty work, just keeping order and routine criminal cases, and my in-laws are hiding a Jewish child. Let's go to Praga; I'll show you and you can meet my wife!"

We ride over to Praga. Targowa Street is packed; we enter a building near the Różycki Market and go to a room on the second story in the left wing overlooking the courtyard. Inside I meet an older man wearing a policeman's uniform and his wife—Rysiek's in-laws. A little girl is playing on the floor. The home is very poor, sad. His mother-in-law explains. "Things are difficult, we have to watch out that no one bothers the little girl. We registered her as our niece; they might figure out it's all a ruse. We have papers that say she was born in the country; it's a good thing it's a girl; we couldn't have taken a boy. Maybe some family will come for her after the war; then we'll give her back. If not, she'll be ours. We've become attached to her."

Rysiek and I walk over to the second courtyard. He and Halinka live in a tiny rented room inside a larger apartment. Unfortunately they have to cross a common room to get there, which is uncomfortable for both landlords and tenants.

Rysiek introduces me to his wife. Halinka is young, nice, eight months pregnant. "How will you manage in this tiny room?"

"We'll make out somehow; the main thing is that Halinka's parents are living in the same building."

I tell them quietly about my situation, about the escape and the nightmare of the past weeks. Rysiek asks about my parents, about people from our street. "Ach," says Halinka, "better not talk about all that now. We have to figure out how to help Stefa—Jadwiga."

Unfortunately I can't live with them because of the landlord and the common room. It's possible to spend the night there now and then, but only on a down comforter on the floor. Rysiek has friends in the Schicht soap factory, and as soon as I have my Kennkarte he can find work for me there. But he can't arrange the documents, and without a Kennkarte you can't do a thing. I feel good in their home; that night I'll be able to sleep without fear. I feel safe here, free from any threats or danger. Halinka fixes supper, but all I can think about is a washbowl full of hot water. Even going to the toilet requires a whole operation. I have to cross the room with Halinka; she watches out for a moment when nobody is around. She's right, better avoid the eyes of strangers, better avoid any questions. Rysiek fetches a pot of hot water from the kitchen and then goes outside while I undress and wash. Even at Ania's I couldn't undress and wash that peacefully. Here I'm able to relax a bit. Halinka hands me a towel and some soap. I don't rush, I'm not afraid someone will come barging in all of a sudden, that I'll have to escape: Halinka is with me, and Rysiek is keeping watch downstairs.

When Rysiek comes back we sit down to a modest supper. They're pretty poor since Rysiek's pay is miserably low; when he has some time off he goes to the country for fatback, meat, and lard and smuggles it into the city. He sells a little and keeps some for himself. It's already late; we have to open the sofa bed for Rysiek and Halinka. I have a spot on the floor, but I'll be more than comfortable on top of the down.

We get up from the table and suddenly hear voices in the next room. Someone knocks on our door and opens it at the same time. Two young men step inside. Halinka turns pale; Rysiek looks at me, and even though I'm terrified I put on my silly smile and right away Rysiek has come to and is greeting the new arrivals. Halinka explains that her cousin from the country has come to visit. "I'd like you to meet Jadwiga—and these are Rysiek's colleagues from work." We shake hands. The men are already a little primed with drink. They set two bottles of vodka on the table and pull out a string of sausages.

"So we've brought something to drink and some bread and pickles to chew on—all you need to come up with is the mustard. We know you never have any food around."

Halinka brings some glasses and we sit down at the table. I have to watch out so not to give myself away and endanger Rysiek and Halinka. I hardly say a word, just giggle at all the questions and look at Halinka, who makes something up about my passing through and then skillfully changes the subject.

Unfortunately one of the men starts pawing at me more and more aggressively and asking insistent questions. I fend off his hands as well as I can but it's worse with the vodka. They force me to drink and I have no desire to; I sip just a little. I absolutely have to keep my wits about me. The other man offers some sausage and says, "You see, Rysiek, you're an idiot for not going with us after Jews and other illegals. Then you'd have your own vodka and something to eat and you'd be living like a human being. But instead you're about to have a baby and you don't have a thing; what kind of husband are you? We always find somebody. If they have money they pay the ransom, and if they don't, it's kaput. But we're still finding ones with dough; they've all got something they'll give to save their skin. And you? You want to starve to death along with your family?"

I can't look at Rysiek. I just stare at the man speaking and wait for what's coming next. But Halinka says calmly, "I won't let Rysiek do it. He wants to go with you, but I'm afraid he might get a knife in his back. Until I have the baby I'm not letting him go anywhere. After that we'll see. I've got bad nerves and I'm not supposed to get agitated. Rysiek knows that better than anybody."

STEFAN ERNEST. By bearing witness to what actually happened, I want to pay my own debt to fortune for having granted me several more weeks of life. I hope and believe that my voice is not the only one, that there are and will be others whose accounts of these events will be better, broader, more precise. And that when the time comes they will leave pen and paper behind and speak their thoughts out loud, to tell the world everything that happened.

I am hiding in a pit, lingering on without fresh air, without steady nourishment, without sufficient plumbing, without any prospect of change, and every passing hour is worth its weight in gold. I can feel my strength fading away, feel myself suffocating for want of air. The struggle for my personal survival is becoming hopeless. Here, on this side of the wall—but that doesn't matter, because I will finish my account, and I have faith that in the proper time it will see the light of day and people will know how it was. And they will ask if this is the truth. I will answer in advance: No, this is not the truth, it is only a small part, a tiny fraction of the truth. The essential truth, the real truth, cannot be described even with the most powerful pen.

FRANCISZKA GRÜNBERG. About five o'clock our son entered—or really, he burst into the apartment without Maria. He was sweating and out of breath; his face was flushed. He threw his cap on the sofa and said in a solemn voice, "I just saw one thousand happy Jews!"

My first thought was the boy had suffered a nervous shock that had addled his wits. "Rysiek, what on earth are you saying? What kind of nonsense is this? Did something happen on your way over? Are you having hallucinations? What do you mean you saw one thousand Jews, and happy ones at that?"

"But I really did see them, that's why I'm late. I saw one thousand Jews laughing and enjoying themselves, and Lutek [Ludwik] was there too and I talked with him. They're all at the Hotel Polski and they're going to leave the country, maybe even go to

America.[3] They all have papers—that cost money, of course—and they're leaving in two days. We can leave too."

And he explained how he'd been to see this man Jerzy, who reported that Ludwik had said, "It's a shame I don't know where they are. I'd really like to arrange for them to leave; maybe one of them will telephone you or drop by, please put them in touch with me." Then all three of them—Jerzy, Maria, and Rysiek—had ridden over to the Hotel Polski on Długa Street. There they really did see about a thousand Jewish men, women, and children, well dressed, their faces happy and full of the hope that they would be leaving in two or three days. Their eyes were glued to their sure-fire foreign papers, directing them to the camp for interned aliens at Vittel in France or outside Hanover, from where they would soon travel to the countries listed on the papers, mostly Palestine or Paraguay. These people kept leaving the hotel to run errands; there wasn't a German in sight; it was paradise on earth. They found Ludwik there with his wife; he was happy to see Rysiek and claimed he could still arrange something for us, but it would cost so-and-so; he mentioned a sizable sum. Rysiek was enthralled. He said his parents would be sure to agree right away and that he'd come back the next day with his father. He looked awhile longer at the "thousand happy Jews," and he himself was so happy he gave Ludwik a kiss and then ran home. Maria watched everything, said good-bye to Rysiek, and left.

After hearing that we were dumbstruck. Even back in the ghetto people had been talking about foreign documents, and it was known that those who had them had been separated from the rest of the Jews before the notorious "resettlement" of 22 July 1942 and had been taken to Pawiak prison for their own safety. There for a long time they had written letters to their families and friends, not secret messages but regular letters, in which they said they weren't bad off, that they were buying food for themselves and being treated well. People began trying to procure documents. Some had Aryan friends write letters or telegraph their families abroad, asking them to send papers immediately. Back then Ludwik had mentioned he was doing something along those lines. Could his current departure have something to do with that? We figured that papers must have come for many people who were no longer there, so they were taking others in their stead: If pan X from Paraguay later discovered that his cousin wasn't his cousin at all, everyone would just say it was a typical Jewish flimflam, but it made the Germans look good because they'd given Jews the papers. We went back and forth between that thought and the idea that the papers had been faked in a scheme to lure some Jews out of hiding, take their money, and later kill them in some place like Treblinka. Or maybe not? Maybe they were doing it to show the world that the Jews were still here and that the rumors abroad were complete fabrications. We talked and talked until our heads were spinning. We decided to keep Rysiek for the night and send him to Ludwik the next day with a letter containing several questions that were bothering us. And that's what we did. When Rysiek came back from Ludwik he said, "Ludwik doesn't know any more details; he knows that the Germans are doing it for money, but he thinks it will end happily. Ludwik knows for a fact that letters have arrived from people who went out with the first transport to Vittel."

That was the time of the so-called street blockades, or roundups, in different parts of Warsaw. For several weeks Ziuta and Stach had been telling us about them; Stach evidently enjoyed scaring us. We had no place to hide. And every day we heard of new blockades and searches. Apparently they were pulling people out of basements, attics, and all kinds of nooks and crannies. Anyone who wasn't registered was taken to the Gestapo. We were not registered, and we lived in constant fear.

The morning after Rysiek visited the hotel, Stach came over and then Maria. Stach spent several hours with us. Rysiek hadn't left and was with us as well. Stach scared us with the idea that a blockade might come any minute. He encouraged us to leave, telling us we might have a better chance of saving ourselves by leaving with the people at the hotel, since things were getting very bad. Later Krysia showed up and told us not to believe the Germans, that as far as she was concerned leaving meant death and we had a better chance of surviving here since we had a good place, a small, quiet, out-of-the-way house. She advised us to stay. We listened to the two conflicting opinions. Ziuta didn't argue one way or the other. She didn't encourage us to leave, but she did mention the blockades and suggested that it might be a good idea.

We were living in a state of nervous tension. Rysiek was strongly pushing to leave, to the point of crying. According to him we had no choice. He said the people at the hotel knew what they were doing; after all, they had a head on their shoulders too; we could finally get rid of the constant fear; and so on.

My husband disliked the idea. The whole story horrified him. Finally, at my urging, he decided to go to the hotel along with Rysiek and Stach, to see for himself how everything looked and to talk with Ludwik. So one scorching day all three of them went. They were gone several hours. When they came back, Rysiek was so cross and angry he was crying for rage and threw his cap on the sofa in a fit. Stach had a sour face as well. My husband was upset and almost embarrassed, as if he were guilty of something.

What happened was this. They arrived at the hotel and saw the "thousand happy Jews." Ludwik talked about how everyone believed it would all end well. He was in a good mood; his wife, elegantly dressed, was also in good spirits. My husband ran into some other acquaintances too—intelligent, cultured people who told him, "If you can still manage to make arrangements, there's no point in wasting time deciding. Others would give God-knows-what to get out, but they either don't have the means or they don't know about it. The wife of one of the Jewish Gestapo men in charge is going in that transport. If he had the slightest indication that something was wrong, he wouldn't be sending his wife. So don't think about it, just go." Ludwik saw that my husband was undecided and added, "There'll probably be another transport in a few days, so if you decide to go then, you should see Jerzy; he knows his way around and he'll take care of things. I'll try and send you a letter from the road, so you know whether they're taking us west, like the Germans say, or else east to Treblinka or Bełżec."

It was a beautiful July day. Our room was full of flowers. Ziuta's little garden was full of them, and she was constantly bringing them inside for us. In general, the room was very pleasant.

"Look how nice and cozy this room is," my husband said. "Where is it you want to go? God only knows what they'll do with us."

Once again I felt the urge to argue. "Nice and cozy? And here you're shaking from fear day and night! Of course things won't be this comfortable in the camp, but we won't have the fear either."

My husband nodded his head sadly. "Yes, that's true, things aren't so sweet here, but how do I know what's there?" And we each kept going in circles trying to convince the other. In my heart I realized he was right, but I was gripped by some "departure" fever, and although I didn't believe one hundred percent in the affair, I was pushing for him to leave.

Two hours later Rysiek showed up on the path, accompanied by a young person whose strong underbite, glasses, and beret immediately attracted attention. A few minutes later the man stepped into our room. This was Jerzy. He was thirty-two to thirty-four years old, with a face that was intelligent and quick, although I can't say open and frank. On the contrary, his gaze vanished somewhere deep behind the glaring lenses of his large glasses, as if hiding in the shadows of his bushy dark eyebrows. His entire figure, beginning with his jaw and shoulders, was unusually angular and somewhat coiled, like a snake's. He immediately made himself at home, greeted my husband and myself, and took a seat at the table when he was asked. The conversation was lively and engaging from the start. Jerzy was an intelligent person. He spoke of the latest political news, both the official and the unofficial versions, and about the most recent executions, the details of which we hadn't known, and then we moved to the topic of departure. Jerzy said that a transport was leaving from the hotel in two days with three of his friends for whom he arranged everything, but that nobody else could be added to that group. There would be one more, maybe after a week or ten days. At that time it would be possible to go, and he could take care of arranging things. He mentioned the same amount of money as Ludwik had. We asked him for his advice about whether to stay or leave, to which he shrewdly answered, "I can't advise, you have to decide yourselves, but I can assure you that if I were in your place I would definitely leave."

Maria showed up near the end of his visit. She joined us at the table and began quizzing Jerzy about the details of the trip. She said she didn't trust it. Jerzy shrugged his shoulders in reply. He wasn't going to push. He sat there for almost an hour and then rose to leave. We told him we'd think it over and asked him to stop by on such and such a day.

Jerzy came back at the appointed time. We were expecting him to tell us something about the departure, but he didn't say anything other than it was the last chance to make arrangements. Maria came in while we were talking; she was keeping an eye on the matter. We told Jerzy that we'd heard the hotel had been occupied by army troops. He said he knew about that; this time the gendarmes were going to visit every person who filled out the official exit forms. They would take everyone to a designated place, from where they would go to the station. "After all, it's always been the Gestapo who arranged things and they still are, so it doesn't really matter where the assembly point is, whether in the Hotel Polski or some other place, and the truckload of gendarmes is going for the sake of security, so that no one gets stopped on the street." On the one hand the whole thing seemed strange; on the other it was true that the Gestapo handled all such departures. We looked at one another, but evidently whoever feels touched by Destiny abandons all reason. So even though I was thinking rationally that the whole thing, including Jerzy, was very strange, to put it mildly, the finger of destiny was pushing a button inside me that made me say, "It could all easily be true. After all, it's understandable, if also a little odd. So how do we arrange it?"

"I have to receive an advance today, thirty percent of the sum, and in two days I'll bring you a document directing you to one of the South American countries. At that time you pay me the balance."

Two or three days later, Jerzy returned with a photocopy of a paper stamped for Panama and made out to a name that had been well known in Poland before the war. We were happy to see precisely that name. We knew that the person in question had been in America for a long time, so we were certain one of his friends had sent him the exit papers. That name reassured us that the whole thing might be a sure bet after all, and our moods improved. We gave Jerzy a call, and he promised to show up in two or three days to tell us when and how. He told us we should get ready to leave. Maria wanted to bring the clothes she was storing for us, but I resisted; I wanted to leave a few things behind just in case.

I immediately sent Rysiek to pan Stanisław for my fox fur coat with its beautiful otter collar and two brand-new suits, but he explained he didn't have the things at home and it would be a few days before he could fetch them. Rysiek promised to come back at a later date and asked that the things be made ready. Pan Stanisław promised to do so. Three or four days later Rysiek went back to pan Stanisław and got the same answer, but this time in a fairly dry form; once again he was told to return in a few days—even explaining that we were leaving in a day or two didn't help.

Maria bought us a very large wicker trunk and brought it over in a carriage. That wasn't a good idea, since the neighbors might ask themselves, "What does Ziuta need something like that for? Who is it for? Who's living there? Who's traveling?"—but fortunately the other residents of the building were not the prying type. Ziuta washed our underclothes; we packed everything we had at Ziuta's except our travel clothes into the trunk and waited for Jerzy to give the word to leave. He'd been by to see us two or three times, but on each occasion he told us we had to wait another day or two.

Maria was increasingly nervous; she was terribly afraid of the whole trip. She was always there whenever Jerzy came. She would take him into the room next door. I don't know what she said to him there, but when she came out she was flushed and Jerzy had his eyes downcast. Every time he left Maria told us she'd taken Jerzy aside and begged him in private to cancel the entire business if he suspected there was something fishy. She was also afraid lest she, her child Ziuta, and so on end up in the dungeons of the Gestapo. Each time Jerzy assured her that everything was in order and that his information was the best.

Because I no longer wanted to send Rysiek to pan Stanisław for the furs and suits, I asked Maria to go to him in Żoliborz and gave her a letter. But she came back empty-handed, mad and upset, since pan Stanisław had told her he didn't have anything that belonged to anybody else and didn't know what she was talking about.

One day Jerzy came by to tell us we would be leaving the next day; we were supposed to take a carriage to the Gestapo headquarters on Szuch Boulevard, where they had the list of all those scheduled to leave. We gaped at each other as if we'd been sentenced to death and were standing in front of the gallows looking right at the noose. Ziuta was sitting in the armchair knitting a sweater. I saw how the tears were flowing from her eyes onto the wool. Maria was sitting there looking redder than the most crimson rose, her eyes flashing bolts of anger. Jerzy was quietly nibbling sunflower seeds on the sofa. Seeing Ziuta drenched in tears I went over and knelt beside her like a child beside her mother and asked why she was crying. Did she not want us to leave, or was she afraid of something? We didn't have to go; after all, she could just tell us that we could go on living peacefully with her. "I never threw you out," she said, "and God knows whether you should leave or not, but there's something gives me a bad feeling and something that makes me scared. I'm afraid for your sake." I stroked her head and held her close, and at that moment forgave all the bitter moments we had experienced at her place, seeing how honest she was deep down inside. Ziuta soon became ashamed of her tears; she wiped her eyes, snorted loudly into her handkerchief, energetically resumed her handiwork, and was once again silent and impassive. But one such noble reaction was enough for me.

Jerzy promised to come by the next day at ten in the morning and assist with our departure. All through the night we talked to each other without a wink of sleep. What's going to happen? Should we leave? Can we trust Jerzy? Such a bizarre notion, driving right up to the Gestapo! What a sight! Three Jews with their entire luggage drive right up to Gestapo headquarters and announce their arrival: "We're here, we made it." Isn't it grotesque? But didn't some Jews leave by way of the Gestapo, at the very beginning of the occupation? The questions raced one after the other and there were no answers. We were still undecided whether we should embark on a similar adventure.

In the morning we got dressed, as if to leave, although I was convinced that we wouldn't do it; we wouldn't drive up to the Gestapo as Jerzy had determined. Around ten o'clock Maria came by, all wrought up and hot under the collar, and said she would be right back. Ziuta also was milling about, equally nervous. An hour later Maria came back. This time she was no longer nervous, she was hysterical—she, who was always so well dressed and groomed, but at that moment her hair was disheveled, her hat was crooked, her blouse was coming out of her skirt. She stepped in quickly, plopped down into the chair, turned to face the three of us sitting on the sofa, and said, "Do what you want, but my advice is not to go. I just came back from my fortuneteller. Remember how she's always been right? I decided to go see her right before you left and ask her to tell my fortune. I'm coming from her place right now. Imagine what she said: 'I see a journey, strangers—two, I think—death is awaiting them. Unpleasant things for you.' When she said that I jumped up and ran over here. You see? She knows. I also felt it the whole time, that something's bad, but you wanted to go. Do what you think best, but I had to warn you. The money you lost doesn't mean a thing. Save your lives."

My husband was pale as a sheet and said, "I'm not going." I, too, felt I couldn't handle the trip to the Gestapo. Then Jerzy showed up, cool and collected as always. Maria immediately ran up to him and, grabbing him by the hand, said, "Is it already time, pan Jerzy? But it's certain death!"

Jerzy sat down calmly and said, "The trip has been postponed another several days, but don't you go scaring people." When he heard that it was on account of a fortuneteller, he smiled and waved his hand and said his cousin had once believed what a fortuneteller had told her and had acted accordingly and was unhappy her entire life, and if we wanted to believe things like that he wouldn't stop us, but as for him, Jerzy, he wouldn't act that way. He sat for a while and then said good-bye and promised to come back in two or three days. Maria went with him to see him off.

My husband was practically crying in despair. "Now I've lost everything. Jerzy knows where we are. He can do what he wants with us. I've lost my entire fortune and my peace." Maria came back nearly twenty minutes later. Seeing how terribly upset my husband was, she started to calm him down, saying that she didn't think Jerzy would turn us in, she had begged him to have pity on her, her child, Ziuta, and her children. She said we could work out the money somehow, maybe the piano at pan Seweryn W's could be sold along with the things at her place and somehow we'd manage. She spent half the day with us, upset and anxious to be sure but somehow calmed by the fact that for the moment we weren't leaving.

Jerzy didn't show up for another three or four days. We hadn't thought he'd come anymore. But one day while I was in the kitchen fixing dinner and kneading dough for noodles, Rysiek came in to say that Jerzy was on his way. Those words always pinched my heart. Jerzy entered our room. I wanted to stop fixing dinner and listen to what Jerzy had to say, but Rysiek came to the kitchen and told me that Jerzy asked for me to leave them alone for a moment since he had something to say and didn't want a woman to be present. So I stayed where I was. Their conversation lasted fifteen minutes, while I almost died of curiosity. What could be so important I wasn't allowed to hear it? Finally Rysiek came to me with a sullen face and said I could come in, and while I was still in the kitchen he briefly told me what it was about. Evidently Jerzy claimed he had heard something about these departures and temporarily put ours on hold. He had reclaimed the diamond from the Gestapo officers but was unable to recover the rest of the money, worth about half the value of the ring. In fact he didn't even want to, since that would mean locking horns with this person or that. So he'd return whatever was still in his possession—that is, the ring—and meanwhile he'd listen to find out whether there'd be another departure or not, and for any news about those who had left.

I walked into our room. Jerzy and my husband were sitting there with gloomy faces, neither one looking at the other. To let me know what tactic we had to use, my husband immediately started speaking to me more or less like this: "You see, pan Jerzy has learned some very nasty things about what happened to the people who left from the hotel; evidently they were sent to their deaths after all. See how honest pan Jerzy is? He came to tell us right away and brought along the ring. He's afraid to ask those scoundrels to return the money, and he's right, too. The main thing is that he found out the truth." I continued the conversation in the same vein: Naturally we were very thankful to him for having gone to so much trouble to discover the truth, and we would always remember him for that. We also would very much like it if he'd visit us and were very obliged for the ring, since without it we wouldn't have anything left to buy bread. Jerzy asked us for the foreign document he had brought us, since he had obligated himself to return it. We handed it back to him. A few minutes later he left, saying he would stop in to see us after a few days. But we never saw him again.

The summer passed, and soon fall had colored the leaves of the few trees in our park golden. Somehow we managed to survive despite the constant suspicion, the constant expectation that something terrible was about to happen, and the constant nagging thought that Jerzy still had something up his sleeve, and that the closer we got to the end of the war, the sooner he was going to want to get rid of us. And indeed Jerzy had not forgotten us.

First Roland showed up at the beginning of November, to relax a little at home and fatten up on his mother's cooking. My husband passed the evenings playing "one thousand" with the boy, and during the day Roland helped us pass the time with his singing and his healthy sense of humor. So we were sad and sorry when pani Ziuta told us he was going back on Sunday the fourteenth. But there was no question of his staying; people in the factory where he worked might find out he had sneaked off to Warsaw. So mostly he sat at home in a bad mood because he couldn't leave the house.

At 3 P.M. on the fourteenth, pani Ziuta went to put Roland on the train back to Grójec and then go to church for vespers. As she was about to leave we noticed two men on the path outside. They were about forty years old, well dressed and powerfully built. One wore a yellow leather jacket and a cap, the other a black overcoat and a dark hat. Both were complete strangers in the neighborhood. Together they approached the door but didn't knock. A few minutes later we saw them walking away; we guessed they'd gone to the neighbors and hadn't found who they were looking for and felt the fear lift a little that had begun to weigh on our hearts. The unknown men passed our house, turned off somewhere to the left, and disappeared. Ziuta locked the door, put the key under the mat, and left.

It was a gloomy autumn afternoon; we knew we would be alone for a few hours; there wasn't much daylight left, and Ziuta wouldn't be back until after dark—six or seven o'clock. We started reading; my husband lay down on the sofa to read. Since he didn't want to wear out his one pair of pants, he was wearing Rysiek's ski pants. I wrapped myself in a knit shawl, sat down in the armchair from where I could watch what was going on, and every now and then glanced up from my reading at the pathway. After a short while, maybe ten or fifteen minutes, I heard the key turn in the kitchen. Who can that be? Probably Stach, I thought, and content with that I turned to face the door, which opened a moment later— but instead of Stach, there at the threshold of our room was one of the two strangers we had seen earlier in the garden, the one with the overcoat and hat. His face was strong and angular, with a clearly marked jaw. His small, shifty eyes were taking in the entire room. He stomped over to the sofa where my husband was lying down. My husband and I kept our eyes fixed on each other. The stranger took a chair from the table, spun it toward the sofa, and sat down. My husband sat up, and as soon as I recovered from the shock I walked over to the sofa and sat next to him, like a scared child entranced by a bogeyman. For several seconds there was silence. Finally the stranger practically roared, "So here you are! Well, get dressed, let's go!"

"I'm not going anywhere," I responded.

The stranger fixed me with an animal gaze; his lower jaw was sliding left and right. He looks so much like Jerzy, I thought, maybe it's his brother or his cousin.

The stranger was gnashing his teeth. "Get dressed this minute. They'll talk to you over there."

"Listen," I answered. "There's no sense in wasting words; we're not going anywhere. Please just tell us what it is you want."

The man sized me up. My calm manner had evidently thrown him off balance. "You don't want to go? It'll cost you a hundred thousand zloty! Well, out with it! Hand it over!"

I spoke again. "We don't have any money, and we're not giving you anything. There's nothing to discuss."

"So that's how it's going to be, is it?" The criminal was almost shouting. He sprang out of the chair and ran to the wardrobe, tearing open the doors and tossing everything out on the table: my husband's overcoat, his jacket, some English cloth, and six brand-new silk shirts. He paused to look at the label—"Opus, not bad"—and then took my husband's only pair of pants.

My husband jumped up and tried to take the pants back. "Give them here," he said. "They're the only ones I have; that's it. I won't be able to go out!"

"Go out? That's the whole point, you don't go out!" The man tore the pants out of my husband's hands and placed them on the table. "Don't touch," he said, then opened the drawer and dumped all the contents onto the floor. He didn't find anything that caught his interest. Then he took my purse from the wardrobe, rummaged through it, removed my Kennkarte and a silver cigarette case, and put them in his pocket. After that he ran his hand beneath the tabletop, feeling all around.

"Damn it all, where'd you hide the cash? Because I know all about you, pan Górski!"

Górski! The alias we had used with Jerzy. No one else knew it. So of course this was all Jerzy's doing. The man turned both armchairs upside down, feeling everywhere. He tore the bed apart, dumping the pillows and mattress onto the floor, cursing and swearing. He noticed my husband's nice brown hat and added it to the pile on the table. He stood on a chair and looked on top of the wardrobe. He found a box with some rags, threw it on the floor, and rummaged through that. He pulled out a suitcase we had bought for the journey from under the bed and threw our things inside. He grabbed my husband's arm to see if there was a watch. He found a nice Omega and tore it off. He turned to me and wrenched off my wedding ring, nearly breaking my fingers. My husband started to scuffle with him; the man hit him in the face. On my other hand I was wearing a silver ring of no value that my daughter had given me. It was the only memento of her I had. The criminal took that as well. I begged him, practically on my knees, to give it back. "All I can do is sell it to you for ten thousand zloty." I would have happily paid even more, but I had hidden all our money in one place and he would have taken every last penny. And I still had my husband and son to think about.

He packed everything into the suitcase and said, "Now listen! Your son is coming from Piastów tomorrow at noon, and we'll be there to meet him. If we don't get thirty thousand zloty within two days, we'll know what to do!"

My legs were giving way. "So it's Jerzy giving the orders?" I was shouting.

"Jerzy, that's right! What did you think, that Jerzy was going to get you out of the country? Remember: two days, thirty thousand zloty!"

I grabbed his arm. "At least give me back my Kennkarte—I need it to get the money, and I'm the only one who can get it!"

I struggled with him a long time. He pointed to the kitchen door. "You better let go of me because my colleague's standing outside and he might come in." But I refused to let go. What finally convinced him was the thought that he might not get his money. So he took the Kennkarte out of his coat pocket and gave it back to me. Then he left and locked the door behind him.

My husband was beside himself. Tears were streaming from his eyes; he threw himself on the sofa and tore his hair. Oblivious to any danger, he shouted, "My poor child, what's going to happen to

him? I don't have a single pair of pants, how can I go outside? Why
did you ever get involved with that Jerzy, you and your stupid idea
of leaving the country. What's going to happen? What's going to
happen?"

He rolled about on the sofa, tearing at his jacket and shirt in
his despair. His condition alarmed me. I thought he would go mad.
I tried to calm him, telling him not to give up, we had been in
worse situations where danger was more immediate and had managed somehow to come through, so there was a good chance we'd
find a way out of this as well. After all, we had a little time, since
Rysiek was coming tomorrow, so maybe, maybe—

Suddenly we heard the kitchen door open again and Ziuta's
voice. Apparently she was not alone. We tried to listen to the conversation. Maybe it had something to do with what had just happened. We heard a man's voice, but a moment later we realized
that Ziuta had come with the priest, because we could hear her
saying things like, "Right here, Father, it would have to be cut right
here, folded over there, and sewn on right here." They were talking about sewing or repairing something for the church; the conversation dragged on forever. We had managed to lower the thick
paper shades, so our room wasn't just dark; it was pitch black. And
our souls were black, too, even as Ziuta was telling the priest "It'll
turn out white as snow. I'll wash it, iron it, and bring it over. You
can rest assured, Father." The priest asked about Roland, Hanka,
and Ziuta's husband. Our fingers were nearly gnawed to the bone.
Finally, after a hundred thousand questions, how's this and how's
that, how's his health and how's hers, and all sorts of holy chitchat,
the priest left, after the pious Ziuta obsequiously kissed his hand.
We crawled into the kitchen, afraid Ziuta might go out again. I
whispered "Come quickly" and dragged her to our room so she
wouldn't dawdle. Once we were in the room I turned on the light.
When Ziuta saw the way things looked she lost her balance and
had to lean against the wall. With her huge steely-blue eyes wide

open she walked around the room, completely dumbfounded. Finally she managed to mutter, "What happened?" and seeing my husband doubled up on the sofa, sobbing and grabbing at his tangled tufts of hair, she ran to him, shook him by the arm, and said in a terrified voice, "What happened to you? Tell me, for Jesus' sake; get up!"

We told her everything. She clutched at her head. "What are we going to do? What are we going to do? You can't stay here a moment longer. What will you do about the child?" I tried as hard as I could to keep calm and clear-headed.

"Ziuta," I said, "you have to call Stach and Maria right away. The most important thing is to save the child. Don't delay, it's getting late, they have to make it here somehow."

Ziuta ran out of the apartment and telephoned Stach's neighbors. After a few minutes she came back and said that Stach had sounded terrified when she told him to come right away. After about half an hour Stach and Maria showed up. It's difficult to describe their horror when they heard what had happened. We decided they would each watch the stop where Rysiek would get off the tram, and then take him to Stachna, Maria's sister. Earlier, Stachna wouldn't hear about taking Rysiek in, but given the way things were they decided to present her with a done deed. Nothing could be done about us, though, since they didn't have enough room. They quickly said good-bye and left. We sat up with Ziuta late into the night, weighing what to do. We couldn't come up with anything. None of us slept. I talked with my husband in our room, while Ziuta tossed and turned on her creaky bed.

The next morning, Maria showed up before eleven. She came by way of the fields, since she was afraid the blackmailers might see her. She had left Stach on lookout by the streetcar stop and had come to calm us down and see what was going on. She went right back to her watch and promised to return after everything had been taken care of. Ziuta was to act as a messenger between the streetcar stop and us. Ziuta accompanied Maria back through the fields and returned, saying she had noticed a well-built man wearing a dark coat and hat milling about the entrance to the property, with his collar turned up and his hat pulled down over his face. The description fit yesterday's "guest." Then she sneaked back to check the streetcar stop. According to my watch—which the thief had overlooked—it was noon, and our anxiety reached its peak, since that was when we were supposed to have met our child. At ten after twelve Ziuta came running up and I could tell from her expression that everything was all right. She said that no sooner had Rysiek stepped off the tram than Stach and Maria ran up and led him off in the opposite direction, without giving him a chance to catch his breath. They were taking him across the fields to Stachna's place in upper Mokotów. Rysiek was so amazed to see people he knew well that he turned red from astonishment and fear, thinking something bad had happened to us, but they had reassured him right away. Ziuta watched for a long time after the three of them left and then came back to us, having noticed from a distance that the man was still milling about. We sighed with relief. Then we all deliberated what to do about us.

We agreed with Ziuta that we couldn't stay at her place a moment longer; unfortunately, no one could figure out any other place for us to go. There was still some hope Maria might find a way out, as she had for Rysiek. She was supposed to come back once Rysiek had been installed at Stachna's. The fact that my husband had nothing to wear was another severe problem; his pants had been stolen, and Rysiek's ski pants came down only to his knees, which made him look comical. Nor did he have anything to wear on his head. Ziuta sat with her head bowed, gloomily staring off into the corner. We, too, sat brooding without speaking. Then Ziuta jumped up and said, "Things are the way they are. I still have to fix dinner for us and for Maria. With all the running around she's been doing, she's bound to be pretty hungry."

Finally Ziuta declared that after dinner she would go to her very good acquaintance, pani Zofia O, the mother of one of Roland's friends, who lived with her twelve-year-old son in a single room on the same street about 100 meters away. Maybe she would let us stay there temporarily—one room was just too small to remain in permanently. After dinner Ziuta quickly stashed the dishes in the corner and dashed off to pani Zofia's. Maria, who couldn't stay very long, went out with Ziuta, promising to drop in the next morning. Once again we were alone. Every few minutes we would think we heard the door being opened and would wait for the same robber to appear, but Ziuta no longer left the key under the doormat. We couldn't shake the feeling that the men would want to take revenge and send the Germans to get us. The moments seemed to stretch into eternity. It was already getting dark when Ziuta came back. "Well!" she said, still on the threshold. "I did what I could. Pani Zofia agreed right away to take you for a time. I had to tell her everything, though: that we'd been hiding two people for months, and that on account of a careless mistake something very unpleasant had happened and the people now had to leave the apartment. She has three sons. Two were sent to Germany as forced labor; Janusz is somewhere in the east and Tadzik is out in the country at some dairy plant. The third son, Kazik, is twelve years old, and he's with his mother. I said I'd bring you over as soon as it gets completely dark." We were overjoyed. We decided to leave just a few minutes before the curfew, since we didn't have far to go. We were still afraid someone might be watching us and decide to follow, but that person would also have to be back before curfew and no doubt had farther to go than we did.

We were sad to leave the quiet, friendly, cozy apartment to which we had grown so accustomed, but there was no choice. We had nothing to take, since the robber had stripped us bare; our entire bundle consisted of a few worn shirts and an old patched-up summer dress: we left our bedding behind. My husband had to go in the ski pants; Ziuta lent him a short sheepskin coat. I took along my tiny vial of poison, discreetly slipping it in my bag. We ate supper in the old place, and with only ten minutes before curfew we left. On our way out we turned back for a last glimpse of our temporary refuge. As soon as we left the vestibule, Ziuta took both of us by the arm and, as she was familiar with the terrain, led us—in the dark—across the fields and potato patches and back to the street right across from pani Zofia. We could make out the outlines of a modern apartment house; a moment later we were climbing up the dimly lit staircase. To this day I don't know which floor we stayed on, only that Ziuta knocked on one of five or six doors, and it opened at once. We were let in without a word.

POLA GLEZER (WHO ALSO WENT BY THE NAMES AGATA Królak and Franciszka Radomska) owned a tailor shop before the war in her native Warsaw. In 1942 she married Olek, whom the Germans shot nine months later for possessing a weapon. Glezer was pregnant at the time; the child was stillborn in spring 1943. A friend helped her obtain false documents and work. Following the collapse of the Warsaw Uprising, she escaped to a small town outside Warsaw, where she survived until liberation without revealing her identity. Glezer then confessed her background and experiences to her friend Jadwiga, writing her account as a nighttime conversation between two girlfriends. It is unknown what later became of her.

I decided to make my way to Warsaw, where I planned to look up a friend of mine or possibly go to an acquaintance of my husband's. Naturally I had to leave the apartment at dawn, so none of the neighbors would notice; then I'd walk around outside until I could take the first train into Warsaw. So I traipsed through the village, expecting to hear someone shout *Jude!* and then be sentenced without trial and shot. But in the end nobody stopped me and I boarded the train as calmly as I could.

I watched the world passing by and thought how wonderful it really is. The sun was shining so beautifully, the air smelled so nice, the birds were singing. Everyone was hurrying to get someplace, striving for something, taking care of business; everyone had some destination. The man next to me tried to strike up a conversation, which interrupted my sad reflections. After half an hour we became good friends. He asked me the purpose of my trip. I answered evasively. Our conversation turned into a gentle flirtation, and pan X wanted to arrange a date. I wondered why anybody would want to court danger by going out with a Jewish woman. Was he so sensitive he pretended not to realize I was Jewish? Everything was one enormous question mark. When all my attempts to wriggle out of the situation proved in vain, and my acquaintance refused to give up, I asked him to look at me carefully and tell me what he saw. He launched into a string of compliments, not what I expected. Don't be surprised, Jadwiga, that I'm going on so long about this. On the surface it was just an ordinary flirtation, the kind that happens all the time, but there was something about this that was more significant, something that might be called decisive. It took me some time to catch on that he really didn't realize who I was. I wanted to see what kind of impression it would make, so I simply said, "Can't you tell that I'm Jewish?"

He opened his eyes wide. "Unbelievable. I never would have guessed."

Then we had a short frank discussion, and pan X asked me to stay in touch. I promised I'd write if they didn't kill me in the next day or so. But the meeting had a tremendous effect on me. I gained a great deal of self-confidence, which I held onto throughout the occupation. I became imaginative and even inspired; I developed into a sophisticated liar—you see the kind of thing I can boast to you about.

In Warsaw I went to the office of public records and found my friend's address, but unfortunately she had moved and the people at her old home didn't know her new one. I made the care-taker promise that if pani J showed up to have her residency permit stamped, he'd find out her new address. Disappointed, I got back on the train headed for Góra Kalwaria, to try my luck with my husband's acquaintance. On the way I flirted again, this time with pan S, to whom I presented myself as a capricious woman who'd had a fight with her husband and was on her way to her parents. I tell you I was losing all sense of reality. I felt as if I were playing a role in some comedy and—ironic as it sounds—even laughed on cue when pan S unambiguously proposed we spend our vacation together.

Finally I reached my destination, where the Zs received me very well. The husband was taken by my story. He vowed to get hold of a Kennkarte for me and told me to return in a few days. Overjoyed, I took the train back "home."

After a few days I set out again for the promised Kennkarte. After reliving all the difficulties of travel I finally reached the same house, but all my fantasies of survival vanished into thin air. My would-be benefactor said he had tried but nothing had come of it, maybe in a few weeks? It was one thing for an ordinary person to talk about a few weeks, but for me every single moment was filled with danger. "Of course," he said, as if he didn't fully understand my situation, "we could go fishing. Nobody's there and no one would recognize you, but you wouldn't be able to sleep at our place since our neighbors are German and they invite themselves over for vodka and cards." When I didn't answer, he said again, "Let's go fishing," and looked at me suggestively. I thanked him for his cordiality and promised that if I'm still alive I'll come by for the Kennkarte. I shook hands with his wife, who said good-bye with a look that seemed reserved for a rival. I went on my way, with sunken head.

Quo vadis? There was no road for me. No one needed me; on the contrary, I was only a burden. I thought of throwing myself into the pond where the sun was reflected so beautifully. Maybe, I thought, I would find peace there. I looked at the mirrorlike surface and saw the face of my beloved mother—smiling at me—and I saw a pair of big blue eyes. It was my sister from the land of the sun, begging me to struggle and survive: "Even the worst will pass," she said. "We'll see each other again someday, and you'll never again be homeless and alone."

LEON NAJBERG. Captain Miller was waiting for me at Inwalidów Square, as arranged. I was so happy I wanted to run over to him, but he winked and nodded for me to follow him. He led me toward the Vistula, where we hid in the brush. There we greeted each other warmly; the captain said he'd expected to meet someone from Oppel's Jewish workers but never me. His family had already mourned my loss (they knew me from his stories); evidently my comrades from the worksite had assumed up to the day of their deportation that I'd been killed after the fighting broke out in the ghetto. I gave the captain a brief report of the uprising, and he told me about the Jewish workers at the factory. At dusk he took me to his home in Żoliborz at 18 Krasiński Street. I took a bath and threw away my lice-infested rags, and he gave me fresh underclothes and a jacket. After dinner I had to leave the apartment; there were already two Jews hiding there—two brothers from Lwów—a doctor and an engineer.[4]

The captain promised that starting the next day, 28 September 1943, he would do everything possible to help our group—indeed, from our very first encounter he demonstrated an unshakable sincerity in his efforts to help Jews. I arranged to meet him in the same way the next day. At that time he told me that no place had been found for me. But he promised to devote every free minute to the task of locating a temporary situation, even if it was just for a month. And once again the question of money arose, which neither I, nor pani Zemsz, who was hiding in the basement with me, nor Captain Miller possessed.

The days passed without change or any prospect of change. I bought a pair of overalls and wandered the streets of Warsaw during the day, dressed as a worker, while at night I returned to the basement.

One day I learned from the captain that he had located a potential place for us, but that evening, when I returned to the basement, pani Zemsz told me that some children had come in the basement during the day; they had seen her and taken an interest in her. She had pretended to be mute but the experience left her shaken, and when I told her that the search for another hiding place was dragging on, she decided to go to the caretaker of the building at 10 Grzybowski Square, who found her a place nearby. (In March or April of 1944 I saw her picture in an issue of the new *Warsaw Courier*, with the news that a woman had been found murdered in the ruins of a building on Krochmalna, wearing clothes from the Czyste hospital. To this day I don't know how she perished.)

On Saturday I again rode out to Żoliborz, in order to be sure to reach Miller before I left Warsaw. In the evening the captain took me to Bielany, where he had been promised a place for one month for 3,000 zloty. But when we arrived, the landlady had changed her mind about taking in a Jew. It was getting late; I couldn't return to Warsaw, since the curfew for Poles began at 9 P.M. I decided to spend the night in the fields at Bielany, but the captain objected and resolved to arrange for both of us to stay at a friend's in the same part of town.

It was after nine when we reached Chełmżyńska Street (currently Płatnicza), and the captain went up to number 88, a single-family house. A moment later he came back with the joyful news that his friend had agreed I could spend the night there as well. I went inside and met the owner, pan Szczypiorski, who turned out to be an unusually warm person, kind and sensitive to human suffering. After I'd been there a few hours he instructed me that his wife was outside Warsaw; in case she showed up I should introduce myself as a cousin from Ożarów who had come to Warsaw for medical treatment. That was the first home in occupied Warsaw where I experienced genuine familial warmth from the very first moment. I was supposed to spend only one night there and return the following evening (since it was Sunday). Throughout the entire day pan Szczypiorski was very kind and friendly, and at sunset, when Captain Miller arrived, pan Szczypiorski explained that after everything I had experienced he considered it his sacred obligation to keep me there. Miller was happy that he had finally managed to situate me. For the first several days I lay in bed pretending to be sick, which wasn't very difficult, and when pani Teofila came back, she swallowed the tale we had concocted without a moment's hesitation.

The next days were blissfully peaceful, although this did not last long. After I had recuperated some, I decided to write down my experiences in the form of a diary. Captain Miller provided me with pencils, notebooks, and a calendar. I had kept a few scraps of notes made inside the ghetto, and the events were still fresh in my memory. When I sat down to write they simply flowed from my pen; there wasn't space to record everything I had inside my head. I was so engrossed in my writing that I didn't even go down to eat. But I was surrounded by well-meaning people who helped at every step, and when they interrupted me it was only to make sure I didn't get sick from working too hard. At that time pani Teofila still didn't know what I was writing. The work so absorbed me that I couldn't tear myself away and would write until late in the night. Pan Szczypiorski told me several times not to stay up late, since the light could be seen from the street and might attract unwanted attention. Fortunately the house was a two-story dwelling; my room was on the upper story, where no strangers ever ventured.

Pan Szczypiorski (he was a senior cashier in the ticket office and is now a department director for the Warsaw office of transportation; he belonged to the Communist Party before the war) would bring home viciously anti-Semitic pamphlets published by the Propagandeamt and distributed at his work. I used them to decorate my desk; if a stranger were to come upstairs, I would hide my notebook underneath a stack of such "literature." Each notebook that I finished was immediately sealed and buried in the basement. I went on living and writing in this relative peace and quiet until the middle of October 1943.

At that point rumors reached us that the entire city of Warsaw was to be closed off and a general roundup conducted with the goal of uncovering Jews in hiding.[5] All of Bielany, including our street, was suddenly blocked off by gendarmes. Stefanek, the Szczypiorskis' son, came running up, all out of breath, to tell me to escape into the fields. At the time he didn't know I was Jewish; but Polish youth—especially those unable to provide proper documents—were also in danger during such occasions, and he wanted to protect his cousin.

I went into the garden, but the whole area was surrounded and there was no way of getting past the German cordon. From my upstairs room I secretly watched the Germans outside. From the house across the street (home of the Kaczmarski family—he was a streetcar operator), I caught a glimpse of several young men peeking out from one of the windows on the second floor. One glance suggested they were Jewish; my hunch seemed confirmed when I saw the Kaczmarskis suddenly leave the house, locking the door and closing the gate behind them.

A moment later pani Teofila came upstairs and told me to get my papers ready, since the Germans were going through the houses. I said her husband had taken my documents to register me with the Arbeitsamt, and I had no others. Pani Teofila told me to go outside and hide under the currant bushes.

At that moment the doorbell rang long and shrill, and we heard the heavy pounding of rifle butts against the door. Pani Teofila ran down to let in the gendarmes, and in the twinkling of an eye I decided to hide in an attic loft. I had discovered earlier that one of these spaces had a little indentation or niche that could not be seen from any distance. In order to get inside the niche I had to crawl on my hands and knees across eight meters of attic. Once inside the niche, I was sure that this time I was finished. I heard footsteps and the sounds of German words coming from the neighbor's attic. After a moment I could make out the gendarmes' voices, demanding pani Szczypiorska show her papers and asking whether there were any men in the house. She told them there were none. The gendarmes began searching on the ground floor, looking inside the wardrobe and the sofa beds. They checked the basement, the bathroom, and the garden and headed upstairs to my room. They tore the bedding off the bed to see if anyone was hiding inside. They looked into the two storage spaces on either side of the stairs that led to my room, then wrenched open the door that led to the space where I was hiding. Two gendarmes walked inside to a spot where they could stand up comfortably, very close to where the slanted attic led to my little niche. They shone their flashlights through the loft but failed to notice the niche. Someone shouted from outside, *"Hier niemand da"*—There's no one here, but they stopped to look at the empty wine bottles. A moment later the gendarmes left the attic and went back down to the room, where there was a gramophone built into a wooden cabinet. One of them asked pani Szczypiorska to put on a record; they wanted to listen to a little music. I heard her tell them the gramophone was broken. When the gendarmes left I heard the sound of someone collapsing on the floor. Half an hour later I decided to leave my hiding place. There in the room lay pani Szczypiorska, who had fainted; Stefanek, who had come back, was reviving her. The woman had changed beyond recognition. She was very pale, her eyes terrified, and she was shaking from fear. The gendarmes stayed in Bielany throughout the evening. They ferreted out a few dozen people. And on Schroeger Street they found a young Jewish couple who were taken to Pawiak along with the people hiding them—none of them ever came back. Whether by chance or oversight the gendarmes did not go inside the Kaczmarskis' house.

That evening pan Szczypiorski came home worried, since he had heard in Żoliborz that two Jews had been caught in Bielany. He had been convinced that I was one of them, which would have meant a tragedy for his family. Outside the house he nearly fainted when he saw that all the lights were out; pani Szczypiorska had been too afraid to light them, and the dark house only seemed to confirm his fears.

But even after he realized that everyone was still alive his joy was short-lived. Pani Teofila made a scene and threatened to leave with the child if I stayed. (By that time she probably realized I was Jewish.) He wanted to go on sheltering me and refused to concede defeat. The argument lasted several days. Meanwhile, I found a triangular opening between the roof and the ceiling of one of the attic lofts that was located above the door leading to the garden. I decided to convert the space into a hideout and stay there until I received my Kennkarte. Pan Szczypiorski bought some boards, hinges, deadbolts, and cement. We constructed a trapdoor out of the boards, which we fixed to the inside of the roof, like a pigeon screen; if danger threatened I could climb in, lower the trapdoor, and bolt it shut behind. The trapdoor fit flush with the ceiling of the loft, and we daubed cement on the boards to make them blend in. If the searchers were very thorough, and if time permitted, Stefanek, who knew by then that I was Jewish, would camouflage the door and the surrounding area with pieces of wood, empty bottles, and assorted debris.

It turned out I had to use the hideout several times even after I had obtained the Aryan documents, for instance in February 1944 when a Home Army unit carried out an expropriation action against several shopkeepers.* And I used the hideout another time that Easter, when a Home Army execution squad drove up to a house where some women of loose morals were living who were in the service of the Gestapo. The squad shot four women and two German officers who were with them. All of Bielany was immediately surrounded by Germans, but the hideout passed that test as well. The Germans rounded up 150 men from Bielany and executed them.

I think it was a month later when all Warsaw was electrified by the theft of a few armored cars from the German automobile workshop located on Walicôw Street.[6] The Germans searched the entire city and showed up at Bielany as well. Once again, the streets were cordoned off as they launched an intensive search for the dismantled parts.

Some 250 meters from our house was a warehouse where coal had been sold before the war. The place was abandoned, forgotten, and locked up. No one bothered about it. During the search the Germans took an interest, and several gendarmes approached the building to see what was inside. But the strong bars and bolts were not afraid of the Germans and refused to budge. That was too much for the Germans, who started pounding with their rifle butts, trying to break down the door. At that point a strong explosion was heard from inside and several Germans were blown up. The Home Army had been hiding one of the armored cars inside the building, which was equipped with a specially constructed time bomb connected to the lock. The car, the warehouse, and the Germans were blown to pieces and strewn across several dozen square meters. The

---

*The Home Army (AK) was the official underground resistance sanctioned by the Polish government-in-exile in London. An umbrella organization, it contained elements ranging from progressive liberal democrats to anti-Semitic, right-wing nationalists.—PB

explosion shattered windows in all the neighboring apartments. It wasn't long before we felt the consequences. Some higher officers drove out to Bielany, and the whole area resembled a battle zone. This time the searches went on for twenty-four hours. The Germans spared no one—not even children. Everyone had to produce papers. They took another hundred hostages from Bielany and shot them.[7] During those twenty-four hours I lay doubled up inside my hideout (80 centimeters wide by 60 centimeters long by one meter deep), where there was very little air. I was so numb and exhausted I couldn't eat.

Whenever things were calm I continued writing my diary; by May 1944 I had filled sixteen notebooks and hidden them away. Young Kowarski, who was hiding in Warsaw, visited several times (his father, a Jew, had been the manager of Orbis on Nalewki Street). Kowarski knew pan Szczypiorski and came to see him from time to time. Kowarski told him he was receiving aid from the Jewish National Committee, but when I wanted to contact them myself to obtain assistance, pan Szczypiorski and Captain Miller wouldn't let me, claiming that this would only increase the risk of my being found out. Material conditions at the Szczypiorskis' were generally pitiful throughout my stay there. All of us lived off their family's ration cards and pan Aleksander's modest paycheck; now and then pani Szczypiorska would travel to the Lublin district and smuggle things back, which helped a little to improve our income, which was scanty at best.

Once my hideout had weathered several searches, peace returned to the household, and everyone showed me genuine humanitarian concern and sincere attachment. In the middle of the Nazi storm, the Szczypiorskis gave me a warm home, all three treating me like a son and a brother.

I stayed there until the outbreak of the uprising in Warsaw. On the day it started I was in Bielany, fighting with the Home Army until the end.

After the Germans regained control of Bielany all the men hid, and the Germans again began rummaging through the houses looking for the fighters. In those nightmarish days the hideout again proved helpful, and Stefanek's brotherly feelings toward me were invaluable. Pan Szczypiorski was not at home; the uprising had caught him at his work, where he fought alongside the others.

*JOURNALIST **HENRYK RYSZEWSKI** WAS NOT ONLY NOT JEWISH, he was anti-Semitic—until the outrageous Nazi treatment of Jews brought about a change of heart. For almost two years thereafter, the "reborn" Ryszewski and his wife, Irena, hid thirteen people in their apartment. When Ryszewski died in 1972, he was posthumously honored by the Yad Vashem Institute of Jerusalem.*

It's very easy to have a constantly negative attitude toward everything one encounters. "Life is an easy task for the likes of Pyotr Stepanovich," Dostoyevsky once wrote, "since he invented someone else who dwells in the world by his side." After I turned twenty-one a similarly estranged being resided within me, and this person was an anti-Semite. That was when I joined the editorial staff of the *Gazeta Warszawska,* the main organ of the bellicose Endecja. There I gained a classic anti-Semitic education. Nor did these views abate later on, between 1924 and 1939, when I worked as a parliamentary correspondent for the *Dziennik Bydgoski,* vanguard of the anti-Semitic press in Pomerania. In those circumstances I became a steadfast and outspoken anti-Semite and took every opportunity to uphold my convictions, both in my professional work as well as in the Parliamentary Reporter Club. Today I am greatly embarrassed as I recall the noisy disputes I carried on with my talented colleague Bernard Singer, from the Jewish paper *Nasz Przegląd* (Our View), who signed his own reports with the pseudonym "Regnis." It took life itself to show me how sick, how mentally crippled I had been. The war and the terrible cruelties spawned by Nazism and worldwide fascism kindled within me a love of my fellowman that dismantled all barriers of chauvinism and errant nationalism, all prejudices of race and caste. A spark of human sympathy was lit within me; that was all it took. Saint Paul was transformed on the road to Damascus, I on the streets of Warsaw that led from the ghetto to my home on Nowy Zjazd. Once a hardened anti-Semite, I became a staunch defender of Jews.

That was an especially bright day in my life, when something opened up within me and came bursting out. I broke my own bonds; I no longer recognized myself. In one moment everything was simplified, things were absolutely clear and perfectly understood; I looked at the world, people, and events with new eyes.

When my heart and my imagination first stirred, a new person was born inside me. There is an eastern proverb that says, "When you see your friend's beard on fire, douse your own with water." But in my case the opposite happened: My home became a happy harbor for Jews, a cradle of their hopes for survival. Sharing their common oppression and bearing the same burdens, I had no choice but to become reborn.

Rabbi Jehuda Hamnassi once delivered a calf that was seeking shelter into the hands of the butchers, saying, "Go to the slaughter, for that you were born." This one deed caused him many long years of suffering, until one day a servant girl wanted to drown a litter of young kittens. The rabbi reproached her, saying, "Leave them alone; the Lord shows mercy to all his creatures." And from that point on his suffering ceased. My own disease, known as anti-Semitism, was long and protracted. But suddenly I was cured when in the name of our Lord I showed compassion to others and took them under my roof. In the language of theology (I still have a little Latin left from my time at the seminary in Włocławek), I became a *"neofita ex anti-semitismo conversus"*—a convert from anti-Semitism.

We all celebrated Christmas together. The meal was meager but very festive. Nearly everyone helped with the cooking. My own task was to find and decorate a Christmas tree.

A long time ago, from a poor stable in Bethlehem, the true meaning of universal love and the idea of brotherhood among different nations, races, creeds, and skin colors first came into the world. On this particular day the divine rays of that brotherhood warmed the careworn people in our Warsaw apartment. Seated at the table set for Christmas Eve, at that moment they were fortunate beyond measure—cheerful, smiling, and singing.

Christmas awakens our deepest and noblest feelings, and we were truly moved as we shared the Host with our Jewish friends. For each person there was a present—even if it was a small one—underneath the tree. We were happy for ourselves and for the children. The tree with its lighted candles was a joy to behold. Little Linka was particularly delighted by the holiday atmosphere and overwhelmed her mother with questions. Most of all she wanted to make sure she'd always have a Christmas tree when they went back to their own home. Linka's mother was moved and a little embarrassed; she hugged her daughter close and said, "That Christmas tree isn't yours, sweetheart, our people have a different faith. But you'll never forget that tree as long as you live, I'm sure about that!"

We started to sing carols, and everyone felt light at heart. We asked our friends to sing some Jewish folk songs, or hymns. They couldn't turn us down and, humming more than singing, they shared some of their age-old songs, full of yearning and deeply lyrical. Our little Januszek did very well with a short poem penned especially for the occasion. Pan Opal, a banker by profession, composed a rhymed panegyric in our honor, in which he mostly praised the "first lady" pani Irena, expressing his profound gratitude and friendship and pledging to cherish forever the memory of all she had done.

When appropriate, Jews are able to strike the most gracious chords within the human soul, to appeal to the softest nature of the human heart. Years ago, for example, after the ratification of the May Third Constitution, the Jews of Warsaw stood before King Stanisław August, and said, "Praise be to you, good king and lord! The sweet words from your lips give wings to ideas. . . . The truth you speak fills us with confidence; your words stream into our souls like the dew from heaven quenches the thirsty earth. You have but to speak, and we will be of one accord. Let us be uplifted by your grace, kind king! Be merciful to us, as the Lord is merciful to you!"

Pani Irena listened to pan Opal's speech, smiled, and then sincerely thanked everyone for such eloquent demonstrations of their feelings.

Little Linka, gifted with a wonderful memory, also gave a fine performance before the lighted Christmas tree. Her patriotic verse began with the words: "Through all suffering and pogroms, through all struggles and battles, Grandfather Israel, You were with us—Your name was with us in our wanderings." We listened, moved, as Linka declaimed her messianic poem. Then the Christmas Eve celebration came to an end, leaving us all with memories to last a lifetime.

The buildings of Warsaw—and their concierges—have histories, although not always the most honorable ones. And how often, in the current wartime conditions, have these buildings' residents— and not only in Warsaw—become hungry demons lurking for a chance to pounce? How many have eaten of the tree of knowledge, tasted temptation, and allowed their suspicions to guide them to our enemies? Poor souls, it was impossible to enjoy a moment's privacy in their own homes, away from watching eyes. Later, when certain people took to denouncing Jews as an easy and lucrative source of income, we felt we were under surveillance from all sides. The stairwells of the large apartment houses turned to glass under prying, inquisitive eyes, peeking in at all times of the day and night—tireless, ever-present, all-seeing, and all-intrusive. We could literally feel their gaze from the day we started sheltering people who had fled the ghetto. Oh, how we wanted to cast a spell to mask us from everyone who daily passed us on the stairs, even trusted friends and acquaintances! Because at that time no one, not even family, could be trusted—too many people's lives were at stake.

In her ceaseless struggle with the killers operating under the swastika, pani Irena developed a number of ruses and ploys to blunt the alertness of all those with whom she had to have daily contact. With two stairwells at her disposition (one leading to Nowy Zjazd and the other to Mariensztat), she would alternate her use of entrances. To avoid drawing attention to the amount of groceries she needed to obtain, she would go to the market three or four times a day. Whenever she came back, before inserting her key into the lock she would signal to warn the guests not to move about the room.

Managing such a number of "dangerous" tenants was very complicated. They would have to be locked in one room, if a stranger came to visit, or they would hide in the back room underneath the bed (appropriately covered), or else squeeze into two empty wardrobes where holes had been cut in the back panels for ventilation. This state of affairs was extremely precarious and caused great anxiety and stress. We held a common meeting and decided to build a partition out of plywood and wall off a space inside the bathroom just large enough to fit everyone in our care. The entrance consisted of camouflaged sliding doors. A shelter like that wasn't much of a defense against the enemy, but it served well enough for occasional use. From time to time pani Irena would sequester her wards in the bathroom and hold open house, so that anyone could look in the apartment and satisfy his curiosity; now and then we had to convince the neighbors that nobody was staying or hiding with the Ryś family (that was my pen name). We would organize such an event whenever we felt the level of suspicion had risen above the acceptable norm. We were especially concerned about the concierge, for as we all know, the devil never sleeps. These preventive measures evidently helped; we passed the test.

The way life is, one stroke of bad luck or one evil person can wreck everything despite the most careful planning. The most innocent-seeming well-concealed curiosity could invite mortal sin and lead to discovery and disaster. The merest glimpse from behind a curtain through a window—the only window on the world for Jews in hiding—might meet in mid-glance another pair of eyes, equally curious but also greedy. Any letup in vigilance would place everyone in jeopardy, luring evil spirits that would hover invisibly over those in hiding, patiently waiting for a moment of weakness, when they would pounce, armed with some insidious weapon.

The constant dangers threatening the inhabitants of 7 Nowy Zjazd Street demanded organization, discipline, and extreme vigilance, and we devoted ourselves to the sole task of keeping our charges invisible. Unflaggingly we drilled them at every occasion: "Remember, all eyes are on you. Look out the curtain all you want, but stay invisible. Talk quietly, and don't laugh out loud. Walk about the apartment as softly as possible so the downstairs neighbors won't realize how many people are living here. Remember, our building is like glass—everything is transparent—and the walls have ears. There's nothing standing between you and the danger of being discovered. Even though you're behind locked doors, evil shadows are constantly at your heels. Even the ground is treacherous, and every slip carries the threat of death for us all."

Our hearts rebelled at this strict regimen, but our minds recognized the higher logic. That's why everyone agreed to observe the rules; their compliance was simply incredible. There simply was no other choice.

IN 1938, AT AGE TWENTY-TWO, WARSAW-BORN **CAŁEL PERE-CHODNIK** *married Anna Nusfeld and settled in Otwock to run a builder's supply center. A daughter, Athalil, was born two years later. During the occupation, Perechodnik served as an SP functionary in*

Otwock. In August 1942, he lost his wife and daughter during a roundup and went into hiding. Perechodnik perished in Warsaw in October 1944. His older brother, Pesach, survived. Perechodnik's account has appeared in English under the title Am I a Murderer?[8]

Our landlady is past forty, uneducated, unrefined, unattractive, and with a mean and sadistic nature; the only thing she has going for her is a shapely figure and some inexplicable appeal for Wacław. As the days pass by, we talk about when it will all end and when Italy will fall, and we beseech God. What should we Jews beseech of God?

1. That pani Hela, our landlady, not lose her job.
2. That Wacław not lose his job.
3. That they don't argue and split up.
4. That they both stay healthy and not get sick.
5. That Wacław's wife should never catch on to the nature of his relationship with pani Hela.
6. That no suitor shows up on our landlady's doorstep.
7. That there be no air raid and that the house not be bombed.
8. That nobody catches us or realizes that pani Hela is hiding someone.
9. That our landlady has a lot of money so she will lose her craving for more.
10. But that she not dress too elegantly, because people will wonder how she can afford to.
11. That everyone stay healthy, since calling for a doctor is out of the question.
12. That we have enough money to cover the rent and our expenses until the end of the war.

We have to beseech God for all that, yet the strange thing is that we're happy just to ask for those things because, after all, what would it be if we also had to ask God:

1. That our landlady not have bad dreams, such as ones with gray-haired cows, birds with cut-off tails, or any other omens that might augur our being discovered.
2. That she not tell daily yarns about planned roundups in the neighborhood.
3. That she not make a scene every day about being afraid to keep us and then raise the rent.
4. That she not eat up all our savings and then fetch a Polish policeman to do away with us in the night.

For all that, thank God, we need not ask. Wacław's unblemished character and pani Hela's own direct approach guarantee some peace, but there are still enough things on the list to beseech God for.

But what is a person to do who doesn't believe in God?

FRAGMENT OF **CAŁEL PERECHODNIK***'S LETTER TO HIS deceased wife.*

19 AUGUST 1943

Today, dear Anka, is the anniversary of your Golgotha, tomorrow the anniversary of your death. A year has passed since I last saw you. You see, Anka, I do not believe in God and never will, but there is one thing in which I want to and have to believe: the immortality of the soul. Because I can't imagine that there's nothing left of you. Yes, I know very well that the Germans burned your body, your wondrous body I kissed so many times, and used it as fertilizer. Maybe the potatoes I am now consuming grew on your ashes, maybe the rye in the bread I am eating. I don't want to think about that for I'll go out of my mind, but I want and have to think and believe that your soul, your pure and noble soul, is alive and that it's looking down on me from above, that it sees everything I do and praises or reproaches me.

You remember, Anka, how every evening I would tell you about the day's activities? You would listen carefully, perhaps bored by my professional concerns, but you never let that show. You knew my every deed, my every thought. I don't need to tell you that I never lied or hid anything from you. You always knew that very well and were so proud of your Całek. Even at the last moment, when I had a sacred obligation to lie to you, to tell you that they had found the basement where she was hiding and that they killed her, that there was nothing you could have done to save that basement, I broke down; I was unable to lie.

In my introduction to this memoir I wrote that it should be read as my dying confession; in essence, however, it is an accounting presented to you on the anniversary of your death.[9] As I cannot talk to you every evening and share my thoughts and experiences, I had to pour all this down on paper and today I am reading it to you.

Do I need to reassure you that I've left nothing out, that everything I've written is true? You know me, dearest Aneczka; you know I am incapable of lying to you. So you are listening carefully. You probably know not only my past but my future as well.

You may know that I didn't escape the fate of the Jews, you sympathize and pity me for having to endure another year of suffering, for having to see so many horrible things. Are you thinking that it would have been better if I hadn't broken out on that cursed day, if I had bravely accompanied you on your last earthly journey?

Or maybe you know, Anka, that I am fated to survive the war, so that I will remember you always, love you always, always pay homage to you. You see, Anka, I was terribly afraid of dying—not before the Aktion in Otwock but afterward. Before the Aktion I was a fatalist, I believed that whatever is meant to be will be, but I never imagined—and I'm sure you believe me, Anka—that you would perish and I would remain alive.

I was sure we were inseparable and that no force could break us apart. Unfortunately, I was the one who broke us apart—I was indifferent to the fate of the masses and I let you go off into the unknown while I stayed. After that I began to be horribly afraid of dying. Not of death itself, but the shame of dying in this way, while I could have died honorably, trying to sweeten the last minutes of your life.

Today, Anka, I am no longer afraid to die, and in a month I'll no longer be afraid of anything. You're not surprised, Aneczka, at this metamorphosis; after all, you always guessed my thoughts right away, before I even spoke them, before I even formulated them for myself. Maybe that's why I could never lie to you? Or maybe I respected you too much, loved you too much to lie to you? Therefore, Anka, you will understand me perfectly now, as well. Once I wanted to have a child, to remember me in case I died. Now that I am completely alone, now that I am orphaned, I cannot leave a living child for posterity; I had to leave an inanimate object into which I myself breathed life. . . .

This progeny is my account, which I believe will someday be printed so that the whole world will learn of your suffering. I have written it to your glory, to your immortality, and leave it as an eternal monument to you. Now that this child has been brought to life, it must be protected until it grows. . . . Aluśka, our first daughter, perished with you. What great fortune, Aneczka dearest, that on that cursed day you did not know that our lawyer friend hoped to save her, that he wanted to take our daughter to his sister to be raised.

Your heart would have broken if you had known how close our daughter came to being saved, in what good hands she might have been placed. Now you do know, but now all human suffering is alien to you. I on the other hand, who have remained, must suffer and rend my living flesh thinking about our Aluśka, thinking about my guilt. . . .

I have faith that millions of people will read these memories, that they will pity you for the fate that bound you to me in marriage. If you were single, if you had never believed in me so reverently, surely you would have saved yourself. I brought your doom, but I will also achieve your revenge.

Your second child will avenge you, your child born in the pain of death. On the day I place this child with our friend, my soul will regain its balance, I will no longer be afraid of death or the life to come, and I will no longer regret my still being alive, or that at the last moment I betrayed you so basely.

HELENA MIDLER'S ACCOUNT, COVERING A VERY SHORT PERIOD (November–December 1944), provides valuable insight into life in a bunker on the Aryan side after the uprising. Following her account are two numbers of the satiric Bunker Weekly. *Although we know nothing about Helena Midler's background or ultimate fate, her writing attests to her humor and intelligence.*

> Na dworze deszcz pada,
> deszcz pada jesienny,
> i pluszcze o szyby
> jednaki niezmienny.*

THURSDAY, 16 NOVEMBER 1944

I long for the patter of autumn rain, long for the monotonous music of tiny droplets drizzling against the windowpane, for the sad, gray, overcast November sky, and I long for thoughts at twilight, which—sad though they may be—never begin with the words "If I survive" and are never burdened with the heavy doubt that all thinking is pointless and empty, because in the end I won't survive anyway.

Rain is falling outside . . .

---

*The poem, by Leopold Staff, has been paraphrased. The correct version is: O szyby deszcz dzwoni, deszcz dzwoni jesienny/ I pluszcze jednaki, miarowy, niezmienny (Rain is ringing on my windowpane, the steady rhythm of autumn drizzle).—PB

In the morning while everyone is still fast asleep and nothing (except the men's light snoring) interrupts the quiet of the bunker, the muffled melody of raindrops reaches my ears from behind the "door" of our "bungalow" as they ooze their way through the leaky ceiling and drip into the water. A signal from the outside world: Outside, rain is falling. On occasion (rarely, far too rarely), the silence is torn by a distant roar of artillery fire, an exploding shell, or the rhythmic knocking of a machine gun: another signal from the outside world, proof that the Bolsheviks are close and the fighting is going on, but so sluggishly that the end is as distant as ever.

In our seventh week of confinement and complete isolation, this is all we know about the outside world.

We dream of freedom. Freedom! The word has taken on magical powers and now means something different, something much greater than before. It has ceased to be a mere slogan permanently fixed alongside its companions, equality and fraternity. It is no longer a cliché incapable of reaching people's hearts and minds, a tired catchword to be evoked and expounded upon for rhetorical resonance. For us, freedom is a living word; it is our goal and our dream. It is the sky above us and the sun and stars, it is the earth under our feet and the air for our lungs. It is a full stomach and a bold gaze, the end of living like a hunted dog. Everything we don't have and are striving to obtain is freedom, because—for us—freedom is life itself!

Those who believe in God are better off. They are able to hang their head in humility or lift their eyes to heaven and entreat: "From the midst of our sufferings, amid the torment of hopeless longing and inconsolable misery, the countless humiliations, the tears we have shed, the burden that is too great for us weak human beings to bear, we beseech you, Lord, take this load from our shoulders and make us human once again!"

Those who believe that their prayers will reach the just Almighty Being, and that God will hear them and finally send an end to their misfortune are better off.

For those of us who do not believe, things are more difficult. We cannot lighten our hearts with prayer or entrust our troubles to someone who will deliver us from them.

Like a miser I eagerly lock all my pain in the strongbox of my heart, from where, in occasional outbreaks of sincerity, I take out a coin to give to whomever I'm talking to; then I close the box and carefully turn the little key, since there is no one who can help me. The person in the crowd is always alone, always alone.

11 P.M. [THE SAME DAY]

After all the tragedies I have experienced there had to be another, for me personally one of the most painful (evidently my bitter cup is still not full).

My closest surroundings . . . at moments like this I'm ready to blaspheme, since I consider it a great fortune that my parents did not live to see the day their daughter joined with a person of Jacek's class and character. Adek and Jacek are arguing now, in tones sufficiently high for everyone nearby to hear. I picked up my pencil in order to distract myself from the content of their discussion, but it's no use. I am burning with embarrassment. Every moment that prolongs our living together is like dancing on hot coals for me. Simply being connected to my "husband" makes me feel humiliated and maltreated in the company of our companions in misery. Can I possibly feel that this man is my match?

I can't find words to describe the tempest raging in my heart. I want to yowl or howl like a dog, because I feel something inside my heart is going to break, something will explode. I long to transform my heart, which has long since turned to stone, into a boulder, so I will be immune to the stupidity and simplemindedness of those to whom I have been joined by fate.

During the night I had a small attack of hysteria. My nerves couldn't withstand the shame and humiliation I felt while my "husband" argued with my "brother-in-law," so they sought release in an acute burst of spasmodic sobbing. Supposedly hysteria is treated with a slap in the face. Since life itself has already slapped me around quite enough, I was able to calm down on my own. During the night Jacek sought my hand. Perhaps he felt guilty; perhaps he was trying to show he was sorry. I pretended to be asleep . . . although despite everything I felt some kind of sympathy for him. After all, is it his fault that life didn't give him any polish, or that he isn't smart or intelligent enough to realize how he ought to behave? And is it his fault that life played a practical joke on him and connected him with people he would normally never meet within his own sphere? And is it his fault that a cruel fate joined him with a woman of my particular background and is now forcing us to continue our shared life without the slightest chance of going back, despite the fact that we each realized long ago it was a mistake?

Today Jurek reconciled the two brothers-in-law, and for the moment things are "idyllic," although I don't know for how long. But the entire incident left a bad taste that cannot be erased. "It's an ill bird that fouls his own nest."

The entire argument yesterday, the mutual cataloging of injustice and injury, committed or not committed, the petty counting of money—it all seems both more and more ridiculous and painfully tragic in light of our current situation. Our food is running out. We have calculated that we have enough kasha, barley, and wheat to last for another two weeks; we'll run out of fat even sooner, and what then?

For the moment there's no sign of any offensive. Nothing augurs an early liberation, while the possibilities of dying are increasing in number as well as scope. We're placing all our bets on one remaining card. Once again we are preparing to go looting. Maybe this way we will again manage to prolong our lives as we have in the past. When our fuel supply was in danger of running out, which would have meant the remaining provisions would have been unusable, Jacek and Anna went outside and brought back a little kerosene and gasoline. When we were low on candles, a second trip to the shelter secured a kerosene lantern and some wax. A third quest brought a large supply of fuel, one more kerosene lamp, and even barley, coffee, and one little head of cabbage. Who knows whether the next expedition will wind up being so providential.

MONDAY, 20 NOVEMBER

Yesterday no one made it out. Instead, plans were made for the very risky undertaking of breaking into an apartment. Wanda was supposed to go with Hela Domagalska. Such an expedition really is exceedingly dangerous, threatening their lives as well as our own. It's possible that Germans have settled there, or that the area has been closed to civilians; if so, nothing—including their Aryan looks—would be of any help. Wanda's brother Jurek objected to her going, and Michał was opposed to Hela's leaving. The two of them, particularly Hela, are too scared to stand by their decision. So today I hear they've given up on the idea. There's less and less food and the situation is very, very serious. Everyone's nerves are stretched to the breaking point. Thus it's no surprise that the stupidest thing can set off new quarrels and arguments. Something is rotten in the state of Denmark.

Meanwhile, this morning there was a brief noise of motors, a few bursts of antiaircraft guns, and then things were again quiet.

And that is supposed to be our hope of imminent liberation, of life in the face of the death that is constantly hanging over us like the sword of Damocles?

.

For the third day in a row we were awakened by the reports of explosions, the roar of motors, and the din of artillery. All these sounds are muffled and indistinct, because as we learned during the last (our fourth) expedition, the opening to our hideout was buried in rubble during the last few days, limiting our contact with the outside world even more. But such sounds of battle lift our spirits, although I have to confess that, as far as I'm concerned, I'm afraid to let any hope enter my heart. We've been through so many similar situations, when we were uplifted in some new way only to come hurtling down from the heights—and be left with nothing but painful wounds from the crash. So it's no surprise that I'm afraid of any and all hope, so as not to have to experience another disappointment. Inside the bunker we go on economizing with the food, in order to prolong our existence here by at least one more month. The men go hungry, and not just the men; after all, can the women survive on one bowl of slop (soup made of ground barley with chaff) and two pancakes made of wheat bran and fried without any fat?

Hunger and nerves go hand in hand. Everyone has become exceptionally grouchy and quarrelsome. What's more, as if to crown our dog's fate, we have recently acquired all sorts of lice, fleas, and other vermin that sap what little remains of our good humor and our patience for surviving. Since we refuse to delude ourselves with hope, there's nothing else to do except lie wrapped up under our bedding in the morning and listen to the noise of the fighting that is sowing destruction and death all around, while (oh, paradox!) bringing us—who knows—maybe life?

So what did the last week bring, seemingly so full of tempests, so rich in impressions, but that ultimately left nothing more than a bad taste and one more layer of discouragement weighing on our hearts?

Last Saturday Hela and I woke up determined to go out in the night and make our way to the attic of this building in order to observe the situation. Since all the brave girls with Aryan looks failed to come through, and since our fodder is being depleted with every passing moment, there was nothing else left but for us, the most Semitic-looking ladies in the entire group, to undertake this risky step. In the end, however, our courage alone was not enough, since if we were "found out" everyone would be jeopardized. So it was decided that Wanda, Jacek, and Adek would go back to the shelter and give it one last going over, even though they had slim chances of finding anything. But they came back with surprising results: about 20 kilograms of food, a little sugar, some pickled pumpkin, paraffin for candles, wicks for the kerosene lamps, and gasoline. All in all it meant prolonging life to about 1 January 1945, of course unfortunately without increasing the rations. In plain terms, it meant prolonging the hunger strike for one more month.

The people coming back let slip that they had discovered some linens had been sewn up inside a sack. The Domagalskis, who even in those conditions were so keen on material goods it was ridiculous, immediately proposed another trip to the shelter, disregarding the fact that despite everything it was important to maintain at least some semblance of caution, and this kind of daily expedition might set unwanted people on our trail, assuming anyone was left in the area. Attempts to convince them otherwise were in vain, due to the stubbornness and lack of intelligence among the interested parties. Quarrels and conflicts, *comme toujours*. Nevertheless, another attempt was scheduled for Tuesday. A fever of preparations, great plans, great hopes—but also great disappointment. It turned out that the tunnel that connected our shelter with the others, and which was currently our only exit, had been covered up. Some suspected that this might have been done deliberately from outside, but more likely the trapdoor broke off and some rubble fell into the tunnel, since for several weeks we had noticed debris filtering down from the trap, probably as a result of the rain leaking through the seal or else the constant shaking from the fighting.

So we were completely buried: a sad impression, particularly when you know your supply of food is inadequate; after all, what guarantee was there that the war might end within the month, since two months had gone by without the slightest change? The men decided to dig us out, but the very idea frightened them, since they were so weakened by hunger. And then amid all that a new conflict broke out, far more serious than the previous ones, and if it weren't for the psychological effects of hunger the whole thing would have been very shameful indeed. Naturally Jacek set it all off with his unbridled tongue and his unmitigated stupidity. By and large his reproaches were warranted; since Jurek, Wanda, and Anna had behaved inappropriately at the beginning, when we first entered the bunker. While they brought the tastiest morsels of margarine, white bread, wine, and even some canned goods, the rest of us had gathered basic provisions such as wheat, barley, kasha, sugar, and dark bread, things that had largely helped us survive this far. However, instead of acting properly by pooling everything into one common pot, as we had, they withheld some of their provisions as "theirs." From time to time they would share a little with us, I might say as a courtesy. That alone was enough to cause some discord to creep in our ranks. When Anna's housekeeping proved completely irrational, with the result that certain products that might have lasted a long time were consumed at a shocking rate, we thought to save the situation. But even then, despite the semblance of adding extra provisions, it was clear that certain people were being favored. This might have passed unnoticed if everyone had been full, but unfortunately it was bound to set off a quarrel when everyone, especially the men, were hungry. This led to a "chat" between Jacek and Anna, and since he's too

stupid to follow through intelligently and consistently on something once it's been addressed, instead of reproaching her as he
should have, he accused her of eating margarine on the sly.

No wonder, then, that not only did she feel hurt but so did
Jurek, who seems incidentally to be a person of unimpeachable
integrity and generosity. At the same time a conflict broke out
between Wanda and Michał and his wife. The air was heavy and
exceedingly unpleasant. Finally it was decided that all the women
would take turns portioning the food, though in reality that meant
only Hela and Anna; nevertheless, things did take a turn for the
better.

The next day Wanda had another fight with Michał and his
wife, which led Wanda to an unbelievable attack of hysteria, during which she said that if she had to go out because of them, and if
a German caught her, she wouldn't hesitate to give us all away at
the first blow. Later she explained that she would never really do
that and she was just threatening them so they would stop provok-
ing her. Still, that kind of talk was very untoward.

Jurek took both conflicts very much to heart. He felt what I
did during the quarrel between Jacek and Adek, a kind of internal
howl, a sense that his nerves were on the verge of snapping, that
they were about to burst and cause an explosion for which he
could not be held accountable. After all, Jurek's nerves were the
least hardened to our conditions, and lately the lack of cigarettes
was making him suffer even more, since he had always been a passionate smoker. The most recent quarrels were the last straw. So
he decided to leave, together with Wanda. Anna would stay. Of
course, leaving like that meant you had more of a chance of getting killed than of surviving, and besides, he was planning to take
his Colt, and I suspect he wouldn't have hesitated long before
putting a bullet in his brain. Naturally, the mood in the bunker
was awful. Finally we determined that the reason for their leaving were the quarrels started by Jacek and Michał, so Adek had a

short talk with Jacek and then with Michał. That night family peace was restored, and the would-be refugees decided to stay. But the storms had left their mark, and who knows on what day and at which moment a dormant volcano may burst open with renewed force.

Finally, today was the first day of general harmony, and the men set out to dig a tunnel in order to try their luck again at looting.

Yesterday, 1 December, was Szymek's birthday. I thought about you, Szym, my only one; I thought that if you were here with me it would be easier for me to bear my current life, and I thought today—like every day, like always—that I can't believe that you are no longer alive. I had a sad day yesterday, on the twenty-seventh anniversary of your birth. Your life was too short, Szym, a brutal death took you too soon, even though you would be one of the most worthy individuals among the few Jews who are left. But fate doesn't care about justice, nor does it weigh merit or worth on any scale. The good ones, the "fair" ones, are gone, and only the dregs are left. The story of Noah's Ark was not repeated. You visit me at night in my dreams, Szym, you return to me in my thoughts and in my daydreams, because in my heart I am always crying with longing for you alone.

SUNDAY, 31 DECEMBER

The last day of the year 1944. Tomorrow is the dawn of a new year. Despondent, I go through the sad celebrations, without even attempting to recall other New Year's Eves from years past. The memories are too painful. Here we have to live as if life began when we entered the bunker, as if nothing and no one existed beyond ourselves in time and space. We have become such animals, the present time suffers in comparison with even the worst moments of the past. If at times I feel that despair and exhaustion are driving me to the brink of insanity, reason immediately intervenes to interpose its own counterarguments. My only goal, the only love left in my life, is my sister Fela. It is for her sake that I long to survive, for my one and only loving and beloved sister, whom I am convinced is still alive; only the thought of her helps me bear all the suffering, which even the most splendid future will not be able to recompense. For her sake I long to live, so I need to be resolute and not give in. Even though one of my most serious faults is a lack of energy and resourcefulness, I have to counter this with patience and the will to live. But meanwhile the last day of 1944 is passing, the sixth year of this relentlessly brutal war.

BUNKER WEEKLY: NUMBER ONE

7 November 1944   Price: One Cigarette

From the Editors

Today, dear readers, we place in your hands the first number of our bunker newsletter. Our task will be to keep you informed of all major events of interest to the citizens of our tiny but turbulent state. To this end we will provide updates on the political and military situation as well as on internal affairs—social, economic, and others. As our paper grows we will also include an advertising section. As of this writing, the prospects for our new venture seem promising indeed; it is probably the only paper in the world that will be read by all citizens in the land without exception and regardless of creed, gender, nationality, age, or education. Our only momentary complaint is the chronic shortage of paper, which drastically affects the aesthetic format of our weekly. We call upon all people of goodwill to remit to the editorial office any clean piece of paper they chance to find. Contributions are gladly accepted. In presenting to you, dear readers, this first issue, we sincerely wish—for your sake as well as our own—that it will also be the last.

What's Happening on the Front?

As there are no signs in the air or on land that would indicate the launch of a major offensive, we must confine our report to the repeated skirmishes taking place over the past several weeks between our citizens and the local insects. Following fierce battles, we have held our position while inflicting great losses on the enemy. Space will not permit us to recount further details from our interview with our military spokesmen; we plan to include this in our next issue. Here we wish to communicate that, for the moment, none of the dream auguries regarding the war have yet come to pass. Nevertheless we vow that if they do, even at a later date, we will become loyal adherents of such divination to the end of our days and will bring up future generations in the faith, so help us God. Amen.

Market Report

As a result of the change in our monetary system, the cigarette has been declared the official currency of our small state. All attempts to monetize soup or pancakes have proven futile.

Technological Update

He who does not keep abreast of progress is moving backward.

Michał of the golden hands has again made our lives easier by constructing a step intended to replace something that resembled the funicular rail up Kasprowy Wierch. It's true that up to now he's the only one really able to work it, but we hope that with a little experience, some slippers, and a dose of goodwill, our five does on the upper level will soon be leaping aloft from the step with all the nimbleness of their mountain sisters. Meanwhile, we have just heard that our resident genius Michałek is hard at work in his alchemical laboratory on a new paraffin lamp.

Miracle Baby Gets First Teeth

Over the past several days our bunker has witnessed a number of unusually important events. One of the most significant of these is the fact that Ama, our multitalented cooking oil, is beginning to teethe (the editor does not vouch for the reliability of this information) and is showing her first . . . wisdom tooth. Understandably this has created quite a sensation, since in our shelter wisdom is such a rare commodity. Everyone is eagerly awaiting the first results of this potentially significant occurrence.

Dangerous Epidemic

Reports have been confirmed that our shelter has recently been hit by a dangerous and distressing epidemic of hemorrhoids. The worst and most notable case is that of "white" Hela. As the editors possess no medication that might alleviate the suffering, we offer instead this little verse by a major author, who, like Heine, is of unknown origin:

The Suppository and the Tortoise
The suppository was distraught
By the tortoise in his carapace.
"It must be very hard," he thought,
"to live in such restricted space:
How does he fare? It must be hell."
The tortoise then assured his brother,
"I'd rather be penned in my own shell
than pushed into the ass of another."

Corsairs on Quest

Last Sunday, in the quiet of the night, under cover of darkness, our pirate cutter embarked on a raid and returned with a rich store of plunder. Due to limited space we are unable to provide more particulars: Suffice to say the episode was rich in hair-raising moments of danger. We permit ourselves to recall that our most intrepid adventurer, Wandzia, a devotee of such missions, is already hatching plans for new and even bolder quests. Tact compels us to keep these plans shrouded in secrecy, so we must leave the reader in suspense until the next issue.

For Young Housewives

In view of our citizens' growing tendency to put on weight—a trend resulting solely from the climate in which we live—the Housewives Association has conferred with the High Commission and passed a resolution limiting high-lifers to a maximum of two meals a day. In keeping with this resolution we offer all our lady readers an excellent weekly planner for preparing meals, which we present in the form of a calendar:

Monday
   2 wheat pancakes with coffee
   barley soup

Tuesday
   barley soup
   2 wheat pancakes with coffee

Wednesday
   2 wheat pancakes with coffee
   barley soup

Thursday
   barley soup
   2 wheat pancakes with coffee

Friday
   2 wheat pancakes with coffee
   barley soup

Saturday
   barley soup
   2 wheat pancakes with coffee

Sunday
   2 wheat pancakes with coffee
   barley soup and noodles

Official Notice

Wherefore my husband Kubuś, able-bodied seaman aka Jacuś, has managed to escape my subversive influence, I hereby officially proclaim myself not liable for his appearance (see exhibit A: dirty pajama top).

"Black" Hela

(Read but don't pass it on—lest it cost the editors a cigarette.)

BUNKER WEEKLY: NUMBER TWO

24 November 1944   Price: One Cigarette

Military Communiqué

Recent observations indicate the Warsaw front has livened up somewhat. While it's true this does not help our situation in the slightest, as our own positions have yet to reach even Mokotowska Street, it is clear that the war has moved from the foxhole into open terrain, significantly raising our expectations.

Market Report

With the freezing of tobacco assets, the cigarette has been taken out of circulation. For the moment no other currency has been introduced; given our state's catastrophic financial situation it is also unknown whether any currency is even needed.

Travelers' Corner

Traveler! May you turn purple with shame, for I am going to tell you today about a country without peer but, alas, one you have never bothered to visit or even learn about, despite your numerous travels and adventures. Do you know the country, as Goethe might ask, whose panorama is one hundred times more beautiful than Naples, whose monuments and ruins are a hundred times more instructive than Pompeii's, and whose general ambience is a hundred times more romantic than Venice?

Heed my advice, great traveler, visit the land I will describe to you, and your experience will be interesting, enlightening, and romantic.

You who have journeyed to Egypt especially to see the digs at Edfu, you who know the sights of Athens like the back of your hand and the streets of Pompeii as well as your own presumably empty pocket, suddenly are surrounded by ruins you have never seen before. No Parisian *guide* or Roman *cicerone* is there to interrupt your reverie with his monotonous babble. We have too much respect for your intelligence, for your knowledge of history, art, and architecture, to dog you with paid tour guides. Thus you will have to figure out for yourself the history and cultural accomplishments of the town whose ruins you are visiting.

You first head toward the remains of a temple whose architectural structure immediately recalls the Acropolis, though the locals in their naïveté refer to it simply as the shed. What immediately leaps out is the antique form of the toilet, which proves that our ancestors were no less advanced than we in this particular area. As you venture further you may be appalled at the abundant human excrement polluting the temple and offending your delicate nostrils. You may be inclined to avert your eyes, but there is no point, since you'd see the same wherever you looked; besides: Beat your own chest and ask if you too are without fault.

But let us continue. We now move into a ravine that slopes down toward sea level. In this rugged terrain, erudition and archaeological savvy are not enough; you need to be an accomplished mountaineer as well. But what is that for you, world traveler, who has scaled peaks such as Giewont, Mont Blanc, and—who knows—possibly even Everest? So you climb down and cross the couloir, but wait. Rewind your memory and recall whether you ever saw a film with Boris Karloff with the advertisement: *Only for people with strong nerves.* Decide if your own nerves are up to the test; if not, you should turn back; if so, you may proceed—into a land that never sees the light of day, where the darkness is complete. We call this town the *Città della notte eterna*—the city of eternal night. I am sure you are brave enough that, should some errant rat graze your face, you will not panic or screech to high heaven like some silly woman; at the sounds of bat wings whirring overhead you will merely adjust your cap with great sangfroid in the manner of the heroic gentlemen.

Now listen carefully to my advice, traveler: The city you have entered is a land flowing with oil and gas, but do not pause to examine these riches unless you wish to incur the natives' wrath. For they are pirates who divide their plunder even before it's taken.

You now approach the ditch that surrounds the town, which because of its unpleasant odor has earned the name Canale Ammerdante (sewer of shit), although it should properly be called the tunnel of life because of the blessings it provides.

Now whistle lightly, and there will appear before you a gondola with a stout gondolier, Signore Giacobo—gentleman bandit, rogue, and coward all in one, according to his own description, known to the world as the king of plunderers and a bold pirate chieftain. Do not expect, though, to be serenaded with a sentimental Neapolitan song. After all, this is a city of darkness and untrammeled silence.

At first you have the impression that this place is completely deserted, but the closer you come to your goal, the more clearly you realize it is not. Soon you hear voices whose intonations suggest an argument or quarrel. But this impression, too, proves false; these are merely the passionate half-whisper of Signora Helena and the sultry alto of Signora Wanda engaged in friendly chat. Don't suppose they are speaking too loudly; their voices are merely proof that their companions are keeping too quiet.

Finally you have attained the shore. If by chance you step from the gondola less nimbly than you ought and splash into the water, invoking the curses of the dictator, do not be disconcerted: He is a decent person, if somewhat skittish, and your socks will surely dry out within the next several weeks.

Now permit me to leave you on your own as you continue, for at this point in my account I should reveal something of the inhabitants, but since I learned early on that you can be beaten for telling the truth, and since I'm no match for Miecisty, or even Zbyszek Cyganiewicz,* I'd prefer not to provoke the other eight people and will tactfully conclude my article. All in all I am sure you will be impressed, traveler, by the luxury of the fixtures and furnishings and the high standard of living of the inhabitants. If by chance you should find yourself having to choose among the local *pensioni,* I advise you to consider the one run by Signora Buna. There you will find superb company, and the kitchen is noted for its nutritious, delicious, and varied meals. As far as local toilets are concerned, I suggest taking advantage of that attended by the worthy Signora Adka.

Hot Off the Press

In response to the legitimate objections raised that the previous issue neglected to make any mention of our very best boy, pan Jurek, we hereby state that the same is preparing to lead a great reconnaissance expedition, which will undoubtedly earn a golden inscription in the annals of our history.

For now, no further details are known.

Political News

We have learned that a diplomatic hunting party will soon take place within our realm. The object of this hunt is neither bear nor bison but lice, fleas, and possibly rats.

Rumor has it the guests will include Hitler, Göring, Himmler, Goebbels, and the entire German staff and diplomatic corps. One curious aspect of the planned event is that the friendly hosts have agreed to keep a very low profile, leaving as much Lebensraum as possible for their guests, who have displayed an evident sensitivity in this matter.

*Polish boxers.—PB

Chapter 6

LIBERATION

After suppressing the revolt inside the ghetto, the Germans razed the entire district and then sorted through the rubble and salvaged whatever could be used. According to a progress report sent to Heinrich Himmler in April 1944, when the dismantlement had been half completed, 6.73 million cubic feet of buildings had been systematically demolished to yield 22.5 million bricks, 5,006 tons of scrap iron, and 76 tons of copper, brass, and lead. The plan was to level the area and sow it with ash and dung. Eventually the Nazis wished to see the entire city of Warsaw reduced to a small town. In the meantime, they used the ruins of the former ghetto as a site for executions.

By late July 1944, as the Soviet offensive approached the Vistula, the Polish underground Home Army received the go-ahead from London to launch a citywide uprising against the Germans, which they did on 1 August. Many Jews came out of hiding to help. In mid-September the Soviet army reached the eastern bank of the Vistula and occupied the Praga suburbs, but then stopped and refused to provide relief to the insurgents. After two months of fierce fighting, the Polish forces capitulated. During the course of the uprising, some 20,000 combatants were killed; approximately 180,000 civilians also lost their lives, mostly murdered by the Germans and their Ukrainian auxiliaries. The surviving population was evacuated *from the city and dispersed throughout various camps or relocated in the provinces, while special demolition squads were sent from block to block to burn what buildings were still standing. Having destroyed the city, the Germans withdrew, and on 15 January 1945 the Soviet Army, together with the Polish First Army fighting under its command, entered the ruins. Those who had hidden—including a handful of Jews—emerged from their bunkers.*

*BEFORE THE WAR, **IRENA GROCHER** lived in Warsaw with her parents and younger brother Jakub; she had just graduated from the gymnasium when the Germans invaded. After losing her entire family, she escaped from the ghetto with the help of friends. Narrowly avoiding arrest during the Hotel Polski scheme, Grocher remained in hiding before and after the Warsaw Uprising. She emigrated to Israel in 1975.*

Life in the bunker,
5 October 1944
to 17 January 1945

5 OCTOBER

After the surrender of the uprising they ordered the evacuation of Warsaw—or really of the rubble, since by then the city looked like one gigantic battlefield.

Today was the last day and we had to hurry, since anyone found after that date would be punished with a bullet to the head. People left on foot, taking their children with them, carrying their bundles, abandoning their entire fortune to fate, and heading into the unknown, in some cases to death and at best to a long odyssey.

But even so, despite the threat of death there were those who stayed in the city. They equipped themselves with weapons and grenades and created camouflaged shelters, or really what were

called bunkers. I stayed as well, since I had neither Aryan papers
nor "good" looks and I was as afraid of the Germans as of the
plague. I preferred to die, even of hunger, just so I would never
have to lay eyes on another German.

We collected enough food and water in containers to last
for two weeks. We counted on the Germans leaving Warsaw by that
time; the Soviets were already in Praga. There were nine of us: two
other women and six men. Our friends camouflaged us by covering
our shelter with debris from the outside, and then they left with the
idea that they would let us back out once the city was free.

Today Mietek talked the boys into digging a well; little Janek
claimed they had as much chance of finding water as he did of
growing a cactus on his palm, but even so he set to work with
great energy. I helped out as well by filling the bucket with sand;
only Stasia didn't do anything: she "didn't have the strength." We
are rationing our bread very sparingly. It breaks my heart that I
have to divide it like that, but there's no choice. Relations with
Stasia aren't good, since she's so superior; she has a man behind
her, one she snared with her female charms. While they were digging the well the boys found a rabbi's fur wrap and yarmulke.
Everyone agreed it meant good luck and we would find water for
sure. It's such a terrible feeling to wait for water that you have to
deny yourself and measure out with a dropper, so no one will be
shortchanged by a single drop. All of a sudden Liber interrupted
my brooding on our misfortune when he started shouting that
they had hit water. We were happy beyond belief. We jumped for
joy. We felt like wanderers lost in the desert who suddenly stumble
on an oasis. Whoever hasn't experienced that will never understand it; it's like a drunken happiness. But our euphoria was very
brief. Reality began to close in again. There's no more bread. Now
that we have water, we'll have to cook. One would have thought

the water would have brought everyone together, but unfortunately people are quarreling again over who knows what.

Wiśnia took a pillowcase and cut out a blouse for me and some underwear; I'll sew them up quickly. Otherwise I won't have anything to wear after washing up.

I DECEMBER

Today was the beginning of a new era in our life. Two factions have formed: the original people and the new ones. They were dismantling a barricade, so we couldn't sleep in our own place. The new tenant is lying down because she is weak.

2 DECEMBER

Once again we are sleeping all together. It's not worth making a fuss about; anyway, I've already forgotten it. The boys went out once again today to look for loot. (They've dug out over five meters of sewage tunnel.) They ran into a German car. Big Mietek and J walked up to the car to see what was going on and whether they were being watched. They really do have iron nerves. Luckily there was nobody there. After they came back, little Mietek started to panic, saying they were bound to have been seen, they should have covered their tracks and not come here, we were already done for—but no one really took his babble to heart. The main thing they brought back from that expedition was carbide for the lanterns.

3 DECEMBER

Janek and little Mietek are going out again today. Leon's father is setting up a stove. It's the second night we haven't slept in the little cubicle.

4 DECEMBER

Today they're digging an escape to the outside world. We—that is Stasia and I—are sleeping on the wet ground. We managed to do some laundry, since we have a stove. In a word, our life is full of organization. Today the Germans were plundering our courtyard.

We're sleeping on a bed like everyone else. Janek offered his services and constructed a fine bed out of a few boards. Now everyone but Wiśnia is sleeping like that. We had a kind of pre-holiday cleaning. The tunnel is almost finished. We set up a handmade table, very elegant. The boys provided the silverware from their looting, of course. Leon's father cooked some pancakes on the stove.

Stasia is sick all the time (at least so she says), too weak. They want us to work together, but I'd rather work without her, since she's so mad at me she could kill me. I try not to let it worry me, but the worst thing is that other people are getting involved. But it's her fault, because even if there is some dissonance, it should be kept between ourselves. Wiśnia gave me the song "Treblinka" and there were official apologies.

In the digging operation at the sewer, Janek does the least amount of work but has the biggest mouth. Big Mietek does the most, along with the director. It's curious that the ones with the least experience as manual laborers have turned out to be the best and most honest workers. So it's not physical strength that decides but rather psychological attitude, a certain understanding of the situation and a healthy view of life.

Three o'clock at night. They've dug their way to the sewer. This is a big event in our underground life.

Today I worked from four in the afternoon to ten in the morning. I'm completely worn out, but nobody understands that.

Our sewer is almost finished. A toilet is under construction. We are settling down as if for good. We simply forget that there exists some other life. Big Mietek and the director found a torah. Everyone says it will bring us good luck. The new woman is constantly sick; now she is kind enough to get up out of bed, but she doesn't do anything: a genuine *artiste,* by the grace of God. During the night another looting expedition. Sewek went as well—his hand doesn't hurt anymore. They stopped in at Lonia's. Big Mietek brought an encyclopedia. I'm very happy about that.

Janek woke everyone up in the night, since he was hungry and couldn't sleep. I gave him my pancake. It really takes talent. Dear little Janeczek. In the morning I woke up on my own. I took the lamp from the other room; everybody was still asleep. When I came back with the lamp, all dressed, the director was angry that I had taken so long. He claimed I should be ready in fifteen minutes. "But I got up all by myself, without waiting to be woken," I told him. To which he said, "I see you've learned to talk back just like Stasia." That hurt me so much I started to cry. Later Wiśnia started singing and I cooled off. We're planning to have a party on Christmas and invite Lonia and all the people from the neighboring bunker.

The sewer tunnel is already finished. The boys started digging from the other side. Leon fell into the ditch and twisted his arm.

Everybody went out looting except for Leon. Janek heard a Russian march, and we were all very moved. Janek got dressed up to the nines today and went off to a meeting that did not take place.

At 8 A.M. we entered the sewage tunnel. It's hard to describe what you feel going into that infernal hole, which nevertheless saved the lives of twenty-four people. Only Stasia fainted; the other one kept having hysterics the whole time. We sat, or really squatted, in H_2O, unable to see a way out, since the manholes were covered with rubble. Generally speaking we didn't know whether we would be able to get out. We were haunted by the fear that we wouldn't be able to leave, that we would die there of starvation. Everyone was overcome by some kind of wild anxiety. The whole thing lasted until six, when Big Mietek and Tadeusz opened a manhole and let us out. We went outside on the street, completely soaked. It was icy cold and everything we were wearing froze immediately. Later it turned out that Janek had been wounded; he had killed one German.

We learned from our sentries that there had been six cars carrying thirty units of Feldgendarmerie. They dynamited our bunker, but not the one belonging to the Płonek family. When we finally came out of the sewer, we stood in the entranceway to a hospital for about an hour. We were frozen through, wet, hungry, and dazed—but happy to have escaped death. It had been a long time since I had been on the streets of Warsaw. They've destroyed everything. Buildings are burning all around; sparks are flying; you can see as clear as day. We didn't know where to go. The boys went to a bakery and then took everybody there. The other people stayed at the bakery and our boys took the rest of us to a bunker— three men and five women.

Little is eaten. Everything is one big mess. I have lost all my energy for work; maybe it will return in time. The Germans are coming around searching; everyone is scared. In general the situation is difficult and uncertain. Everyone is resigned and apathetic. Who knows what's next? At times I have this premonition that we probably won't survive, that we are struggling to no avail. To punish myself I won't drink any cocoa ("chois"); even if everybody else does, I won't touch it. Tomorrow I'm on kitchen duty. I have to describe one more story. We don't have water. Everyone wants to drink; people are simply burning up. By chance I found one liter of water while I was clearing away rubble. Edka and I each had a little bit and then I took it back—practically full—to our room for the others. Lonia came over; she's terribly thirsty (after dinner). I gave her the bottle and said, "You drink first, then I'll have some as well; I'm very thirsty." "Fine." Marian came over. Lonia drank a third of the water and asked him, "Marian, you want a little water?" "Yes." "Drink some and leave some for Rena; she wants some too." He drank and put down the bottle. I picked it up. There was not a drop left. I felt sick. How could someone drink everything when someone else wants it too? A very ugly character trait. After all, I was the one who had found it and I could have first drunk my fill and then given it to them. That left a bad taste. If I ever find a companion it will probably be someone like Janek, since I won't get very far with my own methods.

Today was my turn for kitchen duty. The work is very tiring, since you have to cook three large pots on a little stove without stopping. And in the end it takes hours before you can eat. The boys are digging a well and a tunnel and clearing rubble. The work is going full steam ahead, so that it's a pleasure. There are different reasons for dividing our forces, for separating, too many people and what-not, but as long as one is there one should do everything one is supposed to.

The boys are already sleeping on beds in their rooms, only the brothers, big Mietek, and I are on the ground, but not only am I not jealous of anyone; I even feel happier than the ones who are lying in their beds. Today for example, when I came back from my watch, I noticed that someone had made my bed for me and there was even a little pillow inside a case. I was truly moved that the boys had thought of me. It must have been Sewek. Mietek had gone so far as to put down his fur jacket. It's all very nice and done without any expectations.

We are now in an attic somewhere on Mariańska Street. We had to run away from the laundry when they started shooting again. We don't know whether it was Germans or some other damned thing. Stasia, Ziuta, Ziuta's husband, and fortunately Lonia, Marian, and Edka are all with us. The boys, even Sewek, aren't interested in us. Evidently they want to break off completely. The situation is hopeless, since women can't manage on their own. In particular, Lonia has told me distinctly that Marian has two women, and that's more than enough for him. I am a psychological wreck and am very afraid of the future, I just want to fall asleep forever and stop struggling. If I had a soulmate none of this would matter, but unfortunately I am all alone and that's the worst thing.

6 JANUARY 1945

In the same attic. Sewek, Mietek, and Artawes came since they had been discovered.

7 JANUARY

The same attic. It's snowing. When we go out we leave tracks, which might be our undoing.

A fright. The boys dug inside to another basement; they thought it was closed, but it turned out there was a window. All that work and energy wasted. Today they plan to work somewhere else. The problem of food, fat—Lonia and Marian.

The same attic.

Inside the same attic. During the night the boys started building a bunker. I was supposed to go with Ignaś to a different bunker, but I didn't want to. I prefer to stay with everyone else; we've been through so much together that I want to stay with them to the end. Is this the right choice? I don't know.

The same attic. They're still working on the bunker.

They're still working on the bunker. Now I want to leave here, because relations are so touchy. There are two camps: Lonia's and Stasia's.

Inside the attic. Edka and I are working on the bunker. Stasia and Lonia are cooking. The new bunker needs a huge amount of work and it's uncertain when we'll move in. Meanwhile, every morning, while it's still dark, we have to clamber like cats up to the third floor. There are no stairs; you could break a leg getting up there. It's a difficult life. If only it all would end well. Is it all really worth the struggle? At times it seems as though it isn't, but the desire to live is so great it overcomes all faltering.

Once again in the infernal attic. Lonia is a real nag. Stasia and I found some shoes. I gave Mietek back the ones he had lent me and put on the new ones. Stasia took the other clothes.

For three days we've been hearing some activity on the front, but far from us. We can't stay on Sosnowa Street anymore, since the looters are coming every day and might surround us one night and catch everybody. Tonight we moved into our bunker, where there's no water and no sewer, but that's the way it is—there isn't any choice. A well can be dug, as can a sewer.

We're in the bunker. The boys are getting ready to fetch water. They are peeing into the carbide lanterns, since there's no water.

One A.M.—liberation.

It's the second day we've been sleeping inside the bunker. Janek came over with Stasiek, who had made a trapdoor for us, and told us we were free. The Russians are in the city. The Germans fled during the night. What joy, what happiness! It's simply impossible to imagine. Everyone is kissing one another. They are happy, laughing; some are crying. Everyone went out into the city. Lonia and I stayed to cook something to eat. After a while some of them came back lugging bread and onions they got from the soldiers. We are now living during the day. How quickly a person gets used to new conditions. It's simply unbelievable. During the night we all washed up, but this time in Lonia's bunker on Mariańska.

Once again I'm sleeping with Lonia inside the bunker; we are cooking.

At one at night I went out of the bunker into the free world. I had a strange feeling. I should have been happy, after all; I should have been jumping for joy. We were struggling to stay alive the whole time just for this moment, to be told that the Germans are gone, that we are allowed to live. Why am I not really happy? All I feel is that my heart has frozen inside me. I am sad for the ones I lost. And what will be next, how will I build a path to the future, all alone in a strange world, with no capital, no trade? Just a student who never graduated. I guess we'll see.

WHEN THE GERMANS INVADED WARSAW, JAKUB SMAKOWSKI was sixteen. Inside the ghetto, he began smuggling food from outside the walls to save his family from starvation. In August 1942, his mother and sister were deported to Treblinka; the following April he led his father to the Aryan side. Smakowski stayed inside the ghetto, where he fought in the uprising. In 1944 he again took arms against the Germans and fought with the Home Army under the pseudonym Czarny Julek. After the collapse of the insurgency he hid in a bunker at 36 Wspólna Street until liberation.

Smakowski's testimony consists of two dictations, both in Yiddish, one from November 1945 in Warsaw, the other nearly a year later, in a DP camp in Leipheim, Germany. Nothing more is known of the author.

In September 1944, Warsaw was in flames. Those were the last weeks of the uprising. German planes were constantly bombarding the capital, sowing terror and despair among the inhabitants; between bombardments you could hear the din of buildings collapsing as they were hit by artillery shells. People were shot en masse on the streets. The Germans chased the Poles through the burning

streets of the city, torturing them and shooting. Here and there
fighting was still going on at the barricades. The fighters threw
grenades out of windows and put up a fierce resistance. Only a few
buildings on Marszałkowska, from the Central Station to Mokotów,
were not bombed because Germans were living there.

Anyone who was in Warsaw at that time experienced the
most frightening, the most tragic moments of his life.

Our company, consisting of a few hundred fighters, was led
by Captain Lech. It contained seventeen Polish Jews as well as a
few Greek Jews: Moszik from Salonika; Alfred Lewi and his
brother Doria. We quartered ourselves in the Mewa cinema at
Hoża 38. We helped construct the barricade on Zielna Street.
Dressed in SS uniforms with Polish insignia we moved to Czerniaków in order to obtain supplies for our company. I shared some of
the food with the Jews hiding in the same building.

In the middle of September, during a heavy bombardment
on Krucza Street, I took shelter in the basement of number 27.
There I ran into a group of Jews; they were starving, anxious, and
deathly afraid. Among them was Matys Sinykamień, his wife
Franka, and their child. I provided them with some food and
placed them in the basement of the building at Krucza 11, in the
same shelter where Eli was staying and which served as a contact
point for Jews connected with the Armia Ludowa. I gave them
some food from the stores of the fighters, and that led to a worsen-
ing of relations with Captain Lech. So I moved to Eli's shelter in
the basement at 11 Krucza Street. There, during the final phase of
the uprising at the end of September 1944, I met Bernard, the
well-known activist from the Bund.* I was just lying down to rest

*Before the war, Bernard had served as general secretary of the Leatherworkers Union.

when a middle-aged man appeared; he had a goatee and was wearing a light suit and a white shirt with a black tie. I seemed familiar to him, so as he looked at me he asked for my name. It turned out that Comrade Bernard knew my father, Welwel, who had been active in the Bund before the war.

Who was Comrade Bernard and what did he stand for? He was the personification of humanitarianism in the deepest sense of the word. In those times and circumstances, his simple appearance did not do him justice. In our encounters with him we felt his deep humanitarian character. In his company we felt safe and close to one another, like brothers.

From time to time my comrade Dudek Landau (known as Janek Cegielski), who had fought in the ghetto uprising, came to Eli's shelter. Before the war his father had had a leather warehouse on Bonifraterska Street. Inside the ghetto he belonged to the bakers group from Bonifraterska, which had contact with the ŻOB. I saw him on Miła Street during the first days of the April uprising in the ghetto. He was dressed in an SS uniform and was with a group of comrades. He was carrying a pistol. When he caught a German he didn't shoot him, he beat him to death with the handle of his pistol. During the Warsaw Uprising he fought with the Armia Ludowa on Warecka Street. Later we met up in liberated Warsaw. At present he is in the Erding camp outside of Munich.

We decided to make our way through the underground sewage tunnels to the Vistula and from there to the Russians in Praga. Once we reached the west bank, one of the comrades who was a good swimmer was to make his way across the river, carrying a line that had been prepared in advance. Upon reaching the Praga side he was to hold the line to make it easier for the others to cross.

There's no point in describing all those terrible experiences. Women also took part in the risky undertaking of attempting to cross the Vistula under the hail of bullets, among the killed and dying. The first group, including Comrade Bernard, said good-bye to those of us who stayed in the shelter and set off in the tunnels toward the Warsaw bank of the river.

After some time Eli's wife came back, practically naked, carrying a package of clothes, and said that the first ten Jews crossing the river had been shot by the Germans. The rest dispersed. Later it turned out that Eli had been killed in the action.

There were fifteen of us left. Early in the morning we constructed a more spacious bunker inside the burned building at Wspólna 26, on the left side of the basement. We camouflaged the entrance to the hideout and closed the trapdoor. The entrance was constantly guarded from the inside by one of us, who kept an eye out for anyone suspicious.

Apart from me, the following people stayed inside the bunker: Tosia, Eli's wife, who before the war sold oil in a little shop at Franciszkańska 22; Moszik, the Greek Jew from Salonika; Matys Sinykamień with his wife and child; the Łucki brothers— Danek with his wife and Henryk, who owned a metal shop at Bagno 8; Jakub Trost, a butcher, along with his wife; and Henryk Majzner, who used to own the store Eugenia on Pańska Street, where they sold down quilts.

A second shelter was constructed on the right side of the basement, where the following people moved in: Aron Walia, with his wife and sister-in-law; Big Mietek, Glazer's brother-in-law, and his wife, Basia; Sewek Glazer and his wife, Frania; Mietek who escaped the death camp at Treblinka and his brother-in-law Władek (last name unknown)—they settled in Israel after the war; Włodarski, the owner of a haberdasher shop on Targowa Street in Praga; and the Christians who had hidden the above-named Jews.

We spent two weeks there deep underground, without any daylight, crammed next to one another, living off a few drops of water and the remains of some crumbling zwieback. In these conditions twenty people buried alive in the basement at 26 Wspólna Street survived the last weeks of occupation by the Nazi bandits and the constant bombing of the remaining ruins of the capital that went on day and night. Our ears burst from the cannonades and the thunder of the exploding bombs. Death was lurking at every corner. We were tormented by hunger and sapped of what strength we had left.

It was decided that one comrade from each bunker—Sewek Glazer and myself—would go out on the steps of our demolished building to gain some orientation. We saw the ruins of buildings, a few dirty figures with torn clothes peeping out of the heaps of bricks and stones, a group of Poles carrying shovels driven on by some Germans.

The Jews from the other bunker moved into ours. We decided that a few of us—Big Mietek and Basia, the Greek Jew Moszik, and I—would have to go out to look for food; otherwise we would all die of starvation.

Under cover of night, armed with a pistol with the safety off, we walked around the ruined houses looking for any kind of food for our group, which we considered the most valuable thing. Warga from Walas's group found a woman with a child inside the ruins (the woman, named Maria, survived to liberation), and we took her back to our bunker. Maria found work with us dividing our modest food rations.

After some time searching the nearby basements, a few members of our group—Big Mietek, the brothers Zygmunt and Fredek, and myself—came across a few Jews in the second courtyard of the ruins of the building at Wspólna 33. These included Zygmunt, the former owner of an apartment building in Warsaw, Henryk Bialer from Nalewki 19 (after liberation he wound up in a camp outside Munich), Abraham from Mokotów, and a baptized Jew whose pseudonym was Piorun. They told us they had been hiding with seventeen people in the basement of a building on Wiejska Street near Three Crosses Square. Some Polish workers under German supervision had discovered them. All the ones who were hiding ran away.

This information aroused my curiosity since I knew that Comrade Bernard had been hiding in a bunker on Wiejska. We took the people we had met to our bunker at Wspólna 26. During the next nights I searched the ruins around Wiejska Street looking for my dear friend Bernard, and to my joy I found him in unusually dramatic circumstances. One night Zygmunt, Ruta, Basia, and myself were searching through the ruins when I noted a spark suddenly going out inside the basement of a building on the corner of Krucha and Wilcza. I released the safety on my pistol and ran right smack into a door, behind which to my great amazement I noticed a man trying to cut his throat with a pair of scissors; with him inside the hideout were two others who were extremely frightened. In a flash I realized that the man with the scissors was Comrade Bernard. My pistol fell out of my hand, and in a panic I called out "Bernard!" and bounded over to him. He embraced and hugged me, repeating "Julek" and "Welwel" (my father's name). We both cried and held each other for a long time. The other two people were Guzik, the director of the Joint, and Samborski, owner of a pharmaceutical warehouse in Warsaw. We spent the whole day on the steps of a burned-out building on Żurawia.

I soon returned to our bunker on Wspólna, in order to prepare some room for Bernard and his comrades. By evening they were already in "our house" at Wspólna 26. A few days later Henryk Bialer, Zygmunt, Samborski, Abraham from Mokotów, and Władek from the Walia group moved out of our bunker to the basement on Hoża.

One evening Big Mietek, Zygmunt, and I went out to look for provisions. Sudenly we heard a conversation in a basement on Wspólna and saw several revolvers aimed at us. I realized they belonged to Jews in hiding, so I called out *"Amhu"* (your own) and disarmed the dangerous situation. Among the people we met were a former Jewish policeman with his wife, and twenty-year-old Bela, a beautiful blonde whom we jokingly called the queen of the bunker.

Bela had been in the ghetto; after being arrested she worked in the tailor's workshop at Pawiak and was then freed during the Warsaw Uprising. Apart from those mentioned there were Bolek from Krakow and a man with the pseudonym "Pistolet," who fought in the ranks of the Home Army and later emigrated to Israel. Meeting with these people allowed us to exchange provisions.

Comrade Bernard became the most respected and well-liked person in our bunker. Thanks to him our mood improved significantly. He spoke in a way that was both interesting and exciting, telling us about his life, prison, work in the party, and the social and economic relations in the country. In vivid, gripping words he described the figure of Baruch Szulman, as well as my father's own activity in the Bund. During this time I grew close to Comrade Bernard and realized that in him I had found a close and devoted friend.

In the middle of January 1945 came the long awaited day of liberation. After a few days of increased attack by Soviet forces, the Germans fled. The victorious units of the Red Army and the Polish Army entered the demolished city.

After six years of bloody Nazi occupation, the handful of Jews who had survived came out of the basements and hiding places, out of the bunkers and sewage tunnels, into freedom. The persecuted, tortured, and hunted could finally straighten their backs and stretch their limbs.

As we dreamed of freedom, we had placed so much hope in that day. For the last time I fired a few shots from my pistol, as a sign of joy that I had finally lived to see the defeat of German imperialism and had satisfied my urge for revenge.

DAWID FOGELMAN WAS BORN IN WARSAW IN 1915. During the occupation he worked at his trade as a turner.

In July 1942, Fogelman's wife and two small children were

deported to Treblinka. He himself was captured during a roundup in March 1943, sent to Umschlagplatz, and loaded on a train bound for Treblinka, but he jumped off and returned to Warsaw. Fogelman was working at the Gdańsk train station when the uprising broke out in the ghetto; at the end of July 1943 all Jewish laborers were moved into the prison on Gęsia Street, where they were dressed as Soviet prisoners and daily sent to outside labor sites. During the Warsaw Uprising, a group of fighters freed the prisoners held on Gęsia Street and incorporated them into their own ranks. The following fragment describes the last days of the fighting. Later, Fogelman survived inside a bunker at Szczęsliwa 5, where he wrote his account. Nothing is known of his further fate.

The situation is hopeless. We set out at the crack of dawn to build a barricade. While we are working, German tanks approach and start shooting at us. By a miracle we manage to stave off the attack; our tanks immediately fire back and burn two German tanks. Three others flee. We go on building barricades. Suddenly some shrapnel explodes, killing two Jews on the spot and badly wounding four others. We break off and run for the shelter. I immediately grab four boys and we carry the dead to the Jewish cemetery, where we bury them; the wounded we take to the first-aid station.

Meanwhile the situation is getting worse by the hour. The Germans are attacking our position from all sides. The AK (Home Army) units are beginning to retreat little by little, escaping through the ghetto to the Old Town. Our leadership has completely lost control, and the chaos is spreading. Seeing this I run to Heniek, since I want to escape to the Old Town as well, but I can't find him. I grab my bags and am about to leave, when a lieutenant suddenly runs up to me; he grabs another boy—a twenty-year-old Jew who was with me at Pawiak—and orders us to carry a kettle of soup to the front line. We set down our knapsacks. I take the soup;

a female medic shows us the way. As soon as we're outside, the shooting is so heavy that I have to dive to the ground several times. I make it to the ghetto, but every few minutes I have to leave the kettle and take cover. As we're heading down Niska Street I see AK units running away in a panic toward the Old Town, while here I am stupidly hauling a hundred-pound kettle of soup. Tough, we have to go on. I reach Zamenhof Street and turn onto Szczęsliwa; the medic looks for the line, but can't find anybody; we enter a courtyard, set down the kettle, and wait. All of a sudden some civilian comes out of a basement carrying a bucket of water. I immediately realize he must have some kind of hiding place nearby. I ask the medic if I may leave and she says yes.

I take the boy (his name was Jacek) and we follow the civilian. I watch him go into the demolished building at Szczęsliwa 5 and follow him inside. Another civilian is standing in the entranceway and I immediately recognize him as Jewish. I approach and ask whether he doesn't have a hiding place for us. At first he was afraid; he didn't believe we were Jewish because we were wearing uniforms. We manage to convince him and he agreed. Next we go to the pickup point for provisions. That wasn't very easy, but there was no other choice. I take Jacek and one of the new companions and we go. The way there is miserable. Planes are flying practically right over our heads and strafing us with machine guns; we have to crawl on our hands and knees. Our companion stays in the ghetto while Jacek and I enter the school. The courtyard is empty. I go inside the workshop and grab a knapsack with bread and some canned goods. Jacek fetches some provisions as well, we take everything that's at hand, and head back. We expect the Germans to show up any minute. We manage to reach the ghetto, find our companion, divide what we are carrying, and make our way to the hideout.

We arrive at 5 Szczęsliwa; inside the courtyard is a pile of rubble. My companion shows us where to go; I see an opening like a cave, I want to walk in, but I can't; you have to wriggle in like a rat. I look around; it's dark; we light candles. Inside it's like a grave; full of rubble, there's no place to turn, you can't stand up, you have to bend, you can smell the stench. I wonder how four people can live here. There's no choice; you can hear the shrapnel whistling overhead. We had to hide since the Germans could come any moment. I set to work. First we start to clear out rubble to make more room. We look for some containers, which we fill with water; we camouflage the entrance and . . . wait for liberation.

A month has passed like that. Once again there is no water. We have to fetch it; we gather all our containers. We go out during the night, make it to the faucet, turn it on, and—no water! I was dumbfounded. Evidently the water plant's been damaged. We look for a water meter in the courtyard but can't find any. I see a hole knocked out of a wall; we go inside and feel a wave of hot air. The building has been burned down, and the heat is still trapped in the basement. We search through several basements and find a lot of food, as much as 28 cans—a treasure for us, since our supply of canned goods is running out. We find lard, wheat flour, different grains, and, most importantly, twenty boxes of matches, some kerosene, and a kerosene lantern. We go inside one of the basements and discover water dripping from a pipe. So there *is* water; I place a washbasin beneath the pipe, so at least it will catch something overnight. We leave our water containers and take everything back to the shelter. We made some decent "brandy" (we had found a little vodka), ate one tin of food with some dried bread, and went to bed.

I have to note that some new tenants have moved in— namely, some rats as big as cats; they keep us up the whole night. Tough. That's the way it is, we'll just have to get used to them as well; who knows what else awaits us?

We've lost our sense of time; we don't know which day of the week it is or which day of September. We live like cattle, dirty, unshaven: utter savages. The Soviets are near Warsaw; we can hear the artillery fire very clearly, even the machine guns. There are air raids at night. We keep living with the hope that it won't last much longer.

But still we have to go out for water. We enter our old building just to make sure there really isn't any. We turn on the faucet, and this time water comes out. We go down into the basement; the basin is full of water. It's hot in the basement; I take off my clothes, bathe, and dress in some underclothes I find in the basement. We take the water and return to the hideout. Now we have enough of everything.

It's cramped, inside the shelter, and horribly moist. You have to lie down the whole day; the ceiling is so low it's impossible to stand. One day I go out hoping maybe I can find some other place to hide. Two of us go searching. I go out a few steps, and several meters away from our hideout I see this large pile of rubble reaching up to the second floor, with an opening at the bottom. We clear some of the rubble, go inside, and light some candles. We find a large, spacious room; the walls and ceiling seem pretty much intact, but the place is filled with rubble. It will need a lot of work, but that's tough—we just have to do it.

We set to work, and after two days and one night the place is all fixed up. I use some bricks to lay a floor. One comrade sets up a large stove with an oven; we want to bake our own bread, but it turns out there is too little draft so we have to give that up. We'll just have to use the smaller stove instead. We make shelves and hangers, and at night we go out for beds. We find three spring beds and a new cot; six soft mattresses and sheets, two down blankets, five pillows, and something to cover them with. We take everything to our room. No one wants to sleep on the cot, so we draw lots. We set up all the beds and put the best mattress, the best down, and the best pillow on the cot. Whoever winds up with the cot won't be the worse for it. We draw lots. The cot goes to me; I was pleased, since that turned out to be the best.

On 3 November the fighting finally resumes. From early in the morning we can hear artillery fire and machine guns, as well as airplanes. Our hearts rejoice; without that music we were sad. Now we know they'll be freeing us soon. We are yearning for that moment.

But once again we are disappointed. After a few days of intensified action the front calms down again. Our spirits are completely broken; never in my life have I been in such despair, although I've lived through so much by now. I just don't know what's going on with me. I fall into a terrible melancholy; I don't speak to anyone the whole day. The nights are awful. There's not a single night that I don't dream of shouts and weeping; I sob in my sleep. In the morning I wake up feeling even more downcast. If it lasts much longer I won't be able to stand it. The hardest thing to bear is the inactivity, the waiting, the insecurity.

Our day looks like this: We wake up at six, with one person getting up at five to start the fire while it's still dark. Breakfast consists of half a kilogram of canned food, seasoned with flour and fried in lard. In addition we have a few canned tomatoes, also seasoned with lard and flour, something like a side dish. Next, a cup of coffee with sugar and a few pancakes—since we are out of dried bread. Each person receives a spoonful of good jam. From my point of view breakfast is beyond reproach.

It's already 15 December [1944]. Once again, two months have passed. The days are gray and monotonous. Everything is moving along the way it has been; these are days of waiting. It's cold. The cold is more and more noticeable; we have to stay in bed. Our provisions are running out, and there are no new ones in sight. We've made a few trips to the basements for food, but all in vain; the Polish laborers being forced to work for the Germans take everything. The situation is catastrophic. Even if we are very frugal, our supplies won't last for more than six weeks. This is very depressing for us. Who would have thought it would go on like this so long?

The worst thing is we have nothing to do. One day I had the idea to write poems. At first it was difficult, but then I composed a poem in Yiddish about our life in the shelter. My companions were delighted by it, so the next day I went on writing. I wrote about the deportation of the Jews from Warsaw, as well as a poem entitled "Winds of War." I wrote four poems in Polish and three in Yiddish.* I have to confess that I found this very engrossing, mostly because it made me forget about the tragic situation I was in. Under normal circumstances I would grow old without ever having written poems like that, but now I felt inspired by my own experiences.

Everything would be all right if it would only end, but unfortunately there's no end in sight.

It's almost New Year's 1945. I have been sitting here hiding for five months and don't know whether I'll live to see the end, but I do know I can't lose hope. We have learned that the situation on the front has taken a turn for the worse. The Germans have dug trenches everywhere. We can't move an inch.

Nevertheless we decide to go out looking for food on Christmas Day. I set out on a long and very dangerous route. I wanted to go as far as Pawia Street, where I knew were several apartment houses near the Tobacco Monopoly building. Getting there was very difficult, the night was bright, the wind was strong; it was hard to puzzle out the ghetto streets. The whole ghetto now is one big open field. I made my way very carefully and finally managed to reach the Monopoly building on Pawia. From far off I could tell it had been burned, but it was a solid structure, made of concrete. One of my companions sneaks up to the entrance and I follow. A light was on in the first basement; inside we saw a German soldier

---

*Two of these poems are included in the Yiddish anthology entitled *Pieśń getta* edited by R. Pups (Warsaw, 1962).

walking about. We stood rooted to the ground in fear, unable to budge. My companion went ahead nevertheless, but when we heard steps we took off running. I ran the whole way. I didn't want to fall into their hands alive. I ran all the way to my hideout. Evidently the wind was so strong they didn't hear us running. I was as if newly born. It was apparently some army station, since they were building new trenches, and the soldiers were taking shelter in the basement because it was cold. If the Germans hadn't been in the basement I would have fallen right into their hands.

After that terrible night we set off the next night in a different direction, toward Powązki. We searched several buildings and found a little food, but it was all spoiled and mildewed. Since we didn't have anything better we took it anyway. During the next nights we searched the entire area and found enough provisions for about three months.

In a word, our circumstances have improved. We are getting ready for the New Year so we decided to have a good supper; 1944 has been the most terrifying year of my life. For the moment I have freed myself from the Germans and lived to see their defeat near at hand. Hundreds of thousands of my brothers would have given much to witness this moment. This past year I have been through so much suffering and fear I don't understand how a person can bear it all. The Soviets have been sitting on the Vistula for four months and not taken a single step. On New Year's Eve we were very sad. Each spoke of his dear ones; I wished each a Happy New Year and read poems in Polish and Yiddish. In the end I cried. I had accumulated so much suffering that I had to cry a little. We went to sleep with the hope that 1945 would bring liberation.

The first days of January 1945 are passing in a very sad mood. It's cold outside. I lie in bed night and day. At night we gather snow, since our water supply is shaky. On 15 January there is fierce artillery fire during the night. We jump out of bed and run outside.

Horrific shooting on all sides. Evidently the offensive has started. The shooting continues without stopping through 17 January. During the day I lie in bed and listen to the airplanes flying low overhead. One of our group gets dressed quickly and goes out to check whose planes they are. Finally he comes back and says they're probably German since he couldn't see any insignia. We grow very sad. And so the whole day and night passes by.

The next day on 18 January I again hear planes. I get dressed and go out with one other person. From the distance I see the sil-houettes of soldiers, but I believe they're Germans. I strain my eyes; the soldiers are growing closer, I can make them out . . . the Polish Army! I grab my companion, we kiss each other, I cry for joy. I can't get a word out, I just point with my finger in that direc-tion. Meanwhile he's also spotted Polish and Russian soldiers. We run down to the shelter to share our happy news. I'm unable to describe our joy; we all went crazy. My companions at first didn't want to believe it and each had to go out and see for himself.

I dress quickly in my best things. I pack my belongings, sling on my knapsack, and leave the bunker. My companions were still not sure; they asked me to lead them. On Dzika Street, opposite Umschlagplatz, I see a few soldiers in the distance. I call out to them that we are Jews. With our hands up we walk toward them; I immediately recognize two officers of the Red Army as Jewish. We kiss each other; the officers are crying for joy along with us, they take us into their quarters. An army barber comes and shaves us and cuts our hair, since we looked like savages. We still had a little grain alcohol and some wine. We drank and played the whole night. I will remember that night for as long as I live. I realized beyond a doubt that I had finally found freedom. I am finishing this account because now I am beginning a completely different life—as a free man. After these experiences I look at life with com-pletely different eyes. I am breaking off from my old life and beginning my new one.

FRANCISZKA GRÜNBERG. Immediately after breakfast the village elder [of Rudki] went with us to Katarzyna's. Her place was a little shack somewhat sunken into the earth; there was no courtyard or garden, and the windows and doors were tiny, like in a house built for gnomes. Two or three hens were pecking around the house, being fed by a fairly young woman who was dirty and sloppily dressed. Hearing our steps, she turned in our direction. Her face was gloomy, with an evil gaze.

The elder greeted her in a friendly tone—"Good morning, pani Katarzyna"—which she answered with a mumbled "Gd mng." The elder asked her to take us to the apartment, but the woman refused to open the door, only relenting after the elder threatened to break it down. We stepped inside a dank, sooty little room that was unbelievably dirty. The woman glared at us and muttered "Whdyou want?" The elder explained that on orders of the regional authorities she was obliged to put up a family from Warsaw. The woman fell into a fury. She wasn't going to agree to anything. She was poor and they should leave her in peace. On top of that we could rob her, since she was gone most of the day. People from Warsaw were roaming through the countryside look-ing for households to rob. The elder finally interrupted her run of words—really, curses—and declared that the village would provide for us. The farmers would supply potatoes, kasha, and fuel, so because of us she would be able to keep warm. The woman started shouting again—that's what they say now but later she would have to feed us herself—and once again the elder assured her this wouldn't be the case, and so they went on arguing like that for a long time.

In the end the elder refused to give in and finally managed to have his way. The woman muttered, "Now just leave me alone—they can go ahead and stay in this filth if that's what they want." I said we would be back inside the hour, since our bundles were with the elder, and we left. However, when we came back an hour later we found the door had been locked and there was no sign of Katarzyna.

One of the farmers saw us standing there outside the locked door, at a loss what to do—by that time the whole village knew who we were—so he stopped and said, "Katarzyna locked her house up? She's a real hornet. But she's bound to be with her relatives across the way: She never visits anybody else." I left my husband and son beside the shack and set off to look for Katarzyna. I entered a crooked house on the other side of the road and found her sitting there. She had an evil look about her, and when she caught sight of me her face took on a predatory expression. I thought she would throw herself on me at any moment.

There was no way out; I realized the only way I would get anywhere was to stay determined and energetic. In that situation I forgot about all danger and focused on the necessity of obtaining a roof over our heads, at least for the time being. So I announced in a very determined voice, "Didn't you hear what the elder said? You won't have to pay any of the costs, but you do have to put us up. If you don't agree, we'll spend tonight at the elder's and in the morning I'll go to the regional administration, and the person in charge there will know what to do. Later you'll regret it. You're better off not trying to fight us; there's no reason to. What's more, you even stand to gain. I have the RGO* and the regional administration behind me, and they will take care of you. So please come along with me and unlock the door. You're being mean and inhuman, and if you don't let us in this minute we'll do whatever we can to make sure people treat you the way you're treating us."

The woman kept glaring at me the whole time, as if she wanted to eat me alive, and in the end she didn't say a word, just

*The Rada Główna Opiekuńcza, or Central Care and Sheltering Council, a charitable organization established in World War I, and reactivated during World War II with help from Herbert Hoover's Polish Relief Commission.—PB

shrugged her shoulders in anger and stayed in her chair. A relative who was in the room had been listening to what I was saying. She started trying to persuade Katarzyna to let us in and not make any trouble for herself and not be so mean to the unfortunate refugees. But the woman just sat there and didn't budge. "Go on now," her relative repeated, and Katarzyna finally stood up, but the look on her face gave me a fright. Surely the mythic harpies had more human faces.

Moving slower than a turtle and still having second thoughts, Katarzyna finally made it to her door. Then she opened it, all the while looking daggers at us. She went in and sat down on a small stool, looking around with wild eyes. We carried in our bags. We had to think about fuel and food. Leaving my husband and son inside the room, I went back to the elder's. It was humiliating to have to beg for help, but what other choice was there? On the way I stopped in at the only store in the village, where there was nothing but cigarettes, matches, cigarette wrappers, vodka, and carbide. I bought some carbide, since we had a lamp.

When the elder saw me he immediately asked how things had gone with Katarzyna. After hearing my report he said, "Yes, she's a real shrew, I don't know if you'll be able to stand it with her." I asked how I should go about obtaining potatoes and fuel. "I'll bring you a basket of peat for burning today, and 50 pounds of potatoes and some ration coupons you can give to the wealthier farmers for potatoes. You'll have to ask the farmers about fuel too; each one will give you a load of peat. I'll tell them."

I thanked him cordially and went back to our new "home" to send Rysiek for the things the elder had promised. It was already quite gray, and dark inside the hut, so I took out the carbide lamp and was on the verge of filling it with carbide when Katarzyna, who had been sitting like a log in the same spot, jumped up. "Whddr you wanting to do? Light that devil? You want to murder me?" I just looked at her, amazed. What was the woman talking about? Had she lost her mind? What a terrible fate we have and what unbelievable circumstances it has led us to! I spoke to Katarzyna calmly. "We'll have some light to see by, and Rysiek is bringing some peat so it will be warm. We'll cook some potatoes and we'll all eat." But the woman didn't even want to listen. Meanwhile, Rysiek went out and came back with a lantern already lit. The woman started shrieking to high heaven that the devil was choking her. She started grunting and wheezing and wrapping her arms around her chest. She grabbed the carbide lamp and put it out, and everything was dark again.

My nerves were completely frazzled. Always on the move, the sword of Damocles constantly hanging over our heads, most recently being put up at a new farmhouse every twenty-four hours, the humiliating treatment by this shrew Katarzyna, and finally her fury over the "devilish" carbide lamp—the whole turmoil completely did me in. I was ready to bite and scratch, even to kill. I don't know how, but by some superhuman effort I took hold of myself, and after a long while I started speaking to Katarzyna in a very gentle voice: We had to light something. We were hungry and cold so we had to cook something hot, there were candles in the store but we couldn't afford them, and so on.

She snorted. "Just go to sleep and that's it." Once again I explained to her that it was only six o'clock and it was as cold as a doghouse, and I went on explaining things over and over until I was worn out. The woman grew calmer and calmer; finally, she went to the larder and came back with the kind of lantern they hang on a wagon, which she then lit. The lantern had a hole in the glass so it smoldered awfully, and the room was full of smoke and soot. That didn't bother Katarzyna in the least. But our eyes were burning and crying, our throats were unbearably scratchy, and we were wheezing and coughing. Katarzyna was wheezing the whole time as well, spitting and blowing her nose on the floor, but she said it was "healthy 'cause the kerosene cleans evrthing out of a person."

Rysiek brought potatoes and a little peat; I started a fire and cooked supper. After supper I asked Katarzyna for a little straw and she gave us a thin sheaf, although very unwillingly and with a good deal of foot-dragging. I took out our little pillow, which had lost half its feathers, and next to it I placed my one and only dress, folded over several times. Then we lay down to sleep, covering ourselves with coats that only reached to the middle of our calves.

No sooner had we fallen asleep than we were wakened by Katarzyna's loud ranting. "Ai! That damned devil's come and got me he's choking me, oh, Most Holy Mother, take him away from me, what's he wanting from me? What's he choking me for?" and on and on like that. After she had gone on awhile without letting up I asked her what was wrong and why she was shouting. "That damned carbide is choking me, it's a horrible devil, keeping ahold of me without letting go."

What was there to say? I told her it had to be the soot from the smoky lantern that was choking her, since it was choking us as well, but the woman wouldn't hear of it. She went on ranting— "Why did I go on and take in these people who have devils like that to make me fall sick? Plague take that elder 'cause he's lost his wits for sure"—and so on over and over. Every half hour she'd get out of bed and drink some water; twice she stepped out to the porch to get some air. She kept tormenting herself and us until finally at four in the morning she got up, dressed, and went outside. We heard her open the door to the adjacent cowshed—there wasn't a single cow there, just a few hens nesting in the corners— and bring back a little wood. She lit a fire, perched on the packed dirt floor like a hen, with her legs curled up beneath her, put a pot of black coffee on the fire, and sat there spitting and snorting the entire time. We also woke up, irritated, cross, and horribly exhausted from the night. I added some peat to the fire, took some coffee out of my bundle, and prepared it. The tasteless fluid warmed us up. I heated a pot of water and carried a little laundry pan from the little porch, since there wasn't any basin, and we used that to wash up. After a breakfast consisting of some overcooked potatoes, a young girl about twenty-five years old came over to see us. She was exceptionally nice and friendly and told us she was a teacher who had run a little school in the village ever since the beginning of the war. She had been deported from Łódź, came to Rudki, and started teaching the village children here. She had heard there was a family from Warsaw and wanted to find out what we needed. When she saw we didn't have any bedding, she promised to bring a straw tick from the cooperative, which she would arrange through the RGO, and then told us she was going at once to fetch a shawl we could wrap ourselves in.

She went out without waiting for an answer and came back half an hour later with a large woolen shawl, a loaf of rationed bread she had obtained from the cooperative at Nowe Miasto (on the Pilica River), some fatback, and a candle. We were taken aback by the gifts, but the girl was so sweet, simply amazing, that there was no room for demurring. She insisted that we drop in to see her and then left, after first promising to drive into town after one or two days to bring the mattresses. We were moved by her kindness, her sweet and engaging manner, her charming personality. She brought a glimmer of light into our dreary lives.

That night passed almost exactly like the first. Katarzyna again complained and snorted, spat, blew her nose, and tormented us with her behavior. After two days we ran out of peat and potatoes. We had to go back to the village to get some more. Rysiek took a large wicker basket from Katarzyna and went with my husband, who had a sack. They came back loaded down with peat and potatoes. Evidently the farmer they had visited had heard from the elder that the wealthier farmers were responsible for supplying us with fuel and potatoes; he received them very hospitably and filled the basket with peat and the sack with potatoes. So we were relatively well off as far as fuel was concerned and had enough to eat—although only potatoes, of course. Thanks to the teacher, we even had a piece of fatback that we put into our soup in pharmaceutical doses.

The teacher kept her word. On the third day we looked through our Lilliputian window and saw a wagon heading toward town, with a woman completely covered in shawls, since it was bitter cold. Katarzyna, who never missed a chance to look out of the window, was also watching when she heard the clatter of the wheels and shouted, "You see, there's that teacher riding into town sure as anything." We never would have recognized the woman all bundled up as our sweet teacher. Toward evening, the same wagon returned and stopped nearby; the woman wrapped in her shawl jumped down, picked up a large bundle, and ran to our cottage. A moment later she came in, and as she took off her shawl we saw our guardian angel's charming face, pink from the cold. She handed us the bundle, saying, "Here's some ticking for mattresses, you'll sleep more comfortably when you stuff them with straw. I'm going back home now because I'm frozen through. Good night." Having said that she hurried out, sealing herself with the shawl, sprang lightly onto the wagon, and drove off.

We immediately set about filling the mattresses with straw. Our old straw wasn't enough, so Katarzyna took pity and gave us one more little sheaf. We placed two stuffed mattresses on the floor next to each other, covered them with the large shawl the teacher had lent us, and found that our bed was fit for a king.

That evening I went to see the teacher. She also boarded with a farmer, inside a tiny hut; actually the farmer lived in the kitchen and the teacher had a fairly large room on the other side of a little porch. The moment I opened the door to her room I was struck by an air of urban sophistication and culture. The room was divided by a special partition. The first section was like a little drawing room; it had a small table with a large embroidered tablecloth, a few armchairs with white covers, some landscapes on the walls, curtains, a small tapestry, and several books lying on the table. The second half of the room served as dining room, bedroom, and kitchen, and the whole place was very clean and nicely ordered. The teacher lived with her sister and the sister's little daughter. She was very happy to see me. I spent an hour conversing cordially with these charming women. Some jam, tea, and country-style bread appeared on the little table. When I left the teacher insisted that I visit her often. I thanked her for everything she had done for me and went home to our dirty, sooty hovel, which was covered with snot and spit.

When we ran out of fuel and nothing was left but the remains of the potatoes, we again had to visit the farmers. No one refused; it was unclear whether they were doing it gladly or not, but each one gave his portion of fuel and potatoes. Still, it was really begging, and although Rysiek never grumbled as he took the basket or the sack and made his rounds to fetch the things we simply couldn't do without, I alone could see how much it cost him, how much determination he was putting into the task. My heart broke as well when he went along with me, or else by himself, bearing the potato sack, with nothing more to offer than a few words from the elder that the farmer in question was obliged to give us so many potatoes. For peat he didn't need any ration coupon; he would come back bending under the weight of the heavy basket.

The war kept going on and on; it seemed it would never end. There was no news of any activity in Poland. A deathly silence reigned around us and it seemed this would never change. And we were rotting away in Rudki, in constant fear, afraid we might learn something terrible at any moment, or that somebody would recognize us, or something even worse might happen. We ate nothing but potatoes, often rotten or frozen, and we were condemned to a constant interchange with the crazy woman Katarzyna, who poisoned our lives with hundreds of different trivial matters. The lice were eating us alive; our "undergarments" were down to their last threads—rags we could no longer wear. The same thing happened with my good shoes. Our bodies had open wounds from the constant scratching. And the last straw was the lack of sleep during the nights when Katarzyna would start her crazy babbling.

The sores my husband and son had on their legs refused to heal, as a result of inadequate nutrition and the poor hygiene we were exposed to. A few of the village women gave me some rags to bind the wounds, but they were constantly leaking pus. I don't know what would have happened if we had had to keep moving.

It was 14 January 1945, I think, when we saw some German soldiers driving wagons loaded down with suitcases and bags. Trudging behind the wagons came the German officers—dirty, without their belts, with drooping heads and downcast eyes, which they would only lift now and then to see what lay ahead. We didn't know what it meant; we thought some German unit was intending to put up here. We were worried; the idea of having Germans right under our noses was no cause for joy. All of a sudden there was a knock at the door. I opened and two officers stepped in, as dirty as the others, with no weapons or any insignia. They sat down and asked for some coffee. Katarzyna lit a fire. They asked me if I was from Warsaw. I nodded my head. They offered me a little roll of candy drops. The idea of taking anything from them disgusted me, so I placed the candy on the stove behind the pots, and there it sat until it melted into a smoking red magma that seemed to me a kind of symbol for the bloody martyrdom of the Jewish nation. I looked those two representatives of German culture right in the eye; I studied them closely and could not fathom how these people, who were created in the likeness of other people on earth, could commit the kind of bestial deeds we all knew so well, of which the mere recollection causes us to shudder.

One of them was a real chatterbox. He started to tell me he had walked all the way from Stalingrad, where the Germans had disgraced themselves by losing the battle. Now he was probably going to continue escaping on foot all the way to Berlin, because

Ivan (the Soviet army) was already in Nowe Miasto. That bit of news took me completely aback. I stared at him so wide-eyed I must have looked half crazed, because he tugged his comrade by the sleeve and said, "Look at the impression my bit of news has made on this woman, Is she scared or what?" Impression? Who knows how it feels to be condemned to death and placed in front of the firing squad when suddenly a messenger comes racing up at the last moment carrying a pardon? Truly the German's words were like a pardon for those of us who had been condemned to die. Now I no longer cared about him. I understood what the wagons loaded with suitcases meant: They were running away. They had been beaten. For us this meant the first spark of freedom. Freedom! The word had lost all meaning for me. I turned away from the German and joined my husband and son in the corner. Their faces, too, showed unbounded astonishment and joy that the long-awaited moment had finally arrived—and calmly, with no more slaughter or battles or similar horrors. The Germans left. I was overcome by a nervous trembling; I was shivering as with fever. Maybe the moment wasn't so close after all. Maybe something unexpected would happen. Maybe tragic moments were still in store for us.

Should we go to Nowe Miasto? Or were the Germans killing people on the road? Maybe they're going to burn down the village without letting anybody out. What should we do? How should we proceed? It was too much for me to handle. I just kept going in circles doing nothing. Meanwhile my son and husband were laughing, and saying that the Germans wouldn't hurt us; they just wanted to get away as quickly as possible. We were crazy, utterly intoxicated with the news, to the point of being delirious. Nobody gave a thought to peat or potatoes, although we didn't have anything; we just stood by the window and watched the fleeing Germans. When evening came we lay down on our straw ticks, covered ourselves with the shawl, and fell asleep, exhausted by the overload of emotions. Katarzyna went to bed as well; evidently she was in a better mood that day because she didn't carry on.

I don't know how long we slept before we were awakened by a loud rumbling from the road, which ran several kilometers away from the house. From all the racket it sounded like several trucks and tanks were passing. What could it mean? Was a battle shaping up here? There was no end to the din; it grew louder and louder. Katarzyna also woke up and immediately started carrying on. She thought they were already shooting, that some big battle was under way. I wanted to open the door and look outside—maybe I could make out what was going on—but she refused to let me. She was afraid of something though she didn't know what; the Germans might think we were spying and burn down the cottage and kill us all, and so on. So we all lay there quietly, with our hearts pounding, listening to what was going on around us.

We had been lying there a few hours when we heard some wagons coming down the little road past our hut. We could hear horses neighing, as well as some voices goading the horses and calling to one another—all just outside our window. It was difficult to make out what the voices meant. But we could see the sky was beginning to turn gray. Katarzyna jumped out of bed and got dressed. Standing by the window, she looked around warily. "A powerful lot of troops are passing through," she said finally. Once again we were worried. Were they Germans? So many? Something's brewing nearby; it's not over yet. We'll have to pass through one more hell. We huddled closely together under the shawl and covered our ears with our coats so as to block out the shouts and rumbling. Meanwhile Katarzyna just stood there staring. It was already light. "These troops sure are dressed funny," she said at last. "They're all wearing sheepskins and fur caps." We looked up at her and poked our heads out of the coats. Katarzyna threw on a shawl and went out. We were afraid to move. Maybe the Germans would show up at any moment. She was gone for nearly twenty minutes.

Finally she came back and told us the troops were all wearing some kind of red star on their caps. As if launched by a spring, we jumped up from our bedding. "Russians!" all three of us shouted in chorus and, pushing her away from the window, pressed our faces against the pane. A long line of wagons was passing from the direction of Nowe Miasto, accompanied by a small number of soldiers. The Soviet troops, dressed in sheepskin coats and fur caps, were calling out to one another other cheerfully, and after a moment we could hear a happy Russian song. Like a madwoman I pounced on my son and started kissing and hugging him, shouting, "You survived the war, my son!" I let the hot tears stream slowly down my cheeks: tears of joy, that I had kept my son from the clutches of the bloody Nazi beast.

WHEN THE GERMANS OCCUPIED WARSAW, **GUSTAWA WILNER** *had to move from an apartment on fashionable Willowa Street to join her parents in the future ghetto, where she was active with the local building committee. In 1942 she secured jobs for herself and her father at a worksite outside the ghetto; later all three managed to escape and hide on the Aryan side until the 1944 Uprising, after which she was evacuated to the countryside. Gustawa's sister Halina was murdered at Trawniki in 1943.*

The account is dedicated to the author's brother Arie (Jurek) Wilner, a leading figure in the Jewish resistance and a liaison to the Żegota group. Along with several other leaders of the Jewish Fighting Organization, Arie Wilner committed suicide on 8 May 1943.

After the war Gustawa Wilner and her parents left Poland and eventually settled in Israel.

Living in the country was the best medicine for me. We still had a little money, which we used to buy eggs, cheese, and butter.

What bothered us most were the filth and cramped conditions. Meanwhile pan Mechner and pani Zofia befriended the village elder, and he promised to give them a tiny place that was unoccupied and had been sitting there locked up for a long time with nobody using it. Evidently it had been set aside for some special purpose.

There was talk in the village about "boys from the forests"— meaning the partisans. People said they came at night to requisition food. We ourselves didn't know the first thing about partisans.

It wasn't long before we had a chance to find out. One night the dogs started barking very loud and woke us up. Pan Mechner was just opening the door to step outside for a moment when he found himself face-to-face with a young man armed with a machine gun, who immediately demanded to see his papers. The man stepped into the room, followed by another man, who instantly turned to us. "You're Jews!" he said. "You have no right to hide here. The whole village might suffer because of you."

Pani Zofia, confident of her own Aryan identity, vigorously jumped to our defense, showing her papers and naming some well-known people in her family, as well as friends who might confirm her racial background, and thereby ours as well, as family members.

That threw them off guard. One of them said, "We'll find out for sure. We'll be back shortly." They left. After no more than ten minutes we once again heard the stamping of feet and people pushing against the door. This time we counted fifteen of them. They were armed with machine guns, hand grenades, and revolvers. One of them shined a flashlight in our eyes and was generally rude.

Pani Zofia once again leapt to our defense. At that point the same person told the others, "She's a Pole who's hiding those two Jews. They have to be taken care of." They began asking questions, demanded our documents, and examined them closely.

At that point pan Mechner addressed them in all his dignity. "You come bursting in here as if we were criminals. Whatever you intend to do, be quick about it. Nothing can scare us anymore. We've been through too much for that. If you want to kill us, don't dally; we'll know we're dying by the hands of our brothers. If you don't have such evil intentions, then take us to the forest so we can fight alongside the partisans against the enemy." After that speech they all went silent. Pani Zofia expressed her sorrow and shame at her fellow countrymen and repeated the idea of taking us to the forest. They began to confer among themselves. One of them came up to me, saying, "And you, ma'am, don't you have anything to say?"

"I have so much to say to you I prefer to keep silent," I answered.

Then he said, "You're still young and beautiful. You have your whole life ahead of you."

"Is it worth living for people like that?" I said, pointing at the mob. He didn't say any more to me and joined the rest. They conferred for a fairly long time. We awaited the verdict in silence.

Finally one of them spoke up. "We'll give you forty-eight hours to clear out or else we'll take care of you."

After they left, each one of us literally went into shock and each for different reasons. We had thought that the "Jewish issue" had disappeared with the Warsaw Uprising. Apart from that, we were faced with the tremendous difficulty of continuing to move from place to place.

Pan Mechner summoned his courage and went to the regional command of the town of Końskie. Using his beautiful German, a certain bravado, and his ability to win over the very devil, he managed to finagle three passes, which at that time was no mean feat.

Pani Zofia decided we would head toward Łowicz, since she knew a lumber merchant there who had a good relationship with her brother. She expected he would help us.

We arrived safe and sound. Pani Zofia at once went to see the merchant, in an attempt to secure some space for us. As it turned out, however, he was not so eager to help. All he agreed to do was give pani Zofia a few boards she could sell for money. We were afraid to go to the RGO lest the reason for our leaving Końskie might come out. But there was no choice; we had nowhere else to turn. Pani Zofia found some excuse, partly by referring to her acquaintance the merchant, and managed to persuade them. They found places for us at two farms in the village of Piotrowice, about twenty kilometers from Łowicz. We drove there in a horse-drawn cart.

The farms were fairly large. They were all connected and belonged to three brothers. Each of them owned 28 morgas* of land, a house with two rooms and a kitchen, and sizable holdings of livestock. The mother lived along with her daughter with one of the brothers, while the father lived with the second. The third brother was the one with the empty room. The Wróblewski family (pan Mechner and pani Zofia) stayed there, while I went to the second farm. That way there were two refugees on each property.

After learning that I was good at handiwork, the farmwives began arguing over me. Each wanted me to stay for some time. Generally speaking, people from Warsaw were treated very badly. The refugees were scattered in barns, stables, cowsheds, or attics. They were given little to eat and frequently made to do heavy physical labor, during which they were ridiculed for their incompetence. The peasants kept repeating, "So Warsaw's come to wait on us now." It was a chance for them to give vent to the antagonism that ran between town and country.

By comparison, my situation wasn't so bad. The young farmwives had aspirations of elegance and wanted an example from the big city, which I was expected to provide.

---

*An old unit of land measurement comprising a little over one-third of an acre.—PB

I set about knitting a skirt and some sweaters for my landlady; she was very proud of them. Thanks to that my conditions improved. I slept in one room along with the grandmother, the mother of the young men. Some of the boards that pani Zofia had obtained were sold; pan Mechner used the rest to make three beds, one for each of us. When I received my bed, the farmers offered me a straw tick, an old sheet, and a pillow; the old lady gave me a down quilt. It was stuffed with chicken feathers, but it kept me warm enough.

This was no small success. I made some warm stockings and some gloves for the grandmother, which won over her heart. From time to time she would give me a little treat such as an apple, a piece of cake, an extra bonus of milk, and so on.

For the most part we went hungry. Pani Zofia and pan Mechner really suffered. Because of her aristocratic background, pani Zofia annoyed the peasants and felt an aversion toward them. She did not spare them her disdain, which made her own condition even worse. Winter was coming. None of us had any warm clothes. Pani Zofia had a fall coat but nothing warm to wear underneath. I didn't even have that much. The winter started off severe. Out of hatred the farmers didn't want to lend her anything, so out of spite she refused to go to church, in order to offend their religious feelings, and threatened that if they didn't give her something to wear she wouldn't even go to midnight mass. That was stupid of her and dangerous to boot.

I on the other hand went to church every Sunday. I wanted to appear very devout, so as not to attract attention.

For Sunday the farmwife gave me warm clothes and I would walk the six kilometers to church. I started to explain to pani Zofia that she was making things worse by her behavior. I asked her to come to church at least once. Besides, I knew she was very religious and went to church every Sunday in Warsaw. But she was inflexible.

Christmas was approaching. Despite my pleas pani Zofia stayed stubborn, absolutely refusing to go to mass, and would not even allow pan Mechner to go either. However, she did encourage me to go.

I was very worried. The mass was supposed to start at seven in the morning, instead of at midnight, because of the curfew. I knew the evening before that I would be going to church early in the morning. The young farmwife didn't go, since she had just given birth; for that she arranged some warm clothes for me: the woolen skirt I had made for her, her fancy sheepskin coat, and a warm shawl to cover my head. For shoes I put on the ski boots that I had worn when I left Warsaw. I was also given some warm socks. Thus equipped I set out on foot at five-thirty for the church in Kiernoź.

Along the way I stopped in again to see my "family," to see if I could persuade them after all, but this was in vain. I couldn't convince them. Pani Zofia, seeing me dressed up like that, shouted, "You look like you own the place!" and whispered in my ear, "The devil himself would never guess you were Jewish."

One day as we were just lying in bed, in the dark, the grandmother suddenly started talking to me: "People in the village are saying your family is Jewish." When I heard that I felt as if somebody had hit me over the head. I was lucky it was dark and she couldn't see my face. I quickly recovered my wits and cried out, "Who's saying that, Grandmother? Tell me right away who it is, and I'll go there and teach them to talk like that. I really want to know their name."

The old woman got a little frightened. "Oh, don't worry, they don't know what they're saying. I told them right off it wasn't true; that lady with me says her prayers and goes to church. She got up in the night to go to midnight mass. A Jewish woman wouldn't do that. Then they told me that the Wróblewskis don't go to church."

I again expressed my indignation.

That morning I ran to see them and told them about my conversation with "Grandma." Zofia didn't seem too worried. She just said, "It's good you've been going to church."

News of German defeats began reaching the village in a steady stream. They started building trenches around the nearby villages. The Germans demanded a work contingent. The peasants immediately took advantage of the situation and sent all the people from Warsaw.

I went as well. They gave me the farmer's old jacket and some galoshes that were twice as big as my legs. They also packed a few slices of bread with some lard; I took this and left.

The nearest trenches had been designated for fourteen kilometers west of the village. Although the Varsovians were assigned to the work contingent, there were supposed to be horses and carts and each farmer was supposed to send two people. I was to go with the farmer.

The day before we left for the trenches we suddenly received word from the elder that the work was called off. At the same time, people said that in some village they had seen Germans running away and that the Russians had taken Łowicz. It was true that for several days we had heard fierce bombardment from heavy artillery. The earth was rumbling.

We couldn't believe it was the beginning of the end. Even as the war was taking its course and liberation was approaching, human evil did not diminish. We learned that a Jewish woman had been discovered in the neighboring village and was handed over to the Germans. Poor woman. She wasn't allowed to see freedom when it was so close at hand!

The next day people came from a third village and said the Soviet Army was already there. I couldn't believe it. The next day, early in the morning—it was 18 January 1945—the farmer's brother came running over and told us that two German officers had come at daybreak and under threat of shooting had forced the peasants to hide them under the straw in the attic. He was shaking with fright as he spoke. He had run away from home, for fear of the consequences. He had left five women in the house: his wife, two daughters, and two women from Warsaw. He himself was so afraid he set off on foot to go to his relatives eight kilometers away. I told him to report the incident, but he wouldn't listen and just ran off.

Several minutes later his wife and daughters came, crying and trembling with fear; they begged me to come to the attic, since I knew German, and explain to the officers that they couldn't hide there; the Soviets were already in the next village, and the men were unnecessarily endangering the lives of the peasants. They said they were prepared to let them have some women's dresses as a disguise to help them escape. I protested vigorously against that last proposal, explaining that if the Germans were caught, which was highly likely, the women would really have to face the consequences of having aided their escape and would probably pay for it with their lives. I did agree to go up and tell them that the Russians were in the neighboring village, so that there was no sense in hiding.

It was a curious role: I, a Jewish woman, was supposed to convince two Germans that their situation was helpless, to order them to leave, witness their shame and defeat. I couldn't believe that things could change like that. I went up and called out loudly in German that I wished to talk to them. When they heard their language, they shook off the straw and jumped up, shouting, *"Was ist das?"* I was facing two young officers, tall and blond, ideal specimens of the Nordic race. Their eyes were wide with fear, their hair unkempt and sprinkled with straw, which made them look funny, like figures from a farce. They were a far cry from the Germans of yesterday: arrogant, elegant, and so pedantically clean—as if external cleanliness could compensate for internal filth and moral gangrene.

I spoke to them briefly, saying I had come in the role of translator. I informed them that Soviet troops were in the next village and could show up here at any moment; it was pointless to hide, and they were only unnecessarily endangering people. I advised them to leave at once.

They both began asking whether they could stay until dusk, when it would be easier for them to escape. They asked us to understand the difficult situation they were in. (What a paradox!) At that moment the farmwife called out, *"Proszę pani,* the Russians are already at Józek's"—at my farmer's.

I repeated the news. They began to panic. They started to run around like poisoned mice, crying, *"Oh, Gott! Es ist schlimm!"*—Oh, God, things are bad! I stood and watched yesterday's heroic representatives of the Herrenvolk acting like cowards. At such a moment they were unable to end their vile lives with dignity.

I didn't speak to them anymore. I went down quickly, leaving them in fear, and ordered the farmwife to immediately report the German officers to the Russians. We all left the house and headed toward the farm where I was staying. An old Russian officer was coming our way, with a cordial greeting. I was in front, so he stopped me. He immediately saw I didn't belong to the village (he knew about the refugees). I told him I was from Warsaw and wanted to get back there as quickly as possible. Then he explained that Warsaw was still mined and advised me to wait a couple of weeks.

I cued the farmwoman to report the Germans immediately, which she did. Meanwhile we went inside my cottage, where there were about twenty soldiers half naked, washing up and singing Russian army songs. At that point someone from the courtyard shouted in Russian: *"German'tsi!"* The soldiers grabbed their rifles and ran outside just as they were, half naked. Someone pointed the way to the second farm. A few minutes later we heard some fierce shooting. After nearly twenty minutes they brought both German officers to our farm. I was surprised they were still alive. They were without caps, without their officers' insignia, pale, frightened, trembling: an unbelievable picture. They were searched. On one of them, who was married, they found a wedding picture, party card, military ID, and a photo of his family. Each of us examined that picture, unable to believe that they, too, had fathers, mothers, children: that the same men who smashed the heads of innocent children before the eyes of their horrified mothers, who tore husbands away from wives, children from their parents, who had profaned the most sacred human feelings, had any kind of family feelings at all.

After searching them, the Russians ordered my landlord to give the Germans some old caps, since it was bitter cold. When I asked one of the soldiers why they were treating them in such a humane way, he answered with pathos, "Stalin says that the enemy is on the front; opponents are to be taken prisoner." How nice; I didn't know Stalin was such a humanitarian.

They led the Germans away. The women went quickly to work, as ordered, to fix the Soviet soldiers something to eat. I was so taken aback by the speed of events I didn't fully grasp what had happened. Pan Mechner and pani Zofia came, not knowing how to express their feelings. Pan Mechner came up to me and said, "So it's true. We lived to see the moment of freedom. Is it not a dream?"

SAMUEL PUTERMAN. There's nobody here! And yet I'm surrounded by so many people. I'm back. I survived the hell of the Warsaw Ghetto; I survived the flames. I survived the hell of the Aryan side; I survived the uprising in Warsaw. I survived Sachsenhausen and Oranienburg. I survived Himmler. I came back. I'm back, but there's no one happy to see me. My heart was pounding, throbbing, burning as I walked to the place where they separated us a year ago, where a brutal hand tore me from what was left of my family: my wife, my mother, my sister, and that other poor soul who had been rescued from the ghetto.

I thought you'd be there waiting for me. In the living hell of the concentration camp I wondered what it would be like to be free again—a stupid, naive daydream—and yet it came true. I was freed; I went back. I was free, but you weren't there. You weren't waiting for me in front of our house. You didn't wipe any tears of joy from your face. Your green eyes didn't sparkle with happiness. What greeted me instead was the lingering stench of ashes and the empty sockets of our ruined home. My heart ceased beating; it started to twinge in pain, and to this day it hasn't stopped aching. Only a tiny part of my beautiful dream of freedom came true. The rest shattered right there, in front of the house where you were supposed to be waiting.

Notes

Introduction by Philip Boehm

1. Estimates compiled in 1958 by Tatiana Berenstein and Adam Rutkowski of the Jewish Historical Institute in Warsaw. For more detailed demographic descriptions, see the excellent collection of essays, *The Jews in Warsaw,* edited by W. Bartoszewski and A. Polonsky (Oxford: Basil Blackwell, 1991), as well as Charles G. Roland's thoughtful and well-researched analysis of the medical profession inside the ghetto, *Courage Under Siege: Starvation, Disease, and Death in the Warsaw Ghetto* (New York and Oxford: Oxford University Press, 1992).
2. Jacob Sloan, ed., *Notes from the Warsaw Ghetto: The Journal of Emmanuel Ringelblum* (New York: Shocken, 1974).
3. Isaac Bashevis Singer, *Shosha* (New York: Farrar, Straus & Giroux, 1978), pp. 71–72.
4. For further analysis of the roots of anti-Semitism in Poland, see Hillel Levine, *Economic Origins of Anti-Semitism* (New Haven and London: Yale University Press, 1991).

Chapter 1: LIFE WITHIN THE WALLS

1. *Eksterminacja żydów na ziemiach polskich w okresie okupacji hitlerowskiej,* compiled and edited by Tatiana Berenstein, A. Eisenbach, and Adam Rutkowski (Warsaw, 1957), p. 69, item 27.

2. *Dokumenty i materiały do dziejów okupacji niemieckiej w Polsce, Tom III, Getto łódzkie, cz. I*, edited by A. Eisenbach (Warsaw-Łódź-Kraków, 1946), pp. 35–37.

3. See Abram Lewin's account published in *Biuletyn ŻIH*, 1956, nos. 19–20; 1957, nos. 21–24; 1958, no. 25. See also *Adama Czerniakowa dziennik*, entries for 3, 7, and 12 May 1942, as well as footnote 38, p. 275.

4. See Berenstein, et al., *Eksterminacja*, p. 167, item 79, for a telegram from the head of the security police and SD to the leaders of the SS and police in five districts concerning the confiscation of all manner of fur products, as well as *Adama Czerniakowa dziennik*, entry for 24 December 1941, p. 234.

5. For some of the names of those murdered, see B. Mark, *Walka i zagłada getta warszawskiego* (Warsaw, 1959), p. 86, and *Archiwum Ringelbluma: Getto warszawskie, lipiec 1942–styczeń 1943* (Warsaw, 1980), p. 104.

Chapter 2: GHETTO INSTITUTIONS

1. See Marian Fuks's introduction to *Adama Czerniakowa dziennik*, p. 16.

2. See *Archiwum Ringelbluma*, p. 161, note 97.

3. See B. Mark, *Walka i zagłada*, pp. 266–67.

4. Mawult adds the following: Desk officers in the chancellery included Mieczysław Goldstein and the lawyer Leon Józef Fels. Serving in Division One were the lawyers Stanisław Adler, Aleksander Brewda, Rafał Lederman, and the former associate judge Dr. Ludwik Lindenfeld. Konrad Geller, an industrialist from Bielsko and a former officer of the Austrian Army during the Great War, held the position of translator. In Division Two were Albert Szwalbe, B. Rozenes, Bronisław Lewin, Henryk Nowogrodzki, and Gustaw Wichler (the last three were all lawyers: Nowogrodzki and Wichler were intended to serve as defense counsel in disciplinary cases), and in Division Three were Stanisław Kroszczor, Ignacy Blaupapier, and the engineer Jakub Proszower. The editor Aleksander Szenberg from Łódź, the lawyer Mieczysław Czackis, and retired policeman Stanisław Ejbyszyc—who had long held a similar function at National Police Headquarters—all worked in the chancellery. Over time the staffing underwent various changes: The lawyer Czesław Kornblit was appointed to oversee the Office of Real Estate, so he resigned his police post and left the SP, where he was replaced by Marceli Czapliński.—PB

5. Mawult continues: This job of overseeing the SP was assigned to Department One of the PP, which was headed by Captain Moniak at that time (and possibly for all of 1941), with Captain Poniński in charge of the OPL itself. Beyond that—ex officio—stood the commandant of the PP for the city of Warsaw, Colonel Reszczyński; his deputy, Major Przymusiński, considered the éminence grise within the Polish police and the autonomous administration of the city of Warsaw; further, Major Tarwid, head of the "North" district, as well as the directors of various commissariats in the field.

Chapter 3: ROUNDUPS, SELECTIONS, AND DEPORTATIONS

1. In the archives of the Jewish Historical Institute, this account is attributed to an anonymous author. By corroborating information contained in the text with outside sources, however, it is clear that the account was written by Berman.
2. See Marian Fuks, *Z diariusza muzycznego* (Warsaw, 1977), pp. 42–43.
3. See Ruta Sakowska, *Ludzie z dzielnicy zamkniętej* (Warsaw, 1975), pp. 299–300.
4. See *Archiwum Ringelbluma*, p. 320.
5. See ibid., p. 316.
6. See *Adama Czerniakowa dziennik getta warszawskiego,* p. 288.
7. See *Archiwum Ringelbluma*, p. 36.
8. See Mary Berg, *Dziennik z getta warszawskiego* (Warsaw, 1983), p. 41.
9. See B. Mark, *Powstanie w getcie warszawskim* (Warsaw, 1963), pp. 218–19.

Chapter 4: PASSIVE AND ACTIVE RESISTANCE INSIDE THE GHETTO

1. See *Adama Czerniakowa dziennik,* pp. 303, 310.
2. See Berenstein et al., *Ekstermnacja,* p. 323.
3. Ibid., p. 323, item 170.
4. Ruta Sakowska, *Ludzie z dzielnicy zamkniętej,* p. 255.
5. The specific references are to achievements with Napoleon against the Spanish (1808), in Latvia against the Swedes (1605), against the Turks and Tatars (in present-day Romania, 1620), against Chmielnicki's Cossacks (present-day

Ukraine, 1649). Following references are similar: against the Spanish at Saragossa in 1608 and against the Swedes at Jasna Góra in 1655.—PB

6. The Werterfassungstelle warehouses were located in several buildings along Niska Street. At the height of the deportations, there were approximately 5,000 Jews employed there. Tatiana Berenstein, "Przedsiębiorcy niemieccy a zagłada Żydów w Warszawie," *Biuletyn ŻIH*, 1955, nos. 13–14.

7. See *Archiwum Ringelbluma*, p. 311.

8. This account originally appeared in *Fołks-Sztyme*, 1961, no. 7, p. 89.

9. See *Głos Warszawy*, 20, 23 April 1943; *Walka Młodych*, 5, 1 May 1943; *Gwardzista*, 18, 20 May 1943. The reports are confirmed by a number of accounts, as well as the Stroop report itself (*The Jewish Quarter of Warsaw Is No More: The Stroop Report*, translated by Sybil Miltan [New York: Pantheon, 1979]). See also B. Mark, *Powstanie w getcie warszawskim*, p. 237.

10. This information is confirmed by B. Mark, ibid., p. 64.

Chapter 5: ON THE OTHER SIDE OF THE WALLS

1. First published in the *Fołks-Sztyme*, 1977, no. 11.

2. See B. Mark, *Powstanie w getcie warszawskim*, p. 148.

3. During the war and in the first years that followed, it was thought that the Germans used the Hotel Polski as part of a grand deception designed to lure Jews out of hiding on the Aryan side of the city. The Israeli historian Natan Eck, on the other hand, demonstrated in 1957 ("Yad Vashem Studies" January 1957) that the Nazi authorities intended to trade Jews for Germans who had been interned in South America. The first Jews who reported to the Hotel Polski were taken to internment camps at Vittel (France) and Bergen-Belsen. Some Jews managed to escape annihilation at that time. But the South American governments then withdrew their promises, and the Jews were sent from those camps to Auschwitz. The last transport of Jews from the Hotel Polski (over forty people) was routed to Pawiak, where some perished; the rest were sent to Auschwitz. See also T. Prekerowa, "Sprawa Hotelu Polskiego," *Polityka*, 1987, no. 20.

4. Information from the second version of Najberg's account, written after the war: "Later on, when the Polish population was evacuated from the city, the latter was recognized as a Jew in one of the camps and killed. The doctor is still alive; he's the head doctor of UNRRA in Belgium and is in constant contact with Miller."

5. L. Landau describes the roundups conducted in Żoliborz and Bielany on Saturday, 23 October, as repressions in response to the shooting of two German soldiers and not as a specifically planned roundup of Jews. At that time the Germans were mainly seeking weapons, printing presses, etc.; they detained many people who were not registered, including Jews. L. Landau, *Kronika lat okupackji,* vol. 3 (Warsaw, 1963), pp. 311–14.

6. According to Władysław Bartoszewski, one armored car (not several) was stolen from Walicowa Street on 8 February 1944. See *1859 dni Warszawy* (Kraków, 1984), p. 542.

7. This information is incorrect. The stolen armored car had been hidden in a workshop on Daniłowski Street. But the report that German soldiers were killed there trying to break open the door has not been confirmed, nor has the information regarding the shooting of the hostages at that time.

8. The account has been published in English under the title, *Am I a Murderer? Testament of a Jewish Ghetto Policeman,* edited and translated by Frank Fox (Boulder, Colo.: Westview Press, 1995).—PB

9. See also Całel Perechodnik's Last Will and Testament:

I, Całel Perechodnik, son of Oszer and Sara née Góralska, born 8 September 1916 in Warsaw, being of sound mind and body, do hereby write my testament. In consequence of the decrees of the German authorities I have been condemned to death, I and my entire family, just as all Jews throughout Poland. At the present moment the sentence has been carried out nearly completely; only a few Jews remain, hiding from the Germans, with little chance of surviving the war. Out of my entire family only my mother and I are left. It may eventually turn out that my older brother Pejsach is still alive, if he succeeded in saving himself from the pogrom being carried out on Jews in the eastern territories. I possess no personal property but am at present the legal heir to the property left by my father, Oszer, as well as by my wife, Chana née Nusfeld. The former property left by my father Oszer Perechodnik consists of (a) the single family villa in Otwock at 10 Kościelna Street, deeded as Zaręba "A," (b) the lot in Otwock on Andriolli Street, deeded as Szerespol, (c) the lot in Otwock on Wierzbowa Street, deeded as Wawrzyniec Glinianki—all of this, which legally belongs to me on the day of my death and which according to Polish law I may bequeath, I assign in the event of my death to pan Władysław Błażewski, master of law, employed by the Regional Cooperative in Otwock, currently resident in Warsaw at 14 Chłopicki Street, as well as to pan Stefan Maliszewski, of the parish chancellery in Otwock and resident in that same town at 1

Mickiewicz Street, to be shared in equal parts of 50 percent. Concerning the property left by my wife, Chana née Nusfeld Perechodnik, i.e., the single-family villa in Otwock at 4 Sienkiewicz Street, deeded as Rozalin 130, the entire portion that falls to me I bequeath in the event of my death to pani Maria Erdman née Błażewski, resident in Warsaw at 14 Chłopicki Street. I am under the impression that 42 percent of the entire villa as well as the "Oaza" cinema is presently mine by way of inheritance. After the war a Polish court may determine the exact percent. For my part, as the last living witness, I would like to recount the order in which the Nusfeld siblings, co-owners of the "Oaza" cinema as well as the entire villa, died. Both the villa as well the "Oaza" cinema belonged in equal parts to the Nusfeld brothers Wolf and Motel, and to the sisters Rajzla Frydman and Chana Perechodnik. In September 1939 the bachelor Motel Nusfeld died at the front; on 11 November 1939, the Germans shot Wolf Nusfeld in Śródborów, leaving his son Jezajasz as well as his wife Mindla née Wajnsztok. In June 1942 Jezajasz Nusfeld died in Warsaw as a result of disease, as heir to one third of the entire estate. In light of the fact that he died without siblings, one half of the property passed to his mother, Mindla, while the other half was assigned to the nearest paternal relative according to article 746 of the Civil Code. Thus the estate belonging to the Nusfeld sisters constituted approximately 84 percent of the entire villa. On 19 August 1942, Ukrainians killed Rajzla Nusfeld's husband, Mojżesz Frydman, in Otwock, while Rajzla together with her two small children as well as my wife, Chana, and my little daughter, Athalil, were deported that same day in a freight train to Treblinka, where they found death at the hands of the German executioners. It may be presumed that the children died first and that my wife Chana, as the younger, outlived her older sister Rajzla Frydman. Based on articles 720 and 722 of the Civil Code, my wife, Chana, was before her death the legal co-owner of 84 percent of Rozalin 130. According to article 233 of the Code, 21 percent would pass to me as the surviving husband, or 42 percent in the event no closer relatives up to and including the fourth degree could be found of the deceased Chana Perechodnik née Nusfeld. In whichever event I hereby assign my entire legal share to pani Maria Erdman née Błażewski, as a token of gratitude for her desire to save my daughter, Athalil. Insofar as pan Władysław Błażewski and pan Stefan Maliszewski become the legal possessors of the villa in Otwock at 10 Kościelna Street, I request that they let apartment number 2, consisting of one room with a kitchen as well as a balcony on the second floor inside the new building, be leased at no cost for the remainder of her life to pani Dąbrowska, master pharmacist and owner of the villa in Otwock at 7 Warszawska Street. The apartment consisting of one room, kitchen, and balcony on the second floor in the corner building should be let at no cost for the remainder of her life to pani Magdalena Babis, resident in Warsaw at 104 Poznańska Street. I note that all of these bequests I perform as a sign of my gratitude for the desire to save my life, as well as that of my parents during the anti-Jewish pogroms. I request that pan Władysław Błażewski, master of law, publish the memoirs I have written that are in his possession. Naturally this should be considered a moral obligation in the event they are deemed unfit to print.

Concerning the order of deaths within my own family, my sister Rachela died in August 1942, her husband Jakub Frajnd in January 1943, while my father died on 15 September 1943 in Warsaw, leaving myself and his wife Sara and possibly also my brother. I request that the Polish court see that my testament is fulfilled as here written, in accord both with the letter of the law as well as with the spirit of my wishes. I am not a lawyer by profession and cannot formulate the testament according to the proper form; under the present circumstances, however, I am unable to retain any help. It is written in my own hand; my signature may be easily authenticated in the magisterial archives or by witnesses. It is my wish that in the event of my death the abovementioned persons with a clear conscience make full use of the estate which morally belongs to them 100 percent. Written in Warsaw this 23rd day of October nineteen hundred forty-four.

Glossary

AA—see Arbeitsamt.

AK—Armia Krajowa or Home Army, an umbrella group of underground resistance movements, sanctioned by the Polish government-in-exile in London. It contained elements ranging from progressive liberal democrats to anti-Semitic, right-wing nationalists.

AL—Armia Ludowa or People's Army, a resistance group formed in 1944 chiefly from the Gwardia Ludowa (People's Guard), allied with the PPR or Polish Workers Party and backed by the Soviets.

Arbeitsamt—Employment office.

Arrestanstalt—Jail.

Ausweis—ID.

Blue Police—see PP.

Bund—Algemeyner Yiddisher Arbeter Bund, a Jewish Socialist-unionist party founded in Vilna in 1897.

CENTOS—Centralne Towarzystwo Opieki nad Sierotami, the Central Association for the Care of Orphans.

Dienstausweis—work papers, employment ID.

Dulag—see Durchgangslager.

Durchgangslager—Transit camp.

Endecja—National Democrats, a prewar Polish political party, largely anti-Semitic.

Einsatzgruppen—"Task Force" units of SS and police dispatched on special assignments. When the German Army invaded Soviet territory, these forces conducted mass roundups and executions, primarily of Jews. The Einsatz-gruppen are thought to have murdered some 1.5 million people.

Einsatz Reinhard—Operation Reinhard, cryptonym for the program to exterminate Jews in the Generalgouvernement, headquartered in Lublin.

Ezra—A charitable organization (Hebrew for "Help").

Generalgouvernement—Following the secret Nazi-Soviet pact, the invading German and Soviet forces partitioned Poland in 1939. Some of the German-controlled territories were annexed directly to the Reich; the rest were renamed the Generalgouvernement and administered from Kraków.

Gmina Żydowska—Jewish Community or kehilla, which, in prewar Poland, had some local legislative jurisdiction.

Haskalah—The Jewish "Enlightenment" whose chief proponent was Moses Mendelssohn (1729–1780).

Herrenvolk—Master race.

HIAS—The Hebrew Immigrant Aid Society, founded in New York in 1881.

Inżynier—Various technical and engineering degrees function as a title in Polish, much as M.D.s or Ph.D.s.

JDC—see Joint Distribution Committee.

Jewish Fighting Organization—see ŻOB.

Jewish Self-Help Agency—Jüdische Soziale Selbsthilfe or JSS, an agency that took welfare collections, organized soup kitchens, and so forth.

JHK—see Jüdische Hilfskomitee.

Joint Distribution Committee—also known as the "Joint," founded in the United States at the outbreak of World War I to aid Jews in Palestine.

JSS—Jüdische Soziale Selbsthilfe. See Jewish Self-Help Agency.

Judenrat (pl., Judenräte)—Jewish councils set up by the Germans to administer ghettos in occupied territories. The structure and function of these councils varied greatly.

Jüdische Hilfskomitee—Jewish Aid Committee, a liaison group that represented various social institutions in the ghetto to the German authorities.

Junacy—see Sonderdienst

Kehilla (pl., kehillot)—see Gmina Żydowska.

Kennkarte—ID.

KPP—Komunistyczna Partia Polski, or Communist Party of Poland (prewar), largely purged by Stalin.

KRN—Krajowa Rada Narodowa or National Council, a Polish governmental body consisting of leftist parties, created in 1944 and backed by the Soviets to counter the London government-in-exile.

KSP—Kierownictwo Służby Porządkowej, or SP headquarters.

Kulturträger—Bearers of culture.

Lebensraum—"Living space." The Nazis claimed they needed more land to accommodate the German nation, and invoked the concept of *Lebensraum* to legitimize their aggressive territorial expansion.

Meldekarte—ID or residency permit.

Mikvah—Ritual pool or "bath" for purposes of immersion and purification.

Misnagdim—Hebrew for "opponents," referring to the orthodox opponents of the Hasidic movement. Chief proponent of the Misnagdim was Rabbi Elijah ben Solomon, the Ga'on of Vilna (1720–1797).

Ordnungsdienst—See SP.

Oneg Sabbath—"Joy of Sabbath," the secret archival project conducted by historian Emanuel Ringelblum.

ORT—from the Russian Obshchestvo Remeslennogo i Zemledelcheskogo Truda, loosely the Trades Manufacturing Development Organization.

Personalabteilung—Personnel Department.

PP—Refers both to the prewar Policja Państwowa or State Police, the Polish police force, as well as the Polnische Polizei or Polish Police organized by the Germans and staffed largely with recruits from the prewar institution. During the occupation these police were often called "Blue Police" because of their uniforms.

PPR—Polska Partia Robotnicza or Polish Workers Party.

PPS—Polska Partia Socjalistyczna or Polish Socialist Party.

Raumkommando—This was the name given to the crews assigned to plunder the apartments of deported Jews.

SD—Sicherheitsdienst or Security Service, originally the security branch of the SS. In 1939 it merged with other police departments, including the Gestapo, to form the RSHA or Reich Main Security Office, which was headed by Heydrich who reported to Himmler.

Sonderdienst—"Special Service," a special formation of Volksdeutsche in the service of the Germans. Also known as Junacy.

SP—Służba Porządkowa or Order Service (German Ordnungsdienst), the Jewish police force inside the ghetto.

Szaulisi—Lithuanian units in the service of the Nazis (from Lithuanian *šaulys* or sniper, also the name of a prewar paramilitary organization).

TOPOROL—Towarzystwo Popierania Rozwoju Rolnictwa wśród Żydów, the Jewish Agricultural Development Organization.

TOZ—Towarzystwo Ochrony Zdrowia, the Society for the Preservation of Health.

Transferstelle—Transport Authority, the office that controlled the traffic of goods entering and leaving the ghetto.

Umschlagplatz—"Transshipment Station," the railroad siding first used by the Transferstelle, and later as a collection point for deportations.

Umsiedlungskommando—"Resettlement Squad." See Vernichtungskommando.

Vernichtungskommando—"Extermination commando," the SS squad that oversaw the deportations to Treblinka.

Volksdeutsche—Polish citizens of German background.

Werkschutz—Factory guard service.

ZMS—Związek Młodzieży Socjalistycznej, the Union of Socialist Youth.

ŻOB—Żydowski Organizacja Bojowa, the Jewish Fighting Organization.

ŻTOS—Żydowski Towarzystwo Opieki Społecznej, the Jewish Welfare Association.

ŻZW—Żydowski Związek Wojskowy, the Jewish Military Alliance or Yiddisher Militerisher Farband.

Biographies

The Jewish Historical Institute is located in Warsaw on Tłomackie Street, at the site of the former Main Judaic Library, which once stood next to the Great Synagogue. The institute houses several collections that document German occupation, the most famous being the Ringelblum Archive recovered after the war. A separate group, labeled Relacje, contains over 7000 memoirs written after the war, of which some 1600 are devoted to the Warsaw Ghetto. The testimonies contained in this book are, with one exception, drawn from a third collection, known as Pamiętniki, or diaries, containing 272 records written during the occupation or immediately thereafter. In choosing excerpts for the anthology, Michał Grynberg favored previously unpublished accounts in which the author related personal experiences as examples of general developments, or else attempted a descriptive overview or analysis, such as of the Judenrat.

The following biographies of the writers included in this volume are drawn from the second Polish edition. The Pamiętniki archive comprises thirty-six accounts that treat the Warsaw Ghetto but not all are included in the present anthology.

Anonymous Man

[Untitled typescript in Polish, 253 pp.]

This account was delivered to the Jewish Historical Institute after the war by pan Zalcberg, who did not reveal the author's name. The document, written between April and July 1944, indicates that the author was a lawyer from Włocławek, who served with the SP inside the ghetto and had close contacts in the SP leadership and the Jewish Council.

During the Aktion of January 1943, the author quit the police force; one month later he left the ghetto and went into hiding on the Aryan side, where he survived the war.

While much of this testimony is devoted to the SP, the author also discusses the deportations of 1942 in great detail. In analyzing the apparent lack of resistance during the deportations, he places much blame on the intelligentsia for not fulfilling its obligation to the ghetto population.

No further information on the author could be obtained.

Anonymous Woman

["Recollections from My Time in the Warsaw Ghetto," typescript in Polish, 31 pp.]

This testimony covers the establishment of the ghetto to the end of February 1943, when the author escaped to the Aryan side with her four-year-old son. The last entry bears the date 21 June 1943.

In the ghetto, the author lived for some time on Ogrodowa Street, where she was active in the local building committee, which served thirty families (approximately 150 people). This committee joined with similar groups to set up a soup kitchen that distributed several hundred meals daily.

In 1942 the author lived on Pawia Street, in a building assigned to the hospital where her husband worked. There she and her son survived several roundups inside a group shelter (for 200 people) that was entered through the bottom of a cupboard. On another occasion she and her child hid in the attic at 56 Zamenhof Street with approximately 150 people. This hideout was entered by means of a ladder that was pulled up after the last person was inside. The author describes the desperate situation inside such shelters, the chronic shortage of food and water, and the lack of hygiene—physiological needs were taken care of in the corner.

The author paid close attention to developments inside the ghetto. According to her calculations, by the end of September 1942 only 50,000 inhabitants were left, a figure that accords with that proposed by scholars such as Ber Mark.

The author also considers why the Jews did not resist the deportations—especially as news of Treblinka reached the ghetto as early as August 1942—and attributes this mainly to the fact that the ghetto residents could not bring themselves to believe the Germans would attempt to exterminate the entire Jewish population.

No further information is available about the author or who delivered the document to the Jewish Historical Institute.

Adolf (Abram) Berman (1906–1978)

["The Warsaw Ghetto," typescript in Polish, 56 pp.; first four are missing.]

In the archives of the Jewish Historical Institute, this account is attributed to an anonymous author. By corroborating information in the text with outside sources, however, it is clear that the account was written by Adolf Berman, whose wartime pseudonym was "Adam Borowski."

Before the war Berman, a Ph.D., was a social activist and a member of the Po'alei Tzion–Left. Inside the ghetto he was director of CENTOS, the Central Association for the Care of Orphans. In September 1942, Berman and his wife, Barbara, fled the ghetto to the Aryan side, where he represented the Jewish National Committee and served as secretary for the Żegota group. After the liberation, Berman served in the KRN* and in 1947 he became president of the Central Jewish Committee in Poland. Three years later he emigrated to Israel, where he was active in the Communist Party and in the International Federation of Resistance Fighters (FiR), and ultimately served as a member of the Knesset.

In 1971, Berman published a book in Israel entitled *Żydowski Ruch Oporu*—The Jewish Resistance; a second book in Hebrew came out in 1977 titled *Bemakum Asher yoad li Hogoral*—The Place I Was Fated to Be.

Adolf Berman died on 3 March 1978.

Henryk Bryskier (1899–1945)

["Jews Under the Swastika, or the Warsaw Ghetto," typescript in Polish, 335 pp.]

Henryk Bryskier was born in Warsaw on 3 July 1899. During World War I he fought in the Polish Legions and later was a reserve captain in the Polish army. Trained as a mechanical engineer, he published several monographs on industrial gasses between the world wars. He was also active socially and was president of the Polish Geographic Society.

*Krajowa Rada Narodowa, National Council.

In the ghetto he served as the vice president of ŻTOS, the Jewish Welfare Association, which organized shelters for Jews deported from the provinces. For some time Bryskier also headed the building committee at 15 Leszno Street. In July 1942 he became chief engineer at the H. Brauer factory; his wife found work there as a doctor.

In late January 1943, the Bryskiers managed to move their daughter to the Aryan side, though their plans to follow her soon thereafter were foiled. Bryskier's wife died during the Ghetto Uprising; he was deported to the concentration camp at Majdanek, from where after several months he managed to escape. He returned to Warsaw and found shelter with the Kanigórskis on Chełmska Street. There, while living under the name of Władysław Jankowski, he began writing his account. After various incidents of blackmail he was forced to leave the Kanigórskis, and in May 1944 he joined his daughter hiding in the Praga suburb. There both survived until the east bank of the Vistula was liberated.

At that point Bryskier went to Lublin, where he worked in the PKWN.* Later he returned to Warsaw and became a departmental director in the Ministry of Commerce and Industry. He died in Warsaw in October 1945.

Bryskier's testimony survived the last phase of the war inside a carbide container in the basement where he and his daughter had been hiding. In 1947, Bryskier's daughter delivered it to the Central Jewish Historical Commission. The document describes the beginnings of the ghetto, the hardships of daily life, and the positive role of the Jewish Council in developing trade schools and health services. It also addresses specific institutions such as ŻTOS, the building committees, and the SP.

The author devotes much attention to production inside the ghetto, describing the Brauer factory in great detail, as well as the selections in early September 1942, the Aktion of January 1943, and scenes from Umschlagplatz.

Bryskier prefaced his testimony with the following dedication: "Dear wife and mother, cruelly murdered in Warsaw in May 1943, I cannot construct a granite monument for You, as there is no trace of Your remains, therefore kindly accept this modest notebook of words and paper, which your husband and daughter place on your grave with reverence and love."

---

*Polski Komitet Wyzwolenia Narodowego—the Polish Committee of National Liberation, backed by the Soviets.—PB

Aron Czechowicz and Gurman

["The Ten from Pawiak. Based on the experience of the authors." Typescript in Yiddish, 164 pp., with 5 pp. in Polish.]

Aron Czechowicz was born in Warsaw in 1904. Before his marriage he was a leatherworker; afterward he ran a jewelry shop. His wife and two children perished in Treblinka. Gurman (we have no first name) was Czechowicz's brother-in-law; he owned a tailor shop in a poor Warsaw suburb. The two men wrote their joint account in 1944 in a shelter on the Aryan side. They describe their arrest, their interrogation on Szuch Boulevard, and their life in the Pawiak prison, as well as their successful escape. The document is dated 30 May 1945.

Inside the prison, the authors worked at their respective trades. In January 1944 the authorities moved the workshops outside the prison to a nearby building, which was designated as an *Arbeitserziehungslager,* a reform labor camp run by the Gestapo.

The authors detail the various tortures inflicted on the prisoners (from attack dogs to hanging prisoners by the legs and shooting them in such a way as to prolong their agony), in which Gestapo officers Albert, Müller, and Bürckl earned particular notoriety. They also describe group executions of Jews and Poles.

The authors committed to memory many names of victims and perpetrators alike, and attached to their document a list of 201 Jewish prisoners at Pawiak, including fourteen women incarcerated in the women's ward known as "Serbia." Among the prisoners was Emanuel Ringelblum, whose hideout had been betrayed to the Gestapo on 7 March 1944.* The account indicates that most of the prisoners were Jews who had been arrested on the Aryan side, mostly as a result of denunciations, along with the approximately 400 who had been lured to the Hotel Polski and who also perished in the prison.

Apart from an invaluable source of information, the testimony is also an amazing story of escape, meticulously planned and carried out during the night of 30 May 1944.† The names of the escapees are: Aron Czechowicz, Gurman, Zaremski, Zylberman, Chil [Dubiecki], Datyner, Jakubowicz, Lipszyc, Rosen, and Sawicki. The title "The Ten from Pawiak," alludes to a well-known prewar film.

---

*The bunker was denounced by eighteen-year-old Jan Łakiński, and all those hiding (nearly thirty people), as well as the Poles who had sheltered them, were taken to Pawiak and murdered. Łakiński was later sentenced to death by a tribunal in Warsaw.

†The escape is confirmed by Leon Wanat in his book *Za murami Pawiaka* (Warsaw, 1967), pp. 358–61.

Aron Czechowicz delivered the testimony—originally written in Yiddish—to the Jewish Historical Commission in Łódź after the war; beyond that we have no further information about the authors.

Stefan Ernest

["On the War Between Mighty Germany and the Jews of Warsaw 1939–1943," manuscript in Polish, 306 pp.]

Little is known about Stefan Ernest. He was born in Warsaw and lived on Królewska Street before the German invasion. In the ghetto he worked in the Employment Office of the Jewish Council, at 84 Leszno Street. In late 1942 he was dismissed from his employment, and in January 1943 he crossed to the Aryan side.

Ernest's account, which he calls a report from the ghetto, covers the period from 1940 to January 1943. While the author refrains from commenting on his personal situation, he does not hide his opinion of many of the events and people he describes. He discusses the Jewish Council in detail, rating the performance of several of its members, especially the president, Adam Czerniaków, whom he criticizes sharply for committing suicide. It is unclear how the account reached the Jewish Historical Institute.

While we do not know for certain, Stefan Ernest must have perished shortly after writing his account; its last date is May 1943.

Dawid Fogelman

["Diary Written in a Bunker," typescript in Polish, 41 pp.]

Dawid Fogelman was born in 1915 in Warsaw, where he lived on Dzielna Street. Having finished trade school, he worked as a turner at the Agricultural Machine Factory on Leszno Street until 1939. Both parents died before the war; his mother in 1927 and his father in 1936. Fogelman had a wife and two infant children who were deported to Treblinka in July 1942.

In the ghetto, the author mostly worked in his trade at sites outside the ghetto, such as the Avia factory in Praga, the Eastern Train Station, and the trailer factory in the Bielany suburb.

In March 1943, Fogelman was captured during a roundup, sent to Umschlagplatz, and loaded on a train to Treblinka. He managed to jump out of the boxcar near Otwock; from there he gradually made his way back to Warsaw. At the time of the Ghetto Uprising, he worked at the Gdańsk train station; at the end of July 1943 all the Jewish laborers there were moved into the prison on

Gęsia Street, where they were dressed as Soviet prisoners and daily sent to work at the SD garages in the Dynasy district. At one point he was also in the Pawiak prison, where he helped others escape, though he himself stayed behind.

On 5 August 1944, during the Warsaw Uprising, a group of Polish fighters freed the prisoners on Gęsia Street and incorporated them into their own ranks; Dawid Fogelman played an active role in the revolt. After the capitulation he survived inside a bunker at 5 Szczęsliwa Street, where he wrote his account. Nothing is known of his further fate, or of how the account reached the Jewish Historical Institute.

Pola Glezer (Agata Królak, Franciszka Radomska)
["Unhealed Wounds," manuscript, 79 pp., and typescript in Polish, 23 pp.]

Pola Glezer was born in Warsaw in 1919; her parents were Dawid and Jacheta. Having finished high school, she was proprietress of a tailor shop. Inside the ghetto in 1942 she married Olek, who was employed in a factory the Germans considered important for the war effort. The author survived several narrow escapes from Umschlagplatz; in September 1942 her husband rescued her from the "cauldron" inside a sealed bakery truck.

Nine months after the marriage, Olek was shot for possessing a weapon; Glezer was pregnant, and in the spring of 1943 she delivered a stillborn child.

After escaping from the ghetto, she made her way to a village and stayed with some farmers she knew, but sometime later she went back to the ghetto. Shortly before the Uprising she left again and returned to the same farmhouse.

In June 1943, Glezer again made her way to Warsaw, where she looked up her friend Irena, who helped her obtain papers and work at a seamstress shop on Wilcza Street. After losing that job, she answered an ad for a nanny. This position, too, was short-lived; when she confided to her employers that she was Jewish, they immediately made her leave.

Until the outbreak of the Warsaw Uprising, Glezer worked as a manicurist; afterward, when the Germans forced everyone in the city to march to the camp at Pruszków, she broke away from the column and escaped to a small town outside Warsaw. Under the name of Franciszka Radomska, she found work as a cosmetician and survived until liberation without revealing her identity.

The account is written as a dialogue between two girlfriends on the night after Soviet and Polish troops freed the town. In the conversation, Franciszka (Glezer) confesses her background and relates her experiences to her friend Jadwiga, the daughter of the family with whom she was staying.

She rubbed her eyes. Was it a dream? Had she really lived to see a Polish soldier side by side with one from the Red Army? She waved her hand as hard as she could to greet them. Welcome, welcome! she kept crying out in jubilation. More and more people were gathering on the road, there were more and more hurrahs and shouts of happiness. Hours passed in the highest spirits. Jadzia tugged at her friend: Come on, it's time to go home. They walked back slowly and in silence. Her heart was jumping for joy, but her eyes were filled with tears. In her soul she could hear the quiet protest: Why hadn't They lived to see it? Jadzia's voice suddenly drew her out of her reverie, as if from far away, even though she was standing right beside her. Franka!—she was saying—You're so happy, the way you're greeting them you'd think you were a Communist. . . . Ach, Jadzia, if you only knew, she thought, if you only knew that I was Jewish.

It is unknown what later became of the author or how the account found its way into the archives.

Irena Grocher

["Experiences in a Bunker," typescript in Polish, 31 pp.]

Before the war, Irena Grocher lived in Warsaw with her parents and younger brother Jakub. Her father represented the Bielski weaving shops, and her mother was co-owner of a sporting goods store. She herself had just finished high school when the Germans invaded.

During the occupation Grocher lost her entire family—her father at Auschwitz and her mother and brother at Treblinka. In mid-February 1943, the author escaped from the ghetto with the help of her friend Czesia, a Gentile. At first she lived with Czesia, who was also sheltering the son of her former employers, the Zylberbergs. When the neighbors began to pry, however, both Grocher and the boy had to leave, and Czesia took them to the Nowak family from Kalisz, who were living in Warsaw on fake Aryan documents. A large group of Jews was hiding there. When the Nowaks made arrangements to leave the country through the Hotel Polski scheme, German gendarmes arrested everyone in the building and removed them to Pawiak, where they were killed. As they were being taken from the apartment building, however, Grocher managed to escape. With the help of Wiktor Szpanbok, a family friend also living on Aryan papers, she remained in Warsaw until the 1944 Uprising, after which she stayed with a group of other young people in the basement of a burned-out building in the center of town—outside the former ghetto.

Irena Grocher's account is really a diary in which she systematically recorded what went on in the bunker. Mostly it describes the struggle to stay undetected and the group's efforts to obtain food and water. The first entry is dated 5 October 1944. From the document we learn that the number of people hiding in the bunker grew from nine to twenty-four.

In focusing on life in the bunker, the author relates matters of life and death as well as seemingly trivial events that had a profound influence on the relationships among the people inside. The cramped quarters gave rise to squabbles that had no real cause and unleashed traits that under normal circumstances would have remained dormant:

> Little Mietek and Janek started arguing over tobacco, even though there's enough to last a year. They argued when there wasn't any and now that there is some they're at it again. They didn't stop until the Germans appeared in the courtyard, and we were terrified they might have heard. Now we're all sitting quiet and shaking like gelatin.

Other worries centered on ethics and sexual mores: for instance, the difficulty in arranging a separate sleeping space for the women, which the author solved in the following manner:

> I wondered whether to sleep in one room with the boys. Ultimately I decided that I couldn't care less what people think. The main thing is to have a clean conscience. Besides, anyone who's going to mean anything to me is bound to have 100 percent trust in me, and I'll never let them down.

But the document's primary focus is on how the occupants kept their hiding place secure. In early November, Grocher noted:

> Once again the Germans were in the courtyard for several hours, taking iron out of the warehouse. Their milling about worries us greatly. Particularly W is in a panic, which adversely affects the rest of us. But somehow we get used to our lot and go on living.

Grocher and her comrades were forced to abandon that hideout; shortly afterward the Germans blew up the basement. The party then regrouped; Irena and some others found shelter in various attics. Finally on 15 January they were freed; the last entry is dated 19 January 1945.

After the war Irena Grocher lived in Łódź. She finished medical school and worked in a hospital as a pediatrician. In 1975, together with her husband (also a doctor) and two children, she emigrated to Israel. There she delivered her account to the archives at Yad Vashem; the Jewish Historical Institute acquired a copy as part of a general exchange.

Franciszka Grünberg

["Through Fields and Meadows," manuscript, 621 pp., and typescript in Polish, 327 pp.]

Franciszka Grünberg was born in Warsaw, where she worked as a dentist. Before the war she lived with her husband, Stefan, and their two children on Chłodna Street.

During the selections carried out at the Többens workshop in August 1942, she lost her sixteen-year-old daughter, Liliana, who was working in the factory. The following March she delivered her fourteen-year-old son, Richard, to friends on the Aryan side; she and her husband followed one month later. Her former tenant from Chłodna Street, Alina Wieczorek, helped arrange for the Grünbergs to stay with Józefa (Ziuta) Turska at 21 Chełmska Street, Apartment 19. At that time they were living under the name Łukomski.

The author describes how a blackmailer forced the Grünbergs to leave pani Turska's apartment. With her help they found someone else, who sheltered them through the Warsaw Uprising of 1944, after which they moved to a village called Rudki, not far from Nowe Miasto on the Pilica River. There they survived until liberation and then emigrated from Poland.

The account, which was compiled shortly after the war, covers the period from January 1943 to January 1945; according to the author, her notes from 1939 to 1942 were lost during the war.

Helena Gutman-Staszewska

["Recollections from the German Occupation, August 1939–November 1940," manuscript, 20 pp., and typescript in Polish, 8 pp.]

Before the war, Helena Gutman-Staszewska taught in a public elementary school for Jewish children on Krucza Street in Warsaw. She lived at 20 Chłodna Street, from where she moved to 6 Ogrodowa Street inside the ghetto. There she worked for various soup kitchens, child welfare agencies, and other social institutions, including the Jewish Self-Help Agency.

Her rather short testimony describes the frightening days of early September 1939, the aerial bombardment of the capital, and the self-sacrifice of many residents—Jewish as well as Polish—in building defenses and extinguishing fires.

One significant event revealed in the account took place on 1 December 1939, when approximately four hundred teachers in public schools for Jewish children were dismissed, effectively depriving some 30,000 children of their schooling.

Another section describes the difficulties of moving into the ghetto when it was first established. The constant revision of the boundaries forced thousands of families to leave their homes and lug their belongings from one place to another—a strenuous prelude to the tragedy to come.

Gutman-Staszewska survived the war, although her fate remains unknown.

Chaim Hasenfus
["Two Years of War (Experiences and Reflections)," typescript in Polish, 42 pp.]
Chaim Hasenfus was born in 1906 in Warsaw, where he lived at 33 Nowogrodzka Street. After graduating from the R. Kowalski gymnasium, he went on to earn four higher degrees, one of which seems to have been in philology:

> On 17 November 1939, Professor Ossowski got word to me through my colleague Świszewski of a fairly trivial incident. The Germans were searching the Department of Sociology at the University. Rummaging in Professor Bystroń's desk, they found my work entitled "The Question of Language Among Polish Jews" and took it with them. The paper was to appear in the *Przegląd Socjologiczny*.

To earn a living, Hasenfus worked as an accountant in a bank before the war. In 1940 he had to move into the ghetto, so he arranged an exchange with a commissioner in the PP who lived at 41 Sienna Street. In giving up his apartment, Hasenfus had to leave his library of 400 books.

The account consists of two parts. The first chronicles events inside the ghetto up to July 1941, although the period from 1 February 1940 to 8 January 1941 is not included. The second section offers more general reflections on matters such as Poland's geopolitical situation between the wars, Polish domestic and foreign policy, and the persecution of Jews through the ages. Hasenfus repeatedly quotes Heine on the subject of Germans and Jews. The conclusion of these reflections is dated 30 September 1941.

Nothing further is known of the author or of how the document reached the Jewish Historical Institute.

Jan Mawult (Stanisław Gombiński)

["All Equal (Streets of the Ghetto)," typescript in Polish, 109 pp.; "Purgatory (Ghetto Adminis-tration)," typescript in Polish, 111 pp.]

Jan Mawult was a lawyer by profession; in the ghetto he directed a department of the Jewish police force. His account was written in hiding during the first half of 1944.

The first section portrays the people in the ghetto from its inception to 20 January 1943 and ends with the following entry:

> Remarque begins *All Quiet on the Western Front* with the words, "This book is not intended to be an accusation." These recollections are different; they are not *intended* to be—they *are* an accusation of the sole true perpetrators.

The second section of the account describes and evaluates the Jewish Council, the SP, and other ghetto institutions. Here Mawult attempts to explain why these organizations developed as they did and why the people in their employ behaved as they did.

In reviewing the second Polish edition of this book, Ludwik Hass noted that Jan Mawult survived the war and emigrated to Paris, where he died in the 1980s. Krzysztof Prochaska of Łódź corroborated this information.

Helena Midler

["Diary," typescript in Polish, 8 pp.; Bunker Weekly, typescript in Polish, 6 pp.]

While this account covers a very short period (November–December 1944), it provides valuable insight into life inside a bunker outside the ghetto after the fall of the 1944 Warsaw Uprising. We learn that the bunker housed nine people—five of whom were women—who were evidently hiding to escape deportation. Only one resident, Hela Domagalska, is identified; the others are referred to by first name only.

The account is divided into two parts. The first describes life in the bunker, the problems and dilemmas caused by the living conditions; the second consists of two numbers of the satirical newsletter *Bunker Weekly*.

Both the content and tone of her writing suggest that Helena Midler belonged to the intelligentsia. Beyond that, however, we know nothing about her specific background or fate.

Leon (Arie) Najberg (wartime pseudonym "Marian")
[Untitled, typescripts in Polish, 184 pp. and 44 pp.]

In 1939, Leon Najberg was fourteen years old and a member of Hashomer Hatzair, a Zionist youth movement. His father, Leon, was a shopkeeper; he, his wife, and their four children lived in Warsaw outside the future ghetto.

Najberg's older brother, Izaak, was killed that year while fighting in the Polish Army. His younger brother was recognized as Jewish by a member of the PP, the Polish Police, in 1943 and executed; his mother and sister perished at Treblinka.

Early in the occupation, Najberg and his father traded goods with the Aryan side. Because his "good" appearance allowed him to move freely outside the ghetto walls, Leon also couriered documents to outlying towns for Hashomer Hatzair. In August 1942 he was transferred to the Adam Oppel munitions factory, which according to his account employed sixty Jewish workers. The following April he received permission to return to the ghetto, where he survived the Uprising and stayed for several months before making contact with Stefan Miller of the Gwardia Ludowa, or People's Guard, in September 1943. Miller helped Najberg find shelter with Teofila and Aleksandr Szczypiorski. There he filled some eight hundred notebook pages with his testimony. After the war, this document fell into the wrong hands and the author never recovered it. However, thanks to the initiative of Rachela Auerbach and Klara Mirska of the Central Jewish Historical Commission, Najberg reconstructed the account from memory, thereby preserving one of the most valuable testimonies about the ghetto, particularly its final phase during the Uprising and immediate aftermath.

Leon Najberg survived the war. Today he lives in Israel, where he published his recollections from the occupation in Hebrew under the title *Aharonim b'ketze hamered shel geto Warshe* (*The Last of the Warsaw Ghetto Fighters*).

Całel Perechodnik
["History of a Jewish Family during the Occupation," typescript in Polish, 346 pp.]

Całel Perechodnik was born in Warsaw on 8 August 1916. After earning a degree in agronomy in Toulouse, France, he returned to Poland, where he married Anna Nusfeld in 1938 and settled in Otwock outside Warsaw. There he owned a builder's supply center. A daughter, Athalil, was born in August 1940. Perechodnik was a member of the Zionist organization Betar.

During the occupation, Perechodnik served in the Otwock SP. In August 1942, when local Jews were being deported, he lost his wife and daughter. Then he went into hiding, first in Otwock and later in Warsaw. Perechodnik's parents, Oszer and Sara, also hid with Polish friends, his father under the name Michał Bogdański. Despite his "good" appearance, Perechodnik's father was denounced and executed on 14 September 1942. The author himself perished in Warsaw toward the end of October 1944. His older brother Pejsach survived the war.

The account was written while hiding in Warsaw. It spans the period from 1 September 1939 to 19 August 1944 and covers both personal and family matters as well as more general topics, such as the labor camps for Jews set up outside Warsaw, the relations between Jews and Polish Gentiles in Otwock, and the dangers facing Jews in hiding.

Perechodnik entrusted the account to his friend Władysław Błażewski, then resident in Warsaw at 14 Chłopicki Street. It is unknown how the account reached the archives of the Jewish Historical Institute. This testimony appeared in English in 1995 under the title *Am I a Murderer? Testament of a Jewish Ghetto Policeman.*

Samuel Puterman
["The Warsaw Ghetto," typescript in Polish, 257 pp.]

Samuel Puterman was a member of the SP. After the revolt in the ghetto he hid with the Piotrowskis at 13 Orla Street, Apartment 42, where he stayed through the 1944 Uprising and was sent to Sachsenhausen and Oranienburg.

Puterman's account covers a wide range of topics on daily life in the ghetto, from its creation to the end of the deportations. It is clear that the author was familiar with the operations of the Jewish Council, the SP, the Jewish Gestapo front known as the "Thirteen," and the workshops—as well as very interested in artistic circles and cultural events inside the ghetto. The account relates many details about the deportations of July–August 1942, the tragic scenes that took place on Umschlagplatz, and the actions of various SP members during the roundups.

After the war, Puterman emigrated to France, where he died in 1955, according to information received from his sister, Irena Barbara, who survived the war and now lives in Canada. The author himself delivered the document to the Jewish Historical Institute.

Karol Rotgeber

["An Account, Dedicated to My Thirteen-year-old Son Paweł, Taken from the Többens Factory to Umschlagplatz on 18 August 1942." Transcript in Polish, 215 pp.]

Karol Rotgeber was fifty years old when the war broke out. He had finished the Ubisz business school as well as a course in dentistry at the Szymański School in Warsaw. His wife was a dentist; they lived with their son Paweł (born 1929) at 20 Franciszkańska Street. Immediately before the war, Rotgeber worked as a factory clerk. In the ghetto he paid two thousand zloty and a bottle of grain alcohol for a job in the Carlheintz Müller factory; his wife and son found employment at the brushworks, where Rotgeber eventually joined them. In August 1942 his son was taken away during a selection.

In February, Rotgeber paid people to smuggle him and his wife out of the ghetto. They went into hiding in the Praga suburb, having agreed to pay a one-time sum of 10,000 zloty and a monthly rent of 400. The account was written in hiding; it was concluded on 12 June 1943.

The document shows the author as a devout Jew and patriotic Pole. Evidently Rotgeber was a social activist before the war as well as in the ghetto, where he was particularly interested in the situation of hospitals; at one point he was invited to a session of the Health Department services in the Jewish Council.

The testimony contains much information on the Jewish Council, the "Thirteen," and the factory shops. Rotgeber assesses the importance of employment, the hope that work could save the Jews from complete extermination, and the lengths to which the Germans encouraged this delusion in order to dull vigilance and help avert armed resistance. When the fighting did break out in the ghetto, Rotgeber—in despair at his own inability to help—wrote a dramatic appeal to Archbishop Adam Sapieha, head of the Roman Catholic Church in Poland, in care of the secretary general of the Polish Red Cross. He signed the letter with the pseudonym "Lewap," the reverse of his son's name.

Nothing further is known about Karol Rotgeber.

Henryk Ryszewski (1900–1972)

["No One Wants to Die Voluntarily," typescript in Polish, 61 pp.]

The journalist Henryk Ryszewski was not Jewish—in fact, before the war he was, in his own words, "a frank and consistent anti-Semite." The Nazi treatment of Jews caused Ryszewski to revise his position: For almost two years he and his wife, Irena, hid thirteen people in their apartment, including Leon Fall, editor of the Lwów-based *Chwila*, Anna and Róża Lewin from Łódź, Ludwik Opal of the Bank Dyskontowy in Warsaw, and Leon Funt, along with his wife and daughter. Among other details, Ryszewski's account shows that an underground journalist organization known as the Mutual Aid Society set up a team of three people to help Jewish journalists and booksellers. Ryszewski died in 1972 and was posthumously honored by the Yad Vashem Institute of Jerusalem with the title Righteous Among the Nations, which his daughter Zofia Brusikiewicz accepted in his name in 1985.

Henryk Słobodzki
["Days on the Edge," manuscript, 88 pp., and typescript in Polish, 76 pp.]

Of Henryk Słobodzki we know only that he was a doctor who worked in the ghetto at the Stawki Street hospital, and that he was incarcerated in the Pawiak prison in 1943 from 20 November to 9 December in cell no. 268. There he shared his cell with thirty-three other prisoners, mostly well-educated Jewish professionals who had been arrested on the Aryan side of the city.

We may assume that Słobodzki escaped from a convoy of prisoners on their way to a worksite outside the prison buildings. He is known to have perished in Warsaw; Adolf Berman delivered the account to the Jewish Historical Institute after the war.

If one were to ignore the time and place in which the account was written, it could easily be read as literary fiction, particularly because of the style of the piece, which uses dialogue to relate the nighttime discussions among the prisoners. Locked in their cell, the men debated philosophical subjects prompted by their situation, such as the definition of heroism and whether their sufferings were to some better end or merely in vain.

Jakub Smakowski ("Czarny Julek")
["Life and Struggle," manuscript in Yiddish, 88 pp. and 5 pp., and "Recollections of a Jewish Fighter from the Warsaw Ghetto," manuscript in Yiddish, 47 pp.]

Jakub Smakowski was sixteen years old and training to become an electrician when the Germans invaded Warsaw; he lived with his family at 19 Pańska Street. His father, Welwel, was a housepainter active in the Bund.

Like many young people inside the ghetto, Jakub began smuggling food through the wall from the Aryan side to save his family from starvation. After some time he expanded this operation and began using the sewer system. At one point he held a job at the mechanic shop on Komitetowa Street; later he worked at the "Brunowerke" on Nabielak Street.

On 13 August 1942, his mother and sister were taken to Umschlagplatz and deported to Treblinka. His mother was thirty-eight years old. The following

April, Smakowski led his father to the Aryan side, while he stayed inside the ghetto to fight under Janka Pika (Pinie Finkel). In November 1943, Smakowksi helped free twenty-five Polish resistance fighters of the Home Army, or AK, whom the Germans had taken to the ghetto ruins to be executed. Among those freed was Captain Zygmunt Kazimierczuk, who then sheltered Smakowski's father in his home on Świętojańska Street. From the Aryan side, Jakub Smakowski continued to visit the ruined ghetto, taking provisions to bunkers where Jews were still hiding.

In August 1944 he again took arms against the Germans, fighting with the AK under the pseudonym Czarny Julek. He participated in the storming of the Gęsia Street prison, in which 400 prisoners were freed. Ultimately he attained the rank of staff sergeant.

After the collapse of the insurgency, Smakowski helped lead the fighters out through the sewers and helped construct various bunkers. He himself hid with some two dozen other Jews in a shelter at 36 Wspólna Street until liberation.[*]

Smakowski's testimony consists of two dictations, both originally in Yiddish: The first was completed in November 1945, in Warsaw, the second nearly a year later in a DP camp in Leipheim, Germany. They provide much detail on bunkers that escaped detection during the ghetto uprising and later. They also give a portrait of those who, like the author, displayed great courage and self-sacrifice trying to bring help to others.

Nothing more is known of Jakub Smakowski.

Stefania Staszewska

["Recollections from the Ghetto," manuscript and typescript in Polish, 25 pp.]

Stefania Staszewska, whose conspiratorial alias was "Szochur," was born in Warsaw, where she lived with her family at 11 Szczęśliwa Street. Her father, Samuel Szochur, worked as a part-time laborer in a textile store on Gęsia Street.

In early September 1939, Samuel Szochur fled Warsaw along with thousands of others who believed the war would quickly be over and they would be able to return soon. Stefania stayed with her mother in the capital; she had just

---

[*]Smakowski lists the names of the others as follows: Matys Sinykamień and his wife and child, Jankiel Frost and his son, Aron Walia and his wife, Sewek and his wife, all from Łódź; Berysz Meisner and his wife from Stanisławów; Heniek and Dawid Łucki and their wives, Heniek Szpigel and his brother-in-law, Zygmunt and Fredek Nudelman, Bernard (the Bund activist), Dawid Guzik (director of the Joint Distribution Committee), Heniek (no last name), Warna and Moszika Lewi from Saloniki.

finished her fourth year of the gymnasium, where she was active in Socialist youth groups; inside the ghetto she continued to work for the Polish Workers Party (PPR).

During the deportations, Staszewska lost her mother and was sent to work at the Többens factory. There she helped prepare for the 1943 Uprising. In April she was deported to the Poniatów labor camp, but she managed to escape and return to Warsaw with the help of Maria Grzybowska and Ania Arcara. Staszewska then obtained fake papers under the name Zofia Bartoszewska and found work as a housemaid at the home of Maria Parnowska outside Warsaw. There she survived until liberation.

Staszewska's deposition covers 1941 to 1942 and focuses particularly on the deportations. In Poland she later published other sections detailing her escape from Poniatów and her experiences in hiding.

After the war she settled in Warsaw, where she worked as an actress in the National Yiddish Theater.

Marek Stok

["The Warsaw Ghetto," typescript in Polish, 32 pp.]

Marek Stok, a lawyer, fled Warsaw in early September 1939 together with his family. In April 1940 he returned to the capital, where he found work in a garment workshop at 12 Prosta Street; after losing that position he earned his living with sporadic legal consulting.

Stok lived in the ghetto until the fighting broke out in April 1943, at which time he escaped to the Aryan side. He wrote his account in early 1944 while he was hiding at the home of Marta and Stefan Koper at 6 Ratuszowa Street, Apartment 13.

As he began describing the deportations to Treblinka, the author resolved to stop writing. After listing various reasons, he wrote: "And so I have decided not to recount the next, most important phase—the complete annihilation of hundreds of thousands of Warsaw Jews. I was a witness of this from the beginning to the heroic uprising in the ghetto."

In his testimony, Stok details the status of affairs in various institutions such as the Jewish Council and the SP, which he criticizes for its 1941 role in rounding up people for labor camps. He also censures the health service of the Jewish Council for their inadequate efforts to contain the typhus epidemic. His portrait of life in the ghetto accentuates the contrast in lifestyle between the poor starving masses and the nouveau-riche smugglers who frequented the coffeehouses.

While it is not clear how the document reached the Jewish Historical Institute, we know that Marek Stok survived the war and later emigrated to Brazil.

Stanisław Sznapman
[*"Ghetto Diary," typescript in Polish, 64 pp.*]

This is less a day-to-day chronicle and more a series of reflections and recollections by Stanisław Sznapman, who lived in the ghetto until July 1943. At that point he went into hiding on the Aryan side, where he wrote his story. Presumably he perished there in unknown circumstances; beyond this conjecture we know very little about him.

Apart from relating various historical details (some of which have not been corroborated), the account offers both social and psychological analysis, for instance of individuals attempting to free themselves of familial obligations in the face of death. Sznapman further assesses the progress of the war itself and predicts an imminent German defeat. But he also warns that people will then appear who will whitewash the German crimes and present the Germans themselves as innocent lambs incapable of such atrocities.

Sznapman's journal was delivered to the Jewish Historical Institute after the war by Helena Boguszewska and Henryk Kornacki.

Marysia Szpiro
[*Untitled manuscript and typescript in Polish, 18 pp.*]

Marysia Szpiro wrote her account in 1946, when she was eleven years old. With a child's imagination she reaches back to recall the outbreak of the war and the bombardment of Warsaw. She remembers living on Wolska Street, where her parents had a shop with stationery and kitchen implements. Marysia had five siblings: the eldest, Estera, was sixteen years old at that time. The others were Dora, Halinka, Josek, and three-year-old Mendełe.

Inside the ghetto, the Szpiro family was in dire poverty; the older siblings would sneak over the wall in search of food. Eventually Marysia's parents and two of her siblings died of hunger: "Mendełe had dysentery; he swelled up like a balloon. He died. When my father died, none of the neighbors came to the apartment; death in the ghetto was pretty common. People just stepped past the corpses lying in the way, without paying any attention. Every one of us calmly waited for death."

In July 1942, Marysia and her brother Josek managed to escape from the ghetto. Marysia made her way to a village, where she worked for a farmer without revealing her background. There she survived the war.

Later she was taken to an orphanage near Skierniewice. In time she joined a kibbutz in Łódź and presumably emigrated to Israel.

It is not clear how the document reached the Jewish Historical Institute.

Ber Warm

["Niska i Prosta, * *or, The Last Days of the Warsaw Jews," typescript in Polish, 41 pp.; pp. 30 and 38 missing.]*

As a member of the SP, or the Jewish police force, Ber Warm was assigned to the Befehlstelle, the SS command post for the deportation Aktion, and later to the Werterfassungstelle, or Office for Value Assessment. The account is focused on these two institutions as well as the little ghetto.

Warm estimates that some 4,500 people worked for the Werterfassungstelle; during the deportations the number rose to 6,000. A similar number of Jews lived in the little ghetto, where 3,000 were employed in the factories; the rest were family members.

The section devoted to the Befehlstelle provides much detail on its criminal activities, listing the names of the Germans in command as well as officers from the SP who were stationed there.

Around the time of the Uprising in April 1943, Warm went into hiding. There he wrote his account, which he concluded in October of that year. After the war Adolf Berman delivered the account to the Jewish Historical Institute, explaining that Ber Warm had perished on the Aryan side.

Gustawa Wilner

["Recollections from the Ghetto and the 'Aryan' side of Warsaw," copy of typescript in Polish, 89 pp.]

Until September 1939, Gustawa Wilner lived on Willowa Street in Warsaw. In early 1940 when she had to move to the site of the future ghetto, she joined her parents at 26 Ogrodowa Street. There she worked with the local building committee, where she focused on programs for children, setting up a playground that as she describes it was "without flowers or even a single blade of grass."

---

*A pun. Niska and Prosta were two streets in the ghetto. *Niska* means *low* and *prosta* means *simple:* a rough translation would be "down and out."—PB

During the deportations to Treblinka, the author managed to find a job at a worksite outside the walls, a veneer storage plant the Germans had set up in the basement of the Central Judaic Library of the Great Synagogue on Tło-mackie Street. Sometime later she managed to procure work for her father there as well.

In the fall of 1942, her parents left the ghetto and hid in the Praga suburb at the home of the Trojanowskis. Wilner also left her worksite at that time and found shelter with Zofia Egerdorf-Wróblewska on Marszałkowska Street. After the Warsaw Uprising she and pani Zofia were sent to the Pruszków transit camp, from which they managed to escape. Eventually they made their way to the village of Piotrowice, not far from Łowicz, where they were liberated. Wilner's parents also survived at the Trojanowskis. Her sister Halina, however, was deported to the Trawniki camp, where she died during the massacre of November 1943.

The author prefaces her account with the following: "Dedicated to the memory of my brother, the fighter Arie (Jurek) Wilner, who fell defending the honor of the Jewish nation." Much of the testimony is devoted to Arie Wilner, a leading figure in the Jewish resistance and a liaison to the Żegota group. Describing her brother's appearance, she wrote:

> When he came walking down the street, I was amazed how won-derful he looked. Blond hair, blue eyes, slender, agile, wearing a sporty coat and a small felt hat with a lowered brim and a woven band à la Tirol (that was the fashion then), with his hands in his pockets and smiling as he whistled a mazurka or *kujawiak*.

Although friends on the Aryan side often tried to persuade Arie Wilner not to return to the ghetto, he categorically refused. His sister recalled a conversation after the war with his close friend and comrade-in-arms Maria Jiruska. When Jiruska tried to convince him not to go back to the ghetto, since that would mean certain death, Wilner replied, "That's where my place is, rather you should wish me an honorable death." That wish was granted; on 8 May 1943, when the Germans discovered the bunker housing the command of the Jewish Fighting Organization, Arie Wilner committed suicide along with the others, so as not to fall into the hands of the perpetrators.*

---

*On 19 April 1945, the commander-in-chief of the Polish Army awarded Wilner the Virtuti Militari Cross, Class V.

At the end of 1945, Gustawa Wilner left Poland together with her parents. After staying in Austria and Italy, they finally settled in Israel, where she wrote her account and delivered it to the Yad Vashem Institute; a copy was sent to the Jewish Historical Institute in Warsaw.

Samuel (Szmul) Zylbersztejn
[Untitled typescript in Yiddish, 199 pp.]

Samuel Zylbersztejn was born in Warsaw, where his father owned a small hosiery workshop and store. In the early 1930s, Zylbersztejn worked for his father and in 1936 acquired his own shop in the same trade.

Inside the ghetto he was active in the building committees and in the Jewish Self-Help Agency. He helped prepare for armed resistance at the Többens plant in the spring of 1943. While he managed to escape numerous selections, including the "cauldron," on 30 April he was taken to Umschlagplatz, from where he was sent first to a labor camp in the Lublin district and from there to several others. He was liberated at the camp in Gusen.

The account, originally written in Yiddish, consists of two parts, the first focusing on the ghetto and the second on the author's experiences in the camps.

Nothing more is known about the author or how the document came to be in the archives.

Natan Żelichower (Jan Kurczab)
[Untitled typescript in Polish, 219 pp.]

Natan Żelichower came from Warsaw, where he worked as a dental technician before the war. In 1942, during the deportations, he lost both his wife and daughter, despite his tremendous efforts to free them from Umschlagplatz.

Later Żelichower was assigned to the Raumkommando, until that group (220 people) was sent to Majdanek in April 1943. From there he was sent from one camp to another, until he was liberated at Buchenwald in April 1945.

The first part of the memoir, which was written immediately after Żelichower's return to Poland in 1945, covers his life in the ghetto; the second describes his harrowing odyssey through the camps.

The author ends his account with the following:

> Four months [after the camp was liberated], I was standing amid the ruins of the Warsaw Ghetto; there is no trace of any street or building. A field of mute bricks and rubble. A terrifying illustration of the truth of the experiences I have described.

The author delivered his account to the local Jewish Historical Commission in Kraków.

Michał Grynberg

[Editor of the anthology]

Born in 1909 in the small town, Sławatycze, on the River Bug, Michał Grynberg received his first schooling in a *cheder* before becoming apprenticed to a tailor at the age of thirteen. Eager to expand his horizons, he spent his meager wages to continue his basic education, and hired a local schoolmaster as a private tutor. In the late 1920s he joined a young group of union activists and moved to Warsaw, where he enrolled in evening classes and attended meetings of the Bund. An attempt to visit the neighboring workers' state landed Grynberg in a Soviet jail; shortly after returning to Warsaw he was arrested by Polish authorities and incarcerated with other political prisoners in Rawicz, where he spent two and a half years before being released in 1938 as part of a general amnesty.

Grynberg returned to Warsaw shortly before the German invasion, at which time he made his way back to Sławatycze. When the occupying Soviet troops withdrew as part of the Nazi-Soviet demarcation agreement, Grynberg eventually moved to Białystok and later to Minsk. There he and his future wife, Danka, were trained as teachers of German. In 1941, in the wake of the German invasion, both were evacuated to a kolkhoz in the Urals, and in the summer of 1942 Grynberg was mobilized along with other teachers and sent to the nearby front. He fought in the battle of Stalingrad, after which his unit of engineers moved westward with the Red Army, and by the end of the war Grynberg was in Czech territory. At that time he took a leave to return to his hometown, stopping in Warsaw along the way, where he visited the ruins of the former ghetto.

Sławatycze, too, was in ruins: the town center burned and most of its Jewish inhabitants murdered. Grynberg demobilized and resettled in the newly acquired Western territories, where he was assigned to head the Jewish Committee in Legnica, overseeing the resettlement of thousands of Jewish repatriates returning primarily from the Soviet Union. Later he was transferred to Wrocław, where he directed a network of Jewish cooperatives. From there he was assigned to Warsaw to the Central Office of Small Goods Manufacture, where he stayed for several years, as that office underwent various transformations, ultimately advancing to the post of departmental vice director.

As a result of the 1968 anti-Semitic purge, Grynberg was expelled from the party and removed from his post. Through friends he found employment at a government trade office until the early 1970s, when he joined the staff of the

Jewish Historical Institute, where he worked until his last days. During that time he prepared and published numerous articles and monographs, including the book that became his doctoral dissertation, *Żydzi w Rejencji Ciechanowskiej* (Jews in the Ziechenau regency) *1939–1942*, about the Nazi program of extermination in regions annexed directly to the Reich. Grynberg received his doctorate in 1989. The current anthology was first published in Poland in 1988 and received various awards, including one from the independent trade union Solidarity. Throughout his life Dr. Grynberg devoted much effort to strengthening relations between Jews and Gentiles in Poland, and in 1993 he published a book devoted to Polish Gentiles honored by Yad Vashem as Righteous Among Nations—of which he himself was named an honorary member. In 1998 he completed another book, still awaiting publication, similar to the present work but covering ghettos throughout occupied Poland. Late in life he made several trips to his hometown of Sławatycze, collecting information for a book documenting Jewish life there and its ultimate annihilation. This book appeared posthumously, together with an autobiographical account. Dr. Michał Grynberg died in Warsaw in April 2000.

Translator's
Acknowledgments

Many people have helped see this book into print since the project began years ago. John Reed was of great assistance in preparing the manuscript in the early stages. The late Helena Pawluć of Warsaw helped identify obscure words and local references. Marek Web of the YIVO Institute for Jewish Research has provided constant aid, and Professor Feliks Tych of the Jewish Historical Institute in Warsaw kindly reviewed the final copy. Numerous friends have offered valuable feedback: I would especially like to thank Mark Anderson, Ed Cohen, Pepe Schraibman, and David Van Biema.

Janet Hotson Baker performed a tremendous service in copyediting a very difficult text. Shara Kay and the entire editorial staff of Metropolitan Books have been consistently helpful. I would particularly like to thank Riva Hocherman for her keen and insightful editing, her profound sympathy for this book, and her concern for its integrity. Sara Bershtel deserves special mention for her unwavering commitment to this project, her inexhaustible patience, her equally inexhaustible good advice and abiding friendship.

Jadwiga Krawczyk, daughter of the late Dr. Michał Grynberg, has been very dedicated to seeing her father's work reach the widest possible readership: It is our great sadness that he did not live to see this English edition, which we dedicate to his memory.

Finally I would like to thank Elżbieta Skłodowska for her help clarifying dozens of linguistic and topographic puzzles, and to her steadfast consolation during the years I have been immersed in this book.

Index